the *ultimate*

diabetic LIVING

diabetes

More than **400** healthy,
delicious recipes

cookbook

A **Better Homes and Gardens** Book

Copyright © 2013 by Meredith Corporation, Des Moines, IA.

All rights reserved

Published by Houghton Mifflin Harcourt Publishing Company, New York, New York

Published simultaneously in Canada

For information about permission to reproduce selections from this book, write to Permissions, Houghton Mifflin Harcourt Publishing Company, 215 Park Avenue South, New York, New York 10003.

www.hmhco.com

Library of Congress Cataloging-in-Publication Data

Diabetic living, the ultimate diabetes cookbook : more than 400 healthy, delicious recipes.

    p. cm.

"A better homes and gardens book."

Includes index.

ISBN 978-1-118-62679-5

ISBN 978-1-4351-5650-0 (Barnes & Noble, Inc. edition)

This 2014 edition printed for Barnes & Noble, Inc.

1. Diabetes—Diet therapy.

  RC662.D547 2013

  641.5'6314—dc23

                2013032971

Meredith Corporation

Food and Nutrition Editor: Jessie Shafer

Contributing Project Manager: Shelli McConnell, Purple Pear Publishing, Inc.

Art Director: Michelle Bilyeu

Cover Photographers: Karla Conrad and Kritsada Panichgul

Cover Food Stylist: Charles Worthington

Houghton Mifflin Harcourt

Publisher: Natalie Chapman

Editorial Director: Cindy Kitchel

Executive Editor: Anne Ficklen

Senior Editor: Adam Kowit

Associate Editor: Heather Dabah

Editorial Assistant: Molly Aronica

Managing Editor: Marina Padakis Lowry

Production Editor: Jacqueline Beach

Interior Design and Layout: Holly Wittenberg

Production Director: Tom Hyland

Cover photos
(top row, from left): Banana Split Ice Cream Pie, page 449, Sweet and Spicy Wasabi Snack Mix, page 403, Glazed Pork Chops with Spinach-Pom Salad, page 186; (middle row, from left): Meatballs with Sweet Lemon Glaze, page 250, Hot Ham and Pear Melts, page 167, Pork and Pineapple Tacos, page 292; (bottom row, from left): Teriyaki Shrimp and Edamame Salad, page 105, Cinnamon Streusel Rolls, page 68, Four-Cheese Macaroni and Cheese, page 240.

Printed in China

SCP 10 9 8 7 6 5 4 3 2 1

the ultimate in health and taste

For people with diabetes, an ultimate recipe is one that meets their special dietary needs in every way. It is packed with the right amount of nutrients for *everyone* at the table. An ultimate recipe is also easy to make and uses readily available, everyday ingredients. And of course, an ultimate recipe is satisfying, portioned right, and tantalizing to the taste buds.

We hope you'll put the ultimate recipes in this book to work for you so your meals are more healthful, easier to make, and tastier. Every one of these recipes was tested and tasted in the Better Homes & Gardens® Test Kitchen to ensure it met our requirements for success. In addition, our Test Kitchen dietitians analyzed each recipe to guarantee the best nutrition for you and your family.

Make *Diabetic Living® The Ultimate Diabetes Cookbook* your guide for preparing diabetes-smart, nutritious recipes that taste great. We're certain this recipe collection will become your go-to source for healthful, delicious meals that will please everyone at your table. Congratulations on making your next meal an ultimate one!

Jessie

Jessie Shafer
Food & Nutrition Editor
Diabetic Living

inside our recipes

See how we calculate nutrition information to help you count calories, carbs, and serving sizes.

Precise serving sizes (listed below the recipe title) help you to manage portions.

Kitchen basics such as ice, salt, black pepper, and nonstick cooking spray usually are not listed in the ingredient list; they are italicized in the directions.

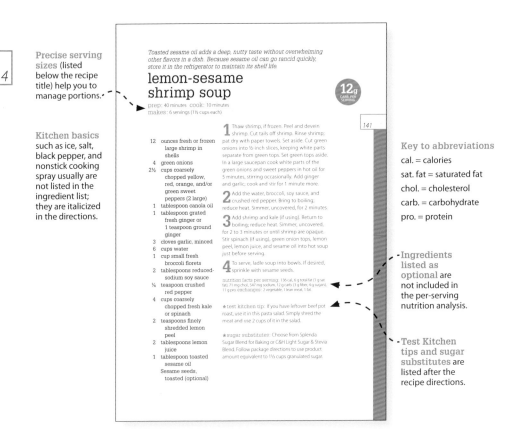

Toasted sesame oil adds a deep, nutty taste without overwhelming other flavors in a dish. Because sesame oil can go rancid quickly, store it in the refrigerator to maintain its shelf life.

lemon-sesame shrimp soup

12g CARB. PER SERVING

prep: 40 minutes cook: 10 minutes
makes: 6 servings (1½ cups each)

141

12 ounces fresh or frozen large shrimp in shells
4 green onions
2½ cups coarsely chopped yellow, red, orange, and/or green sweet peppers (2 large)
1 tablespoon canola oil
1 tablespoon grated fresh ginger or 1 teaspoon ground ginger
3 cloves garlic, minced
6 cups water
1 cup small fresh broccoli florets
2 tablespoons reduced-sodium soy sauce
¼ teaspoon crushed red pepper
4 cups coarsely chopped fresh kale or spinach
2 teaspoons finely shredded lemon peel
2 tablespoons lemon juice
1 tablespoon toasted sesame oil
Sesame seeds, toasted (optional)

1 Thaw shrimp, if frozen. Peel and devein shrimp. Cut tails off shrimp. Rinse shrimp; pat dry with paper towels. Set aside. Cut green onions into ½-inch slices, keeping white parts separate from green tops. Set green tops aside. In a large saucepan cook white parts of the green onions and sweet peppers in hot oil for 5 minutes, stirring occasionally. Add ginger and garlic; cook and stir for 1 minute more.

2 Add the water, broccoli, soy sauce, and crushed red pepper. Bring to boiling; reduce heat. Simmer, uncovered, for 2 minutes.

3 Add shrimp and kale (if using). Return to boiling; reduce heat. Simmer, uncovered, for 2 to 3 minutes or until shrimp are opaque. Stir spinach (if using), green onion tops, lemon peel, lemon juice, and sesame oil into hot soup just before serving.

4 To serve, ladle soup into bowls. If desired, sprinkle with sesame seeds.

nutrition facts per serving: 136 cal, 6 g total fat (1 g sat fat), 71 mg chol, 547 mg sodium, 12 g carb (3 g fiber, 4 g sugars), 11 g pro. exchanges: 2 vegetable, 1 lean meat, 1 fat.

✱test kitchen tip: If you have leftover beef pot roast, use it in this pasta salad. Simply shred the meat and use 2 cups of it in the salad.

✱sugar substitutes: Choose from Splenda Sugar Blend for Baking or C&H Light Sugar & Stevia Blend. Follow package directions to use product amount equivalent to 1⅓ cups granulated sugar.

Key to abbreviations

cal. = calories
sat. fat = saturated fat
chol. = cholesterol
carb. = carbohydrate
pro. = protein

Ingredients listed as optional are not included in the per-serving nutrition analysis.

Test Kitchen tips and sugar substitutes are listed after the recipe directions.

ingredients

- Tub-style vegetable oil spread refers to 60% to 70% vegetable oil product.
- Lean ground beef refers to 95% or leaner ground beef.

nutrition information

- Nutrition facts per serving and food exchanges are noted with each recipe.
- Ingredients listed as optional are not included in the per-serving nutrition analysis.
- When ingredient choices appear, we use the first one to calculate the nutrition analysis.

high standards testing!

This seal assures you every recipe in this book has been tested in the Better Homes and Gardens® Test Kitchen. This means each recipe is practical, reliable, and meets our high standards of taste appeal.

table of
contents

eat **Sm**

The more you understand about diabetes-smart eating habits, the easier you'll find making those practices a seamless part of your life. From what to put into your shopping cart to how to count carbs and downsize servings, these concepts are the first steps to a healthier you.

downsize for better health

Controlling how much you eat can be as big a challenge as deciding what to eat. Try these tips to tackle common portion pitfalls and still satisfy your grumbling stomach.

Keep serving dishes off the table. Dish up your plate from the kitchen counter—not the dinner table. Studies show that if you place a big bowl of pasta on the table, men eat 20 percent more and women eat 10 percent more than when the bowl isn't nearby.

Pick smaller plates and spoons. Research shows that we eat 92 percent of what's on our plates. If you use a 9-inch plate instead of a 12-inch plate, you'll serve yourself less food. And if you use a tablespoon instead of a serving spoon to dish up food, you'll serve yourself less, too.

Think thin. Slim sandwich buns save you up to 15 grams of carbohydrate and 100 calories per serving compared with traditional buns. What's more, thinner buns allow you to better enjoy the flavor of sandwich fillings. Also try thin bagels, very thinly sliced bread, thin-crust pizza, and extra-thin corn tortillas.

Pour a tall glass.
Drinking liquids out of taller, thinner glasses makes us think we are drinking more than we actually are. It's an optical illusion; people tend to focus on the height instead of the width of the liquid in the glass.

Steer clear if you can't eat just one.
Highly pleasurable foods such as chocolate milk shakes, chips, fast food, and candy bars activate the same areas of the brain as when drug addicts see cocaine. Overcoming the urge to eat an addictive food generally takes about two weeks of avoiding the food altogether.

Favor whole foods.
Processing foods tends to concentrate the calories and carbs. Consider this: For 15 grams of carbohydrate, you could eat either 1¼ cups fresh strawberries or a mere 1½ tablespoons all-fruit strawberry preserves. You can usually upsize rather than downsize with whole foods. Whole foods tend to be more filling, too.

Follow food with fun. If you're eating a favorite food and are worried you'll have a tough time quitting after one serving, plan something enjoyable to do as soon as you're done eating—you'll have a rewarding reason to stop.

plan your plate

Getting your eating on track is a cinch if you use this visual guide to meals that offer the right mix of nutrients for better control of glucose and weight.

the plate method

The Idaho Plate Method is a simple strategy to help your whole family eat better—whether you count carbohydrate, exchanges, or nothing at all. If you focus too much on carbohydrates, it's easy to overlook other foods and nutrients needed for good health, including antioxidants and fiber. The plate method makes planning a nutritious, balanced meal while controlling calories and carbohydrate easy.

¼ plate starch or grain

½ plate nonstarchy vegetables

¼ plate protein

start with a 9-inch plate

Portion control is easier when your plate is smaller. Along with a right-size plate, use a 1-cup glass for milk, a ½-cup dish for fruit or desserts, and a 1-cup bowl for cereal or soup. (Hint: Picture the small soup cups used by restaurants.)

partition your plate

Fill half the plate with one or two nonstarchy vegetables (asparagus, broccoli, carrots, green beans, salad greens, zucchini, or others). For a quarter of the plate, choose a lean meat (chicken, lean beef, or pork), fish, or other protein (tofu, eggs, cheese, or nuts). Fill the remaining quarter with a starchy vegetable or whole grain (bread, tortilla, pasta, rice, beans, potatoes, corn, or peas).

add a side

In addition to your full plate, you can enjoy a cup of fat-free milk or light yogurt and a small piece of fresh fruit or ½ cup canned fruit on the side. If you make low-fat choices, a meal with these sides and each of the three plate components totals 55–60 grams of carbohydrate and 350–450 calories.

measure the height

Don't fall into the trap of piling food too high on your plate to make up for the plate's smaller size. Foods should be no more than ½ inch high (about the thickness of your index finger). Nonstarchy vegetables should be the tallest section.

apportion combinations

You can use the plate method with mixed dishes such as casseroles, pizza, tacos, and sandwiches, too. Just think of the ingredients separately. A salad with grilled chicken and croutons could cover every section of the plate: greens, carrots, and tomatoes for the nonstarchy vegetables; chicken for the protein; and croutons for the starch or grain. Assemble casseroles in layers so you can see how much meat versus vegetables you're getting. When in doubt, put the serving for a casserole with pasta, rice, or beans in the starch section of the plate.

go easy on extras

When using items like salad dressings, sauces, and spreads, choose a low-fat version and keep the servings as skimpy as you can. When dining out, ask for dressing on the side and don't be afraid to ask for substitutions. For example, if grilled chicken breast comes with corn, mashed potatoes, and a dinner roll, which are all starches, ask to swap two of them for steamed or sautéed vegetables.

make fair trades

When you are calculating your servings (or exchanges) of fruit, milk, and starch, feel free to trade one for another to keep your carbs in check. For example, if you want two pieces of bread for a sandwich, skip the milk or fruit for that meal. The fruit, milk, or starch serving can also be traded for a cup of broth-based soup or even ½ cup low-fat ice cream for dessert.

divide the breakfast plate

You can use the plate method for breakfast, too. Omit the nonstarchy vegetable and protein servings and just use the starch, fruit, and milk servings. Or pair a hunger-satisfying protein such as scrambled egg whites or lean pork cutlets with a small whole grain pancake.

carb-counting tips

Carb counting takes practice, but you can get better at spotting carbs (see "What Foods Contain Carbs?," page 14) and nailing your carbohydrate counts. Here are some helpful tips.

2 be predictable

Buy the same products—at least at first. You'll learn their carb counts and the ways they affect your blood glucose. Try new products and foods as you get more familiar with the numbers.

3 pick produce by size

Fruits, vegetables, potatoes, and other produce come in a wide range of sizes. The difference between small and large apples easily can be 15 grams of carb. Take a few minutes on occasion to weigh pieces of produce. Look up the carb counts based on the weights you buy. Then try to choose similar sizes each time you shop.

1 be a label reader

The most accurate carb count is from a Nutrition Facts label on a food package. The total carbohydrate number is the sum of fibers, sugars, and starches. Use the total number when counting carb grams per serving. Be sure to check the serving size on the label, too. How accurately does it fit what you eat?

4 eyeball accurate portions

Keep your eyes honest by double-checking your portions every once in a while. Use measuring cups to put oatmeal, cold cereal, pasta, rice, and other starches in your usual serving bowl or plate so you can see how the food looks after it's served. (See "Right-Size Portions," page 15.)

5 use your tools

Invest in a good food scale. Look for models that provide the gram weight of foods. Some can even calculate carb counts based on an internal database. To increase the likelihood you'll reach for your measuring cups and food scale, keep them available on the counter.

6 record recipe counts

Do you have a file of favorite recipes? Take the time to figure carb counts and appropriate serving sizes.

calculating combos

Casseroles, pasta salads, soups, and other mixed dishes present a slight challenge when estimating carb counts. Here is a good rule of thumb for starch-heavy mixed foods (with pasta, rice, potatoes, beans, or corn): For a ¼-cup serving, estimate 7 grams carb.; for ½ cup, estimate 15 grams carb.; and for 1 cup, estimate 30 grams carb.

¼ cup   ½ cup   1 cup

what foods contain carbs?

Carbohydrate is important. It's your main source of daily fuel to keep your body and brain going. It also affects your blood glucose the most. Not all carbohydrate sources are created equal, however, so be sure you eat the most nutritious carbs.

Dairy: Dairy foods (milk, yogurt, cottage cheese) contain lactose, a sugar that breaks down to glucose when digested. Choose low-fat versions of these foods.

Fruits: Fruits contain carbohydrate from fiber and natural sugars. Pick fresh or frozen fruit rather than dried—you'll get a bigger serving for the same carb amount.

Whole grains, starchy vegetables, and legumes: Whole grains (brown rice, whole grain pasta and breads, oatmeal), starchy vegetables (potatoes with skin, corn, peas), and legumes (beans, edamame, lentils) all contain carbohydrate. They are good choices because they are higher in fiber than highly processed grain foods.

Nonstarchy vegetables: All vegetables contain some carbohydrate, but nonstarchy vegetables (broccoli, green beans, spinach, lettuce, sweet and hot peppers, tomatoes) contain much less than starchy vegetables and are full of good-for-you nutrients.

Refined grains, desserts, and sugary drinks: Limit these. Sweets (candy, ice cream, cake, and chocolate) and foods made from refined grains (bagels, white pasta, sugary cereals, white rice) are carb sources that lack many healthful nutrients. Regular soda and energy drinks are high in sugar.

right-size portions

The most accurate way to measure and monitor how much you're eating is to use measuring cups and a food scale. Learning how to visually size up your food will help you keep calories and carbs in check.

everyday objects can help you determine what a regular serving looks like.

handy ways to measure serving sizes A quick tool for estimating amounts is just an arm's length away.

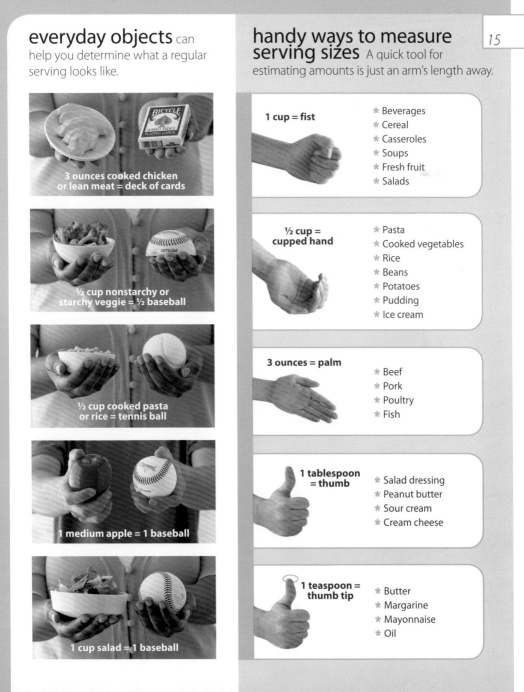

3 ounces cooked chicken or lean meat = deck of cards

½ cup nonstarchy or starchy veggie = ½ baseball

½ cup cooked pasta or rice = tennis ball

1 medium apple = 1 baseball

1 cup salad = 1 baseball

1 cup = fist
* Beverages
* Cereal
* Casseroles
* Soups
* Fresh fruit
* Salads

½ cup = cupped hand
* Pasta
* Cooked vegetables
* Rice
* Beans
* Potatoes
* Pudding
* Ice cream

3 ounces = palm
* Beef
* Pork
* Poultry
* Fish

1 tablespoon = thumb
* Salad dressing
* Peanut butter
* Sour cream
* Cream cheese

1 teaspoon = thumb tip
* Butter
* Margarine
* Mayonnaise
* Oil

get cart smart

Grocery shopping with good health in mind can feel overwhelming. Foods with labels that make claims such as "fat-free" and "low-sodium" can leave you confused. Here's a guide for some of the more perplexing sections of the supermarket.

bakery aisle

Bread's bad-boy reputation is not deserved. As with all carbohydrate-containing foods, quality counts and portion size rules.

- Buy breads that identify 100 percent whole wheat or other whole grain as the first ingredient. "Enriched wheat flour," "multigrain," and "high fiber" don't guarantee a whole grain product.

- Look for the Whole Grain Stamp to ensure a product has at least 8 grams of whole grains per serving. (One whole grain serving is 16 grams.) Aim for 48 grams each day.

- Bread should contain at least 2 grams of fiber per slice.

- Mix up your bread options. Try tortillas, pitas, and flatbreads, too.

cart smarts

People eat more of products making claims such as "low fat." Ignore front-of-package words; go straight to the Nutrition Facts label.

meat counter

In the meat and deli sections, zero in on lean choices to limit calories and saturated fat, the type of fat linked to heart disease and insulin resistance.

- The leanest cuts are the best choices. Look for those with "round" or "loin" in the name, such as round steak and tenderloin.

- Look for ground beef and ground poultry that are at least 90 percent lean. Make sure ground chicken and poultry are ground breast meat and do not include the fat-laden skin.

- Twice a week eat fish high in omega-3 fatty acids, the type of fat that can help prevent heart disease. These include salmon, lake or rainbow trout, tuna, and herring.

cart smarts

Mentally divide your grocery cart into food groups. Pick up healthful items for each group, such as whole grains, vegetables, fruit, lean protein, and low-fat dairy.

0.58

WEIGHT lb &lb PRICE $/lb TOTAL PRICE $

Capacity 30 x 0.01 lb

dairy case

The dairy aisle can be a saturated-fat minefield. Always pick fat-free or reduced-fat options.

- Choose high-quality, flavorful cheeses, such as sharp cheddar, feta, and Parmesan. A small amount will add a lot of flavor to meals.

- Try Greek yogurt if you haven't already. Its high protein content makes it more satisfying than regular yogurt. Even the fat-free varieties are thick, creamy, and indulgent.

- Look for a soft, buttery spread with no trans fat and no more than 1 gram of saturated fat per tablespoon. But be careful. It is legal to claim 0 trans fat for anything less than 0.5 gram per serving. If you see partially hydrogenated oils on the label, leave the product on the shelf.

cart smarts

Place unhealthful items in the cart's child seat. Before checkout, consider each item to reassess whether you want it or need it.

great cereal grains

For a quick, budget-friendly start to your day, cereal is a good bet. But watch out—this aisle is a sea of screaming health claims.

- For a satisfying, diabetes-friendly breakfast option, cereals should meet these nutritional guidelines per serving: 150 calories or less, 30 grams of carbohydrate or less, no more than 8 grams of sugars, and at least 3 grams of fiber.

- Opt for oatmeal. The fiber in oats may help lower cholesterol and steady blood glucose levels. Skip instant varieties to avoid added sugars, flavorings, and salt. Instead, stir in a little ground cinnamon and top with fresh fruit and toasted nuts for a healthful flavor boost.

- When comparing cereals, make note of the serving sizes listed. They range from ½ cup to more than 1 cup.

eye-opening

A great breakfast helps you stay on the healthful-eating track all day. So start weekdays right with one of these breakfast bars, wraps, parfaits, or smoothies. During the weekend, slow down and savor our diabetes-smart pancakes, egg dishes, coffee cakes, and other sensible options.

break

mocha coffee cake, *page 44*

fasts

Placing the ramekins on a baking sheet makes moving them to and from the oven easier.

2g
CARB. PER
SERVING

baked eggs with tomato topper

prep: 20 minutes bake: 16 minutes
makes: 4 servings (1 egg dish and 2 tablespoons tomato topper each)

1   medium roma tomato,
      finely chopped
      (⅓ cup)
1   tablespoon finely
      chopped green
      onion
1   tablespoon snipped
      fresh cilantro
1   teaspoon finely
      chopped jalapeño
      pepper*
1   teaspoon lime juice
⅛   teaspoon salt
      Nonstick cooking
      spray
4   egg whites
4   eggs
4   tablespoons fat-free
      milk
¼   teaspoon black
      pepper
2   tablespoons finely
      shredded reduced-
      fat cheddar cheese

1 For tomato topper, in a small bowl combine tomato, green onion, cilantro, jalapeño pepper, lime juice, and salt; set aside.

2 Preheat oven to 350°F. Coat four 8-ounce ramekins with cooking spray. Place an egg white in each dish. Top each with a whole egg, positioning the yolk in the center of the ramekin. Add 1 tablespoon milk to each ramekin. Top evenly with black pepper, then cheese. Place ramekins on a baking sheet.

3 Bake, uncovered, for 16 to 18 minutes or until eggs are set around edges but still a little jiggly in the center. Top each serving evenly with the tomato topper.

nutrition facts per serving: 107 cal., 6 g total fat (2 g sat. fat), 214 mg chol., 231 mg sodium, 2 g carb. (0 g fiber, 2 g sugars), 12 g pro. exchanges: 2 lean meat, 0.5 fat.

*test kitchen tip: Because chile peppers contain volatile oils that can burn your skin and eyes, avoid direct contact with them as much as possible. When working with chile peppers, wear plastic or rubber gloves. If your bare hands do touch the peppers, wash your hands and nails well with soap and warm water.

*Most cooks have a favorite way
to poach eggs. If you prefer to use
an egg-poaching pan or silicone
poaching cups, do so.*

eggs benedict
with avocado cream

18g
CARB. PER
SERVING

prep: 15 minutes   cook: 3 minutes
makes: 4 servings (1 egg, 2 tablespoons Avocado Cream, 1 muffin half, 1 tomato slice, and ½ slice bacon each)

4   eggs
1   recipe Avocado Cream
2   whole wheat English
    muffins, split and
    toasted
4   slices tomato
2   slices bacon, halved,
    crisp-cooked, and
    drained

avocado cream:
In a blender or food
processor combine
1 small ripe avocado,
halved, seeded, and
peeled; ¼ cup fat-free
plain Greek yogurt;
2 tablespoons snipped
fresh cilantro; 1 tablespoon
lime juice; ¼ teaspoon
bottled hot pepper
sauce (optional); and
⅛ teaspoon salt.

1 Half-fill a nonstick skillet with water. Bring water to boiling; reduce heat to simmering (bubbles should begin to break the surface of the water). Break one of the eggs into a measuring cup. Holding the lip of the cup as close to the water as possible, carefully slide the egg into the simmering water. Repeat with remaining eggs, allowing each egg an equal amount of space.

2 Simmer eggs, uncovered, for 3 to 5 minutes or until the whites are completely set and yolks begin to thicken but are not hard. Remove eggs with a slotted spoon and place them in a large pan of warm water to keep them warm. Prepare Avocado Cream.

3 Place a freshly toasted muffin half on each of four serving plates. Top each with Avocado Cream, a tomato slice, an egg, and a bacon piece.

nutrition facts per serving: 210 cal., 11 g total fat (3 g sat. fat), 216 mg chol., 400 mg sodium, 18 g carb. (4 g fiber, 4 g sugars), 13 g pro. exchanges: 1 starch, 1.5 medium-fat meat, 0.5 fat.

If your supermarket doesn't carry queso fresco, look for it at Mexican food stores or substitute feta cheese.

poblano-chorizo strata

prep: 40 minutes chill: 2 hours bake: 1 hour stand: 10 minutes
makes: 12 servings (¾ cup each)

8   ounces uncooked
    chorizo sausage
2   medium onions,
    thinly sliced
2   medium fresh
    poblano chile
    peppers, seeded
    and thinly sliced*
1   medium red sweet
    pepper, thinly sliced
8   cups 1-inch cubes
    Mexican bolillo rolls
    or crusty Italian
    bread
6   eggs, lightly beaten
2½ cups fat-free milk
1   teaspoon dried
    Mexican oregano
    or regular oregano,
    crushed
½   teaspoon paprika
½   cup queso fresco,
    crumbled
    Snipped fresh cilantro
    (optional)

1 In a large skillet cook chorizo over medium heat until browned. Using a slotted spoon, transfer chorizo to a bowl, reserving 1 tablespoon drippings in skillet. Add onions to drippings in skillet; cook and stir over medium heat about 10 minutes or just until tender. Stir in chile peppers and sweet pepper; cook about 5 minutes or just until peppers are tender. Remove from heat. Stir in chorizo.

2 Lightly grease a 3-quart rectangular or oval baking dish. Spread half of the bread cubes into the prepared dish. Spoon half of the chorizo mixture over bread. Repeat layers.

3 In a large bowl whisk together eggs, milk, oregano, and paprika. Pour egg mixture evenly over layers in baking dish. Cover with foil and chill for at least 2 hours or up to 24 hours.

4 Preheat oven to 325°F. Bake, covered, for 30 minutes. Uncover. Bake for 30 to 45 minutes more or until an instant-read thermometer inserted into the center registers 170°F. Sprinkle with cheese the last 5 minutes of baking. Let stand for 10 minutes before serving. If desired, sprinkle with cilantro.

nutrition facts per serving: 222 cal., 11 g total fat (4 g sat. fat), 114 mg chol., 364 mg sodium, 17 g carb. (1 g fiber, 4 g sugars), 13 g pro. exchanges: 0.5 vegetable, 1 starch, 1 medium-fat meat, 1 fat.

*test kitchen tip: Because chile peppers contain volatile oils that can burn your skin and eyes, avoid direct contact with them as much as possible. When working with chile peppers, wear plastic or rubber gloves. If your bare hands do touch the peppers, wash your hands and nails well with soap and warm water.

Roasted veggies nestle the eggs during the baking. For easy serving, use a large spoon to lift out some of the veggies along with each egg.

baked eggs with roasted vegetables

21g
CARB. PER SERVING

prep: 25 minutes **chill:** 8 hours **stand:** 30 minutes **bake:** 15 minutes
makes: 6 servings (1 egg and ¾ cup vegetables each)

Nonstick cooking spray
3 cups small broccoli florets (about 1 inch in size)
12 ounces yellow potatoes, such as Yukon gold, cut into ½- to ¾-inch pieces (about 2 cups)
1 large sweet potato, cut into ½- to ¾-inch pieces (about 1 cup)
1 small red onion, cut into thin wedges
2 tablespoons olive oil
¼ teaspoon salt
6 eggs
½ cup shredded Manchego cheese (2 ounces)
½ teaspoon cracked black pepper

1 Preheat oven to 425°F. Coat a 2-quart rectangular baking dish with cooking spray. In a large bowl combine broccoli, yellow potatoes, sweet potato, onion, olive oil, and salt; toss to coat vegetables.

2 Spread vegetables evenly into the prepared pan. Roast for 10 minutes. Stir vegetables; roast about 5 minutes more or until vegetables are tender and starting to brown. Remove from oven. Spread vegetables evenly in the prepared baking dish; cool. Cover and chill for 8 to 24 hours.

3 Let chilled vegetables stand at room temperature for 30 minutes. Meanwhile, preheat oven to 375°F.

4 Bake vegetables, uncovered, for 5 minutes. Remove from oven; make six wells in the layer of vegetables. Break an egg into each well. Bake for 5 minutes more. Sprinkle with cheese. Bake for 5 to 10 minutes more or until egg whites are set and yolks start to thicken. Sprinkle with pepper.

nutrition facts per serving: 232 cal., 12 g total fat (4 g sat. fat), 218 mg chol., 332 mg sodium, 21 g carb. (4 g fiber, 4 g sugars), 11 g pro. **exchanges:** 1 vegetable, 1 starch, 1 medium-fat meat, 1 fat.

4 g
CARB. PER
SERVING

Kalamata olives are greenish black-purple in color and have a lingering tangy flavor. In the evening, serve a few as part of an appetizer spread.

mushroom-olive frittata

prep: 30 minutes broil: 2 minutes stand: 5 minutes
makes: 4 servings (1 wedge each)

1 tablespoon olive oil
1 cup sliced fresh
    cremini mushrooms
2 cups coarsely
    shredded fresh
    Swiss chard or
    spinach
1 large shallot, thinly
    sliced
4 eggs*
2 egg whites*
2 teaspoons snipped
    fresh rosemary or
    ½ teaspoon dried
    rosemary, crushed
¼ teaspoon black pepper
⅛ teaspoon salt
¼ cup thinly sliced
    pitted Kalamata
    olives
⅓ cup shredded
    Parmesan cheese

1 Preheat broiler. In a broilerproof medium nonstick skillet heat oil over medium heat. Add mushrooms to skillet; cook for 3 minutes, stirring occasionally. Add Swiss chard and shallot. Cook about 5 minutes or until mushrooms and chard are tender, stirring occasionally.

2 Meanwhile, in a medium bowl whisk together eggs, egg whites, rosemary, pepper, and salt. Pour egg mixture over vegetables in skillet. Cook over medium heat. As mixture sets, run a spatula around edge of skillet, lifting egg mixture so the uncooked portion flows underneath. Continue cooking and lifting edges until egg mixture is almost set and surface is just slightly moist.

3 Sprinkle with olives; top with cheese. Broil about 4 inches from the heat about 2 minutes or until top is lightly browned and center is set. Let stand for 5 minutes. To serve, cut into four wedges.

nutrition facts per serving: 165 cal., 11 g total fat (3 g sat. fat), 216 mg chol., 416 mg sodium, 4 g carb. (1 g fiber, 1 g sugars), 12 g pro. exchanges: 1 vegetable, 1.5 medium-fat meat, 0.5 fat.

*test kitchen tip: If desired, substitute 1¼ cups refrigerated or frozen egg product, thawed, for the 4 eggs and 2 egg whites.

*Tired of limiting yourself to an itty-bitty wedge of quiche?
Thanks to the healthful options in this recipe, each serving
is a full one-fourth of the pie!*

roasted tomato and
asparagus crustless quiche

11g
CARB. PER
SERVING

prep: 20 minutes   **roast:** 10 minutes   **bake:** 40 minutes
makes: 4 servings (1 wedge each)

8   ounces fresh
      asparagus, cut into
      1-inch pieces
4   ounces cherry
      tomatoes or grape
      tomatoes, halved
      Nonstick cooking
      spray
2   cups refrigerated or
      frozen egg product,
      thawed, or 8 eggs,
      lightly beaten
1   cup fat-free cottage
      cheese
¼   cup finely chopped
      red onion
2   tablespoons flour
2   teaspoons snipped
      fresh rosemary
¼   teaspoon black
      pepper
¼   cup finely shredded
      Asiago cheese
      (1 ounce)

1 Preheat oven to 400°F. Arrange
asparagus and tomatoes, cut sides up,
in a single layer in a 15×10×1-inch baking
pan. Coat vegetables with cooking spray.
Roast, uncovered, for 10 to 12 minutes or
until browned and tomatoes are soft. Set
aside and let cool.

2 Reduce oven temperature to 375°F. In a
large mixing bowl combine egg, cottage
cheese, onion, flour, rosemary, and pepper.
Stir in the asparagus and tomatoes.

3 Coat a 9-inch deep-dish pie plate
with cooking spray. Pour egg mixture
into the prepared pie plate. Bake, uncovered,
about 40 minutes or until a knife inserted
near the center comes out clean. Sprinkle
with cheese. To serve, cut into four wedges.
Serve immediately.

nutrition facts per serving: 157 cal., 2 g total fat
(2 g sat. fat), 10 mg chol., 537 mg sodium, 11 g carb. (1 g fiber,
3 g sugars), 21 g pro. exchanges: 1 vegetable, 0.5 starch,
2.5 lean meat.

Andouille sausage, typically made of pork and garlic, is a staple of Cajun cooking. Look for the leaner chicken variety to use in this Southern-style breakfast.

11g
CARB. PER
SERVING

cajun breakfast skillet

prep: 15 minutes cook: 18 minutes stand: 2 minutes
makes: 4 servings (1½ cups each)

Nonstick cooking
   spray
1 medium sweet potato,
   peeled and cut into
   ½-inch cubes
1 small onion, chopped
¼ cup water
1 medium green sweet
   pepper, cut into thin
   bite-size strips
2 3-ounce links chicken
   andouille sausage
   or desired-flavor
   chicken sausage,
   halved lengthwise
   and cut crosswise
   into ½-inch-thick
   slices
¼ cup thinly sliced
   celery
2 teaspoons canola oil
½ teaspoon Cajun
   seasoning
4 eggs
4 egg whites
¼ cup fat-free milk

1 Coat an unheated large nonstick skillet with cooking spray. In the skillet cook sweet potato, onion, and the water, covered, over medium heat for 8 minutes, stirring once or twice. Add the sweet pepper, sausage, celery, and oil. Cook, uncovered, over medium heat about 5 minutes or until vegetables are tender and sausage is lightly browned, stirring occasionally. Stir the Cajun seasoning into the vegetable mixture.

2 Meanwhile, in a medium bowl beat together eggs, egg whites, and milk with a rotary beater or whisk.

3 Pour the egg mixture over the vegetable mixture. Cook over medium heat, without stirring, until mixture begins to set on the bottom and around edges. Using a spatula or large spoon, lift and fold the partially cooked egg mixture so the uncooked portion flows underneath. Continue cooking about 4 minutes more or until egg mixture is cooked through but still slightly moist. Remove from heat and let stand 2 minutes before serving.

nutrition facts per serving: 230 cal., 11 g total fat (3 g sat. fat), 223 mg chol., 411 mg sodium, 11 g carb. (2 g fiber, 4 g sugars), 20 g pro. exchanges: 0.5 vegetable, 0.5 starch, 2 medium-fat meat.

Nachos in the morning may sound a bit indulgent, but this recipe has all the right ingredients for a healthful, breakfast-perfect version.

huevos rancheros breakfast nachos

prep: 20 minutes cook: 10 minutes
makes: 4 servings (11 chips, 3 tablespoons salsa mixture, and ¼ cup egg each)

26g
CARB. PER
SERVING

3   ounces baked tortilla
     chips
¼   teaspoon cumin
     seeds
½   cup canned black
     beans, rinsed and
     drained
½   cup bottled salsa
2   eggs
3   egg whites
3   tablespoons fat-free
     milk
⅛   teaspoon black
     pepper
     Nonstick cooking
     spray
½   cup shredded
     reduced-fat Mexican-
     style cheese blend
     (2 ounces)

1 Divide chips among four serving plates, spreading into single layers; set aside. In a dry small saucepan heat cumin seeds over medium heat about 1 minute or until aromatic, stirring frequently. Stir in black beans and salsa. Cook for 1 to 2 minutes or until heated through, stirring occasionally. Remove from heat; cover and keep warm.

2 In a medium bowl whisk together eggs, egg whites, milk, and pepper. Coat an unheated medium nonstick skillet with cooking spray; heat skillet over medium heat. Pour in egg mixture. Cook over medium heat, without stirring, until mixture starts to set on the bottom and around edges. Using a spatula or a large spoon, lift and fold the partially cooked egg mixture so the uncooked portion flows underneath. Continue cooking for 2 to 3 minutes or until egg mixture is cooked through but still glossy and moist. Remove from heat immediately.

3 Break up cooked eggs and spoon over tortilla chips. Top with salsa mixture and cheese. Serve immediately.

nutrition facts per serving: 207 cal., 6 g total fat (3 g sat. fat), 113 mg chol., 503 mg sodium, 26 g carb. (4 g fiber, 2 g sugars), 14 g pro. exchanges: 1.5 starch, 1.5 medium-fat meat.

6 g
CARB. PER
SERVING

Cheese, Italian sausage, and colorful veggies make this quiche irresistible. Using frozen egg product and omitting the crust makes it easy on the diet, too.

italian sausage and zucchini quiche

prep: 25 minutes bake: 25 minutes cool: 10 minutes
makes: 4 servings (1 individual dish each)

Nonstick cooking
  spray
4 ounces uncooked
  turkey Italian
  sausage links,
  casings removed
1 small red sweet
  pepper, chopped
1 cup coarsely
  shredded, unpeeled
  zucchini
¼ cup finely shredded
  Parmesan cheese
1½ cups refrigerated or
  frozen egg product,
  thawed, or 6 eggs,
  lightly beaten
¼ cup fat-free milk
⅛ teaspoon black
  pepper
⅓ cup shredded part-
  skim or reduced-fat
  mozzarella cheese

1 Preheat oven to 325°F. Coat four 8-ounce shallow ramekins or quiche dishes or one 9-inch pie plate with cooking spray. Set aside.

2 In a medium skillet cook turkey sausage, sweet pepper, and zucchini until turkey is cooked through and pepper is just tender, stirring to break up turkey as it cooks. Combine cooked turkey mixture and Parmesan cheese. Divide mixture among the prepared dishes or spoon into pie plate. In a medium bowl whisk together egg, milk, and black pepper. Pour egg mixture evenly into the ramekins or pie plate. Sprinkle with mozzarella cheese.

3 Bake individual servings about 25 minutes or pie plate about 35 minutes or until a knife inserted in center(s) comes out clean. Cool on a wire rack for 10 minutes before serving.

nutrition facts per serving: 151 cal., 5 g total fat (3 g sat. fat), 25 mg chol., 588 mg sodium, 6 g carb. (1 g fiber, 4 g sugars), 18 g pro. exchanges: 0.5 vegetable, 2.5 lean meat, 0.5 fat.

This recipe is reminiscent of a stylish breakfast you'd find at a chic little corner cafe. Prepare it at home with egg substitute to make it more healthful.

tomato-arugula omelets

start to finish: 25 minutes
makes: 4 servings (1 omelet each)

Nonstick cooking
  spray
2 cups refrigerated or
  frozen egg product,
  thawed, or 8 eggs,
  lightly beaten
⅛ teaspoon black
  pepper
1 cup torn fresh
  arugula or spinach
1 cup seeded, chopped
  tomato
½ cup crumbled
  reduced-fat feta
  cheese (2 ounces)
¼ cup pitted Kalamata
  olives, sliced

1 Coat a medium nonstick skillet with flared sides with cooking spray. Heat skillet over medium heat.

2 In a medium bowl combine the egg and pepper. Pour one-fourth of the egg mixture into prepared skillet. Immediately begin stirring the eggs gently but continuously with a wooden or plastic spatula until mixture resembles small pieces of cooked egg surrounded by liquid egg. Stop stirring. Cook for 30 to 60 seconds more or until egg is set but shiny.

3 When egg is set but still shiny, sprinkle one-fourth of the arugula, one-fourth of the tomato, one-fourth of the cheese, and one-fourth of the olives over half of the egg. With a spatula, lift and fold the other half of the egg up over filling. Transfer omelet to a serving plate. (If necessary, wipe out skillet with a clean paper towel and coat with nonstick cooking spray between omelets.) Repeat with remaining egg mixture, arugula, tomato, cheese, and olives to make three more omelets.

nutrition facts per serving: 118 cal., 4 g total fat (2 g sat. fat), 5 mg chol., 562 mg sodium, 5 g carb. (1 g fiber, 2 g sugars), 16 g pro. exchanges: 0.5 vegetable, 2 lean meat, 0.5 fat.

A wedge of your favorite foil-wrapped spreadable cheese adds a luscious ooziness to the filling.

asparagus-cheese omelet

4g
CARB. PER SERVING

start to finish: 20 minutes
makes: 1 serving (1 omelet)

Nonstick cooking
   spray
3 to 5 thin spears
   asparagus
1 tablespoon red sweet
   pepper slivers
3 egg whites, or
   2 egg whites and
   1 whole egg, or
   ½ cup refrigerated
   or frozen egg
   product, thawed
⅛ teaspoon freshly
   ground black
   pepper
½ teaspoon olive oil
1 0.75-ounce desired-
   flavor individually
   foil-wrapped
   spreadable cheese
   wedge, cut up
1 teaspoon snipped
   fresh basil or
   parsley

1 Lightly coat an unheated large nonstick skillet with cooking spray. Add asparagus and sweet pepper to skillet; pan-roast over medium-high heat about 7 minutes or until crisp-tender, turning occasionally. Set aside.

2 In a medium bowl combine egg whites and black pepper. Using a fork, beat until combined but not frothy. In a medium nonstick skillet heat oil over medium-high heat. Add egg whites to skillet. Reduce heat to medium. As egg white starts to set, use a spatula to gently lift edges of set egg white, tilting pan to allow liquid egg white to run under set egg. Continue until egg is set but still shiny.

3 Arrange the asparagus and sweet pepper on half of the set egg in skillet. Top vegetables evenly with cheese. Fold the unfilled half of the egg over the vegetables and cheese. Gently slide the omelet out of the skillet onto a serving plate. Sprinkle omelet with basil.

nutrition facts per serving: 116 cal., 5 g total fat (1 g sat. fat), 10 mg chol., 427 mg sodium, 4 g carb. (1 g fiber, 3 g sugars), 15 g pro. exchanges: 0.5 vegetable, 2 lean meat, 0.5 fat.

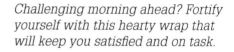

34

18g
CARB. PER
SERVING

*Challenging morning ahead? Fortify
yourself with this hearty wrap that
will keep you satisfied and on task.*

bacon and egg breakfast wraps

start to finish: 25 minutes
makes: 4 servings (1 wrap each)

4   slices bacon, chopped
1   cup chopped fresh
    mushrooms
1   small green sweet
    pepper, chopped
    (½ cup)
¼   teaspoon chili
    powder
¼   teaspoon black
    pepper
⅛   teaspoon salt
1   cup refrigerated or
    frozen egg product,
    thawed
¼   cup chopped, seeded
    tomato
    Bottled hot pepper
    sauce
4   8-inch flour tortillas,
    warmed*

1 In a large nonstick skillet cook bacon over
medium heat until crisp. Using a slotted
spoon, remove bacon from skillet, reserving
1 tablespoon of the drippings in the skillet
(discard the remaining drippings). Drain bacon
on paper towels.

2 Add mushrooms, sweet pepper, chili
powder, black pepper, and salt to the
reserved drippings in skillet; cook and stir
about 3 minutes or until vegetables are tender.

3 Pour egg over vegetable mixture in skillet.
Cook over medium heat. As mixture sets,
run a spatula around edge of skillet, lifting and
folding egg mixture so the uncooked portion
flows underneath. Continue cooking over
medium heat about 2 minutes or until egg is
cooked through but still glossy and moist. Stir
in cooked bacon, tomato, and hot pepper sauce
to taste. Divide egg mixture among tortillas; roll
up tortillas. To serve, cut wraps in half.

nutrition facts per serving: 195 cal., 9 g total fat
(3 g sat. fat), 11 mg chol., 462 mg sodium, 18 g carb. (1 g fiber,
2 g sugars), 11 g pro. exchanges: 0.5 vegetable, 1 starch,
1 lean meat, 1.5 fat.

*test kitchen tip: To warm tortillas, preheat
oven to 350°F. Wrap tortillas tightly in foil. Bake
about 10 minutes or until heated through.

Drain the bottled roasted peppers on paper towels before cutting them into strips.

italian egg breakfast sandwiches

29g CARB. PER SERVING

start to finish: 25 minutes
makes: 4 servings (1 sandwich each)

Nonstick cooking spray
1 cup refrigerated or frozen egg product, thawed, or 4 eggs, lightly beaten
¼ teaspoon dried Italian seasoning, crushed
⅛ teaspoon salt
4 whole grain English muffins, split and toasted
2 tablespoons bottled refrigerated reduced-fat or regular basil pesto
4 ounces shredded cooked chicken breast
¼ cup chopped bottled roasted red sweet peppers

1 Lightly coat an unheated large nonstick skillet with cooking spray. In a small bowl combine egg, Italian seasoning, and salt. Heat skillet over medium heat; pour in egg mixture. Cook, without stirring, until mixture begins to set on the bottom and around edges. With a spatula or a large spoon, lift and fold the partially cooked egg mixture so the uncooked portion flows underneath. Continue cooking for 2 to 3 minutes or until egg mixture is cooked through but still glossy and moist. Immediately remove from heat.

2 Spread cut sides of English muffins with pesto. Top bottom halves of muffins with egg mixture, chicken, and chopped peppers; add muffin tops. Serve warm.

nutrition facts per serving: 243 cal., 5 g total fat (1 g sat. fat), 26 mg chol., 588 mg sodium, 29 g carb. (5 g fiber, 6 g sugars), 22 g pro. exchanges: 2 starch, 2.5 lean meat.

36

Thanks to the whole wheat tortillas, you can enjoy all the flavors of bagels and lox (smoked salmon) without an overdose of carbs.

14g
CARB. PER
SERVING

smoked salmon breakfast wraps

start to finish: 20 minutes
makes: 4 servings (1 wrap each)

⅓ cup light cream
    cheese spread
1 tablespoon snipped
    fresh chives
1 teaspoon finely
    shredded lemon
    peel
1 tablespoon lemon
    juice
4 6- to 7-inch whole
    wheat flour tortillas
3 ounces thinly sliced
    smoked salmon
    (lox-style), cut into
    strips
1 small zucchini,
    trimmed
    Lemon wedges
    (optional)

1 In a small bowl stir together cream cheese spread, chives, lemon peel, and lemon juice until smooth. Spread evenly over tortillas, leaving a ½-inch border around the edges.

2 Divide salmon among tortillas, placing it on the bottom half of each tortilla. To make zucchini ribbons, draw a sharp vegetable peeler lengthwise along the zucchini to cut very thin slices. Place zucchini ribbons on top of salmon. Starting from the bottom, roll up tortillas. Cut in half. If desired, serve with lemon wedges.

nutrition facts per serving: 124 cal., 6 g total fat (2 g sat. fat), 15 mg chol., 451 mg sodium, 14 g carb. (9 g fiber, 2 g sugars), 12 g pro. exchanges: 1 starch, 1 lean meat.

Bananas and blueberries add color and nutrients to the maple syrup topping.

oatmeal pancakes with maple fruit

31g
CARB. PER SERVING

prep: 20 minutes   stand: 10 minutes   cook: 2 minutes per batch
makes: 8 servings (2 pancakes and ⅓ cup maple fruit each)

3   medium bananas, peeled and sliced
½   cup fresh blueberries
¼   cup sugar-free maple-flavored syrup
2   teaspoons lemon juice
¼   teaspoon ground cinnamon
1   cup flour
½   cup quick-cooking rolled oats
1½ teaspoons baking powder
½   teaspoon baking soda
⅛   teaspoon salt
1   cup low-fat buttermilk or sour milk*
¼   cup refrigerated or frozen egg product, thawed, or 1 egg, lightly beaten
1   tablespoon canola oil
1   tablespoon sugar-free maple-flavored syrup
1   teaspoon vanilla

1 For maple fruit, in a medium bowl stir together bananas, blueberries, the ¼ cup syrup, the lemon juice, and cinnamon. Set aside.

2 In a large bowl stir together flour, oats, baking powder, baking soda, and salt. In a medium bowl use a fork to combine buttermilk, egg, oil, 1 tablespoon syrup, and the vanilla. Add buttermilk mixture all at once to flour mixture. Stir just until moistened. Let stand for 10 minutes to soften oats.

3 For each pancake, spoon 2 slightly rounded tablespoons batter onto a hot, lightly greased griddle or heavy skillet; spread to a 3- to 4-inch circle. Cook over medium heat for 1 to 2 minutes on each side or until pancakes are golden brown. Turn over when edges are slightly dry and bottoms are browned. Serve warm topped with maple fruit.

nutrition facts per serving: 159 cal., 3 g total fat (0 g sat. fat), 1 mg chol., 246 mg sodium, 31 g carb. (2 g fiber, 8 g sugars), 5 g pro. exchanges: 0.5 fruit, 1 starch, 0.5 carb., 0.5 fat.

*test kitchen tip: To make 1 cup sour milk, place 1 tablespoon lemon juice or vinegar in a glass measuring cup. Add enough fat-free milk to make 1 cup total liquid; stir. Let the mixture stand for 5 minutes before using.

39g
CARB. PER
SERVING

Little bits of chopped pear add a sweet surprise to these morning treats.

pear-ginger pancakes

prep: 20 minutes cook: 2 minutes per batch
makes: 4 servings (2 pancakes and about 2 tablespoons syrup each)

- ½ cup all-purpose flour
- ½ cup whole wheat flour
- 1 tablespoon packed brown sugar *
- 2 teaspoons baking powder
- ¼ teaspoon ground ginger
- ⅛ teaspoon salt
- ¾ cup fat-free milk
- ¼ cup refrigerated or frozen egg product, thawed, or 1 egg
- 2 tablespoons canola oil
- ½ of a medium pear, cored and finely chopped (½ cup)
- 1 recipe Apricot-Pear Syrup

1 In a medium bowl combine all-purpose flour, whole wheat flour, brown sugar, baking powder, ginger, and salt. Make a well in the center of flour mixture; set aside. In a small bowl whisk together milk, egg, and oil; stir in chopped pear. Add egg mixture all at once to flour mixture; stir just until moistened.

2 For each pancake, pour ¼ cup of the batter onto a hot, lightly greased griddle, spreading batter into an even layer if necessary. Cook over medium heat for 2 to 4 minutes or until pancakes are golden, turning to second sides when pancakes have bubbly surfaces and edges are slightly dry. Keep pancakes warm in a 300°F oven while cooking the remaining pancakes. Serve pancakes with warm Apricot-Pear Syrup.

nutrition facts per serving: 242 cal., 7 g total fat (1 g sat. fat), 1 mg chol., 243 mg sodium, 39 g carb. (4 g fiber, 13 g sugars), 7 g pro. exchanges: 0.5 fruit, 2 starch, 1 fat.

nutrition facts per serving with substitute: Same as original, except. 229 cal., 35 g carb. (9 g sugars), 242 mg sodium.

＊sugar substitutes: Choose from Sweet'N Low Brown or Sugar Twin Granulated Brown. Follow package directions to use product amount equivalent to 1 tablespoon brown sugar.

apricot-pear syrup: In a small saucepan combine ½ cup finely chopped pear and 1 tablespoon lemon juice. Stir in 2 tablespoons low-sugar apricot preserves, 1 tablespoon water, and ⅛ teaspoon ground ginger. Heat and stir over low heat until preserves are melted and mixture is warm.

The colorful Cranberry Syrup adds an irresistible burst of sweet-tart flavor to these hearty waffles.

sweet potato waffles with cranberry syrup

33g CARB. PER SERVING

prep: 30 minutes cook: 3 minutes per batch
makes: 10 servings (2 waffle squares and 2½ tablespoons syrup each)

1 recipe Cranberry Syrup
1¼ cups whole wheat pastry flour
½ cup all-purpose flour
2 tablespoons packed brown sugar∗
1 tablespoon baking powder
¼ teaspoon salt
¼ teaspoon ground cinnamon
1½ cups fat-free milk
1 cup pureed, cooked sweet potatoes
½ cup refrigerated or frozen egg product, thawed
2 tablespoons canola oil

1 Prepare Cranberry Syrup; set aside. In a large bowl combine flours, brown sugar, baking powder, salt, and cinnamon. In a medium bowl combine milk, sweet potatoes, eggs, and oil; add all at once to flour mixture. Stir just until moistened (batter should be lumpy).

2 Pour about ¾ cup batter onto grids of a preheated, lightly greased waffle baker. Close lid quickly; do not open until done. Bake according to manufacturer's directions. When done, use a fork to lift waffle off grids. Repeat with remaining batter. Serve waffles with syrup.

nutrition facts per serving: 172 cal., 3 g total fat (0 g sat. fat), 1 mg chol., 246 mg sodium, 33 g carb. (3 g fiber, 13 g sugars), 5 g pro. exchanges: 2 starch.

∗ sugar substitute: We do not recommend using a sugar substitute for this recipe.

cranberry syrup: In a medium saucepan combine 1½ cups fresh cranberries, ¾ cup reduced-calorie maple-flavored syrup, ⅓ cup orange juice, and ½ teaspoon ground cinnamon. Cook and stir over medium-high heat until boiling. Reduce heat and simmer, uncovered, for 3 to 5 minutes or until cranberries pop. Mash cranberries slightly. Remove from heat and set aside.

Get a head start on breakfast: Stir together the dry ingredients of this gingerbread-like cake the day before. Then prep the rest and pop it in the oven in the morning.

overnight blueberry coffee cake

25g
CARB. PER SERVING

prep: 25 minutes **chill:** 8 hours **bake:** 35 minutes
makes: 12 servings (1 piece each)

Nonstick cooking spray
1 cup whole wheat pastry flour
¾ cup yellow cornmeal
⅓ cup granulated sugar✻
1½ teaspoons ground cinnamon
1 teaspoon baking soda
½ teaspoon ground ginger
¼ teaspoon salt
1 cup plain fat-free Greek yogurt
¾ cup refrigerated or frozen egg product, thawed, or 3 eggs, lightly beaten
⅓ cup canola oil
¼ cup unsweetened applesauce
1 tablespoon butter flavoring
2 cups frozen blueberries
2 tablespoons packed dark brown sugar✻
Frozen light whipped dessert topping, thawed (optional)
Ground ginger (optional)

1 Lightly coat a 2-quart rectangular baking dish with cooking spray; set aside. In a large bowl stir together pastry flour, cornmeal, granulated sugar, 1 teaspoon of the cinnamon, the baking soda, the ½ teaspoon ginger, and salt.

2 In a medium bowl whisk together yogurt, egg, oil, applesauce, and butter flavoring until well mixed; add to the flour mixture, stirring just until combined. Spread half of the batter into the prepared dish.

3 Sprinkle with 1 cup of the frozen blueberries. Spread the remaining batter evenly over top. Cover and chill for 8 to 24 hours.

4 Allow the coffee cake to stand at room temperature while the oven preheats to 350° F. In a small bowl toss together the remaining 1 cup frozen blueberries, the brown sugar, and the remaining ½ teaspoon cinnamon; sprinkle over the batter.

5 Bake, uncovered, about 35 minutes or until a toothpick inserted near the center comes out clean. Serve warm. If desired, serve with whipped topping and sprinkle with additional ginger.

nutrition facts per serving: 175 cal., 7 g total fat (0 g sat. fat), 0 mg chol., 195 mg sodium, 25 g carb. (2 g fiber, 12 g sugars), 5 g pro. exchanges: 1 starch, 0.5 carb., 1 fat.

nutrition facts per serving with substitutes: Same as original, except 152 cal., 19 g carb. (5 g sugars). exchanges: 0 carb.

✻sugar substitutes: Choose from Splenda Granular or Sweet'N Low bulk or packets for the granulated sugar. Choose Splenda Brown Sugar Blend for the brown sugar. Follow package directions to use product amounts equivalent to ⅓ cup granulated sugar and 2 tablespoons brown sugar.

Enjoy everything you love about French toast plus a little extra fiber from the whole grain baguette.

maple-apple drenched french toast

35g CARB. PER SERVING

start to finish: 30 minutes

makes: 4 servings (2 slices toast and ⅓ cup topping each)

1 recipe Maple-Apple Topping
½ cup refrigerated or frozen egg product, thawed, or 2 eggs, beaten
½ cup fat-free milk
¼ teaspoon vanilla
⅛ teaspoon ground cinnamon or ground nutmeg
8 ¾-inch-thick slices whole grain baguette-style bread (6 ounces total)
Nonstick cooking spray
¼ cup coarsely chopped pecans, toasted

1 Prepare Maple-Apple Topping; set aside. In a shallow bowl whisk together egg, milk, vanilla, and cinnamon. Dip bread slices into egg mixture, turning to coat both sides (let soak in egg mixture about 1 minute per side).

2 Coat an unheated large nonstick skillet or griddle with cooking spray. Preheat over medium heat. Place bread on hot skillet or griddle; cook for 4 to 6 minutes or until golden brown, turning once. Divide bread slices among four serving plates. Spoon on Maple-Apple Topping and sprinkle with pecans.

nutrition facts per serving: 229 cal., 7 g total fat (0 g sat. fat), 1 mg chol., 251 mg sodium, 35 g carb. (7 g fiber, 10 g sugars), 11 g pro. exchanges: 2 starch, 0.5 lean meat, 1 fat.

maple-apple topping: In a small saucepan combine 1 large red-skin cooking apple, cored, quartered, and thinly sliced, and 2 tablespoons water. Bring to boiling over medium heat. Cover and cook for 2 to 3 minutes or until apple is just tender, stirring occasionally. Add ½ cup sugar-free or light pancake syrup. Cook, uncovered, about 2 minutes or until slightly thickened and heated through.

Coffee cakes freeze well for up to 3 months. Freeze individual servings in freezer wrap and you can enjoy a sweet treat for weeks to come.

hazelnut coffee cake

23g
CARB. PER
SERVING

prep: 25 minutes bake: 20 minutes cool: 15 minutes
makes: 12 servings (1 piece each)

¼ cup rolled oats
1 tablespoon packed brown sugar*
¼ teaspoon ground cinnamon
1 tablespoon tub-style vegetable oil spread
¼ cup chopped hazelnuts, toasted**
1⅓ cups all-purpose flour
½ cup granulated sugar*
½ teaspoon baking powder
¼ teaspoon baking soda
⅛ teaspoon salt
1 egg, lightly beaten
½ cup light sour cream
¼ cup water
3 tablespoons canola oil
2 tablespoons unsweetened cocoa powder
1 tablespoon fat-free milk
½ teaspoon vanilla

1 Preheat oven to 350°F. Grease a 9×9×2-inch baking pan or dish; set aside. For topping, in a small bowl combine oats, brown sugar, and cinnamon. Using a pastry blender, cut in vegetable oil spread until mixture is crumbly. Stir in hazelnuts. Set aside.

2 In a medium bowl combine flour, granulated sugar, baking powder, baking soda, and salt. In a small bowl combine egg, sour cream, the water, and oil. Add to flour mixture; stir just until combined. Place ½ cup of the batter into a clean small bowl. Stir in cocoa powder, milk, and vanilla until smooth. Spoon the light-color batter into prepared pan, spreading evenly (batter will be shallow in the pan). Spoon the chocolate batter in small mounds over batter in pan. Using a thin metal spatula, slightly marble batters. Sprinkle with topping.

3 Bake for 20 to 25 minutes or until a toothpick inserted in the center comes out clean. Cool in pan on a wire rack for 15 minutes. Cut into 12 pieces. Serve warm.

nutrition facts per serving: 170 cal., 7 g total fat (1 g sat. fat), 20 mg chol., 81 mg sodium, 23 g carb. (1 g fiber, 10 g sugars), 3 g pro. exchanges: 1.5 carb., 1.5 fat.

nutrition facts per serving with substitutes: Same as original, except 153 cal., 80 mg sodium, 17 g carb. (4 g sugars). exchanges: 1 carb.

*sugar substitutes: Choose from Sweet'N Low Brown or Sugar Twin Granulated Brown to substitute for the brown sugar. Use Splenda Sugar Blend to substitute for the granulated sugar. Follow package directions to use product amounts equivalent to 1 tablespoon brown sugar and ½ cup granulated sugar.

**test kitchen tip: To toast hazelnuts, preheat oven to 350°F. Spread nuts in a single layer in a shallow baking pan. Bake for 8 to 10 minutes or until lightly toasted, stirring a few times to toast evenly. Remove nuts from oven. Let nuts cool for 5 minutes. Rub hazelnuts in a clean kitchen towel to remove skins.

24g
CARB. PER
SERVING

This deliciously chocolaty morning-style cake pairs perfectly with a cup of coffee anytime. Pictured on page 21.

mocha coffee cake

prep: 20 minutes bake: 25 minutes
makes: 12 servings (1 piece each)

Nonstick cooking
  spray
3 tablespoons packed
  brown sugar✱
2 tablespoons flour
1 tablespoon
  unsweetened cocoa
  powder
½ teaspoon ground
  cinnamon
2 tablespoons cold
  butter
1½ cups flour
½ cup packed brown
  sugar✱✱
2 tablespoons
  unsweetened cocoa
  powder
1 tablespoon instant
  espresso coffee
  powder
1 teaspoon baking
  powder
¼ teaspoon baking soda
¼ teaspoon salt
2 eggs, lightly beaten,
  or ½ cup refrigerated
  or frozen egg
  product, thawed
½ cup fat-free sour
  cream or plain
  low-fat yogurt
¼ cup water
3 tablespoons canola
  oil
1 teaspoon vanilla

1 Preheat oven to 350°F. Lightly coat an 8×8×2-inch or 9×9×2-inch baking pan with cooking spray; set aside. For topping, in a bowl combine the 3 tablespoons brown sugar, 2 tablespoons flour, 1 tablespoon cocoa powder, and the cinnamon. Cut in butter until mixture resembles coarse crumbs. Set aside.

2 In a large bowl stir together the 1½ cups flour, ½ cup brown sugar, 2 tablespoons cocoa powder, the espresso powder, baking powder, baking soda, and salt. Make a well in the center of the flour mixture; set aside.

3 In a medium bowl combine eggs, sour cream, the water, canola oil, and vanilla. Add to flour mixture; stir just until combined. Spread batter evenly into prepared pan. Sprinkle evenly with topping.

4 Bake for 25 to 30 minutes or until a wooden toothpick inserted in the center comes out clean. Cool in pan on a wire rack for 15 minutes. Cut into 12 pieces; serve warm.

nutrition facts per serving: 165 cal., 6 g total fat (2 g sat. fat), 41 mg chol., 148 mg sodium, 24 g carb. (1 g fiber, 8 g sugars), 3 g pro. exchanges: 1 starch, 0.5 carb., 1 medium-fat meat, 0.5 fat.

nutrition facts per serving with substitute: Same as original, except 162 cal., 147 mg sodium, 22 g carb. (6 g sugars). exchanges: 0.5 medium-fat meat.

✱sugar substitute: We do not recommend using sugar substitute for the 3 tablespoons brown sugar in the topping.

✱✱sugar substitute: Choose Splenda Brown Sugar Blend for the brown sugar in the batter. Follow package directions to use product amount equivalent to ½ cup brown sugar.

These bars are just the ticket when everyone's on a different schedule in the morning. The kids can serve themselves, and you can grab one to enjoy on the way to work.

breakfast bars to go

prep: 25 minutes microwave: 1½ minutes chill: 2 hours
makes: 24 servings (1 bar each)

2 cups crisp rice cereal
2 cups quick-cooking
   rolled oats
½ cup dry-roasted
   peanuts
½ cup sunflower
   kernels
2 cups chopped dried
   fruit, such as raisins,
   apricots, cherries,
   blueberries, and/or
   cranberries
¾ cup honey
¾ cup creamy natural
   peanut butter
¼ cup packed brown
   sugar*
1 teaspoon vanilla

1 Line a 13×9×2-inch baking pan with foil; set aside. In a large bowl combine cereal, oats, peanuts, sunflower kernels, and chopped fruit. Set aside.

2 In a medium microwave-safe bowl combine honey, peanut butter, and brown sugar. Microwave, uncovered, on 100 percent power (high) for 1½ to 2½ minutes or until mixture is bubbly, stirring once. Stir in vanilla. Pour mixture over cereal mixture. Stir until just combined. Press into the prepared pan to form an even layer.

3 Cover and chill for 2 to 24 hours. Cut into 24 bars. If desired, wrap individual bars in plastic wrap and chill for up to 1 week.

nutrition facts per serving: 196 cal., 8 g total fat (1 g sat. fat), 0 mg chol., 53 mg sodium, 30 g carb. (2 g fiber, 19 g sugars), 5 g pro. exchanges: 1 starch, 1 carb., 1.5 fat.

nutrition facts per serving with substitute: Same as original, except 193 calories, 28 g carb. (18 g sugars), 52 mg sodium.

＊sugar substitute: Choose Splenda Brown Sugar Blend. Follow package directions to use product amount equivalent to ¼ cup brown sugar.

Quinoa, a protein-rich grain commonly used in pilafs, salads, and soups, makes a tasty breakfast cereal when spiced with cinnamon and drizzled with honey.

45g CARB. PER SERVING

fruit and nut quinoa

prep: 10 minutes   cook: 15 minutes   stand: 5 minutes
makes: 4 servings (¾ cup quinoa mixture, ½ cup berries, and 1 teaspoon honey each)

1   cup quinoa, rinsed and well drained
1   cup fat-free milk
1   cup water
½   teaspoon ground cinnamon
     Dash salt
½   cup chopped pecans, toasted
1   cup fresh blackberries
1   cup fresh raspberries
4   teaspoons honey

1 In a medium saucepan stir together quinoa, milk, the water, cinnamon, and salt. Bring to boiling over medium-high heat; reduce heat. Simmer, covered, about 15 minutes or until most of the liquid is absorbed. Remove from heat; let stand, covered, for 5 minutes.

2 Stir in pecans. Top each serving evenly with fresh berries. Drizzle each serving with 1 teaspoon honey.

nutrition facts per serving: 325 cal., 13 g total fat (1 g sat. fat), 1 mg chol., 67 mg sodium, 45 g carb. (8 g fiber, 13 g sugars), 10 g pro. exchanges: 0.5 fruit, 2.5 starch, 2 fat.

With apples, nuts, spice, and a crunchy granola topping, this is like having dessert for breakfast—except it's full of healthful nutrients and fiber.

apple crisp hot cereal

start to finish: 10 minutes
makes: 1 serving (¾ cup)

29g
CARB. PER
SERVING

½ cup hot cooked cereal (such as oatmeal)
¼ cup chopped apple∗
2 tablespoons low-fat granola without raisins
1 tablespoon chopped almonds
⅛ teaspoon apple pie spice

Place cooked cereal in a serving bowl. Top with apple, granola, and almonds. Sprinkle with apple pie spice.

nutrition facts per serving: 179 cal., 5 g total fat (1 g sat. fat), 0 mg chol., 35 mg sodium, 29 g carb (4 g fiber, 7 g sugars), 5 g pro. exchanges: 2 starch, 0.5 fat.

∗test kitchen tip: Use peach or nectarine when in peak season as an option to apple.

48

34g
CARB. PER
SERVING

If peaches are out of season, use strawberries or raspberries in this elegant parfait.

peach-blueberry parfaits

start to finish: 10 minutes
makes: 2 servings (1 parfait each [about 1¼ cups])

1   6-ounce carton
vanilla, peach, or
blueberry fat-free
yogurt
1   cup lightly sweetened
multigrain clusters
cereal or low-fat
granola cereal
1   ripe peach, pitted and
cut up
½   cup fresh blueberries
¼   teaspoon ground
cinnamon

Divide half of the yogurt between two dessert glasses or bowls; top with half of the cereal. Top with half of the peach, half of the blueberries, and the cinnamon. Repeat layers with the remaining yogurt, cereal, peach, and blueberries.

nutrition facts per serving: 166 cal., 1 g total fat (0 g sat. fat), 2 mg chol., 95 mg sodium, 34 g carb. (7 g fiber, 19 g sugars), 11 g pro. exchanges: 0.5 milk, 0.5 fruit, 1 starch.

If fresh mangoes are not at their peak, substitute chopped refrigerated mango slices, available in jars in the produce department.

cinnamon toast and fruit breakfast parfaits

43g
CARB. PER SERVING

prep: 15 minutes cook: 3 minutes
makes: 4 servings (1 parfait each [about ¾ cup])

1 tablespoon light stick butter (not margarine)
½ teaspoon ground cinnamon
2 slices light oatmeal bread, cut into cubes
2 6-ounce cartons plain fat-free Greek yogurt
¼ cup strawberry spreadable fruit
1 medium banana, coarsely chopped or thinly sliced (about 1 cup)
¾ cup fresh blueberries
1 medium mango, peeled, seeded, and cubed
4 teaspoons honey

1 In a medium skillet combine butter and cinnamon. Heat over medium heat until melted. Add bread cubes and toss to coat. Continue to cook over medium heat for 3 to 4 minutes or until bread cubes are lightly browned and crisp, stirring occasionally. Remove from heat and set aside to cool.

2 In a small bowl combine yogurt and spreadable fruit. In a large bowl combine banana, blueberries, and mango.

3 To serve, spoon one-third of the fruit evenly into four parfait glasses or 8-ounce clear drinking glasses. Top with half of the bread cubes. Spoon half of the yogurt mixture on top of the bread cubes. Repeat layers once, using half of the remaining fruit, all of the remaining bread cubes, and all of the remaining yogurt mixture. Top evenly with remaining fruit. Drizzle with honey. Serve immediately.

nutrition facts per serving: 217 cal., 2 g total fat (1 g sat. fat), 4 mg chol., 106 mg sodium, 43 g carb. (3 g fiber, 31 g sugars), 10 g pro. exchanges: 0.5 milk, 1 fruit, 1.5 starch.

Wow overnight guests when you present this beautiful fruit salad on your breakfast table.

sunrise fruit salad

start to finish: 25 minutes
makes: 6 servings (¾ cup each)

½ of an 8-ounce tub
    light cream cheese
1 6-ounce carton plain
    fat-free Greek yogurt
1 tablespoon honey
1 teaspoon finely
    shredded lemon
    peel
1 teaspoon finely
    shredded orange
    peel
1 medium orange,
    peeled and
    sectioned
3 medium kiwifruits,
    peeled and sliced
1 medium mango,
    seeded, peeled, and
    cubed
1 cup fresh blueberries

1 In a medium bowl beat cream cheese with an electric mixer on medium speed until smooth. Beat in yogurt and honey until smooth. Stir in lemon peel and orange peel.

2 Divide cream cheese mixture among six serving dishes; top with fruit. Serve immediately or cover loosely and chill for up to 4 hours.

nutrition facts per serving: 131 cal., 3 g total fat (2 g sat. fat), 9 mg chol., 102 mg sodium, 23 g carb. (3 g fiber, 18 g sugars), 5 g pro. exchanges: 0.5 milk, 1 fruit, 0.5 fat.

If you have leftover peach nectar from this recipe, pour a splash into hot tea to add sweetness and satisfying fruit flavor.

peach sunrise refresher

start to finish: 5 minutes
makes: 4 servings (1 cup each)

12g
CARB. PER
SERVING

2 cups ice
1⅓ cups diet cranberry
   juice drink
1⅓ cups peach nectar
   Mint sprigs (optional)
   Quartered orange
   slices (optional)

Place ½ cup ice in each of four glasses. Add ⅓ cup of the cranberry juice to each glass. Slowly fill each glass with ⅓ cup of the peach nectar. If desired, garnish with mint sprigs and orange slices.

nutrition facts per serving: 46 cal., 0 g total fat, 0 mg chol., 24 mg sodium, 12 g carb. (0 g fiber, 12 g sugars), 0 g pro. exchanges: 1 carb.

52

With its pleasantly sweet flavor and lightly nutty aftertaste, almond milk makes a tasty choice for smoothies. Better yet, it's cholesterol-free. Find it in the health food section of the supermarket.

30 g
CARB. PER
SERVING

pb and j smoothies

start to finish: 10 minutes
makes: 2 servings (1¾ cups each)

In a blender combine tofu, berries, almond milk, juice, and peanut butter. Cover and blend until smooth. Gradually add ice through hole in lid of blender; blend until smooth. Pour into two tall glasses. If desired, garnish each serving with a few fresh or frozen blueberries.

6   ounces light soft
       silken tofu
⅔   cup frozen
       blueberries
1¼   cups vanilla-flavor
       almond milk, chilled
½   cup grape juice,
       chilled
2   tablespoons creamy
       peanut butter
½   cup small ice cubes
       or crushed ice
       Fresh or frozen
       blueberries
       (optional)

nutrition facts per serving: 247 cal., 11 g total fat
(2 g sat. fat), 0 mg chol., 243 mg sodium, 30 g carb. (3 g fiber,
25 g sugars), 11 g pro. exchanges: 1 fruit, 1 carb.,
1.5 medium-fat meat, 0.5 fat.

A dusting of chocolate-covered espresso beans crowns this creamy-topped, icy-cold coffee.

iced caramel-cream coffee

20g
CARB. PER
SERVING

start to finish: 5 minutes
makes: 2 servings (1 cup each)

2   cups cold strong-
    brewed coffee
2   tablespoons
    no-sugar-added
    French vanilla–
    flavor instant
    breakfast mix
2   tablespoons sugar-
    free caramel ice
    cream topping
    Ice cubes
2   tablespoons frozen
    light whipped
    dessert topping,
    thawed
2   teaspoons sugar-free
    caramel ice cream
    topping
    Coarsely crushed
    chocolate-covered
    coffee beans
    (optional)

In a blender combine coffee, instant breakfast mix, and 2 tablespoons ice cream topping. Cover and blend until smooth. Pour over ice in two glasses. Top with dessert topping and drizzle with the 2 teaspoons ice cream topping. If desired, sprinkle with coarsely crushed coffee beans.

nutrition facts per serving: 87 cal., 1 g total fat (1 g sat. fat), 1 mg chol., 62 mg sodium, 20 g carb. (1 g fiber, 3 g sugars), 2 g pro. exchanges: 1 carb.

cinnamon streusel
rolls, *page 68*

home-baked

bre

Go ahead! Bake a batch of fragrant cinnamon rolls. Stretch a soup into a meal with a muffin or biscuit. Bring out your best yeast breads for the holidays. With these recipes, you can do it all—and still stay true to your meal plan.

ads

23g
CARB. PER
SERVING

New to bread baking? This basic recipe is a great place to start. It's easy—yet yummy enough to do you proud.

classic bread loaf

prep: 25 minutes   chill: overnight   stand: 30 minutes   rise: 1 hour
bake: 25 minutes
makes: 12 servings (1 slice each)

¾   cup warm water
      (105°F to 115°F)
1   package active dry
      yeast
½   cup fat-free milk
2   tablespoons sugar*
2   tablespoons butter
½   teaspoon salt
2½   cups flour
      Nonstick cooking
      spray or olive oil
      Cornmeal
1   egg, lightly beaten
2   teaspoons water

*sugar substitutes:
Choose from Splenda Granular
or Sweet'N Low bulk or packets.
Follow package directions to
use product amount equivalent
to 2 tablespoons sugar.

**nutrition facts per serving with
substitute:** Same as original, except
127 cal., 21 g carb. (1 g sugars).

make-ahead directions: Prepare and
bake as directed. Cover tightly with plastic
wrap; overwrap with foil. Place in a resealable
plastic freezer bag. Seal, label, and freeze for
up to 2 months. Thaw at room temperature.

1 In a large bowl stir together the ¾ cup water and the yeast. Let stand for 5 minutes. Meanwhile, in a small saucepan heat and stir milk, sugar, butter, and salt just until warm (120°F to 130°F) and butter almost melts. Stir milk mixture into yeast mixture until combined. Stir in flour (dough will be sticky). Lightly coat a medium bowl with cooking spray; transfer dough to the greased bowl. Lightly coat a sheet of plastic wrap with cooking spray; cover bowl with the greased plastic wrap and chill dough overnight.

2 Using a dough scraper or spatula, carefully loosen dough from bowl and turn out onto a floured surface. Cover with the greased plastic wrap and let stand for 30 minutes.

3 Grease a baking sheet; sprinkle lightly with cornmeal. Gently shape dough into an oval loaf (about 6×5 inches). Using a dough scraper or spatula if necessary, transfer loaf to the prepared baking sheet. Cover and let rise in a warm place until nearly double in size (about 1 hour).

4 Preheat oven to 400°F. In a small bowl whisk together egg and the 2 teaspoons water; brush over loaf. Bake about 25 minutes or until an instant-read thermometer inserted in loaf registers at least 200°F and bread sounds hollow when tapped. If necessary, cover with foil during the last 5 minutes of baking to prevent overbrowning. Remove from baking sheet; cool on a wire rack.

nutrition facts per serving: 134 cal., 3 g total fat (1 g sat. fat), 21 mg chol., 125 mg sodium, 23 g carb. (1 g fiber, 3 g sugars), 4 g pro. **exchanges:** 1.5 starch, 0.5 fat.

Here's the perfect loaf to serve with lasagna and other robust, red-sauced Italian specialties.

roasted garlic-herb bread

12g
CARB. PER
SERVING

prep: 15 minutes   roast: 25 minutes   bake: 12 minutes
makes: 12 servings (1 slice each)

2   heads fresh garlic
2   tablespoons olive oil
3   tablespoons snipped
    fresh Italian (flat-
    leaf) parsley
1   tablespoon snipped
    fresh basil, oregano,
    and/or thyme
¼   teaspoon salt
¼   teaspoon freshly
    ground black
    pepper
1   10- to 12-ounce loaf
    whole grain Italian
    bread

1 Preheat oven to 425°F. Peel away the dry outer layers of skin from heads of garlic, leaving skins and cloves intact. Cut off the pointed top portions (about ¼ inch), leaving bulbs intact but exposing the individual cloves. Place each garlic head, cut side up, in a custard cup. Drizzle each with about ¼ teaspoon of the olive oil. Cover with foil. Bake for 25 to 35 minutes or until the cloves feel soft when pressed. Set aside until cool enough to handle.

2 Squeeze out the garlic paste from individual cloves into a small bowl. Mash garlic cloves with a fork. Stir in remaining olive oil, the parsley, basil, salt, and pepper.

3 Without cutting through bottom crust, cut bread into 12 slices. Spread garlic mixture between slices, spreading on one side only of each slice. Wrap loaf in heavy foil. Bake about 12 minutes or until heated through. Serve warm.

nutrition facts per serving: 88 cal., 3 g total fat (0 g sat. fat), 0 mg chol., 122 mg sodium, 12 g carb. (3 g fiber, 1 g sugars), 4 g pro. exchanges: 1 starch.

23g CARB. PER SERVING

Once you taste this spicy-sweet bread, you'll think of all kinds of occasions for bringing it to your table. It's perfect for brunch, holidays, Sunday soup suppers, and more.

spicy apricot and sausage braid

prep: 1 hour **rise:** 1 hour 40 minutes **stand:** 10 minutes **bake:** 20 minutes
makes: 16 servings (1 slice each)

4 ounces andouille sausage, finely chopped
½ cup finely chopped dried apricots
½ to 1 teaspoon crushed red pepper
½ cup snipped fresh cilantro
2 tablespoons honey
3 to 3½ cups flour
1 package active dry yeast
¾ teaspoon salt
⅔ cup warm water (105°F to 115°F)
2 eggs, lightly beaten
¼ cup olive oil
1 egg, lightly beaten
1 teaspoon water

1 In a large nonstick skillet cook sausage over medium-high heat until it starts to brown. Stir in apricots and crushed red pepper. Cook and stir for 1 minute. Stir in cilantro and honey. Remove from heat; cool.

2 Meanwhile, in a large bowl combine 1 cup of the flour, the yeast, and salt. Add the ⅔ cup warm water, the 2 eggs, and the oil. Beat with an electric mixer on low to medium speed for 30 seconds, scraping sides of bowl constantly. Beat on high speed for 3 minutes. Stir in sausage mixture. Using a wooden spoon, stir in as much of the remaining flour as you can.

3 Turn dough out onto a lightly floured surface. Knead in enough of the remaining flour to make a soft dough that is smooth and elastic (3 to 5 minutes total). Shape dough into a ball. Place dough in a lightly greased bowl, turning once to grease surface of dough. Cover; let rise in a warm place until double in size (about 1 hour).

4 Punch dough down. Turn dough out onto a lightly floured surface; divide dough into three portions. Cover; let rest for 10 minutes. Meanwhile, line a large baking sheet with parchment paper.

5 Gently roll each dough portion into a 16-inch-long rope. Place the ropes 1 inch apart on the prepared baking sheet; braid.

6 Cover. Let rise in a warm place until nearly double in size (about 40 minutes).

7 Preheat oven to 350°F. In a small bowl combine the 1 egg and the 1 teaspoon water; brush over braid. Bake for 20 to 25 minutes or until loaf sounds hollow when lightly tapped. Cool on a wire rack. Store in the refrigerator.

make-ahead directions: Prepare dough as directed through Step 5. Chill dough for at least 2 hours or up to 24 hours. Let stand at room temperature for 30 minutes before baking. Continue as directed in Step 7.

nutrition facts per serving: 158 cal., 5 g total fat (1 g sat. fat), 41 mg chol., 177 mg sodium, 23 g carb. (1 g fiber, 4 g sugars), 5 g pro. **exchanges:** 1.5 starch, 1 fat.

15g CARB. PER SERVING

Keep Dijon mustard in your fridge and you'll always have a low-fat ingredient to flavor-charge your cooking.

multigrain mustard baguette

prep: 30 minutes rise: 1 hour bake: 25 minutes
makes: 16 servings (1 slice each)

1   16-ounce loaf frozen
    wheat bread dough
½   cup seeds and/or
    chopped nuts✱
1   egg
1   tablespoon water
1   tablespoon Dijon-
    style mustard
2   tablespoons seeds✱

1 Thaw dough according to package directions. Grease a large baking sheet; set aside. On a lightly floured surface roll dough into a 1-inch-thick rectangle. Sprinkle dough with some of the ½ cup seeds and/or nuts. Using a rolling pin, roll seeds and/or nuts into the dough. Fold dough in half crosswise; repeat sprinkling and rolling until seeds and/or nuts are all added and are evenly distributed throughout dough.

2 Using floured hands, gently roll dough rectangle into a spiral and shape into a 16-inch-long baguette. Place shaped dough, seam side down, on prepared baking sheet. Cover loosely and let rise in a warm place until double in size (1 to 1½ hours).

3 Preheat oven to 350°F. In a small bowl whisk together egg and the water. Brush loaf with mustard and then brush with egg mixture. Sprinkle with the 2 tablespoons seeds. Snip small slits diagonally down the top of the loaf. Bake for 25 to 30 minutes or until bread sounds hollow when lightly tapped.

nutrition facts per serving: 111 cal., 4 g total fat (0 g sat. fat), 12 mg chol., 185 mg sodium, 15 g carb. (2 g fiber, 0 g sugars), 5 g pro. exchanges: 1 starch, 0.5 fat.

✱ test kitchen tip: For seeds, try sesame, poppy, or fennel. For nuts, try pecans, walnuts, or pine nuts.

make-ahead directions: Prepare as directed in Steps 1 and 2, except after shaping dough and covering loosely, chill in the refrigerator for up to 24 hours. Let stand at room temperature for 30 minutes before baking. Bake as directed in Step 3.

To loosen the edges from the casserole, run a table knife or straight-sided spreader around the side of the dish.

easy focaccia casserole bread

prep: 20 minutes   rise: 25 minutes   bake: 30 minutes
makes: 12 servings (1 slice each)

25g
CARB. PER
SERVING

Nonstick cooking
   spray
3 cups flour
1 package fast-rising
   active dry yeast
1 cup warm water
   (120°F to 130°F)
1 egg
1 tablespoon sugar✱
2 tablespoons olive oil
½ teaspoon salt
½ teaspoon dried Italian
   seasoning, crushed
2 tablespoons grated
   Romano cheese or
   Parmesan cheese
2 tablespoons sliced
   green onion (1)
   (optional)
2 tablespoons Kalamata
   olives, quartered
   lengthwise (optional)

1 Coat a 1½-quart casserole with cooking spray; set aside. In a medium bowl stir together 1½ cups of the flour and the yeast. Add the water, egg, sugar, 1 tablespoon of the olive oil, and the salt. Beat with an electric mixer on low speed for 30 seconds, scraping sides of bowl constantly. Beat on high speed for 3 minutes. Using a wooden spoon, stir in the remaining 1½ cups flour (batter will be stiff).

2 Spoon batter into prepared casserole. Brush with the remaining 1 tablespoon olive oil. Sprinkle with Italian seasoning. Sprinkle with cheese and, if desired, green onion and olives. Cover; let rise in a warm place until nearly double in size (25 to 30 minutes).

3 Preheat oven to 375°F. Bake for 30 to 35 minutes or until bread sounds hollow when lightly tapped. Remove from casserole; cool completely on a wire rack.

nutrition facts per serving: 149 cal., 3 g total fat (1 g sat. fat), 16 mg chol., 117 mg sodium, 25 g carb. (1 g fiber, 1 g sugars), 4 g pro. exchanges: 1.5 starch, 0.5 fat.

nutrition facts per serving with substitute: Same as original, except 146 cal., 24 g carb. (0 g sugars).

✱sugar substitutes: Choose from Splenda Granular or Sweet'N Low bulk or packets. Follow package directions to use product amount equivalent to 1 tablespoon sugar.

26g
CARB. PER
SERVING

*This pizzalike bread will stand out at all kinds of occasions,
from potluck picnics to glamorous dinner parties.*

tomato-artichoke focaccia

prep: 30 minutes   rise: 1 hour 15 minutes   bake: 25 minutes
makes: 16 servings (1 piece each)

3½ to 4 cups flour
1   package active dry
    yeast
1   teaspoon salt
1¼ cups warm water
    (120°F to 130°F)
2   tablespoons olive oil
¼   cup cornmeal
    Nonstick cooking
    spray
1¼ pounds roma tomatoes
    and/or green or
    yellow tomatoes,
    thinly sliced
1   14-ounce can
    artichoke hearts,
    drained and
    quartered
1   tablespoon olive oil
1   tablespoon snipped
    fresh rosemary or
    1 teaspoon dried
    rosemary, crushed
1   small red onion, very
    thinly sliced and
    separated into rings
4   cloves garlic, cut into
    thin slivers

1 In a large bowl combine 1½ cups of the
flour, the yeast, and salt. Add the warm
water and the 2 tablespoons olive oil. Beat
with an electric mixer on low to medium
speed for 30 seconds, scraping bowl. Beat on
high speed for 3 minutes. Stir in cornmeal and
as much of the remaining flour as you can.

2 Turn out dough onto a lightly floured
surface. Knead in enough of the remaining
flour to make a moderately soft dough that is
smooth and elastic (3 to 5 minutes total). Shape
dough into a ball. Place dough in a lightly
greased bowl, turning once to grease surface.

3 Cover and let dough rise in a warm place
until double in size (45 to 60 minutes).
Punch dough down; let rest for 10 minutes.
Grease a 15×10×1-inch baking pan. Place dough
in prepared baking pan. Gently pull and stretch
dough in the baking pan into a 15×8-inch
rectangle, being careful not to overwork dough.

4 Lightly coat dough with cooking spray.
Cover; let dough rise in a warm place until
nearly double in size (about 30 minutes).

5 Preheat oven to 450°F. Arrange tomato slices
and artichoke quarters on paper towels. Let
stand for 15 minutes. Change paper towels as
necessary so all of the excess liquid is absorbed
from tomatoes and artichokes. Using your
fingers, press deep indentations in the dough
1½ to 2 inches apart. Brush dough with the
1 tablespoon olive oil. Sprinkle with rosemary.
Arrange tomato slices, artichoke quarters, onion
rings, and garlic slivers on top of dough.

6 Bake about 25 minutes or until golden
brown. Transfer to a wire rack to cool. Cut
into pieces. Serve warm or at room temperature.

nutrition facts per serving: 148 cal., 3 g total fat (0 g sat.
fat), 0 mg chol., 232 mg sodium, 26 g carb. (2 g fiber, 2 g sugars),
4 g pro. exchanges: 2 starch.

make-ahead directions: Prepare
dough as directed through Step 2. Cover
and chill dough in the refrigerator for 16 to
24 hours. Punch dough down and continue
as directed in Step 3, except increase the
rising time in Step 4 to about 45 minutes.

Thanks to a tube of pizza dough, these luscious tomato- and cheese-filled twists are ready for the oven in just 15 minutes.

focaccia breadsticks

12g CARB. PER SERVING

prep: 15 minutes   bake: 15 minutes
makes: 16 servings (1 breadstick each)

¼   cup oil-packed dried tomatoes
¼   cup grated Romano cheese
2   teaspoons water
⅛   teaspoon cracked black pepper
1   13.8-ounce package refrigerated pizza dough

1 Preheat oven to 350°F. Lightly grease a baking sheet; set aside. Drain dried tomatoes, reserving 2 teaspoons of the oil; finely snip tomatoes. In a large bowl combine tomatoes, the 2 teaspoons reserved oil, the cheese, water, and pepper. Set aside.

2 Unroll the pizza dough. On a lightly floured surface roll the dough into a 14×8-inch rectangle. Spread the tomato mixture crosswise over half of the dough. Fold plain half of the dough over filled half of the dough (rectangle should now be 7×8 inches); press lightly to seal edges. Cut the folded dough crosswise into sixteen ½-inch-wide strips. Twist each strip two or three times. Place twisted strips 1 inch apart on prepared baking sheet. Bake for 15 to 18 minutes or until golden brown. Transfer to a wire rack; cool slightly. Serve warm or at room temperature.

nutrition facts per serving: 72 cal., 1 g total fat (0 g sat. fat), 1 mg chol., 159 mg sodium, 12 g carb. (0 g fiber, 0 g sugars), 3 g pro. exchanges: 1 starch.

64

15g CARB. PER SERVING

Sesame seeds add a satisfying crunch to these fuss-free rolls.

easy sesame dinner rolls

prep: 20 minutes rise: 45 minutes bake: 25 minutes
makes: 16 servings (1 roll each)

1 16-ounce loaf frozen white or wheat bread dough
¼ cup sesame seeds
2 tablespoons yellow cornmeal
2 tablespoons grated or finely shredded Parmesan cheese
1 teaspoon salt-free lemon-pepper seasoning
3 tablespoons butter, melted

1 Thaw dough according to package directions. Grease a 9×9×2-inch square baking pan; set aside. In a shallow dish combine sesame seeds, cornmeal, Parmesan cheese, and lemon-pepper seasoning. Place butter in a second dish. Cut the bread dough into 16 equal pieces. Shape each piece into a ball by pulling and pinching dough underneath. Roll dough pieces in butter, then in the seasoning mixture to lightly coat. Arrange dough pieces, smooth sides up, in prepared pan.

2 Cover pan with waxed paper and let rise in a warm place until nearly double in size (45 to 60 minutes).

3 Preheat oven to 375°F. Bake, uncovered, about 25 minutes or until golden brown. Remove rolls from pan to a wire rack. Cool slightly before serving.

nutrition facts per serving: 109 cal., 4 g total fat (2 g sat. fat), 6 mg chol., 180 mg sodium, 15 g carb. (1 g fiber, 1 g sugars), 2 g pro. exchanges: 1 starch, 0.5 fat.

garlic-herb rolls: Prepare as directed, except omit lemon-pepper seasoning and add 1 teaspoon dried Italian seasoning, crushed, and ½ teaspoon garlic powder.

Remember this recipe when Easter and the year-end holidays roll around—the rolls are fabulous with baked ham.

pumpernickel rosettes

prep: 40 minutes rise: 1 hour 30 minutes stand: 10 minutes bake: 12 minutes
makes: 20 servings (1 roll each)

2¼ to 2¾ cups
    all-purpose flour
1 package active dry
    yeast
1⅓ cups water
¼ cup molasses
2 tablespoons tub-style
    vegetable oil spread
1 teaspoon salt
1½ cups rye flour
2 teaspoons caraway
    seeds
1 egg white
1 tablespoon water

1 In a large mixing bowl combine 1½ cups of the all-purpose flour and the yeast; set aside. In a medium saucepan heat and stir the water, molasses, vegetable oil spread, and salt just until warm (120°F to 130°F). Add water mixture to flour mixture. Beat with an electric mixer on low to medium speed for 30 seconds, scraping sides of bowl constantly. Beat on high speed for 3 minutes. Using a wooden spoon, stir in rye flour, caraway seeds, and as much of the remaining all-purpose flour as you can.

2 Turn dough out onto a lightly floured surface. Knead in enough of the remaining all-purpose flour to make a moderately stiff dough that is smooth and elastic (6 to 8 minutes total). Shape dough into a ball. Place in a lightly greased bowl, turning once to grease surface of dough. Cover; let rise in a warm place until double in size (1 to 1½ hours).

3 Punch dough down. Turn out onto a lightly floured surface. Divide in half. Cover; let rest for 10 minutes. Lightly grease two large baking sheets; set aside.

4 Divide each dough half into 10 equal portions. On a lightly floured surface roll each portion into a 12-inch-long rope. Tie each rope loosely in a knot, leaving two long ends. Tuck top end under knot and bottom end into top center of the knot. Place rosettes 2 to 3 inches apart on prepared baking sheets. Cover; let rise in a warm place until nearly double in size (30 to 45 minutes).

5 Preheat oven to 375°F. In a small bowl lightly beat egg white and 1 tablespoon water; brush over rosettes. Bake about 12 minutes or until tops are golden brown and rolls sound hollow when lightly tapped.

nutrition facts per serving: 101 cal., 1 g total fat (0 g sat. fat), 0 mg chol., 129 mg sodium, 20 g carb. (2 g fiber, 2 g sugars), 3 g pro. exchanges: 1 starch.

Rosemary pairs beautifully with roast pork, chicken, and turkey, so choose these rolls when serving those meats for your main dish.

honey-rosemary bowknots

27g
CARB. PER
SERVING

prep: 45 minutes **rise:** 1 hour 30 minutes **stand:** 10 minutes **bake:** 12 minutes
makes: 18 servings (1 roll each)

3¼ to 3¾ cups flour
1 package active dry
   yeast
1 cup fat-free milk
¼ cup tub-style
   vegetable oil spread
¼ cup honey
½ teaspoon salt
¼ cup refrigerated or
   frozen egg product,
   thawed, or 1 egg
¾ cup yellow cornmeal
1 tablespoon snipped
   fresh rosemary
   Nonstick cooking
   spray

1 In a large mixing bowl combine 1½ cups of the flour and the yeast; set aside. In a medium saucepan heat and stir milk, vegetable oil spread, honey, and salt just until warm (120°F to 130°F); add to flour mixture along with egg. Beat with an electric mixer on low to medium speed for 30 seconds, scraping sides of bowl. Beat on high speed for 3 minutes. Using a wooden spoon, stir in cornmeal, rosemary, and as much of the remaining flour as you can.

2 Turn dough out onto a lightly floured surface. Knead in enough remaining flour to make a moderately soft dough that is smooth and elastic (3 to 5 minutes total). Shape dough into a ball. Place in a lightly greased bowl, turning once to grease surface of dough. Cover; let rise in a warm place until double in size (about 1 hour).

3 Punch dough down. Turn out onto a lightly floured surface. Divide in half. Cover and let rest for 10 minutes. Coat two large baking sheets with cooking spray; set aside.

4 Divide each dough half into nine portions. Roll each portion into a 6-inch-long rope. Tie each rope loosely in a knot. Place knots 2 inches apart on prepared baking sheets. Cover; let rise in a warm place until nearly double in size (about 30 minutes).

5 Preheat oven to 375°F. Bake for 12 to 14 minutes or until golden. Immediately remove from baking sheets. Cool slightly on wire racks; serve warm.

nutrition facts per serving: 144 cal., 2 g total fat (1 g sat. fat), 0 mg chol., 95 mg sodium, 27 g carb. (1 g fiber, 5 g sugars), 4 g pro. **exchanges:** 2 starch.

home-baked breads

33g CARB. PER SERVING

To toast oats, place oats in a large skillet; heat over medium heat until oats are toasted, stirring often. Pictured on page 54.

cinnamon streusel rolls

prep: 45 minutes rise: 1 hour 30 minutes bake: 25 minutes cool: 5 minutes
makes: 15 servings (1 roll each)

1   cup fat-free milk
2   tablespoons packed
      brown sugar✳
2   tablespoons tub-style
      vegetable oil spread
1   teaspoon salt
¼   cup warm water
      (110°F to 115°F)
1   package active dry
      yeast
¼   cup refrigerated or
      frozen egg product,
      thawed, or 1 egg,
      lightly beaten
4   to 4½ cups flour
½   cup rolled oats,
      toasted
2   teaspoons ground
      cinnamon
2   tablespoons tub-style
      vegetable oil spread
¼   cup chopped pecans,
      toasted
1   recipe Sour Cream
      Icing

✳ sugar substitutes: Choose
from Sweet'N Low Brown or
Sugar Twin Granulated Brown.
Follow package directions to
use product amount equivalent
to 2 tablespoons brown sugar.

1 In a small saucepan heat and stir milk, brown sugar, 2 tablespoons vegetable oil spread, and the salt just until warm (110°F to 115°F); set aside. In a large bowl combine the warm water and the yeast; let stand for 10 minutes. Add egg and milk mixture to yeast mixture. Using a wooden spoon, stir in as much of the flour as you can.

2 On a lightly floured surface knead in enough of the remaining flour to make a moderately soft dough that is smooth and elastic (3 to 5 minutes total). Shape dough into a ball. Place in a lightly greased bowl; turn once. Cover; let rise in a warm place until double (about 1 hour). Punch dough down. Turn out onto a lightly floured surface. Cover; let rest 10 minutes.

3 Lightly grease a 13×9×2-inch baking pan; set aside. Combine oats and cinnamon. Blend in 2 tablespoons vegetable oil spread until mixture is crumbly. Stir in pecans.

4 Roll dough into a 15×8-inch rectangle. Sprinkle with oat mixture, leaving a 1-inch space along one of the long sides. Starting from the long side with topping, roll up dough into a spiral. Pinch to seal seam. Slice into 15 pieces. Arrange pieces, cut sides up, in prepared baking pan. Cover; let rise in a warm place until nearly double (about 30 minutes).

5 Preheat oven to 375°F. Bake for 25 to 30 minutes or until golden. Cool in pan on a wire rack for 5 minutes. Remove rolls from pan. Drizzle with Sour Cream Icing. Serve warm.

sour cream icing: In a small bowl combine ⅓ cup light sour cream, ¼ cup powdered sugar, ¼ teaspoon vanilla, and enough fat-free milk (2 to 3 teaspoons) to make drizzling consistency.

nutrition facts per serving: 196 cal., 5 g total fat (1 g sat. fat), 2 mg chol., 199 mg sodium, 33 g carb. (2 g fiber, 5 g sugars), 5 g pro. exchanges: 2 starch, 1 fat.

nutrition facts per serving with substitute:
Same as basic recipe, except 189 cal., 31 g carb.

Change the flavor of this stir-together quick loaf by using white cheddar cheese instead of the Gruyère.

gruyère beer bread

prep: 20 minutes bake: 40 minutes cool: 10 minutes
makes: 12 servings (1 slice each)

1¼ cups all-purpose flour
¾ cup whole wheat pastry flour or whole wheat flour
2 teaspoons baking powder
¼ teaspoon salt
2 tablespoons butter
2 tablespoons light stick butter (not margarine)
3 ounces Gruyère cheese, shredded (¾ cup)
½ cup light beer or nonalcoholic beer
¼ cup fat-free milk
¼ cup refrigerated or frozen egg product, thawed, or 1 egg, lightly beaten
2 tablespoons snipped fresh chives
2 tablespoons honey

1 Preheat oven to 350°F. Lightly grease an 8×4×2-inch loaf pan. In a large bowl stir together flours, baking powder, and salt. Using a pastry blender, cut in butter and light butter until mixture resembles coarse crumbs. Stir in cheese. In a medium bowl combine beer, milk, egg, chives, and honey. Add to flour mixture all at once. Stir with a fork just until combined.

2 Spoon into prepared pan and spread evenly. Bake for 40 to 45 minutes or until a wooden toothpick inserted in center comes out clean. Cool in pan on a wire rack for 10 minutes. Remove loaf from the pan and cool completely. Store any leftover bread in an airtight container in the refrigerator.

nutrition facts per serving: 139 cal., 5 g total fat (3 g sat. fat), 15 mg chol., 179 mg sodium, 18 g carb. (1 g fiber, 3 g sugars), 5 g pro. exchanges: 1 starch, 1 fat.

27 g
CARB. PER SERVING

Flag this recipe for the holidays. The bread is filled with festive flavors you can enjoy and still eat healthfully.

cranberry-almond bread

prep: 25 minutes **bake:** 50 minutes **cool:** 10 minutes
makes: 12 servings (1 slice each)

1½ cups whole wheat
     pastry flour
½   cup all-purpose flour
½   cup granulated
     sugar*
1   tablespoon baking
     powder
¼   teaspoon salt
⅓   cup almond paste
¼   cup refrigerated or
     frozen egg product,
     thawed, or 1 egg,
     lightly beaten
3   tablespoons canola oil
1   cup fat-free milk
⅔   cup fresh cranberries,
     chopped
⅓   cup chopped almonds,
     toasted**
2   teaspoons powdered
     sugar

1 Preheat oven to 350°F. Grease the bottom and ½ inch up the sides of an 8×4×2-inch loaf pan; set aside. In a large bowl stir together whole wheat flour, all-purpose flour, sugar, baking powder, and salt. Make a well in the center of the flour mixture; set aside.

2 In a medium bowl stir together almond paste, egg, and oil until smooth. Stir in milk. Add milk mixture all at once to flour mixture; stir just until moistened (batter should be lumpy). Fold in cranberries and almonds. Spoon batter into prepared loaf pan.

3 Bake for 50 to 55 minutes or until a toothpick inserted near the center comes out clean. Cool in pan on a wire rack for 10 minutes. Remove from pan. Cool completely on wire rack. Wrap and store overnight before slicing. Sprinkle lightly with powdered sugar before serving.

nutrition facts per serving: 177 cal., 7 g total fat (1 g sat. fat), 0 mg chol., 158 mg sodium, 27 g carb. (2 g fiber, 13 g sugars), 4 g pro. **exchanges:** 1 starch, 1 carb., 1 fat.

nutrition facts per serving with substitute: Same as original, except 165 cal., 22 g carb.

✱ **sugar substitute:** Choose Splenda Sugar Blend for Baking. Follow package directions to use product amount equivalent to ½ cup granulated sugar.

✱✱ **test kitchen tip:** To toast nuts, spread nuts in a single layer in a shallow baking pan. Bake in a 350°F oven for 5 to 10 minutes until nuts are golden brown.

Just a touch of coconut milk adds richness to this loaf. Stir leftover coconut milk into light hot chocolate for a dessertlike treat.

banana-coconut bread

24g
CARB. PER
SERVING

prep: 20 minutes bake: 45 minutes cool: 2 hours stand: overnight
makes: 12 servings (1 slice each)

1 cup all-purpose flour
½ cup whole wheat pastry flour or whole wheat flour
2 teaspoons baking powder
½ teaspoon pumpkin pie spice
¼ teaspoon baking soda
¼ teaspoon salt
1 cup mashed bananas (2 to 3 medium)
½ cup packed brown sugar*
⅓ cup unsweetened lite coconut milk**
¼ cup refrigerated or frozen egg product, thawed, or 1 egg, lightly beaten
2 tablespoons canola oil
¼ cup chopped macadamia nuts or sliced almonds
¼ cup raw chip coconut or shredded coconut

1 Preheat oven to 350°F. Grease the bottom and ½ inch up the sides of an 8×4×2-inch loaf pan; set aside.

2 In a bowl combine all-purpose flour, whole wheat flour, baking powder, pumpkin pie spice, baking soda, and salt. Make a well in the center of the flour mixture; set aside.

3 In a medium bowl combine mashed bananas, brown sugar, coconut milk, egg, and oil. Add banana mixture all at once to flour mixture; stir just until moistened (batter should be lumpy). Spoon batter into prepared loaf pan. Sprinkle with macadamia nuts and coconut.

4 Bake for 45 to 50 minutes or until a toothpick inserted near the center comes out clean, covering loaf loosely with foil for the last 20 minutes of baking to prevent overbrowning. Cool in pan on a wire rack for 10 minutes. Remove from pan. Cool completely on wire rack. Wrap and store overnight before slicing.

nutrition facts per serving: 154 cal., 6 g total fat (1 g sat. fat), 0 mg chol., 130 mg sodium, 24 g carb. (2 g fiber, 11 g sugars), 3 g pro. exchanges: 0.5 starch, 1 carb., 1 fat.

nutrition facts per serving with substitute: Same as original, except 139 cal., 19 g carb., 127 mg sodium. exchanges: 0.5 carb.

*sugar substitute: Choose Splenda Brown Sugar Blend. Follow package directions to use product amount equivalent to ½ cup brown sugar.

**test kitchen tip: Be sure to stir the can of coconut milk well before measuring out the ⅓ cup to use in this bread.

You can substitute a lightly beaten egg for each ¼ cup refrigerated or frozen egg product called for in most recipes.

16g
CARB. PER
SERVING

rosemary red pepper muffins

prep: 20 minutes **bake:** 15 minutes **cool:** 5 minutes
makes: 12 servings (1 muffin and 2 teaspoons Goat Cheese Butter each)

Nonstick cooking
  spray
1 medium red sweet
  pepper, chopped
  (¾ cup)
2 cloves garlic, minced
1 cup all-purpose flour
¾ cup whole wheat
  pastry flour or
  brown rice flour
2 tablespoons sugar*
2 teaspoons baking
  powder
2 teaspoons snipped
  fresh rosemary
½ teaspoon salt
1 cup fat-free milk
¼ cup refrigerated or
  frozen egg product,
  thawed
¼ cup light stick butter
  (not margarine),
  melted
1 recipe Goat Cheese
  Butter

1 Preheat oven to 375°F. Generously coat twelve 2½-inch muffin cups with cooking spray, or line cups with paper bake cups and generously coat paper cups with cooking spray. Coat an unheated large nonstick skillet with cooking spray; heat skillet over medium heat. Add sweet pepper; cook about 5 minutes or just until tender, stirring occasionally. Add garlic; cook and stir for 30 seconds. Remove from heat.

2 In a large bowl stir together flours, sugar, baking powder, rosemary, and salt. In a medium bowl whisk together milk, egg, and ¼ cup melted light butter. Add all at once to flour mixture; stir just until combined. Add sweet pepper mixture; stir just until combined. Spoon batter into prepared muffin cups.

3 Bake for 15 to 18 minutes or until a wooden toothpick inserted in centers comes out clean. Cool in muffin cups on a wire rack for 5 minutes. Remove from muffin cups. Serve Goat Cheese Butter with warm muffins.

nutrition facts per serving: 122 cal., 5 g total fat (3 g sat. fat), 11 mg chol., 252 mg sodium, 16 g carb. (1 g fiber, 4 g sugars), 4 g pro. **exchanges:** 1 starch, 1 fat.

nutrition facts per serving with substitute: Same as original, except 115 cal., 14 g carb. (2 g sugars).

*sugar substitutes: Choose from Splenda Granular or Sweet'N Low bulk or packets. Follow package directions to use product amount equivalent to 2 tablespoons sugar.

goat cheese butter: In a small bowl stir together 3 ounces soft goat cheese (chèvre), softened; 2 tablespoons light stick butter (not margarine), softened, or tub-style vegetable oil spread; and, if desired, 2 teaspoons snipped fresh chives until well combined.

Call on these hearty muffins to help boost a soup, stew, chili, or salad into a filling meal.

corn muffins

19g
CARB. PER SERVING

prep: 10 minutes bake: 15 minutes
makes: 12 servings (1 muffin each)

Nonstick cooking
   spray
1   cup flour
¾   cup cornmeal
¼   cup sugar✳
2½ teaspoons baking
     powder
¾   teaspoon salt
2   eggs, beaten
1   cup fat-free milk
¼   cup vegetable oil or
     melted butter

1 Preheat oven to 400°F. Coat twelve 2½-inch muffin cups with cooking spray. In a medium bowl combine flour, cornmeal, sugar, baking powder, and salt; set aside.

2 In a small bowl combine eggs, milk, and oil. Add egg mixture all at once to flour mixture. Stir just until moistened. Spoon batter into prepared muffin cups, filling each cup two-thirds full. Bake about 15 minutes or until lightly browned and a toothpick inserted near centers comes out clean. Serve warm.

nutrition facts per serving: 141 cal., 6 g total fat (1 g sat. fat), 31 mg chol., 244 mg sodium, 19 g carb. (1 g fiber, 5 g sugars), 3 g pro. exchanges: 1 starch, 1 fat.

nutrition facts per serving with substitute: Same as original, except 135 cal., 17 g carb. (3 g sugars).

✳sugar substitutes: Choose from C&H Light Sugar and Stevia Blend, Splenda Sugar Blend for Baking, or Sun Crystals Granulated Blend. Follow package directions to use product amount equivalent to ¼ cup sugar.

20g CARB. PER SERVING

The medley of spices and the richness of winter squash prove once again that you don't need loads of fat to add loads of flavor.

curried squash muffins

prep: 25 minutes bake: 20 minutes cool: 5 minutes
makes: 16 servings (1 muffin each)

1 cup all-purpose flour
½ cup white whole wheat flour
2 teaspoons baking powder
2 teaspoons ground cinnamon
1 teaspoon curry powder
½ teaspoon salt
½ teaspoon cayenne pepper (optional)
½ cup butter, softened
½ cup packed brown sugar*
1 cup mashed roasted butternut squash or 1 cup frozen cooked winter squash, thawed
¼ cup finely chopped crystalized ginger (about 1½ ounces)
1 egg
1 teaspoon vanilla
⅓ cup light vanilla soymilk
Powdered sugar (optional)

1 Preheat oven to 350°F. Line sixteen 2½-inch muffin cups with paper bake cups; set aside. In a medium bowl combine all-purpose flour, white whole wheat flour, baking powder, cinnamon, curry powder, salt, and cayenne pepper (if using); set aside.

2 In a large bowl beat butter with an electric mixer on medium to high speed for 30 seconds. Add brown sugar; beat until combined. Add squash, ginger, egg, and vanilla; beat until combined. Alternately add the flour mixture and soymilk to squash mixture, beating on low speed after each addition just until combined.

3 Spoon batter into prepared muffin cups, filling each about two-thirds full.

4 Bake about 20 minutes or until muffin tops spring back when lightly touched. Cool in muffin cups on a wire rack for 5 minutes. Remove from muffin cups. If desired, sprinkle lightly with powdered sugar. Serve warm.

nutrition facts per serving: 140 cal., 6 g total fat (4 g sat. fat), 27 mg chol., 179 mg sodium, 20 g carb. (1 g fiber, 7 g sugars), 2 g pro. exchanges: 1 starch, 1 fat.

nutrition facts per serving with substitute: Same as original, except 129 cal., 177 mg sodium, 16 g carb. (3 g sugars).

*sugar substitute: Choose Splenda Brown Sugar Blend. Follow package directions to use product amount equivalent to ½ cup brown sugar.

By switching vegetable oil spread for some of the butter and using fat-free milk, we've reduced the fat in each biscuit by 4 grams.

three-seed biscuit squares

17 g CARB. PER SERVING

prep: 15 minutes bake: 10 minutes
makes: 9 servings (1 biscuit each)

1   cup all-purpose flour
½   cup whole wheat flour or white whole wheat flour
2   teaspoons baking powder
¼   teaspoon cream of tartar
¼   teaspoon salt
¼   cup tub-style vegetable oil spread, chilled
2   tablespoons butter
½   cup plus 1 tablespoon fat-free milk
1   egg white, beaten
2   teaspoons sesame seeds
1   teaspoon cumin seeds
1   teaspoon poppy seeds
    Low-sugar orange marmalade or low-sugar fruit spread (optional)

1 Preheat oven to 450°F. In a medium bowl stir together flours, baking powder, cream of tartar, and salt. Using a pastry blender, cut in vegetable oil spread and butter until mixture resembles coarse crumbs. Make a well in the center of the flour mixture. Add milk all at once; stir just until dough clings together.

2 Turn dough out onto a lightly floured surface. Knead by folding and gently pressing dough for four to six strokes or until nearly smooth. Pat or lightly roll dough into a 7×7-inch square. Brush with egg white and sprinkle dough with sesame seeds, cumin seeds, and poppy seeds. Press seeds in lightly with your fingers.

3 Cut dough into nine squares. Place squares 1 inch apart on an ungreased baking sheet. Bake for 10 to 12 minutes or until golden brown. Serve warm. If desired, serve with marmalade or fruit spread.

nutrition facts per serving: 148 cal., 8 g total fat (3 g sat. fat), 7 mg chol., 211 mg sodium, 17 g carb. (1 g fiber, 1 g sugars), 4 g pro. exchanges: 1 starch, 1 fat.

18g CARB. PER SERVING

Crushed tea leaves subtly flavor these biscuits; ginger and peaches add spicy and sweet notes.

ginger peach tea biscuits

prep: 25 minutes   bake: 12 minutes
makes: 12 servings (1 biscuit each)

Nonstick cooking
    spray
1   cup all-purpose flour
½   cup whole wheat
        pastry flour or
        whole wheat flour
2   tablespoons sugar✳
1   tablespoon loose-leaf
        green, white, or
        black tea, crushed
2   teaspoons baking
        powder
1   teaspoon ground
        ginger
¼   teaspoon salt
¼   cup butter
½   cup finely chopped
        dried peaches
1   6-ounce carton plain
        low-fat yogurt
¼   cup refrigerated or
        frozen egg product,
        thawed, or 1 egg,
        lightly beaten

1 Preheat oven to 375°F. Coat a large baking sheet with cooking spray or line with parchment paper; set aside. In a large bowl stir together flours, sugar, tea, baking powder, ginger, and salt. Using a pastry blender, cut in butter until mixture resembles coarse crumbs. Stir in peaches. Make a well in the center of the flour mixture.

2 In a small bowl combine yogurt and egg. Add yogurt mixture all at once to flour mixture. Using a fork, stir until combined. Drop dough into 12 mounds 2 inches apart on prepared baking sheet.

3 Bake for 12 to 15 minutes or until tops are lightly browned. Transfer biscuits to wire racks; serve warm.

nutrition facts per serving: 121 cal., 4 g total fat (3 g sat. fat), 11 mg chol., 157 mg sodium, 18 g carb. (1 g fiber, 5 g sugars), 3 g pro. exchanges: 1 starch, 1 fat.

nutrition facts per serving with substitute: Same as original, except 114 cal., 16 g carb.

✳sugar substitutes: Choose from Splenda Granular or Sweet'N Low bulk or packets. Follow package directions to use product amount equivalent to 2 tablespoons sugar.

A touch of regular butter adds flavor and flakiness; light stick butter helps keep the fat in check.

peppery shallot scone bites

17g
CARB. PER SERVING

prep: 20 minutes   bake: 12 minutes
makes: 9 servings (1 scone each)

¾   cup all-purpose flour
¾   cup whole wheat pastry flour or whole wheat flour
2   teaspoons baking powder
¼   teaspoon cream of tartar
¼   teaspoon salt
¼   teaspoon freshly ground black pepper
¼   cup light stick butter (not margarine)
2   tablespoons butter
⅓   cup thinly sliced green onion tops
½   cup fat-free milk
1   to 2 teaspoons fat-free milk (optional)
9   very thin shallot slices
     Olive oil nonstick cooking spray
     Freshly ground black pepper

1 Preheat oven to 450°F. In a medium bowl stir together flours, baking powder, cream of tartar, salt, and ¼ teaspoon pepper. Using a pastry blender, cut in light butter and butter until mixture resembles coarse crumbs. Stir in green onion tops. Make a well in the center of the flour mixture. Add ½ cup milk all at once to flour mixture; stir just until dough clings together. If needed, add an additional 1 to 2 teaspoons fat-free milk to reach a soft dough consistency.

2 Turn dough out onto a lightly floured surface. Knead by folding and gently pressing dough for four to six strokes or until nearly smooth. Pat or lightly roll dough into a 7×7-inch square. Cut dough into nine squares. Place 1 shallot slice on top of each square. Coat the tops of the shallot slices with cooking spray and sprinkle with additional pepper. Place squares 1 inch apart on an ungreased baking sheet.

3 Bake for 12 to 14 minutes or until lightly browned. Serve warm.

nutrition facts per serving: 128 cal., 6 g total fat (3 g sat. fat), 14 mg chol., 219 mg sodium, 17 g carb. (2 g fiber, 1 g sugars), 3 g pro. exchanges: 1 starch, 1 fat.

Pick your pleasure! Keep it casual with easygoing options such as Buffalo Chicken Salad, or go upscale with stylish choices that star shrimp, salmon, and seared tuna. Whatever you choose, you'll find satisfying salad meals you can feel good about eating.

main-dish

sal

chilled salmon and tabbouleh,
page 103

salads

17g CARB. PER SERVING

Resembling green tomatoes with papery husks, tomatillos bring fascinating hints of citrus, herb, and apple flavors to dishes. Look for firm, dry tomatillos and avoid those with moist, loose-fitting husks.

carne asada salad

prep: 35 minutes **grill:** 17 minutes **stand:** 10 minutes
makes: 6 servings (1 cup lettuce, ⅔ cup bean mixture, and 2½ ounces cooked beef each)

1   1-pound beef flank steak
1   teaspoon ground ancho chile pepper
½   teaspoon dried oregano, crushed
½   teaspoon ground cumin
¼   teaspoon salt
    Dash ground cinnamon
1   small sweet onion, cut into ¼-inch slices
4   medium tomatillos, halved and stems removed
1   15-ounce can black beans, rinsed and drained
1   medium tomato, seeded and chopped (½ cup)
1   small fresh jalapeño chile pepper, seeded and finely chopped*
¼   cup snipped fresh cilantro
¼   cup lime juice
¼   teaspoon ground cumin
6   cups coarsely torn romaine lettuce

1 Trim fat from steak. Score both sides of steak in a diamond pattern, making shallow diagonal cuts at 1-inch intervals. In a small bowl stir together the ground chile pepper, oregano, ½ teaspoon cumin, salt, and cinnamon. Sprinkle spice mixture evenly over the steak, rubbing it in with your fingers.

2 For a charcoal grill, place steak, onion slices, and tomatillo halves on the grill rack directly over medium coals. Grill steak, uncovered, for 17 to 21 minutes for medium (160°F), turning once halfway through grilling. Grill onion and tomatillos for 10 to 12 minutes or until tender and browned, turning once halfway through grilling. (For a gas grill, preheat grill. Reduce heat to medium. Place steak and then vegetables on grill rack over heat. Cover and grill as directed.)

3 Transfer steak, onion, and tomatillos to a cutting board. Cover steak with foil; let stand for 10 minutes. Meanwhile, chop the onion slices and tomatillos. In a large bowl combine chopped onion and tomatillos, beans, tomato, jalapeño pepper, and cilantro. Add lime juice and ¼ teaspoon cumin; toss to combine. Thinly slice steak across the grain. To serve, arrange romaine on six serving plates. Top with bean mixture and steak slices.

nutrition facts per serving: 191 cal., 5 g total fat (2 g sat. fat), 31 mg chol., 329 mg sodium, 17 g carb. (6 g fiber, 4 g sugars), 22 g pro. exchanges: 1 vegetable, 1 starch, 2.5 lean meat.

*test kitchen tip: Because chile peppers contain volatile oils that can burn your skin and eyes, avoid direct contact with them as much as possible. When working with chile peppers, wear plastic or rubber gloves. If your bare hands do touch the peppers, wash your hands and nails well with soap and warm water.

If using wooden skewers, soak them in water for 30 minutes before using to prevent flare-ups.

southwestern beef, rice, and black bean salad

prep: 45 minutes   grill: 4 minutes
makes: 6 servings (2 skewers and ⅔ cup rice mixture each)

- 1 pound beef top sirloin steak, cut 1 inch thick
- 2 teaspoons salt-free Southwest seasoning blend
- 1 teaspoon olive oil
- 4 green onions, cut into 1-inch lengths
- 12 6- to 8-inch skewers
- 1½ cups cooked brown rice
- 1 15-ounce can no-salt-added black beans, rinsed and drained
- ½ cup chopped, seeded tomato (1 medium)
- ¼ cup snipped fresh cilantro
- 1 cup frozen whole kernel corn
- ¾ cup chopped green sweet pepper (1 medium)
- ½ cup chopped sweet onion (1 small)
- 2 teaspoons olive oil
- ½ cup bottled salsa
- ¼ cup lime juice
- ½ teaspoon ground cumin

1 Cut steak into 2×¼-inch strips. In a medium bowl toss steak, seasoning blend, and 1 teaspoon olive oil. Thread steak strips and green onions evenly onto skewers; set aside.

2 In a large bowl combine rice, black beans, tomato, and cilantro; set aside. In a large nonstick skillet cook corn, sweet pepper, and sweet onion in 2 teaspoons olive oil over medium-high heat for 5 minutes or until corn is slightly blackened, stirring frequently. Add to rice mixture. In a small bowl stir together salsa, lime juice, and cumin. Add to rice mixture; toss to combine. Set salad aside.

3 For a charcoal grill, place skewers on the grill rack directly over medium coals. Grill, uncovered, for 4 to 6 minutes or until meat is just pink in the center, turning once. (For a gas grill, preheat grill. Reduce heat to medium. Place skewers on grill rack over heat. Cover and grill as directed.) To serve, spoon rice salad onto six serving plates and top with beef skewers.

nutrition facts per serving: 271 cal., 6 g total fat (2 g sat. fat), 45 mg chol., 185 mg sodium, 32 g carb. (6 g fiber, 3 g sugars), 23 g pro. exchanges: 2 starch, 3 lean meat.

17 g
CARB. PER
SERVING

For succulent results, cover the cooked steak with foil and let it stand about 10 minutes before slicing.

beef and arugula with raspberry-chipotle dressing

prep: 15 minutes grill: 8 minutes

makes: 4 servings (2½ cups salad, about 4 ounces steak, and 2 tablespoons dressing each)

1 pound lean boneless beef sirloin steak, cut 1 inch thick
¼ teaspoon salt
¼ teaspoon black pepper
6 cups arugula leaves
2 cups halved red and/ or yellow cherry tomatoes
2 cups fresh raspberries
2 tablespoons soft goat cheese (chèvre)
1 recipe Raspberry Chipotle Dressing

1 Sprinkle steak with the salt and pepper. For a gas or charcoal grill, place steak on the grill rack directly over medium heat. Grill, covered, to desired doneness, turning steak once halfway through grilling. (Allow 8 to 12 minutes for medium rare and 12 to 15 minutes for medium.) Slice steak.

2 To serve, place arugula on a serving platter. Arrange cherry tomatoes, steak, and raspberries on arugula. Dot with goat cheese. Drizzle with Raspberry Chipotle Dressing.

nutrition facts per serving: 249 cal., 10 g total fat (3 g sat. fat), 61 mg chol., 246 mg sodium, 17 g carb. (7 g fiber, 9 g sugars), 23 g pro. exchanges: 2 vegetable, 0.5 fruit, 3 lean meat, 1 fat.

raspberry-chipotle dressing: Mash ½ cup fresh raspberries. In a screw-top jar combine mashed berries, 2 tablespoons white wine vinegar, 1 tablespoon canola oil, 2 teaspoons honey, and 1 teaspoon chopped canned chipotle peppers in adobo sauce.✱ Cover and shake to combine. Makes about ½ cup.

✱ test kitchen tip: Because chile peppers contain volatile oils that can burn your skin and eyes, avoid direct contact with them as much as possible. When working with chile peppers, wear plastic or rubber gloves. If your bare hands do touch the peppers, wash your hands and nails well with soap and warm water.

Lean beef, fiber-rich multigrain pasta, and summer-fresh corn, tomatoes, and basil make this recipe a delicious choice for a diabetes-friendly meal.

beefy pasta salad

start to finish: 30 minutes
makes: 4 servings (1⅓ cups each)

1 cup dried multigrain penne pasta (about 3½ ounces)
2 ears fresh sweet corn, husks and silks removed
Nonstick cooking spray
12 ounces boneless beef sirloin steak, trimmed of fat and cut into thin bite-size strips, or 2 cups shredded cooked beef pot roast (10 ounces)*
1 cup cherry tomatoes, halved
¼ cup shredded fresh basil
2 tablespoons finely shredded Parmesan cheese
3 tablespoons white wine vinegar
1 tablespoon olive oil
1 clove garlic, minced
¼ teaspoon salt
⅛ teaspoon black pepper
¼ cup finely shredded Parmesan cheese

1 In a 4- to 6-quart Dutch oven cook pasta according to package directions, adding corn for the last 3 minutes of cooking time. Using tongs, transfer corn to a large cutting board. Drain pasta. Rinse pasta in cold water and drain again; set aside. Cool corn until easy to handle.

2 Meanwhile, coat an unheated large nonstick skillet with cooking spray. Preheat skillet over medium-high heat. Add beef strips. Cook for 4 to 6 minutes or until slightly pink in the center, stirring occasionally. (If using shredded beef, cook until heated through.) Remove from heat and cool slightly.

3 On a cutting board place an ear of corn pointed end down. While holding corn firmly at stem end to keep in place, use a sharp knife to cut corn from cobs, leaving corn in planks; rotate cob as needed to cut corn from all sides. Repeat with the remaining ear of corn. In a large bowl combine pasta, beef, tomatoes, basil, and the 2 tablespoons Parmesan cheese.

4 In a screw-top jar combine vinegar, oil, garlic, salt, and pepper. Cover and shake well. Pour over pasta mixture; toss gently to coat. Gently fold in corn planks or place corn planks on top of individual servings. Serve immediately. Garnish with the ¼ cup Parmesan cheese.

nutrition facts per serving: 313 cal., 10 g total fat (3 g sat. fat), 41 mg chol., 341 mg sodium, 28 g carb. (4 g fiber, 3 g sugars), 28 g pro. exchanges: 0.5 vegetable, 1.5 starch, 3 lean meat, 1 fat.

*test kitchen tip: If you have leftover beef pot roast, use it in this pasta salad. Simply shred the meat and use 2 cups of it in the salad.

Arugula's bold, peppery flavor stands up well to meaty pork tenderloin. If you can't find baby arugula, use large arugula leaves but trim the stems.

citrus pork and arugula salad

19g CARB. PER SERVING

84

start to finish: 30 minutes

makes: 4 servings (1½ cups arugula, 2½ to 3 ounces cooked meat, and 2 tablespoons dressing each)

1   1-pound pork tenderloin
¼   teaspoon salt
¼   teaspoon black pepper
1   tablespoon canola oil
½   teaspoon finely shredded orange peel
⅓   cup orange juice
1   tablespoon rice vinegar or white wine vinegar
2   teaspoons reduced-sodium soy sauce
2   teaspoons honey
1   teaspoon toasted sesame oil
½   teaspoon grated fresh ginger or ⅛ teaspoon ground ginger
6   cups baby arugula
½   cup canned unpeeled apricot halves in light syrup, * drained and quartered
1   small avocado, peeled, seeded, and sliced or chopped
¼   cup dried apricots, sliced

1 Trim fat from pork. Cut pork crosswise into ¼-inch slices. Sprinkle with the salt and pepper.

2 In an extra-large skillet cook pork, half at a time, in hot canola oil over medium-high heat for 2 to 3 minutes or until meat is just slightly pink in center, turning once. Remove from skillet and set aside.

3 For dressing, in a screw-top jar combine orange peel and juice, vinegar, soy sauce, honey, sesame oil, and ginger. Cover and shake well.

4 Place arugula on a serving platter. Top with pork slices, canned apricots, avocado slices, and dried apricots. Drizzle with salad dressing.

nutrition facts per serving: 272 cal., 11 g total fat (2 g sat. fat), 74 mg chol., 314 mg sodium, 19 g carb. (3 g fiber, 15 g sugars), 26 g pro. exchanges: 2 vegetable, 0.5 fruit, 3 lean meat, 1 fat.

* test kitchen tip: If fresh apricots are available, use 2 medium fresh apricots, halved, seeded, and quartered.

Prepare this summery recipe when peaches are at their ripest, juiciest best. And if picked-that-day greens are available at the farmer's market, take advantage!

grilled pork and peach salad

prep: 20 minutes **grill:** 10 minutes
makes: 4 servings (1½ cups lettuce, ¾ cup pork mixture, and 1 tablespoon green onions each)

20 g CARB. PER SERVING

1	1-pound pork tenderloin
2	medium peaches or nectarines
2	tablespoons honey
2	tablespoons orange juice
1	tablespoon low-sodium soy sauce
½	teaspoon curry powder
¼	teaspoon black pepper
3	cups torn Bibb lettuce
3	cups packaged fresh baby spinach
2	green onions, bias-sliced (¼ cup)

1 Trim pork and cut pork into 1-inch cubes. Pit peaches and cut into 1-inch cubes. On four 10-inch skewers✱ thread pork cubes. On three more 10-inch skewers✱ thread peach cubes. For a charcoal grill, place skewers on the grill rack directly over medium coals. Grill pork, uncovered, for 10 to 12 minutes or until pork is slightly pink in the center, turning occasionally. Grill peaches for 8 to 10 minutes or until peaches are browned. (For a gas grill, preheat grill. Reduce heat to medium. Place skewers on grill rack over heat. Cover and grill as directed.)

2 Meanwhile, in a large bowl stir together honey, orange juice, soy sauce, curry powder, and pepper. When pork skewers are done, remove pork and peaches from skewers and place in honey mixture; toss to coat.

3 To serve, arrange lettuce and spinach on four serving plates. Spoon pork and peaches evenly over greens. Sprinkle with green onions.

✱**test kitchen tip:** If using wooden skewers, soak them in enough water to cover for at least 30 minutes before using.

nutrition facts per serving: 207 cal., 3 g total fat (1 g sat. fat), 54 mg chol., 444 mg sodium, 20 g carb. (3 g fiber, 17 g sugars), 26 g pro. **exchanges:** 1 vegetable, 0.5 fruit, 0.5 carb., 3.5 lean meat.

When corn is at peak-season freshness, uncooked kernels are sweet, milky, and tender—just right to use in a salad.

pork with fresh corn salad

24g
CARB. PER SERVING

prep: 20 minutes   cook: 5 minutes   roast: 15 minutes   stand: 3 minutes
makes: 4 servings (4 ounces pork and 1¾ cups corn mixture each)

1   teaspoon paprika
½   teaspoon garlic powder
½   teaspoon ground cumin
½   teaspoon black pepper
¼   teaspoon salt
1   1-pound pork tenderloin
    Nonstick cooking spray
3   ears fresh sweet corn, husks and silks removed
2   cups packaged fresh baby spinach
1   cup fresh blackberries
¼   of a medium jicama, peeled and cut into matchstick-size pieces (½ cup)
1   recipe Honey-Rosemary Vinaigrette

1 Preheat oven to 400°F. For rub, in a small bowl combine paprika, garlic powder, cumin, pepper, and salt. Sprinkle rub evenly over all sides of tenderloin; rub in with your fingers.

2 Coat an unheated large nonstick oven-going skillet with cooking spray; heat over medium-high heat. Add tenderloin to the hot skillet; cook, turning occasionally, for 5 to 6 minutes or until well browned on all sides. Place skillet in oven. Roast for 15 to 20 minutes or until an instant-read thermometer inserted into thickest part of the tenderloin registers 145°F.

3 Remove tenderloin from oven. Cover tightly with foil; let stand for 3 minutes. Thinly slice pork crosswise.

4 Meanwhile, cut corn kernels off the cobs. Place corn in a large bowl. Add spinach, blackberries, and jicama. Add Honey-Rosemary Vinaigrette; toss to coat. To serve, divide corn mixture among four serving plates. Top with pork slices.

nutrition facts per serving: 264 cal., 7 g total fat (1 g sat. fat), 74 mg chol., 313 mg sodium, 24 g carb. (6 g fiber, 8 g sugars), 27 g pro. exchanges: 0.5 vegetable, 1.5 starch, 3 lean meat.

honey-rosemary vinaigrette: In a small screw-top jar combine ¼ cup cider vinegar, 1 tablespoon canola oil, 1 tablespoon honey, 1 teaspoon snipped fresh rosemary, and ⅛ teaspoon salt. Cover and shake well. Makes about ⅓ cup.

34g CARB. PER SERVING

Instead of tearing the lettuce, peel whole leaves from the head.
Use the cuplike leaves to cradle each serving of the barley mixture.

pork barley salad

prep: 30 minutes   cook: 45 minutes   grill: 25 minutes   stand: 3 minutes
makes: 6 servings (2 ounces pork, ¾ cup barley mixture, and 1 cup greens each)

5	cups water
1	cup pearl barley
1	cup frozen sweet soybeans (edamame)
1	recipe Dijon Vinaigrette
1	medium red sweet pepper, chopped (¾ cup)
⅓	cup sliced green onions
¼	cup chopped cornichons
¼	cup snipped fresh parsley
1	1-pound pork tenderloin, trimmed
¼	teaspoon black pepper
6	cups torn Bibb or Boston lettuce

1 In a large saucepan bring the water to boiling over high heat. Stir in barley; reduce heat. Cover and simmer for 45 to 50 minutes or just until barley is tender, adding edamame for the last 10 minutes of cooking; drain. Place barley and edamame in a large bowl. Pour Dijon Vinaigrette over warm barley mixture; toss to coat. Add the sweet pepper, green onions, cornichons, and parsley to barley mixture; mix well. Set aside.

2 Sprinkle pork tenderloin evenly with the black pepper. For a charcoal grill, arrange hot coals around a drip pan. Test for medium-high heat above pan. Place meat on grill rack over pan. Cover; grill for 25 to 30 minutes or until a meat thermometer registers 145°F. (For a gas grill, preheat grill. Reduce heat to medium. Adjust for indirect cooking. Grill as directed.)

3 Transfer pork to a cutting board. Cover tightly with foil; let stand for 3 minutes. Cut into ¼-inch-thick slices; cut slices into strips. Add pork to barley mixture; stir to combine. Arrange lettuce on six serving plates; spoon warm salad over lettuce.

nutrition facts per serving: 308 cal., 8 g total fat (1 g sat. fat), 49 mg chol., 130 mg sodium, 34 g carb. (8 g fiber, 4 g sugars), 24 g pro. exchanges: 1 vegetable, 2 starch, 2 lean meat, 0.5 fat.

dijon vinaigrette: In a screw-top jar combine ¼ cup white wine vinegar; 2 tablespoons finely chopped red onion; 2 tablespoons olive oil; 2 teaspoons Dijon-style mustard; 2 cloves garlic, minced; and ¼ teaspoon black pepper. Cover and shake well. Makes about ½ cup.

Skip a step! Start with 2 cups packaged precooked farro, such as Archer Farms brand, and you'll shave 15 minutes from the prep time.

greek pork and farro salad

26g CARB. PER SERVING

prep: 20 minutes cook: 25 minutes
makes: 5 servings (1 cup spinach, about 1¼ cups salad mixture, and about 2 tablespoons dressing each)

89

- ¾ cup uncooked farro
- 3 cups water
- 12 ounces pork tenderloin, trimmed
- 1 teaspoon Greek seasoning
  Nonstick cooking spray
- 1 cup chopped tomato (1 large)
- 1 cup chopped cucumber (1 small)
- ¾ cup chopped yellow sweet pepper (1 medium)
- ¼ cup red wine vinegar
- 3 tablespoons olive oil
- 2 tablespoons snipped fresh oregano
- 1 teaspoon Dijon-style mustard
- ¼ teaspoon black pepper
- 1 clove garlic, minced
- 5 cups fresh baby spinach
- 2 ounces reduced-fat feta cheese, crumbled

1 In a medium saucepan combine farro and water. Bring to boiling; reduce heat. Simmer, uncovered, for 15 to 20 minutes or until farro is desired tenderness. Drain. Place farro in a large bowl.

2 Meanwhile, cut tenderloin into 1-inch pieces. Toss pork cubes with Greek seasoning. Coat an unheated large nonstick skillet with cooking spray. Cook tenderloin in hot skillet over medium heat for 5 to 6 minutes or until no longer pink. Add to farro. Cool slightly.

3 Add tomato, cucumber, and sweet pepper to farro mixture.

4 For dressing, in a screw-top jar combine vinegar, olive oil, oregano, mustard, black pepper, and garlic; shake to combine. Toss with farro mixture until combined. Serve farro salad either at room temperature or chilled. To serve, arrange spinach on a platter or five serving plates. Spoon farro salad over spinach and sprinkle with feta cheese.

nutrition facts per serving: 299 cal., 11 g total fat (3 g sat. fat), 45 mg chol., 275 mg sodium, 26 g carb. (4 g fiber, 2 g sugars), 22 g pro. exchanges: 1 vegetable, 1.5 starch, 2.5 lean meat, 1.5 fat.

If you're cooking for one, eat this as a salad one day, then spoon it into a pita bread half as a sandwich filling the next.

13g CARB. PER SERVING

light and tangy chicken salad

start to finish: 15 minutes
makes: 4 servings (¾ cup each)

6 tablespoons light mayonnaise
¼ cup chopped mango chutney
2 cups diced cooked chicken breast
½ cup halved seedless red grapes
½ cup finely chopped celery
2 tablespoons finely chopped red onion
¼ teaspoon salt
¼ teaspoon black pepper
   Leaf lettuce (optional)
2 tablespoons sliced almonds, toasted

In a medium bowl combine mayonnaise and mango chutney. Add chicken, grapes, celery, and red onion. Season with the salt and pepper. To serve, if desired, line two serving plates with lettuce and spoon chicken mixture over lettuce. Sprinkle chicken salad with almonds.

nutrition facts per serving: 249 cal., 11 g total fat (2 g sat. fat), 67 mg chol., 391 mg sodium, 13 g carb. (1 g fiber, 10 g sugars), 23 g pro. exchanges: 1 fruit, 3 lean meat, 1.5 fat.

You can also broil the chicken: Preheat the broiler and cook the chicken 4 to 5 inches from the heat for 12 to 15 minutes or until done, turning once halfway through broiling time.

warm chicken and new potato salad

prep: 20 minutes grill: 12 minutes cook: 13 minutes
makes: 4 servings (2 cups each)

30g CARB. PER SERVING

12 ounces skinless, boneless chicken breast halves
¼ teaspoon salt
1 pound 2-inch round red-skinned potatoes, scrubbed and quartered
1 pound asparagus, trimmed and cut into 2-inch pieces
1 medium onion, chopped (½ cup)
1 stalk celery, thinly sliced (½ cup)
1 tablespoon light butter
⅓ cup water
¼ cup white wine vinegar
2 tablespoons snipped fresh chives
1 tablespoon sugar*
1 tablespoon coarse-ground mustard
¾ teaspoon cornstarch
2 cups packaged fresh baby spinach
4 slices turkey bacon, cooked according to package directions and chopped

1 Sprinkle chicken with ⅛ teaspoon of the salt. For a charcoal grill, place chicken on the grill rack directly over medium coals. Grill, uncovered, for 12 to 15 minutes or until chicken is no longer pink (170°F), turning once halfway through grilling. (For a gas grill, preheat grill. Reduce heat to medium. Place chicken on grill rack over heat. Cover and grill as directed.) Thinly slice chicken.

2 In a large saucepan cook potatoes in enough gently boiling water to cover for 12 to 15 minutes or until tender, adding asparagus pieces for the last 2 minutes of cooking. Drain potatoes and asparagus.

3 Meanwhile, in a large skillet cook onion and celery in hot butter over medium heat for 5 minutes or just until tender, stirring occasionally. In a small bowl combine the water, vinegar, chives, sugar, mustard, cornstarch, and remaining ⅛ teaspoon salt. Stir until cornstarch is dissolved. Add to onion mixture. Cook and stir until thickened and bubbly. Gently stir in the potato mixture and chicken. Cook, stirring gently, for 1 to 2 minutes more or until heated through. Stir in spinach and bacon just before serving.

nutrition facts per serving: 293 cal., 6 g total fat (2 g sat. fat), 64 mg chol., 608 mg sodium, 30 g carb. (6 g fiber, 8 g sugars), 29 g pro. exchanges: 1 vegetable, 1.5 starch, 3 lean meat.

nutrition facts per serving with substitute: Same as original, except 282 calories, 28 g carb. (5 g sugars).

*sugar substitutes: Choose from Splenda Granular or Sweet'N Low bulk or packets. Follow package directions to use product amount equivalent to 1 tablespoon sugar.

This salad is as tasty served cold as it is warm. Tote leftovers to work in a cooler for a delicious lunch.

10g
CARB. PER
SERVING

italian roasted chicken and vegetable toss

prep: 25 minutes roast: 50 minutes
makes: 6 servings (1⅓ cups greens and 1 cup chicken mixture each)

Nonstick cooking
   spray
2 bone-in chicken
   breast halves (about
   2 pounds total)
1 cup packaged peeled
   fresh baby carrots
1 medium onion, cut
   into 8 wedges
2 medium zucchini, cut
   into 1-inch chunks
   (about 3 cups)
1 medium red or green
   sweet pepper, cut
   into 1-inch chunks
   (about 1 cup)
8 ounces fresh
   mushrooms
3 tablespoons olive oil
¼ teaspoon salt
¼ teaspoon black
   pepper
2 tablespoons balsamic
   vinegar
1 teaspoon dried Italian
   seasoning, crushed
8 ounces
   Mediterranean-
   blend salad greens
   (8 cups)
¼ cup shredded
   Parmesan cheese
   (1 ounce)

1 Preheat oven to 375°F. Coat a shallow roasting pan with cooking spray. Arrange chicken, skin sides up, in half of the roasting pan. In the other half of the pan arrange the carrots and onion wedges. Roast, uncovered, for 25 minutes.

2 Remove roasting pan from oven. Add zucchini, sweet pepper, and mushrooms to the carrots and onion. Drizzle chicken and vegetables with 2 tablespoons of the oil and sprinkle with the salt and black pepper.

3 Roast, uncovered, about 25 minutes more or until chicken is no longer pink (170°F) and vegetables are tender. Remove and set aside until cool enough to handle (5 to 10 minutes). Transfer vegetables to a large bowl.

4 Remove and discard chicken skin and bones. Using two forks, pull chicken apart into big shreds. Add chicken and any juices in pan to vegetables; toss. In a small bowl whisk together vinegar, the remaining 1 tablespoon olive oil, and the Italian seasoning. Add to chicken mixture; toss to coat.

5 To serve, arrange salad greens on a serving platter or divide among four serving plates. Spoon chicken mixture over greens. Sprinkle with cheese.

nutrition facts per serving: 219 cal., 10 g total fat (2 g sat. fat), 51 mg chol., 217 mg sodium, 10 g carb. (2 g fiber, 5 g sugars), 22 g pro. exchanges: 2 vegetable, 3 lean meat, 1 fat.

Food from your favorite barbecue restaurant can really blow your fat-and-calorie budget, but using great barbecue flavors in your cooking doesn't have to.

bbq chicken and roasted corn salad

30g CARB. PER SERVING

prep: 25 minutes broil: 6 minutes

makes: 4 servings (1¾ cups salad, 4 ounces chicken, and about 1 tablespoon dressing each)

94

- 1 to 1¼ pounds skinless, boneless chicken breast halves
- 2 teaspoons ground ancho chile pepper or chili powder
- 1 teaspoon dried oregano, crushed
- 1 teaspoon dried thyme, crushed
- ¼ teaspoon salt
- ¼ teaspoon black pepper
- 1 15-ounce can no-salt-added black beans, rinsed and drained
- 1 cup frozen whole kernel corn, thawed
- 1 tablespoon canola oil
- 2 tablespoons light ranch salad dressing
- 2 tablespoons low-sodium barbecue sauce
- 1 tablespoon white wine vinegar
- 4 cups chopped romaine lettuce
- 1 cup cherry tomatoes, halved
- 1 ounce queso fresco, crumbled, or Monterey Jack cheese, shredded (¼ cup)

1 Place each chicken breast half between two pieces of plastic wrap. Using the flat side of a meat mallet, pound chicken to about ½-inch thickness. Remove plastic wrap.

2 Preheat broiler. In a small bowl stir together ground chile pepper, oregano, thyme, salt, and black pepper. Sprinkle half of the spice mixture evenly over chicken pieces; rub in with your fingers.

3 In a medium bowl combine beans, corn, oil, and the remaining half of the spice mixture. Stir to combine.

4 Line a 15×10×1-inch baking pan with foil. Place chicken on one side of the pan. Add bean mixture to the other side of the pan. Broil 4 to 5 inches from the heat for 6 to 8 minutes or until chicken is tender and no longer pink (170°F), turning chicken and stirring bean mixture once halfway through broiling.

5 Meanwhile, in a small bowl combine salad dressing, barbecue sauce, and vinegar; set aside.

6 To assemble, divide romaine among four serving plates. Slice chicken. Top romaine with bean mixture, chicken, and tomatoes, dividing evenly. Sprinkle with queso fresco and serve with salad dressing mixture.

nutrition facts per serving: 345 cal., 11 g total fat (2 g sat. fat), 80 mg chol., 435 mg sodium, 30 g carb. (8 g fiber, 5 g sugars), 33 g pro. exchanges: 1.5 vegetable, 1 starch, 0.5 carb., 0.5 fat.

Read the nutrition labels on the Buffalo wing sauces available at your grocery store and choose the sauce lowest in sodium.

buffalo chicken salad

start to finish: 15 minutes

makes: 4 servings (½ of a romaine heart, ¾ cup chicken, 1 wedge cheese, 1 tablespoon dressing, and 1 stalk celery each)

2 hearts romaine, sliced

3 cups coarsely chopped cooked chicken breast

½ cup Buffalo wing sauce, such as Wing Time brand

4 21-gram wedges light blue cheese, such as Laughing Cow brand, crumbled

1 teaspoon cracked black pepper

¼ cup bottled fat-free blue cheese salad dressing

4 teaspoons fat-free milk

4 stalks celery, each cut into 4 sticks

1 Divide romaine among four serving plates or bowls. In a medium microwave-safe bowl combine chicken and wing sauce. Microwave on 100 percent power (high) about 60 seconds or until heated through. Evenly divide chicken mixture and spoon over romaine. Top with crumbled cheese and pepper.

2 In a small bowl combine salad dressing and milk; drizzle over salad. Serve with celery sticks.

nutrition facts per serving: 297 cal., 10 g total fat (3 g sat. fat), 99 mg chol., 596 mg sodium, 13 g carb. (3 g fiber, 4 g sugars), 37 g pro. exchanges: 2.5 vegetable, 4.5 lean meat, 0.5 fat.

Many cooks prefer to leave the tapered tail ends of beans intact; some prefer to remove the tails. To prep fresh green beans, line up the stem ends and trim the ends with a paring knife.

chicken salad with tarragon-shallot dressing

11 g CARB. PER SERVING

prep: 20 minutes   grill: 12 minutes   cook: 15 minutes
makes: 4 servings (2 cups salad, 1 chicken thigh, and about 3 tablespoons dressing each)

4   skinless, boneless chicken thighs (about 12 ounces total)
⅛   teaspoon salt
⅛   teaspoon black pepper
8   ounces fresh green beans
    Nonstick cooking spray
1½ cups sliced fresh mushrooms
6   cups torn Bibb lettuce
4   hard-cooked eggs, peeled and thinly sliced
¾   cup grape or cherry tomatoes, halved (optional)
1   recipe Creamy Tarragon-Shallot Dressing

1 Trim fat from chicken. Sprinkle chicken with the salt and pepper. For a charcoal grill, place chicken thighs on the grill rack directly over medium coals. Grill, uncovered, for 12 to 15 minutes or until no longer pink (180°F), turning once halfway through grilling. (For a gas grill, preheat grill. Reduce heat to medium. Place chicken thighs on grill rack over heat. Cover and grill as directed.) Slice chicken thighs into strips. Set aside.

2 Meanwhile, in a medium saucepan cook beans, covered, in enough boiling water to cover for 8 to 10 minutes or until tender. Drain and rinse with cold water to cool quickly; drain again and set aside.

3 Coat an unheated large nonstick skillet with cooking spray; heat over medium heat. Cook mushrooms in hot skillet for 5 to 7 minutes or until tender and lightly browned, stirring occasionally. Remove from heat and cool slightly.

4 To serve, divide torn lettuce among four serving bowls. Top with green beans, cooked mushrooms, sliced eggs, and, if desired, tomatoes. Arrange grilled chicken strips on salads. Drizzle with Creamy Tarragon-Shallot Dressing.

nutrition facts per serving: 259 cal., 12 g total fat (3 g sat. fat), 287 mg chol., 359 mg sodium, 11 g carb. (3 g fiber, 5 g sugars), 27 g pro. exchanges: 1 vegetable, 0.5 starch, 3.5 lean meat, 1 fat.

creamy tarragon-shallot dressing: In a small bowl whisk together ⅓ cup buttermilk and 2 tablespoons light mayonnaise. Stir in ¼ cup finely chopped shallots, 1 tablespoon snipped fresh tarragon, ⅛ teaspoon salt, and a dash black pepper.

If you have curly parsley thriving in the garden or stored in the fridge, use it instead of the flat-leaf variety. Either will add delicious fresh flavor.

cajun chicken pasta salad

prep: 25 minutes grill: 12 minutes
makes: 6 servings (1½ cups salad each)

1 pound skinless, boneless chicken breast halves
1 tablespoon Cajun seasoning or salt-free Cajun seasoning
1 small green sweet pepper, halved
1 small red sweet pepper, halved
1 small onion, cut into ¼-inch-thick slices
8 ounces dried whole-grain penne pasta
½ cup sliced celery (1 stalk)
¼ cup snipped fresh Italian (flat-leaf) parsley
3 tablespoons apple juice
2 tablespoons cider vinegar
2 tablespoons canola oil
1 tablespoon snipped fresh thyme
½ to 1 teaspoon bottled hot pepper sauce
1 clove garlic, minced

1 Sprinkle chicken evenly with Cajun seasoning. For a charcoal grill, place chicken on the greased grill rack directly over medium coals. Grill, uncovered, for 4 minutes. Add sweet peppers and onion. Continue to grill for 8 to 11 minutes more or until chicken is no longer pink (170°F) and vegetables are slightly charred and tender, turning occasionally. (For a gas grill, preheat grill. Reduce heat to medium. Place chicken on grill rack over heat. Cover and grill as directed.) Transfer to a cutting board. Chop chicken and vegetables into bite-size pieces.

2 Cook pasta according to package directions; drain. Place pasta in a large bowl. Add chicken, grilled vegetables, celery, and parsley; stir to combine.

3 For dressing, in a small bowl whisk together the apple juice, cider vinegar, oil, thyme, hot pepper sauce, and garlic. Pour dressing over pasta mixture; toss to coat. Serve immediately or cover and chill. To serve, spoon salad onto six serving plates.

nutrition facts per serving: 293 cal., 8 g total fat (1 g sat. fat), 48 mg chol., 227 mg sodium, 34 g carb. (1 g fiber, 4 g sugars), 21 g pro. exchanges: 1 vegetable, 2 starch, 2 lean meat, 1 fat.

Pumpkin seeds are rich in protein and essential fatty acids. Roast in a 350°F oven for 10 minutes, stirring once. Sprinkle over salads, stir into cereal, and swirl into yogurt.

29g
CARB. PER SERVING

turkey and mango salad with chutney vinaigrette

prep: 15 minutes cook: 6 minutes
makes: 4 servings (2 cups salad, 2½ ounces turkey, and about 1½ tablespoons vinaigrette each)

1	teaspoon ground coriander
1	teaspoon ground cumin
¼	teaspoon salt
¼	teaspoon ground ginger
¼	teaspoon black pepper
⅛	teaspoon cayenne pepper
1	12-ounce turkey breast tenderloin
2	teaspoons canola oil
6	cups packaged fresh baby spinach
¼	of a medium red onion, thinly sliced
1	cup fresh snow pea pods, trimmed
1	medium mango, seeded, peeled, and cubed
1	recipe Chutney Vinaigrette
2	tablespoons roasted pumpkin seeds (pepitas)

1 In a small bowl combine coriander, cumin, salt, ginger, black pepper, and cayenne pepper. Cut turkey tenderloin in half horizontally to make two thin steaks. Sprinkle both sides of turkey pieces evenly with coriander mixture; rub in with your fingers.

2 In a large skillet cook turkey tenderloin pieces in oil over medium heat for 6 to 8 minutes or until no longer pink (170°F), turning once halfway through cooking. Transfer turkey to a cutting board and thinly slice.

3 Toss spinach, red onion, pea pods, mango, and Chutney Vinaigrette in a large bowl to coat. To serve, divide salad among four serving plates. Arrange turkey slices on top. Sprinkle with pumpkin seeds.

nutrition facts per serving: 308 cal., 9 g total fat (1 g sat. fat), 53 mg chol., 426 mg sodium, 29 g carb. (4 g fiber, 18 g sugars), 26 g pro. exchanges: 1.5 vegetable, 1.5 starch, 2.5 lean meat, 1 fat.

chutney vinaigrette: Spoon ¼ cup mango chutney into a small bowl. Use kitchen shears to finely snip any large pieces in the chutney. Stir 1 tablespoon canola oil and 4½ teaspoons rice vinegar into the chutney.

For a healthful dose of antioxidants, substitute fresh spinach for the butterhead lettuce.

cherry, turkey, and wild rice salad

prep: 25 minutes cook: 45 minutes chill: up to 24 hours
makes: 6 servings (1 cup rice mixture and 1 cup greens each)

30 g
CARB. PER
SERVING

4 cups water
1 cup uncooked wild
   rice
2 cups chopped cooked
   turkey breast
1½ cups halved, pitted
   fresh sweet cherries
½ cup sliced celery
   (1 stalk)
1 teaspoon finely
   shredded orange
   peel
3 tablespoons orange
   juice
2 tablespoons canola oil
2 tablespoons white
   wine vinegar
1 teaspoon sugar✳
¼ teaspoon salt
¼ teaspoon black
   pepper
6 cups torn butterhead
   (Boston or Bibb)
   lettuce
¼ cup chopped pecans,
   toasted

1 In a medium saucepan combine water and rice. Bring to boiling; reduce heat. Simmer, covered, for 45 to 50 minutes or until rice is tender. Drain. Place rice in a large mixing bowl; cool.

2 Add turkey, cherries, and celery to the cooled rice.

3 For dressing, in a small bowl whisk together orange peel, orange juice, oil, vinegar, sugar, salt, and pepper. Pour over rice mixture. Toss to combine. Cover; chill for up to 24 hours.

4 To serve, divide lettuce or spinach among six serving bowls. Spoon rice mixture over lettuce. Sprinkle with pecans.

nutrition facts per serving: 287 cal., 11 g total fat (1 g sat. fat), 35 mg chol., 141 mg sodium, 30 g carb. (4 g fiber, 8 g sugars), 19 g pro. exchanges: 0.5 fruit, 1.5 starch, 2 lean meat, 1 fat.

nutrition facts per serving with substitute: Same as original, except 285 cal., 29 g carb. (7 g sugars).

✳sugar substitutes: Choose from Splenda Granular, Equal Spoonful or packets, Truvia Spoonable or packets, or Sweet'N Low bulk or packets. Follow package directions to use product amount equivalent to 1 teaspoon sugar.

15g CARB. PER SERVING

Orange marmalade stars two ways in this recipe: It glazes the roast turkey and adds extra body and flavor to the vinaigrette.

orange cranberry club salad

prep: 30 minutes roast: 1 hour 15 minutes stand: 15 minutes
makes: 4 servings (1¾ cups salad, 2½ ounces turkey, and 2 tablespoons dressing each)

¼ cup low-sugar orange marmalade
2 tablespoons Dijon-style mustard
1 2½-pound turkey breast half with bone
2 slices turkey bacon
2 tablespoons cider vinegar
2 tablespoons olive oil
2 tablespoons low-sugar orange marmalade
1½ teaspoons Dijon-style mustard
2 tablespoons snipped dried cranberries
1 to 2 tablespoons orange juice
6 cups chopped romaine lettuce
1 cup chopped tomato
¼ cup shredded reduced-fat cheddar cheese
2 tablespoons shredded Swiss cheese
2 tablespoons low-sodium or unsalted croutons

1 Preheat oven to 325°F. In a small bowl stir together the ¼ cup marmalade and 2 tablespoons mustard. Remove skin from turkey breast. Rinse turkey; pat dry with paper towels. Insert an oven-going meat thermometer into the center of the turkey breast. The tip should not touch bone.

2 Place turkey breast, bone side down, on a rack in a shallow roasting pan. Roast, uncovered, for 1¼ to 1½ hours or until juices run clear and turkey is no longer pink (170°F), brushing occasionally with marmalade mixture during the last 15 minutes of roasting. Remove turkey from oven; cover with foil. Let stand for 15 minutes before slicing.

3 Meanwhile, cook turkey bacon according to package directions. Drain on paper towels. Coarsely chop bacon.

4 For dressing, in a small bowl whisk together vinegar, olive oil, 2 tablespoons orange marmalade, and 1½ teaspoons mustard. Stir in the dried cranberries and enough orange juice to reach desired consistency.

5 Coarsely shred half of the turkey for the salad. Cover and chill remaining half of the turkey and save for another use.

6 To serve, arrange romaine on a large serving platter. Top with turkey, tomato, turkey bacon, cheddar cheese, Swiss cheese, and croutons.

nutrition facts per serving: 310 cal., 12 g total fat (3 g sat. fat), 84 mg chol., 370 mg sodium, 15 g carb. (2 g fiber, 10 g sugars), 33 g pro. exchanges: 1 starch, 4 lean meat, 1 fat.

Give the salad a gentle toss before serving. This will help mix in the spinach so all of it will become partially wilted.

warm yukon gold and sweet potato salad

26 g
CARB. PER SERVING

prep: 20 minutes **cook:** 15 minutes
makes: 4 servings (2 cups spinach, ¾ cup potatoes, and ⅓ cup sausage mixture each)

8   ounces Yukon gold potatoes, scrubbed and cut into ½-inch slices
8   ounces sweet potato, peeled, and cut into ½-inch slices (1 medium)
7   ounces smoked turkey sausage, cut into ½-inch slices
1   small red onion, cut into thin wedges
1   stalk celery, thinly sliced (½ cup)
2   tablespoons olive oil
2   tablespoons cider vinegar
1   teaspoon Dusseldorf or spicy brown mustard
1   teaspoon snipped fresh sage or ½ teaspoon dried sage, crushed
¼   teaspoon black pepper
⅛   teaspoon celery seeds
1   5- to 6-ounce package fresh baby spinach

1 In a large saucepan cook potatoes and sweet potatoes in enough boiling salted water to cover about 10 minutes or until tender; drain.

2 Meanwhile, in a large skillet cook sausage, onion, and celery in hot olive oil over medium heat about 5 minutes or until onion is tender and sausage is browned. Stir in vinegar, mustard, sage, pepper, and celery seeds.

3 Place spinach on a serving platter. Top with potatoes and sweet potato. Spoon sausage mixture over top.

nutrition facts per serving: 253 cal., 12 g total fat (2 g sat. fat), 33 mg chol., 560 mg sodium, 26 g carb. (4 g fiber, 5 g sugars), 10 g pro. exchanges: 1.5 vegetables, 1 starch, 0.5 medium-fat meat, 1.5 fat.

Reach for a mandoline or your sharpest knife to cut the fennel bulbs into the thinnest slices possible. If you like, save the feathery fennel fronds to garnish the plate.

main-dish salads

seared tuna with fennel salad

prep: 20 minutes cook: 6 minutes
makes: 4 servings (1¾ cups salad, 4 ounces tuna, and 2 tablespoons dressing each)

1 pound fresh or frozen tuna steaks, cut 1 inch thick
¼ teaspoon salt
¼ teaspoon freshly ground black pepper
3 cups torn fresh curly endive or frisée
2 medium fennel bulbs, trimmed, cored, and very thinly sliced (3 cups)
¼ of a medium red onion, thinly sliced
¼ cup pitted Kalamata olives, halved
Nonstick cooking spray
1 recipe Garlic-Lime Aïoli Dressing

1 Thaw fish, if frozen. Rinse fish and pat dry with paper towels. Sprinkle fish evenly with salt and pepper; set aside. In a large bowl toss together endive, fennel, and red onion; divide mixture among four serving plates. Sprinkle evenly with olives. Set aside.

2 Coat an unheated grill pan with cooking spray; heat pan over medium-high heat. Add tuna steaks to the hot pan. Cook for 6 minutes or until steaks are well browned on the outside, turning once; steaks will be pink in the center. Transfer steaks to a cutting board. Cut steaks into ¼-inch-thick slices.

3 To serve, arrange tuna slices on salads. Drizzle with Garlic-Lime Aïoli Dressing.

nutrition facts per serving: 234 cal., 9 g total fat (1 g sat. fat), 58 mg chol., 443 mg sodium, 10 g carb. (4 g fiber, 2 g sugars), 29 g pro. exchanges: 1 vegetable, 4 lean meat, 0.5 fat.

garlic-lime aïoli dressing: In a small bowl combine ⅓ cup light mayonnaise; 3 tablespoons fat-free milk; ½ teaspoon finely shredded lime peel; 1 tablespoon lime juice; and 2 cloves garlic, minced.

Popular in Middle Eastern cooking, tabbouleh combines fiber-rich bulgur with sprightly seasonings. It's a refreshing match for the salmon. Pictured on page 79.

chilled salmon and tabbouleh

22g
CARB. PER
SERVING

prep: 25 minutes stand: 1 hour cook: 8 minutes chill: 2 hours
makes: 4 servings (1½ cups each)

1 pound fresh or frozen skinless salmon fillets
1 cup water
½ teaspoon salt
¼ teaspoon black pepper
2 cloves garlic, minced
1 teaspoon finely shredded lemon peel
1½ cups water
½ cup bulgur
⅓ cup lemon juice
2 tablespoons olive oil
1 cup grape tomatoes or cherry tomatoes, halved
1 cup frozen artichoke hearts, thawed, drained, and coarsely chopped
1 cup chopped, seeded cucumber
½ cup snipped fresh Italian (flat-leaf) parsley
¼ cup snipped fresh mint
2 green onions, thinly sliced

1 Thaw fish, if frozen. Rinse fish; pat dry with paper towels. In a large skillet bring the 1 cup water to boiling. Add salmon in a single layer. Simmer, covered, for 8 to 10 minutes or until fish flakes easily when tested with a fork. Using a slotted spatula, carefully transfer fish to a platter. Sprinkle all sides of the fish with ¼ teaspoon of the salt and ⅛ teaspoon of the pepper. In a small bowl combine garlic and lemon peel; sprinkle evenly over one side of each fish fillet, pressing in with your fingers. Cover and chill salmon.

2 Meanwhile, in a large bowl combine the 1½ cups water and the bulgur. Let stand for 1 hour. Drain bulgur through a fine-mesh sieve, using a large spoon to press out any excess water.

3 In the same large bowl whisk together lemon juice, oil, the remaining ¼ teaspoon salt, and the remaining ⅛ teaspoon pepper. Add drained bulgur, tomatoes, artichoke hearts, cucumber, parsley, mint, and green onions. Toss to combine. Break salmon into large chunks. Gently toss salmon into bulgur mixture. Cover and chill for 2 to 24 hours.

4 To serve, divide salmon-bulgur mixture among four serving plates.

nutrition facts per serving: 393 cal., 22 g total fat (4 g sat. fat), 62 mg chol., 390 mg sodium, 22 g carb. (6 g fiber, 3 g sugars), 27 g pro. exchanges: 1 vegetable, 1 starch, 3 lean meat, 3 fat.

Keep edamame on hand in your freezer and add the tasty gems to your next vegetarian stir-fry for a boost of protein and fiber.

teriyaki shrimp and edamame salad

15g
CARB. PER SERVING

prep: 25 minutes
makes: 4 servings (2⅓ cups each)

½ cup frozen sweet soybeans (edamame)

2 ounces dried radiatore or rotini pasta

3 cups packaged fresh baby spinach

2 cups shredded romaine lettuce

¾ cup coarsely shredded carrots

¾ cup fresh pea pods, trimmed, strings removed, and halved

1 small red or yellow sweet pepper, cut into thin strips

¼ cup thinly sliced green onions (2)

6 ounces cooked medium shrimp, halved horizontally

3 tablespoons rice vinegar or cider vinegar

1 tablespoon canola oil

1 tablespoon reduced-sodium soy sauce

4 cloves garlic, minced

1 teaspoon toasted sesame oil

1 teaspoon grated fresh ginger

⅛ teaspoon crushed red pepper

1 Cook soybeans according to package directions; drain. Cook pasta according to package directions; drain and rinse with cold water.

2 Divide spinach and romaine among four shallow bowls. Top each with carrots, pea pods, sweet pepper, sweet soybeans, and green onions. In a medium bowl combine shrimp and cooked pasta; set aside.

3 For dressing, in a screw-top jar combine vinegar, canola oil, soy sauce, garlic, toasted sesame oil, ginger, and crushed red pepper. Cover and shake well to combine. Pour half of the dressing mixture over the shrimp and pasta; toss to coat.

4 Top each salad in bowls with shrimp mixture. Drizzle salads with remaining salad dressing mixture.

nutrition facts per serving: 181 cal., 7 g total fat (1 g sat. fat), 90 mg chol., 593 mg sodium, 15 g carb. (4 g fiber, 3 g sugars), 15 g pro. exchanges: 1.5 vegetable, 0.5 starch, 1.5 lean meat, 1 fat.

37 g
CARB. PER
SERVING

Mahi mahi, also known as dolphinfish, is a firm saltwater fish with a mild flavor. If you need a substitute, try grouper or red snapper.

maple mahi mahi salad

start to finish: 30 minutes

makes: 2 servings (3 ounces cooked fish and 2½ cups cabbage mixture each)

½ cup frozen shelled sweet soybeans (edamame)

8 ounces fresh or frozen skinless mahi mahi fillets

2 tablespoons pure maple syrup

1 tablespoon balsamic vinegar

1 tablespoon finely chopped onion

1 tablespoon honey mustard

2 teaspoons olive oil

⅛ teaspoon salt

⅛ teaspoon black pepper

4 cups coarsely shredded napa cabbage

½ cup fresh snow pea pods, trimmed and halved crosswise

2 tablespoons snipped dried cherries

2 tablespoons sliced almonds, toasted

1 Cook edamame according to package directions; drain. Set aside to cool.

2 Preheat broiler. Thaw fish, if frozen. Rinse fish; pat dry with paper towels. Cut fish into two portions. Measure thickness of fish; set aside.

3 For dressing, in a small bowl whisk together maple syrup, vinegar, onion, honey mustard, oil, salt, and pepper.

4 Remove 2 tablespoons of the dressing and brush on all sides of the fish pieces.

5 Place fish on the unheated greased rack of a broiler pan. Broil 4 inches from heat until fish flakes easily when tested with a fork. Allow 4 to 6 minutes per ½-inch thickness of fish.

6 Meanwhile, in a large bowl combine napa cabbage, snow pea pods, and cooked edamame. Pour the remaining dressing over cabbage mixture; toss to coat. To serve, divide cabbage mixture between two serving plates. Sprinkle with cherries and almonds. Top with fish.

nutrition facts per serving: 359 cal., 11 g total fat (1 g sat. fat), 83 mg chol., 313 mg sodium, 37 g carb. (6 g fiber, 24 g sugars), 30 g pro. exchanges: 2 vegetable, 0.5 fruit, 1 carb., 3.5 lean meat, 1 fat.

Asparagus packs some major nutrients, including vitamins A, C, and K. Showcase it in this vibrant citrus- and tarragon-laced salad.

asparagus and shrimp salad

17g
CARB. PER SERVING

start to finish: 30 minutes
makes: 4 servings (2½ cups each)

12 ounces fresh or frozen medium shrimp in shells
½ teaspoon finely shredded orange peel
2 tablespoons orange juice
1 pound fresh asparagus, trimmed
3 oranges
Orange juice (optional)
1 tablespoon olive oil or salad oil
1 tablespoon white wine vinegar
1 clove garlic, minced
1 teaspoon chopped fresh tarragon
¼ teaspoon black pepper
⅛ teaspoon salt
6 cups torn mixed salad greens
¼ cup sliced green onions (2)

1 Thaw shrimp, if frozen. Peel and devein shrimp, leaving tails intact if desired. Rinse shrimp; pat dry with paper towels. In a large saucepan bring 4 cups water to boiling. Add shrimp; reduce heat. Simmer, uncovered, for 1 to 3 minutes or until shrimp are opaque. Drain in a colander. Rinse with cold water; drain again. Transfer shrimp to a bowl. Add orange peel and the 2 tablespoons orange juice; toss gently to coat.

2 In a medium saucepan cook asparagus, covered, in a small amount of boiling water for 4 to 6 minutes or until crisp-tender. Drain in a colander. Rinse with cold water; drain again.

3 Peel oranges. Working over a bowl, cut oranges into sections; reserve ⅓ cup of the juice. (If necessary, add additional orange juice to make ⅓ cup.) For dressing, in a small bowl whisk together the ⅓ cup orange juice, the oil, vinegar, garlic, tarragon, pepper, and salt.

4 In a large bowl combine shrimp, asparagus, orange sections, greens, and green onions. Pour dressing over all; toss gently to coat. To serve, divide salad among four serving plates.

nutrition facts per serving: 174 cal., 5 g total fat (1 g sat. fat), 107 mg chol., 504 mg sodium, 17 g carb. (5 g fiber, 12 g sugars), 16 g pro. exchanges: 1 vegetable, 1 fruit, 2 lean meat.

9g
CARB. PER
SERVING

main-dish salads

When peeling and deveining the shrimp, you can leave the tails intact for an eye-catching presentation.

grilled shrimp salad with creamy garlic dressing

prep: 25 minutes grill: 6 minutes
makes: 4 servings (1 shrimp skewer and 1½ cups salad each)

1 pound fresh or frozen
   large shrimp in
   shells
¼ teaspoon salt
⅛ teaspoon black
   pepper
6 cups mixed spring
   salad greens
1 cup coarsely chopped
   cucumber
½ cup shaved, peeled
   jicama*
4 radishes, thinly sliced
1 recipe Creamy Garlic
   Dressing
2 ounces semisoft goat
   cheese (chèvre),
   crumbled (optional)

1 Thaw shrimp, if frozen. Peel and devein shrimp. Rinse shrimp; pat dry with paper towels. Thread shrimp onto four 12-inch skewers,** leaving a ¼-inch space between each shrimp. Sprinkle shrimp with salt and pepper.

2 For a charcoal grill, place shrimp skewers on the grill rack directly over medium coals. Grill, uncovered, for 6 to 8 minutes or until shrimp are opaque, turning once halfway through grilling. (For a gas grill, preheat grill. Reduce heat to medium. Place skewers on grill rack over heat. Cover and grill as directed.)

3 To serve, divide salad greens among four serving bowls. Top with cucumber, jicama, and radishes. Top each salad with a shrimp skewer. Spoon Creamy Garlic Dressing over salads. If desired, sprinkle with goat cheese. Serve immediately.

nutrition facts per serving: 165 cal., 2 g total fat (0 g sat. fat), 173 mg chol., 429 mg sodium, 9 g carb. (2 g fiber, 4 g sugars), 27 g pro. exchanges: 1.5 vegetable, 3 lean meat.

*test kitchen tip: Use a vegetable peeler to shave enough wide strips of the peeled jicama to make ½ cup.

**test kitchen tip: If using wooden skewers, soak them in enough water to cover for at least 30 minutes before using.

creamy garlic dressing: In a small bowl combine ½ cup plain fat-free yogurt; 3 tablespoons fat-free milk; 2 tablespoons snipped fresh mint; 2 teaspoons snipped fresh dill; 1 large clove garlic, minced; ⅛ teaspoon salt; and dash black pepper.

Cooking sesame seeds for a few minutes in a dry skillet turns them extra nutty, crunchy, and golden. If there's an Asian market nearby, you can save a step by buying them already toasted.

sesame scallop salad

35g
CARB. PER
SERVING

start to finish: 30 minutes
makes: 4 servings (2½ cups salad and 2 scallops each)

8 fresh or frozen sea scallops or peeled and deveined large shrimp
4 ounces dried multigrain spaghetti
6 cups shredded napa cabbage and/or shredded romaine lettuce
1 cup coarsely shredded carrot
½ cup quartered and thinly sliced red onion
¼ cup rice vinegar or white wine vinegar
2 tablespoons reduced-sodium soy sauce
4 teaspoons canola oil
1 tablespoon honey
½ teaspoon crushed red pepper
4 teaspoons canola oil
2 teaspoon sesame seeds, toasted

1 Thaw scallops or shrimp, if frozen. Rinse and pat dry with paper towels. Cut scallops in half and set aside.

2 Cook spaghetti according to package directions; drain. Rinse with cold water; drain again. In a large bowl toss together spaghetti, cabbage, carrot, and red onion. Transfer mixture to a serving bowl.

3 For dressing, in a small bowl whisk together vinegar, soy sauce, 4 teaspoons oil, the honey, and crushed red pepper. Set aside.

4 In a large skillet heat the 4 teaspoons oil over medium heat. Add scallops or shrimp; cook for 3 to 4 minutes or until opaque, turning once to brown evenly. Place scallops or shrimp over the cabbage mixture. Drizzle dressing over all; sprinkle with sesame seeds. Gently toss to coat. To serve, divide salad among four serving plates.

nutrition facts per serving: 355 cal., 12 g total fat (1 g sat. fat), 37 mg chol., 514 mg sodium, 35 g carb. (5 g fiber, 9 g sugars), 27 g pro. exchanges: 2 vegetable, 1.5 starch, 3 lean meat, 1 fat.

You'll find going meatless easy when hearty roasted mushrooms and rich, creamy cannellini beans are in the picture!

35g CARB. PER SERVING

roasted tomato and mushroom pasta salad

prep: 20 minutes   roast: 20 minutes   cool: 30 minutes
makes: 6 servings (1¼ cups each)

8   ounces fresh mushrooms, sliced
8   ounces grape tomatoes or cherry tomatoes, halved
4   cloves garlic, thinly sliced
2   teaspoons dried oregano, crushed
1   tablespoon olive oil
6   ounces dried whole grain penne pasta
2   tablespoons olive oil
2   tablespoons white wine vinegar
½   teaspoon cracked black pepper
1   15-ounce can cannellini beans (white kidney beans), rinsed and drained
½   cup snipped fresh basil
2   ounces Parmesan cheese, shaved

1 Preheat oven to 450°F. Line a 15×10×1-inch baking pan with foil. Arrange mushrooms and tomato halves, cut sides up, in the prepared pan. Sprinkle with garlic and oregano. Drizzle with 1 tablespoon olive oil. Roast, uncovered, for 20 to 25 minutes or until tomatoes are soft and skins begin to split and mushrooms are lightly browned.

2 Meanwhile, cook pasta according to package directions, in lightly salted water; drain. In a large bowl whisk together 2 tablespoons olive oil, the vinegar, and pepper. Add warm pasta to the bowl; toss to coat. Let cool to room temperature, stirring occasionally.

3 Add mushroom-tomato mixture and any drippings from the pan, beans, basil, and shaved Parmesan to pasta. Toss to combine. Serve at room temperature.

nutrition facts per serving: 264 cal., 10 g total fat (3 g sat. fat), 6 mg chol., 271 mg sodium, 35 g carb. (4 g fiber, 2 g sugars), 13 g pro. exchanges: 1 vegetable, 2 starch, 1 lean meat, 1 fat.

For a dramatic presentation, bring this salad to the table arranged as directed. Just before passing, toss with tongs so each serving will contain all the ingredients.

mexican edamame and couscous salad

start to finish: 30 minutes

makes: 4 servings (2 cups romaine, ½ cup couscous, 2 tablespoons edamame, 2 tablespoons beans, ½ cup vegetables, ½ tablespoon queso fresco, and 2 tablespoons dressing each)

¼ cup cider vinegar
3 tablespoons snipped fresh cilantro
3 tablespoons olive oil
1 to 2 teaspoons chopped canned chipotle chile peppers in adobo sauce (see tip, *page 82*)
1 clove garlic, minced
¼ teaspoon salt
¼ teaspoon black pepper
8 cups coarsely shredded romaine lettuce
2 cups cooked Israeli (large pearl) couscous✳ or whole grain small pasta
10 grape tomatoes, halved
1 medium yellow sweet pepper, cut into bite-size pieces
½ cup frozen shelled sweet soybeans (edamame), cooked according to package directions
½ cup canned no-salt-added black beans, rinsed and drained
1 lime, cut into thin wedges
2 tablespoons crumbled queso fresco

1 For dressing, in a screw-top jar combine vinegar, cilantro, oil, chopped chile pepper, garlic, salt, and black pepper. Cover and shake well to combine; set aside.

2 Cover a large serving platter with romaine. Toss couscous with 1 tablespoon of the dressing. In a small bowl combine tomatoes and sweet pepper. Arrange tomato mixture, couscous, edamame, black beans, and lime wedges on romaine on the platter. To serve, drizzle with the remaining dressing; sprinkle with queso fresco.

nutrition facts per serving: 290 cal., 12 g total fat (2 g sat. fat), 3 mg chol., 184 mg sodium, 37 g carb. (7 g fiber, 4 g sugars), 10 g pro. exchanges: 1 vegetable, 2 starch, 0.5 lean meat, 2 fat.

✳ test kitchen tip: To cook the couscous, in a small saucepan combine 1 cup water and ¾ cup Israeli (large pearl) couscous. Bring to boiling; reduce heat. Simmer, covered, for 8 minutes. Remove from heat. Let stand, covered, for 5 minutes. Makes about 2 cups cooked couscous.

Be sure to use quick-cooking barley for this recipe. It takes only about 10 minutes to cook; regular requires at least 45 minutes.

cucumber-radish barley salad

34g
CARB. PER SERVING

main-dish salads

prep: 15 minutes cook: 10 minutes
makes: 5 servings (1¼ cups barley salad and ¾ cup spinach each)

1½   cups water
¾   cup uncooked quick-cooking barley
1   15-ounce can no-salt-added garbanzo beans (chickpeas), rinsed and drained
2   cups chopped peeled cucumber (1 medium)
1   cup thinly sliced radishes
½   cup sliced green onions (4)
3   tablespoons cider vinegar
2   tablespoons olive oil
2   tablespoons apple juice or orange juice
2   tablespoons snipped fresh oregano
½   teaspoon black pepper
¼   teaspoon salt
4   cups torn fresh spinach
2   ounces feta cheese, crumbled

1 In a medium saucepan bring water to boiling. Add barley; reduce heat. Simmer, covered, for 10 to 12 minutes or until barley is tender and water is absorbed. Transfer barley to a colander and rinse with cold water; drain well.

2 In a large bowl combine barley, garbanzo beans, cucumber, radishes, and green onions; set aside.

3 For dressing, in a small bowl stir together the vinegar, olive oil, apple juice, oregano, pepper, and salt. Add to barley mixture; toss to coat. To serve, arrange spinach on a platter or five serving plates. Spoon barley mixture over spinach and sprinkle with feta cheese.

nutrition facts per serving: 251 cal., 9 g total fat (2 g sat. fat), 10 mg chol., 283 mg sodium, 34 g carb. (7 g fiber, 3 g sugars), 10 g pro. exchanges: 2 starch, 1 lean meat, 1 fat.

Marinate tofu in chili sauce and peanut butter, then sauté it in sesame oil for a tantalizing protein addition to this salad.

asian tofu salad

prep: 20 minutes marinate: 30 minutes cook: 5 minutes
makes: 6 servings (1¼ cups salad and 2 slices tofu each)

¼	cup reduced-sodium soy sauce
¼	cup sweet chili sauce
1	tablespoon creamy peanut butter
1	clove garlic, minced
1	teaspoon grated fresh ginger
1	16- to 18-ounce package firm water-packed tofu (fresh bean curd)
1	teaspoon toasted sesame oil
4	cups shredded romaine lettuce
1½	cups chopped, peeled jicama
1	medium red sweet pepper, seeded and thinly sliced
1	cup coarsely shredded carrots
2	tablespoons unsalted dry-roasted peanuts
2	tablespoons snipped fresh cilantro

1 In a small bowl whisk together soy sauce, chili sauce, peanut butter, garlic, and ginger. Pat tofu dry with paper towels. Cut tofu crosswise into 12 slices. Place tofu in a 2-quart rectangular baking dish. Drizzle with 3 tablespoons of the soy sauce mixture, turning to coat tofu. Let marinate at room temperature for 30 minutes, turning tofu occasionally. Set aside the remaining soy sauce mixture for dressing.

2 In a very large nonstick skillet heat sesame oil over medium-high heat. Remove tofu slices from the marinade. Add remaining marinade to the skillet. Add tofu slices. Cook for 5 to 6 minutes or until lightly browned, turning once halfway through cooking.

3 In a large bowl combine lettuce, jicama, sweet pepper, and carrots. Divide among six serving plates. Top with tofu, peanuts, and cilantro. Serve with reserved dressing mixture.

nutrition facts per serving: 179 cal., 7 g total fat (1 g sat. fat), 0 mg chol., 515 mg sodium, 18 g carb. (3 g fiber, 9 g sugars), 11 g pro. exchanges: 1.5 vegetable, 0.5 carb., 1 medium-fat meat, 0.5 fat.

chicken pot pie stew, *page 134*

satisfying

soups

Find the perfect bowl for all seasons and occasions: robust chilies and hearty stews to warm you up on winter nights, chilled fruit soups to cool you down on summer days, and irresistible serve-alongs for salads and sandwiches. Check out how well they fit into your meal plan—and get cooking!

&stews

A pistou *is the French version of Italian basil pesto. A spoonful of this cold sauce adds a burst of freshness to each bite.*

french beef stew au pistou

35g CARB. PER SERVING

start to finish: 1 hour
makes: 6 servings (2 cups stew and 1½ tablespoons pistou each)

satisfying soups & stews

2 cups fresh basil
leaves
½ cup grated Parmesan
cheese
3 tablespoons olive oil
2 tablespoons minced
garlic
1 pound lean beef stew
meat, trimmed of fat
and cut into ½-inch
pieces
2 large onions, chopped
(1 cup)
1 pound roma tomatoes,
chopped (about
3 cups)
2 cups diced red
potatoes (about
12 ounces)
2 medium carrots,
diced (1 cup)
4 cups lower-sodium
beef broth
2 cups water
2 cups chopped
zucchini
8 ounces green beans,
trimmed and halved
(2 cups)
4 cups chopped fresh
spinach
1 15-ounce can no-salt-
added red kidney
beans, rinsed and
drained
½ teaspoon crushed
red pepper

1 For pistou, in a food processor combine basil, Parmesan cheese, 2 tablespoons of the oil, and the garlic. Cover and process until a paste forms; set aside.

2 In a 5- to 6-quart Dutch oven heat the remaining 1 tablespoon oil over medium-high heat. Brown stew meat, half at a time, in hot oil, stirring frequently. Remove meat from Dutch oven; set aside. Add onions to Dutch oven; cook over medium heat about 5 minutes or until tender. Return meat to Dutch oven.

3 Add tomatoes, potatoes, and carrots; cook and stir for 4 minutes more. Stir in broth, the water, zucchini, and green beans. Bring to boiling; reduce heat. Simmer, covered, about 15 minutes or until meat and vegetables are tender.

4 Stir in spinach, kidney beans, and crushed red pepper. Cook about 2 minutes more or just until spinach is wilted. Serve with the pistou.

nutrition facts per serving: 374 cal., 14 g total fat (4 g sat. fat), 49 mg chol., 506 mg sodium, 35 g carb. (11 g fiber, 7 g sugars), 29 g pro. exchanges: 2 vegetable, 1.5 starch, 3 lean meat, 1.5 fat.

Cutting the beef into thin strips will be much easier if you place it in the freezer for 30 minutes before slicing.

beef fajita soup

start to finish: 40 minutes
makes: 4 servings (2 cups each)

16g
CARB. PER
SERVING

½ teaspoon garlic powder
½ teaspoon ground cumin
½ teaspoon paprika
⅛ teaspoon cayenne pepper
12 ounces boneless beef sirloin steak, trimmed and cut into very thin bite-size strips
Nonstick cooking spray
2 teaspoons canola oil
2 cups yellow or green sweet peppers cut into thin bite-size strips (2 medium)
1 medium onion, halved and thinly sliced
2 14.5-ounce cans lower-sodium beef broth
1 14.5-ounce can no-salt-added diced tomatoes, undrained
¼ cup light sour cream
½ teaspoon finely shredded lime peel
1 ounce baked tortilla chips, coarsely crushed (⅔ cup) (optional)
½ of an avocado, seeded, peeled, and chopped or sliced (optional)
¼ cup snipped fresh cilantro (optional)

1 In a medium bowl combine garlic powder, cumin, paprika, and cayenne pepper. Add steak strips and toss to coat.

2 Coat an unheated 4-quart nonstick Dutch oven with cooking spray. Heat over medium-high heat. Add half of the steak strips; cook for 2 to 4 minutes or until browned, stirring occasionally. Remove meat from the pan and repeat with remaining steak strips.

3 Add the oil to the Dutch oven. Add sweet peppers and onion. Cook over medium heat about 5 minutes or until lightly browned and just tender, stirring occasionally. Add broth and tomatoes. Bring to boiling. Stir in steak strips and heat through.

4 To serve, ladle soup into bowls. Add a spoonful of sour cream to individual servings and sprinkle with lime peel. If desired, top with tortilla chips, avocado, and cilantro.

nutrition facts per serving: 221 cal., 7 g total fat (2 g sat. fat), 55 mg chol., 443 mg sodium, 16 g carb. (3 g fiber, 8 g sugars), 24 g pro. exchanges: 3 vegetable, 1 starch, 3 lean meat, 1 fat.

11g
CARB. PER
SERVING

*Kale adds vitamins and an enticing cabbage flavor to this soup.
Be sure to use the kale within 2 or 3 days; it can become pungent
if stored longer.*

mushroom and beef soup

prep: 30 minutes cook: 25 minutes
makes: 6 servings (1½ cups each)

12 ounces beef sirloin
     steak, trimmed
1 tablespoon canola oil
4 cups sliced assorted
     mushrooms, such
     as white, cremini,
     shiitake, and morel
¼ cup chopped shallot
2 cloves garlic, minced
4 cups low-sodium beef
     broth
1 14.5-ounce can
     no-salt-added
     diced tomatoes,
     undrained
1 cup chopped carrot
½ cup chopped celery
1 bay leaf
½ teaspoon dried leaf
     thyme, crushed
½ teaspoon salt
¼ teaspoon black
     pepper
2 cups loosely packed
     chopped fresh kale

1 Cut beef into ¾-inch cubes. In a 4- to
5-quart Dutch oven brown beef in hot
oil over medium-high heat. Remove beef;
set aside. Add mushrooms, shallot, and
garlic to pan. Cook for 4 to 5 minutes or until
mushrooms are tender and lightly browned,
stirring occasionally. Return beef to pan.
Add broth, tomatoes, carrot, celery, bay leaf,
thyme, salt, and pepper, stirring to loosen any
browned bits from bottom of pan. Bring to
boiling; reduce heat. Simmer, covered, for
20 to 25 minutes or until carrot is tender.

2 Stir in kale. Simmer for 5 to 10 minutes or
until kale is tender. Discard bay leaf before
ladling into bowls.

nutrition facts per serving: 139 cal., 5 g total fat
(1 g sat. fat), 30 mg chol., 541 mg sodium, 11 g carb. (3 g fiber,
6 g sugars), 15 g pro. exchanges: 2 vegetable, 1.5 lean meat,
0.5 fat.

35g
CARB. PER
SERVING

No-salt-added products help make this classic chili recipe fit into your meal plan. Corn adds extra color and texture to the mix, and the chipotle pepper brings smoky-spicy appeal.

adobo black bean chili

prep: 20 minutes   cook: 20 minutes
makes: 4 servings (1½ cups each)

12   ounces lean ground beef
½   cup chopped onion (1 medium)
¾   cup chopped green sweet pepper (1 medium)
2   cloves garlic, minced
1   15-ounce can no-salt added black beans, rinsed and drained, or 1¾ cups cooked black beans
1   14.5-ounce can no-salt-added diced tomatoes, undrained
1   8-ounce can no-salt-added tomato sauce
½   cup frozen whole kernel corn
1   tablespoon canned chipotle chile peppers in adobo sauce, finely chopped*
2   teaspoons chili powder
1   teaspoon dried oregano, crushed
1   teaspoon ground cumin
¼   teaspoon black pepper
¼   cup light sour cream
2   tablespoons shredded reduced-fat cheddar cheese

1 In a 4-quart Dutch oven cook ground beef, onion, sweet pepper, and garlic until meat is brown and onion is tender; drain fat. Stir in beans, diced tomatoes, tomato sauce, corn, chile peppers, chili powder, oregano, cumin, and black pepper. Bring to boiling; reduce heat. Simmer, covered, for 20 minutes, stirring occasionally.

2 Ladle chili into bowls. Top each serving with sour cream and cheddar cheese.

nutrition facts per serving: 317 cal., 7 g total fat (3 g sat. fat), 59 mg chol., 184 mg sodium, 35 g carb. (10 g fiber, 9 g sugars), 28 g pro. exchanges: 1.5 vegetable, 2 starch, 2.5 lean meat, 0.5 fat.

∗test kitchen tip: Because chile peppers contain volatile oils that can burn your skin and eyes, avoid direct contact with them as much as possible. When working with chile peppers, wear plastic or rubber gloves. If your bare hands do touch the peppers, wash your hands and nails well with soap and warm water.

Yes, even something as indulgent-sounding as cheeseburger soup can fit into your meal plan when you swap a few healthful ingredients for some not-so-healthful ones.

cheeseburger soup

start to finish: 45 minutes
makes: 6 servings (1⅓ cups each)

1 pound 93% or leaner
ground beef
2 cups sliced fresh
mushrooms
1 medium red or green
sweet pepper, cut
into thin bite-size
strips (1 cup)
1 medium onion, cut
into thin wedges
(½ cup)
1 cup lower-sodium
beef broth
¼ cup all-purpose flour
3½ cups fat-free milk
8 slices reduced-fat
process American
cheese product,
torn (5 ounces)
⅛ teaspoon black
pepper
3 cups coarsely chopped
fresh spinach (about
2½ ounces)
½ of a medium
cucumber, sliced
(optional)
1 medium tomato,
thinly sliced or
chopped
1 cup whole grain
croutons
2 tablespoons snipped
fresh chives

1 In a 4-quart Dutch oven cook ground beef, mushrooms, sweet pepper, and onion over medium heat until beef is browned and vegetables are tender, stirring to break up meat as it cooks. Drain off fat.

2 In a small bowl whisk together broth and flour until smooth. Add broth mixture to beef mixture; bring to boiling. Stir in milk. Cook and stir until bubbly; cook and stir for 1 minute more. Reduce heat to low. Add cheese and black pepper. Cook and stir until cheese is melted. Stir in spinach just before serving. To serve, ladle soup into bowls. If desired, top with cucumber. Garnish individual servings with tomato, croutons, and chives.

nutrition facts per serving: 313 cal., 12 g total fat (4 g sat. fat), 56 mg chol., 619 mg sodium, 23 g carb. (3 g fiber, 11 g sugars), 29 g pro. exchanges: 0.5 milk, 1 vegetable, 1 starch, 3 lean meat, 1 fat.

14g CARB. PER SERVING

Made from fermented soybeans, miso paste adds protein and rich flavor to recipes. Look for it in the Asian food section of large supermarkets or in Asian food markets.

miso soup
with pork and edamame

start to finish: 35 minutes
makes: 6 servings (1¾ cups each)

12	ounces boneless pork loin roast
4	teaspoons canola oil
1	medium red sweet pepper, chopped (¾ cup)
1	medium onion, chopped (½ cup)
1	tablespoon grated fresh ginger
2	cloves garlic, minced
¼	teaspoon black pepper
8	cups water
¼	cup red miso paste
1	10- to 12-ounce package frozen shelled sweet soybeans (edamame)
4	cups thinly sliced savoy cabbage
2	to 3 medium radishes, very thinly sliced

1 Trim fat from pork. Cut pork into 1-inch cubes. In a 4-quart nonstick Dutch oven cook pork in 2 teaspoons of the oil over medium-high heat until browned, stirring occasionally. Remove pork from pan and set aside. Drain off any fat from the pan.

2 In the same pan cook sweet pepper and onion in the remaining 2 teaspoons oil over medium heat for 5 minutes, stirring occasionally. Add ginger, garlic, and black pepper; cook and stir 30 seconds more. Add 7 cups of the water. In a small bowl gradually whisk remaining 1 cup water into the miso paste. Add to pan and bring to boiling.

3 Add soybeans and pork to the soup. Return to boiling; reduce heat. Simmer, covered, for 3 minutes. Add cabbage. Cook for 2 minutes more, stirring occasionally. To serve, ladle soup into bowls. Garnish individual servings with radish slices.

nutrition facts per serving: 216 cal., 9 g total fat (1 g sat. fat), 39 mg chol., 486 mg sodium, 14 g carb. (5 g fiber, 6 g sugars), 20 g pro. exchanges: 1 vegetable, 0.5 starch, 2.5 lean meat, 1 fat.

When fresh sweet corn is out of season, use frozen whole kernel corn.

summer corn tortilla soup

27 g
CARB. PER SERVING

start to finish: 40 minutes
makes: 8 servings (1½ cups each)

½ cup chopped onion
  (1 medium)
12 cloves garlic, minced
1 tablespoon olive oil
2 cups fresh sweet corn
  kernels (4 ears of
  corn)
2 cups chopped
  tomatoes
2 cups diced yellow
  summer squash or
  zucchini
1 15-ounce can no-salt-
  added black beans,
  rinsed and drained
8 ounces coarsely
  chopped boneless
  pork loin
4 6-inch corn tortillas
8 cups reduced-sodium
  chicken broth
½ teaspoon chili
  powder
½ teaspoon ground
  cumin
¼ cup snipped fresh
  cilantro
  Nonstick cooking
  spray
1 ripe avocado, halved,
  seeded, peeled, and
  thinly sliced

1 In a 4-quart Dutch oven cook onion and garlic in hot oil about 5 minutes or until tender. Stir in corn, tomatoes, squash, beans, and pork. Cook and stir until heated through. Chop 2 of the corn tortillas. Stir chopped tortillas, broth, chili powder, and cumin into mixture in Dutch oven. Cook and stir about 5 minutes or until tortillas dissolve and meat is done. Stir in cilantro.

2 Meanwhile, preheat broiler. Place the remaining 2 tortillas on a baking sheet. Coat both sides of each tortilla with cooking spray. Broil 4 to 5 inches from the heat for 2 to 3 minutes or until crisp and golden brown, turning once halfway through broiling time. Using a long knife, cut tortillas into thin strips. While still warm, gently scrunch the strips to create wavy tortilla strips. Carefully place on a paper towel; cool.

3 To serve, ladle soup into bowls. Top individual servings with tortilla strips and avocado slices.

nutrition facts per serving: 224 cal., 7 g total fat (1 g sat. fat), 17 mg chol., 595 mg sodium, 27 g carb (7 g fiber, 4 g sugars), 15 g pro. exchanges: 1 vegetable, 1.5 starch, 1.5 lean meat, 1 fat.

Bottled minced garlic is convenient and easy to use, but if you prefer fresh garlic, substitute 18 cloves.

26g
CARB. PER
SERVING

spicy pork tenderloin green chili

prep: 45 minutes   roast: 25 minutes   stand: 10 minutes   cook: 20 minutes
makes: 6 servings (1½ cups each)

8   ounces fresh Anaheim
    chile peppers (3 to 4
    peppers)
1½ pounds pork
    tenderloin, trimmed
    of fat and cut into
    ¾-inch pieces
2   tablespoons canola oil
3   large onions, chopped
    (3 cups)
3   tablespoons bottled
    minced garlic
1   pound fresh tomatillos,
    peeled and diced
    (about 4 cups)
1   tablespoon ground
    cumin
2   teaspoons dried
    oregano, crushed
3   cups reduced-sodium
    chicken broth
1   cup water
1   15-ounce can no-salt-
    added navy beans,
    rinsed and drained
1   tablespoon lime juice
2   tablespoons snipped
    fresh cilantro

1 Preheat oven to 400°F. Arrange chile peppers on a baking sheet. Roast for 25 to 30 minutes or until skins are dark, turning once halfway through roasting. Place chile peppers in a bowl; cover with plastic wrap and let stand for 10 minutes. Carefully remove skins, stems, and seeds; chop chile peppers. (See tip, *page 120*.) Set aside.

2 Trim pork. Cut pork into ¾-inch pieces. In a 5- to 6-quart Dutch oven cook pork in hot oil over medium-high heat until browned. Add onions and garlic; cook about 5 minutes more or just until onions are tender, stirring occasionally. Add tomatillos, cumin, and oregano; cook for 3 minutes more, stirring occasionally.

3 Stir in broth and the water. Bring to boiling; reduce heat. Simmer, uncovered, for 15 minutes, stirring occasionally. Stir in beans, lime juice, and chopped chile peppers. Simmer for 5 minutes more. To serve, ladle chili into bowls. Sprinkle with cilantro.

nutrition facts per serving: 304 cal., 8 g total fat (1 g sat. fat), 74 mg chol., 364 mg sodium, 26 g carb. (10 g fiber, 8 g sugars), 32 g pro. exchanges: 1.5 vegetable, 1.5 starch, 3.5 lean meat.

Chorizo adds a little heat to the meatballs (albóndigas) *in this classic Mexican soup.*

sausage albóndigas soup

12g CARB. PER SERVING

prep: 20 minutes bake: 15 minutes cook: 12 minutes
makes: 6 servings (1⅓ cups each)

12 ounces lean ground pork
4 ounces uncooked chorizo sausage, casing removed
½ cup cooked brown rice
¼ cup finely shredded carrot
¼ cup snipped fresh cilantro
2 cloves garlic, minced
1 teaspoon ground cumin
¼ teaspoon black pepper
1 egg, beaten, or ¼ cup refrigerated or frozen egg product, thawed
½ cup chopped onion (1 medium)
2 teaspoons canola oil
2 14.5-ounce cans reduced-sodium chicken broth
1 14.5-ounce can no-salt-added diced tomatoes, undrained
1 teaspoon dried oregano, crushed
½ teaspoon ground cumin
2 cups coarsely chopped zucchini
¼ cup fresh cilantro leaves

1 Preheat oven to 350°F. Line a 15×10×1-inch baking pan with foil; set aside.

2 In a medium bowl combine pork, chorizo, rice, carrot, ¼ cup snipped cilantro, garlic, 1 teaspoon cumin, and the black pepper. Mix to combine thoroughly. Add egg and stir to combine. Shape into 24 meatballs. Place meatballs on prepared baking pan. Bake about 15 to 20 minutes or until browned and cooked through (160°F). Remove from baking sheet with a slotted spoon.

3 Meanwhile, in a 4-quart Dutch oven cook onion in hot oil over medium heat for 5 minutes or until just tender. Add broth, tomatoes, oregano, and ½ teaspoon cumin. Bring to boiling. Stir in zucchini; return to boiling. Cook about 2 minutes or until zucchini is just tender. Remove from heat. Stir in ¼ cup cilantro leaves and the cooked meatballs. To serve, ladle soup into bowls.

nutrition facts per serving: 241 cal., 12 g total fat (4 g sat. fat), 81 mg chol., 635 mg sodium, 12 g carb. (2 g fiber, 4 g sugars), 21 g pro. exchanges: 2 vegetable, 2.5 lean meat, 1.5 fat.

Pork tenderloin often comes two to a pack. Freeze the extra uncooked tenderloin in a freezer bag or wrapped in freezer wrap for up to 12 months.

18g
CARB. PER
SERVING

poblano, pork, and squash soup

prep: 20 minutes   cook: 30 minutes   roast: 25 minutes   stand: 15 minutes
makes: 4 servings (1½ cups each)

126

12   ounces pork
       tenderloin, trimmed
1   tablespoon olive oil
½   cup chopped onion
2   cloves garlic, minced
2   14.5-ounce cans
       reduced-sodium
       chicken broth
2   cups cubed peeled
       butternut squash
       (½-inch cubes)
½   cup water
1   teaspoon chili powder
2   fresh poblano chile
       peppers, roasted✳
       and chopped✳✳
⅓   cup snipped fresh
       cilantro
¼   cup pumpkin seeds
       (pepitas), toasted
       Lime wedges

1 Cut pork into ½-inch cubes. In a large saucepan brown the pork in hot oil over medium-high heat. Using a slotted spoon, remove pork from saucepan and set aside. Reduce heat to medium. Add onion and garlic to saucepan. Cook and stir for 4 to 5 minutes or until onion is tender. Add pork, broth, squash, water, and chili powder to saucepan, stirring to loosen any browned bits from bottom of pan. Bring to boiling; reduce heat. Simmer, covered, for 30 minutes, stirring occasionally.

2 Stir chile peppers and cilantro into soup. To serve, ladle soup into bowls and top with pumpkin seeds. Serve each with a lime wedge for squeezing over the soup.

nutrition facts per serving: 274 cal., 12 g total fat (2 g sat. fat), 52 mg chol., 537 mg sodium, 18 g carb. (4 g fiber, 5 g sugars), 26 g pro. exchanges: 0.5 vegetable, 1 starch, 3 lean meat, 1 fat.

✳ test kitchen tip: To roast poblano chile peppers, preheat oven to 425°F. Cut peppers in half lengthwise; remove stems, seeds, and membranes. Place pepper halves, cut sides down, on a foil-lined baking sheet. Bake for 20 to 25 minutes or until peppers are charred and very tender. Remove from oven and bring the foil up around peppers; fold edges together to enclose. Let stand about 15 minutes or until cool enough to handle. Use a sharp knife to loosen edges of the skins; gently pull off the skins in strips and discard the skins.

✳✳ test kitchen tip: Because chile peppers contain volatile oils that can burn your skin and eyes, avoid direct contact with them as much as possible. When working with chile peppers, wear plastic or rubber gloves. If your bare hands do touch the peppers, wash your hands and nails well with soap and warm water.

If heirloom potatoes are popping up at the farmer's market, try some other waxy potato varieties, such as fingerling, creamer ruby gold, and creamer yellow Dutch. Avoid starchy russets, which will fall apart during cooking.

spinach and potato soup

prep: 20 minutes cook: 15 minutes
makes: 5 servings (1½ cups each)

½ cup chopped onion
2 cloves garlic, minced
½ teaspoon salt
¼ teaspoon black pepper
2 teaspoons olive oil
4 cups unsalted chicken stock
3 cups coarsely chopped yellow potatoes
5 ounces packaged fresh baby spinach (about 6 cups)
2 teaspoons snipped fresh rosemary or ½ teaspoon dried rosemary, crushed
2 6-ounce containers plain reduced-fat Greek yogurt
½ cup chopped reduced-sodium ham (2½ ounces)
¼ cup chopped toasted almonds

1 In a large saucepan cook onion, garlic, salt, and pepper in hot oil over medium heat for 3 to 4 minutes or until onion is tender. Add 3 cups of the chicken stock and the potatoes. Bring to boiling; reduce heat. Cover and simmer for 15 to 20 minutes or until potatoes are tender.

2 Meanwhile, in a food processor or blender combine half of the spinach and rosemary and ½ cup of the remaining stock. Cover and process or blend until smooth. Add blended spinach mixture to the saucepan. Repeat with remaining spinach, rosemary, and ½ cup stock; add to saucepan. Whisk yogurt into mixture in saucepan until combined. Stir in ham and heat through (do not boil). To serve, ladle soup into bowls and top with almonds.

nutrition facts per serving: 225 cal., 7 g total fat (2 g sat. fat), 11 mg chol., 540 mg sodium, 24 g carb. (3 g fiber, 4 g sugars), 17 g pro. exchanges: 0.5 milk, 0.5 vegetable, 1 starch, 1 lean meat, 1 fat.

24g
CARB. PER
SERVING

Dried herbs are usually added to mixtures at the beginning of the cooking time so the flavors have time to release. Fresh herbs should be stirred in during the last few minutes of cooking.

lamb and chickpea stew

prep: 25 minutes   cook: 45 minutes
makes: 6 servings (1½ cups)

satisfying soups & stews

1   pound boneless
     leg of lamb
4   teaspoons olive oil
1   medium onion, cut
     into thin wedges
     (½ cup)
2   cups water
1   14.5-ounce can
     reduced-sodium
     chicken broth
1   15-ounce can
     garbanzo beans
     (chickpeas), rinsed
     and drained
1   cup fresh green
     beans, trimmed and
     cut into 1½-inch
     pieces
1   tablespoon snipped
     fresh oregano or
     1 teaspoon dried
     oregano, crushed
2   teaspoons snipped
     fresh rosemary or
     ½ teaspoon dried
     rosemary, crushed
¼   teaspoon black
     pepper
4   cups coarsely chopped
     fresh spinach
2   medium tomatoes,
     chopped (1 cup)
½   of a 6-ounce can
     (⅓ cup) no-salt-
     added tomato paste

1 Trim fat from lamb. Cut lamb into 1-inch cubes. In a 4-quart Dutch oven cook half the lamb in 2 teaspoons of the oil over medium-high heat until browned, stirring occasionally. Remove lamb from pan. Add remaining oil to the pan. Add remaining lamb and the onion wedges. Cook until lamb is browned, stirring occasionally. Drain off any fat. Return all the lamb to the pan.

2 Add the water and broth. Bring to boiling; reduce heat. Simmer, covered, for 45 minutes to 1 hour. Add garbanzo beans, green beans, dried oregano (if using), dried rosemary (if using), and pepper. Return to boiling; reduce heat. Simmer, covered, for 5 to 10 minutes or until lamb and green beans are tender.

3 Stir in spinach, tomatoes, tomato paste, fresh oregano (if using), and fresh rosemary (if using). Heat through. To serve, ladle stew into bowls.

nutrition facts per serving: 249 cal., 7 g total fat (2 g sat. fat), 47 mg chol., 393 mg sodium, 24 g carb. (6 g fiber, 7 g sugars), 22 g pro. exchanges: 1 vegetable, 1.5 starch, 2 lean meat, 0.5 fat.

Speed up the prep time by purchasing sliced fresh mushrooms and shredded carrot.

cream of chicken and rice florentine

prep: 25 minutes   cook: 40 minutes
makes: 6 servings (1⅓ cups each)

2   tablespoons olive oil
1   pound skinless, boneless chicken breast halves
3   medium onions, finely chopped (1½ cups)
1   8-ounce package fresh mushrooms, sliced
1   medium carrot, shredded (½ cup)
6   cloves garlic, minced
⅓   cup uncooked long grain rice
1   14.5-ounce can reduced-sodium chicken broth
1   cup water
½   teaspoon black pepper
¼   teaspoon ground nutmeg
2   12-ounce cans fat-free evaporated milk
2   tablespoons flour
4   cups packed fresh spinach
2   teaspoons finely shredded lemon peel
2   tablespoons lemon juice
     Black pepper (optional)

1 In a Dutch oven heat oil over medium-high heat; reduce heat to medium. Add chicken; cook for 12 to 15 minutes or until no longer pink (170°F), turning once halfway through cooking. Transfer chicken to a plate and let cool. When cool enough to handle, use two forks to pull chicken apart into coarse shreds.

2 Meanwhile, add onions, mushrooms, carrot, and garlic to the Dutch oven; cook for 5 minutes, stirring occasionally. Stir in rice; cook for 1 minute more. Add broth, the water, the ½ teaspoon pepper, and the nutmeg. Bring to boiling; reduce heat. Simmer, covered, for 15 minutes.

3 In a small bowl stir together 1 can evaporated milk and flour; stir into mixture in Dutch oven. Stir in remaining can of milk. Cook and stir until bubbly.

4 Stir in spinach and the shredded chicken. Simmer for 5 minutes. Stir in lemon peel and lemon juice. To serve, ladle soup into bowls. If desired, sprinkle with additional pepper.

nutrition facts per serving: 300 cal., 6 g total fat (1 g sat. fat), 48 mg chol., 365 mg sodium, 31 g carb. (2 g fiber, 16 g sugars), 30 g pro. exchanges: 1 vegetable, 1.5 starch, 3.5 lean meat.

Look for whole grain soba noodles in the Asian food aisle of the supermarket. Use them in other soups when you want to add extra whole grain goodness to the mix.

indonesian chicken and soba noodle soup

35g CARB. PER SERVING

start to finish: 45 minutes

makes: 6 servings (1 cup soup and ⅔ cup cooked noodles each)

satisfying soups & stews

1 cup sliced onion

2 tablespoons grated fresh ginger

1 tablespoon canola oil

2 cups shredded green cabbage or napa cabbage

1 small sweet potato, peeled and diced (1 cup)

1 stalk celery, sliced (½ cup)

4 cups reduced-sodium chicken broth

1 tablespoon reduced-sodium soy sauce

½ teaspoon crushed red pepper

8 ounces cooked chicken breast, coarsely chopped

1 tablespoon lime juice

¼ cup chopped green onions (2)

¼ cup snipped fresh cilantro

8 ounces whole grain soba or udon noodles, cooked according to package directions

1 In a large saucepan cook onion and ginger in hot oil over medium-high heat for 3 minutes, stirring occasionally.

2 Add cabbage, sweet potato, and celery. Cook for 4 minutes more, stirring occasionally. Stir in broth, soy sauce, and crushed red pepper. Bring to boiling; reduce heat. Simmer, covered, about 15 minutes or until vegetables are tender.

3 Stir in chicken and lime juice. Just before serving, stir in green onions and cilantro. To serve, ladle soup and noodles into bowls.

nutrition facts per serving: 266 cal., 5 g total fat (1 g sat. fat), 32 mg chol., 581 mg sodium, 35 g carb. (4 g fiber, 4 g sugars), 20 g pro. exchanges: 0.5 vegetable, 2 starch, 2 lean meat.

Barley is a great choice when you're showcasing mushrooms—the grain's mild taste lets the subtle flavors of the mushrooms really come through.

fresh herb chicken and barley soup

24g
CARB. PER
SERVING

prep: 20 minutes cook: 25 minutes
makes: 6 servings (1⅓ cups each)

2 cups sliced fresh
   shiitake mushrooms
2 teaspoons olive oil
6 cups reduced-sodium
   chicken broth
¾ cup chopped red
   sweet pepper
½ cup quick-cooking
   barley
2 cups chopped cooked
   chicken or turkey
2 cups chopped
   asparagus
3 tablespoons snipped
   fresh chives
2 tablespoons snipped
   fresh marjoram
   or oregano or
   2 teaspoons dried
   leaf marjoram or
   oregano, crushed
½ teaspoon black
   pepper

In a 4- to 5-quart Dutch oven cook mushrooms in hot oil over medium-high heat for 4 minutes or until mushrooms are tender. Stir in broth, sweet pepper, and barley. Bring to boiling; reduce heat. Simmer, covered, about 15 minutes or until barley is tender. Stir in chicken, asparagus, chives, marjoram, and black pepper. Heat through. To serve, ladle soup into bowls.

nutrition facts per serving: 220 cal., 5 g total fat (1 g sat. fat), 42 mg chol., 600 mg sodium, 24 g carb. (5 g fiber, 2 g sugars), 20 g pro. exchanges: 1 vegetable, 1 starch, 2 lean meat, 0.5 fat.

Farro, a filling whole grain, and a medley of vegetables help you stretch 1¼ pounds of chicken into eight healthful servings of chili.

farro and vegetable chicken chili

prep: 50 minutes cook: 20 minutes
makes: 8 servings (1½ cups chili and 2 tablespoons cheese each)

31g
CARB. PER
SERVING

1 cup semipearled farro
1¼ pounds skinless, boneless chicken breast halves
2 cups chopped onions (2 large)
2 cups chopped zucchini (2 small)
1 cup chopped carrots (2 medium)
1 fresh jalapeño chile pepper, stemmed, seeded (if desired), and finely chopped (see tip, *page 126*)
2 teaspoons olive oil
2 tablespoons chili powder
2 teaspoons ground cumin
½ teaspoon crushed red pepper
2 14.5-ounce cans reduced-sodium chicken broth
1 14.5-ounce can no-salt-added diced tomatoes, undrained
1 6-ounce can tomato paste
1 cup shredded cheddar cheese (4 ounces)

1 Rinse farro. In a medium saucepan bring 2 cups water to boiling. Stir in farro. Return to boiling; reduce heat. Simmer, covered, for 20 to 25 minutes or until farro is tender. Drain off any excess water.

2 In a large skillet bring 2 cups water to boiling. Add chicken breasts. Reduce heat. Simmer, covered, for 12 to 15 minutes or until chicken is no longer pink (170° F). Transfer chicken to a cutting board. Cool slightly. Coarsely chop or shred chicken. Set aside.

3 Meanwhile, in a 4-quart Dutch oven cook onions, zucchini, carrots, and chile pepper in hot oil about 5 minutes or until tender. Stir in chili powder, cumin, and crushed red pepper. Stir in broth, tomatoes, tomato paste, and another 2 cups water. Bring to boiling; reduce heat. Simmer, covered, for 20 minutes. Stir in cooked farro and chopped or shredded chicken. Cook and stir until heated through. Top individual servings with 2 tablespoons of the cheddar cheese each.

nutrition facts per serving: 305 cal., 8 g total fat (4 g sat. fat), 60 mg chol., 504 mg sodium, 31 g carb. (5 g fiber, 7 g sugars), 26 g pro. exchanges: 2 vegetable, 1.5 starch, 3 lean meat, 0.5 fat.

To store extra piecrust strips, place them in an airtight container and freeze for up to 1 month. Use as soup toppers or salad toppers. Pictured on page 114.

30g CARB. PER SERVING

chicken pot pie stew

prep: 25 minutes bake: 6 minutes cook: 25 minutes
makes: 6 servings (1⅛ cups and about 3 piecrust leaves each)

4 teaspoons canola oil
1 pound skinless, boneless chicken thighs, cut into ¾-inch pieces
1 cup chopped celery (2 stalks)
1 cup chopped carrots (2 medium)
½ cup chopped onion (1 medium)
2 cloves garlic, minced
2½ cups reduced-sodium chicken broth
2 cups fresh mushrooms, sliced
1 cup fresh sweet corn kernels or frozen whole kernel corn, thawed
½ cup frozen peas, thawed
1 12-ounce can evaporated fat-free milk
¼ cup flour
1 teaspoon snipped fresh thyme
½ teaspoon snipped fresh oregano
¼ teaspoon salt
¼ teaspoon black pepper
1 recipe Piecrust Strips (use about ¼ of the recipe)

1 In a 4- to 5-quart nonstick Dutch oven heat 2 teaspoons of the oil over medium heat. Add chicken. Cook and stir about 4 to 5 minutes or until chicken pieces are browned on all sides. Remove from Dutch oven; set aside.

2 In the same Dutch oven heat the remaining 2 teaspoons oil over medium heat. Add celery, carrots, onion, and garlic. Cook and stir 8 to 10 minutes or until vegetables are tender.

3 Add chicken broth to pot; bring to boiling. Add chicken, mushrooms, corn, and peas. Return to boiling; reduce heat. Simmer, uncovered, about 8 minutes or until chicken is no longer pink and vegetables are just tender.

4 In a small bowl whisk together evaporated milk and flour. Add flour mixture to soup mixture. Cook and stir until mixture thickens and bubbles. Cook and stir for 2 minutes more to thicken soup mixture. Stir in fresh thyme, fresh oregano, salt, and pepper. To serve, ladle soup into bowls. Garnish individual servings with a couple Piecrust Strips.

nutrition facts per serving: 295 cal., 9 g total fat (2 g sat. fat), 72 mg chol., 557 mg sodium, 30 g carb. (3 g fiber, 12 g sugars), 24 g pro. exchanges: 1 vegetable, 1.5 starch, 3 lean eat.

piecrust strips: Preheat oven to 400°F. Let ½ of a 15-ounce package rolled refrigerated unbaked piecrust (1 crust) stand according to package directions. Unroll piecrust onto a lightly floured surface. Cut piecrust into strips. Place piecrust strips on a baking sheet. Bake for 6 to 8 minutes or until golden brown. Cool on baking sheet.

Special enough to serve for the holidays yet easy enough to dish up every day, this soup warms the taste buds with a touch of cinnamon.

turkey and cranberry roasted squash soup

23g
CARB. PER
SERVING

prep: 30 minutes cook: 20 minutes roast: 20 minutes
makes: 6 servings (1 cup each)

3 cups ¾-inch pieces peeled butternut or acorn squash or pumpkin
1 medium sweet onion, cut into thin wedges
2 tablespoons canola oil
1 pound skinless, boneless turkey breast tenderloin, cut into ¾-inch pieces
2 14.5-ounce cans reduced-sodium chicken broth
¾ cup thinly sliced carrot
½ cup dried cranberries
¼ teaspoon ground cinnamon
2 teaspoons snipped fresh sage
1 teaspoon snipped fresh thyme
6 tablespoons chopped pecans, toasted (optional)

1 Preheat oven to 400°F. Line a 15×10×1-inch baking pan with foil. Toss squash or pumpkin and onion with 1 tablespoon of the oil in the prepared baking pan. Roast, uncovered, for 20 to 25 minutes or until squash is tender and lightly browned, gently tossing once. Remove from oven.

2 Meanwhile, in a 4-quart Dutch oven heat remaining 1 tablespoon oil over medium heat. Add turkey pieces. Cook and stir to brown turkey on all sides. Carefully add broth, carrot, cranberries, and cinnamon to pan. Bring to boiling; reduce heat. Simmer, covered, about 10 minutes or until turkey is done and carrot is tender. Stir in roasted squash mixture, sage, and thyme. Heat through.

3 To serve, ladle soup into bowls. If desired, garnish with toasted pecans.

nutrition facts per serving: 203 cal., 5 g total fat (1 g sat. fat), 33 mg chol., 588 mg sodium, 23 g carb. (3 g fiber, 12 g sugars), 17 g pro. exchanges: 0.5 fruit, 1 starch, 2 lean meat, 1 fat.

20g
CARB. PER
SERVING

*To make equal-size meatballs, use a measuring teaspoon
to portion out the turkey mixture and then roll it into balls.*

turkey meatball soup

prep: 30 minutes bake: 10 minutes cook: 25 minutes
makes: 6 servings (1⅓ cups each)

Nonstick cooking
    spray
¾ cup soft whole wheat
    bread crumbs
    (1½ slices)
¼ cup bottled light
    ranch salad dressing
1 egg white, lightly
    beaten
¼ teaspoon black
    pepper
1 pound ground turkey
    breast
2 medium carrots,
    thinly sliced (1 cup)
1 stalk celery, thinly
    sliced (½ cup)
1 tablespoon olive oil
3 cups water
1 14.5-ounce can
    reduced-sodium
    chicken broth
1 cup multigrain elbow
    macaroni
1 cup cherry or grape
    tomatoes, halved
4 cups packaged fresh
    baby spinach
2 ounces Parmesan
    cheese, coarsely
    shredded (optional)

1 Preheat oven to 350°F. Line a 15×10×1-inch baking pan with foil; coat foil with cooking spray. In a large bowl combine bread crumbs, dressing, egg white, and pepper. Add ground turkey; mix well. Shape mixture into ¾-inch meatballs (about 72). Place meatballs on the prepared baking pan. Bake about 10 minutes or until done (165°F). Set aside.

2 In a 4-quart Dutch oven cook carrots and celery in hot oil over medium heat for 5 minutes, stirring occasionally. Add the water and broth; bring to boiling. Add macaroni. Return to boiling; reduce heat. Simmer, covered, for 7 minutes or until macaroni is just tender, stirring occasionally.

3 Add meatballs and tomatoes to soup; heat through. Stir in spinach just before serving. To serve, ladle soup into bowls. If desired, sprinkle with Parmesan cheese.

nutrition facts per serving: 230 cal., 6 g total fat (1 g sat. fat), 39 mg chol., 409 mg sodium, 20 g carb. (3 g fiber, 3 g sugars), 24 g pro. exchanges: 1 vegetable, 1 starch, 3 lean meat.

Hominy, onion, garlic, and chile peppers are classic ingredients in this soup from Mexico. It's often made with pork or chicken, but turkey breast makes a flavorful substitute.

turkey posole

30g
CARB. PER SERVING

prep: 15 minutes cook: 28 minutes
makes: 4 servings (2 cups each)

1 pound ground turkey breast
¾ cup chopped red or green sweet pepper
½ cup chopped onion
½ cup chopped fresh poblano chile pepper*
2 teaspoons canola oil
2 teaspoons unsweetened cocoa powder
1 teaspoon dried oregano, crushed
½ teaspoon salt
½ teaspoon ground cumin
½ teaspoon ground ancho chile pepper
¼ teaspoon ground cinnamon
2 14.5-ounce cans no-salt-added diced tomatoes, undrained
1 15.5-ounce can golden hominy, rinsed and drained
1 cup water or reduced-sodium chicken broth
1 8-ounce can no-salt-added tomato sauce
¼ cup sliced green onions (2)
¼ cup thinly sliced radishes
Lime wedges

1 In a 4-quart Dutch oven cook turkey, sweet pepper, onion, and poblano chile in hot oil until meat is no longer pink and vegetables are tender. Drain off fat. Stir in cocoa powder, oregano, salt, cumin, ancho chile pepper, and cinnamon. Cook and stir for 1 minute. Stir in tomatoes, hominy, water, and tomato sauce.

2 Bring to boiling; reduce heat. Simmer, covered, for 20 minutes to blend flavors, stirring occasionally. Garnish with green onions and radishes. Serve with lime wedges.

nutrition facts per serving: 271 cal., 4 g total fat (1 g sat. fat), 55 mg chol., 590 mg sodium, 30 g carb. (9 g fiber, 12 g sugars), 31 g pro. exchanges: 1 vegetable, 1.5 starch, 3 lean meat.

*test kitchen tip: Because chile peppers contain volatile oils that can burn your skin and eyes, avoid contact with them as much as possible. When working with chile peppers, wear plastic or rubber gloves. If your bare hands do touch the peppers, wash your hands and nails well with soap and warm water.

25g
CARB. PER
SERVING

*Ask your fishmonger to skin the salmon for you or use
a long, thin-blade knife to cut the skin from the meat.*

dilled salmon and asparagus soup

prep: 25 minutes   roast: 4 minutes   cook: 12 minutes
makes: 5 servings (1½ cups each)

12 ounces fresh or
     frozen skinless
     salmon fillet
     Nonstick cooking
     spray
1   pound fresh
     asparagus, trimmed
     and cut into 1-inch
     pieces
1   medium onion,
     chopped (½ cup)
1   tablespoon canola oil
2   14.5-ounce cans
     reduced-sodium
     chicken broth
2½ cups fat-free milk
½   cup flour
⅛   teaspoon salt
1   tablespoon snipped
     fresh dill weed or
     1 teaspoon dried
     dill weed
2   cups coarsely
     chopped fresh
     spinach
5   tablespoons light
     sour cream
1   slice rye bread,
     toasted and cut into
     ½-inch cubes
⅓   cup chopped
     cucumber

1 Thaw salmon, if frozen. Rinse salmon and
pat dry with paper towels. Preheat oven
to 450°F. Line a 15×10×1-inch baking pan with
foil. Coat foil with cooking spray. Place salmon
on one side of the pan. Measure thickness of
fish. Add asparagus to the other side of the
pan, spreading in an even layer. Lightly coat
asparagus with cooking spray. Roast asparagus
and salmon, uncovered, for 4 to 6 minutes per
½-inch thickness of salmon or until salmon
flakes easily when tested with a fork and
asparagus is just tender. Using two forks, flake
salmon, removing and discarding any bones.

2 In a 4-quart Dutch oven cook onion in
hot oil over medium heat about 5 minutes
or until tender but not browned, stirring
occasionally. Add broth. In a medium bowl
whisk together milk, flour, and salt until smooth.
Add all at once to broth mixture. Cook and stir
over medium heat until thickened and bubbly.
Cook and stir for 1 minute more.

3 Add flaked salmon, asparagus pieces, and
dill to the soup. Cook for 1 to 2 minutes
or until heated through. Stir in spinach just
before serving.

4 To serve, ladle soup into shallow bowls.
Top individual servings with a spoonful of
sour cream and sprinkle with rye bread cubes
and chopped cucumber.

nutrition facts per serving: 318 cal., 14 g total fat
(3 g sat. fat), 44 mg chol., 603 mg sodium, 25 g carb. (2 g fiber,
9 g sugars), 24 g pro. exchanges: 1 vegetable, 1 starch,
2.5 medium-fat meat.

The baguette slices should be crispy like croutons, so cut them about ½ inch thick and then toast.

29g
CARB. PER
SERVING

seafood stew with toasted baguette slices

prep: 15 minutes   cook: 30 minutes
makes: 4 servings (2 cups stew and 2 baguette slices each)

8   ounces fresh or
    frozen large shrimp
    in shells
8   ounces fresh or
    frozen skinless
    halibut, cut 1 inch
    thick
4   medium fresh or
    frozen sea scallops
2   tablespoons canola oil
    Nonstick cooking
    spray
1   medium green sweet
    pepper, chopped
    (¾ cup)
1   medium onion,
    chopped (½ cup)
1   medium jalapeño
    pepper, seeded and
    finely chopped (see
    tip, *page 137*)
3   cloves garlic, minced
2   cups water
1   14.5-ounce can
    no-salt-added
    stewed tomatoes,
    undrained
1   14.5-ounce can
    reduced-sodium
    chicken broth
½   cup snipped fresh
    cilantro
8   small baguette slices,
    toasted

1 Thaw shrimp, halibut, and scallops, if frozen. Peel and devein shrimp. Rinse shrimp, halibut and scallops and pat dry with paper towels. In a large nonstick skillet heat 1 tablespoon of the oil over medium heat. Add shrimp, halibut, and scallops to separate spots in the hot skillet. Cook shrimp and scallops for 2 to 4 minutes or until opaque, turning once halfway through cooking and transferring them to a plate when they are finished cooking. Cook halibut for 8 to 12 minutes or until fish flakes when tested with a fork. Transfer halibut to a cutting board; cut into 1-inch pieces. Cut scallops in half. Set seafood aside.

2 Meanwhile, coat an unheated nonstick 4-quart Dutch oven with cooking spray; heat over medium heat. Add sweet pepper and onion. Cook for 8 minutes or until vegetables are tender, stirring occasionally. Add jalapeño pepper and garlic; cook and stir for 2 minutes more. Add the water, tomatoes, and broth. Bring to boiling; reduce heat. Simmer, covered, for 10 minutes.

3 Add shrimp, scallops and halibut pieces to the hot stew. Cook for 1 to 2 minutes or until heated through. Stir in cilantro just before serving. To serve, ladle stew into bowls. Top individual servings with toasted baguette slices.

nutrition facts per serving: 368 cal., 11 g total fat (1 g sat. fat), 123 mg chol., 666 mg sodium, 29 g carb. (4 g fiber, 8 g sugars), 38 g pro. exchanges: 1 vegetable, 1.5 starch, 4.5 lean meat, 0.5 fat.

Toasted sesame oil adds a deep, nutty taste without overwhelming other flavors in a dish. Because sesame oil can go rancid quickly, store it in the refrigerator to maintain its shelf life.

lemon-sesame shrimp soup

prep: 40 minutes cook: 10 minutes
makes: 6 servings (1½ cups each)

12g
CARB. PER SERVING

12 ounces fresh or frozen large shrimp in shells
4 green onions
2½ cups coarsely chopped yellow, red, orange, and/or green sweet peppers (2 large)
1 tablespoon canola oil
1 tablespoon grated fresh ginger or 1 teaspoon ground ginger
3 cloves garlic, minced
6 cups water
1 cup small fresh broccoli florets
2 tablespoons reduced-sodium soy sauce
¼ teaspoon crushed red pepper
4 cups coarsely chopped fresh kale or spinach
2 teaspoons finely shredded lemon peel
2 tablespoons lemon juice
1 tablespoon toasted sesame oil
Sesame seeds, toasted (optional)

1 Thaw shrimp, if frozen. Peel and devein shrimp. Cut tails off shrimp. Rinse shrimp; pat dry with paper towels. Set aside. Cut green onions into ½-inch slices, keeping white parts separate from green tops. Set green tops aside. In a large saucepan cook white parts of the green onions and sweet peppers in hot oil for 5 minutes, stirring occasionally. Add ginger and garlic; cook and stir for 1 minute more.

2 Add the water, broccoli, soy sauce, and crushed red pepper. Bring to boiling; reduce heat. Simmer, uncovered, for 2 minutes.

3 Add shrimp and kale (if using). Return to boiling; reduce heat. Simmer, uncovered, for 2 to 3 minutes or until shrimp are opaque. Stir spinach (if using), green onion tops, lemon peel, lemon juice, and sesame oil into hot soup just before serving.

4 To serve, ladle soup into bowls. If desired, sprinkle with sesame seeds.

nutrition facts per serving: 136 cal., 6 g total fat (1 g sat. fat), 71 mg chol., 547 mg sodium, 12 g carb. (3 g fiber, 4 g sugars), 11 g pro. exchanges: 2 vegetable, 1 lean meat, 1 fat.

Why evaporated low-fat milk? It adds creaminess—without the fat and calories of cream.

35g
CARB. PER
SERVING

creamy bean, potato, and roasted garlic soup

prep: 25 minutes roast: 25 minutes cook: 15 minutes
makes: 6 servings (1 cup each)

satisfying soups & stews

2   bulbs garlic
1   teaspoon olive oil
3   cups reduced-sodium vegetable broth or chicken broth
1   large russet potato, peeled and cubed (2 cups)
1   cup cubed, peeled sweet potato
½   cup sliced celery
1   15-ounce can no-salt-added cannellini beans (white kidney beans), rinsed and drained
1   teaspoon snipped fresh thyme
¼   teaspoon salt
⅛   teaspoon cayenne pepper
1   12-ounce can evaporated low-fat milk
1   ounce goat cheese (chèvre)
6   slices whole grain baguette-style French bread, toasted (2 ounces total)
    Snipped fresh chives

1 Preheat oven to 400°F. Cut off the top ½ inch of garlic bulbs to expose the ends of the individual cloves. Place bulbs, cut ends up, on a double thickness of foil. Drizzle with the olive oil. Bring foil up around bulbs and fold edges together to loosely enclose. Roast about 25 minutes or until garlic feels soft when squeezed. Let cool; squeeze bulbs from the bottom of the papery husks to pop out cloves; set aside.

2 Meanwhile, in a large saucepan combine broth, potatoes, and celery. Bring to boiling; reduce heat. Simmer, covered, for 15 to 20 minutes or until potatoes are tender. Add the beans, reserved garlic, thyme, salt, and cayenne. Transfer soup mixture, half at a time, to a blender or food processor. Cover and blend or process just until smooth. (Do not overprocess or potatoes will get gummy.) Return soup to saucepan. Stir in evaporated milk. Heat through.

3 Spread goat cheese evenly on warm toasted baguette slices. To serve, ladle soup into bowls. Top each serving with a toast and sprinkle with chives.

nutrition facts per serving: 221 cal., 4 g total fat (1 g sat. fat), 13 mg chol., 509 mg sodium, 35 g carb. (4 g fiber, 3 g sugars), 10 g pro. exchanges: 0.5 milk, 2 starch, 0.5 fat.

To save the remaining tomato paste for another use, spoon it in 1-tablespoon portions on a waxed paper–lined baking sheet and freeze. Transfer the portions to a freezer bag and store in the freezer until needed.

red lentil soup

43g
CARB. PER
SERVING

prep: 20 minutes   cook: 30 minutes
makes: 6 servings (1 cup each)

1   tablespoon butter
½   cup chopped onion
      (1 medium)
½   cup chopped carrot
      (1 medium)
2   cloves garlic, minced
1   teaspoon ground
      cumin
½   teaspoon salt
¼   teaspoon crushed
      red pepper
1   32-ounce carton no-
      salt-added or low-
      sodium vegetable
      broth (4 cups)
3   tablespoons no-salt-
      added tomato paste
8   ounces dried red
      lentils, rinsed and
      drained (1 cup plus
      2 tablespoons)
8   ounces peeled russet
      potato, cut into
      ½-inch pieces
      (1½ cups)
1   to 2 cups hot water
1   tablespoon lemon
      juice
1   recipe Pita Croutons

1 In a 4-quart Dutch oven heat butter over medium heat. Add onion, carrot, and garlic. Cook and stir for 5 to 8 minutes or until onion starts to brown. Stir in cumin, salt, and crushed red pepper. Carefully add vegetable broth and tomato paste; bring to boiling. Add lentils and potato. Return to boiling; reduce heat. Simmer, uncovered, for 25 to 30 minutes or until lentils are tender, stirring frequently and adding hot water as needed to keep mixture from going dry.

2 Transfer one-third of the lentil mixture to a bowl; set aside. Transfer remaining mixture, half at a time, to a food processor or blender. Cover; process or blend until smooth. Return pureed mixture, chunky lentil mixture, and lemon juice to the Dutch oven and heat through.

3 To serve, ladle soup into bowls. Garnish individual servings with Pita Croutons.

nutrition facts per serving: 244 cal., 3 g total fat (1 g sat. fat), 5 mg chol., 379 mg sodium, 43 g carb. (15 g fiber, 5 g sugars), 12 g pro. exchanges: 1 vegetable, 2 starch, 1 lean meat, 0.5 fat.

pita croutons: Preheat oven to 350°F. Split 1 whole wheat pita bread round horizontally. Coat the cut sides of the pita rounds with nonstick olive oil cooking spray; sprinkle with ⅛ teaspoon paprika. Cut each pita half into four wedges. Spread wedges in a single layer in a 15×10×1-inch baking pan. Bake for 8 to 10 minutes or until crisp. When cool enough to handle, break into bite-size pieces.

For the chicken breast, use leftover chicken or thawed frozen chicken. You can also poach your own: Simmer 12 ounces boneless chicken breast in 1½ cups water in a large covered skillet for 12 to 14 minutes or until cooked through (170°F).

31g
CARB. PER
SERVING

black bean and tomato soup

prep: 25 minutes cook: 22 minutes
makes: 6 servings (1⅔ cups each)

satisfying soups & stews

¾ cup chopped sweet
     onion
3 cloves garlic, minced
¼ teaspoon black
     pepper
⅛ teaspoon salt
1 tablespoon olive oil
¾ cup chopped red
     sweet pepper
3 cups reduced-sodium
     chicken broth
2 14.5-ounce cans
     no-salt-added
     fire-roasted
     diced tomatoes,
     undrained
2 cups no-salt-added
     black beans, rinsed
     and drained
1 teaspoon dried Italian
     seasoning, crushed
2 cups chopped or
     shredded cooked
     chicken breast
1 tablespoon lime juice
3 ounces blue corn
     tortilla chips,
     coarsely crushed
2 tablespoons snipped
     fresh basil, oregano,
     and/or parsley

1 In a 4-quart Dutch oven cook onion, garlic, black pepper, and salt in hot oil over medium heat for 4 to 6 minutes or until onion is tender. Add sweet pepper. Cook for 3 to 5 minutes or until sweet pepper is tender, stirring occasionally. Stir in broth, tomatoes, beans, and Italian seasoning. Bring to boiling; reduce heat. Simmer, uncovered, for 15 minutes.✶

2 Stir in chicken and lime juice; heat through. Ladle soup into bowls. Garnish with tortilla chips and fresh herb.

nutrition facts per serving: 291 cal., 8 g total fat (1 g sat. fat), 40 mg chol., 438 mg sodium, 31 g carb. (7 g fiber, 5 g sugars), 24 g pro. exchanges: 0.5 vegetable, 2 starch, 2 lean meat, 0.5 fat.

✶test kitchen tip: To puree the soup, after Step 1, let soup cool slightly. Using an immersion blender or regular blender, puree soup until nearly smooth. Return to Dutch oven (if using regular blender); continue with Step 2. Serve as directed.

Use a chef's knife to cut the firm squash.
One small squash will yield the 4 cups you need.

butternut squash corn chowder

19g CARB. PER SERVING

prep: 30 minutes   roast: 25 minutes
makes: 8 servings (¾ cup each)

4 ears fresh sweet corn
 or 2 cups frozen
 whole kernel corn
 Nonstick cooking
 spray
4 cups diced, peeled
 butternut squash
 (about 1 small
 squash)
1 tablespoon butter,
 melted
½ cup chopped onion
 (1 medium)
⅓ cup chopped leek
 (1 medium)
2 14.5-ounce cans
 reduced-sodium
 chicken broth
¼ cup half-and-half
 or milk
2 teaspoons snipped
 fresh sage
¼ teaspoon ground
 white pepper
2 tablespoons honey
 (optional)
 Fresh sage leaves

1 If using fresh corn, use a sharp knife to cut the kernels off the cobs (you should have about 2 cups corn kernels). Set aside.

2 Preheat oven to 425°F. Coat the bottom and sides of a roasting pan with cooking spray. Arrange squash in the bottom of the pan. Drizzle with melted butter; toss to coat. Roast for 10 minutes, stirring once. Remove from oven. Add corn, onion, and leek to pan. Toss to combine. Return to oven and roast about 15 minutes more or until vegetables are tender, stirring once.

3 Place one-third of the squash mixture and one-third of the broth in a food processor or blender. Cover and process or blend until almost smooth. Repeat with half of the remaining squash mixture and remaining broth at a time. Transfer processed mixture to a 4-quart Dutch oven. Add the half-and-half, snipped sage, and white pepper. Heat through.

4 To serve, ladle chowder into bowls. If desired, drizzle a little honey over individual servings. Garnish with fresh sage leaves.

nutrition facts per serving: 107 cal., 3 g total fat (2 g sat. fat), 7 mg chol., 264 mg sodium, 19 g carb. (3 g fiber, 5 g sugars), 4 g pro. exchanges: 1 starch, 0.5 fat.

146

36g CARB. PER SERVING

Minestrone *is Italian for "big soup." Beans, zucchini, onion, carrot, and tomatoes make this version big indeed.*

chunky minestrone

prep: 20 minutes   cook: 40 minutes
makes: 4 servings (1⅔ cups each)

1   cup chopped onion
    (1 large)
1   medium carrot, halved
    lengthwise and
    thinly sliced
2   cloves garlic, minced
1   tablespoon olive oil
1   14.5-ounce can
    no-salt-added
    diced tomatoes,
    undrained
1   14.5-ounce can
    reduced-sodium
    chicken broth
1   cup water
¼   cup uncooked brown
    rice
1   teaspoon dried Italian
    seasoning, crushed
3   cups fresh baby
    spinach
1   15-ounce can no-salt-
    added navy beans,
    rinsed and drained
1   medium zucchini,
    quartered
    lengthwise and
    sliced (about
    1½ cups)
¼   teaspoon black
    pepper
⅛   teaspoon salt
    Shredded Parmesan
    cheese (optional)

1 In a 4-quart Dutch oven cook onion, carrot, and garlic in hot oil about 5 minutes or until onion is tender, stirring occasionally.

2 Stir in tomatoes, broth, the water, rice, and Italian seasoning. Bring to boiling; reduce heat. Cover and simmer for 35 to 40 minutes or until rice is tender.

3 Stir in spinach, beans, zucchini, pepper, and salt. Return to boiling; reduce heat. Cover and simmer for 5 minutes more.

4 To serve, ladle soup into bowls. If desired, sprinkle with Parmesan cheese.

nutrition facts per serving: 215 cal., 4 g total fat (1 g sat. fat), 0 mg chol., 399 mg sodium, 36 g carb. (12 g fiber, 7 g sugars), 11 g pro. exchanges: 2 vegetable, 1.5 starch, 1 lean meat, 1 fat.

Pair this creamy blended soup with toasted cheese sandwiches made with low-fat cheese and whole grain bread for a healthful twist on a time-honored combo.

roasted tomato soup and grilled cheese sandwiches

29g
CARB. PER SERVING

prep: 40 minutes roast: 30 minutes
makes: 4 servings (1⅓ cups soup and 2 sandwich quarters each)

3½	pounds roma tomatoes, halved
½	cup chopped onion (1 medium)
¼	cup shredded carrot
¼	cup finely chopped celery
1	clove garlic, minced
2	teaspoons olive oil
1	cup unsalted chicken stock or reduced-sodium chicken broth
1	tablespoon snipped fresh thyme
1	teaspoon snipped fresh rosemary
1	tablespoon snipped fresh basil
¼	teaspoon salt
¼	teaspoon black pepper
2	tablespoons plain fat-free Greek yogurt
	Plain fat-free Greek yogurt
	Snipped fresh basil (optional)
1	recipe Grilled Cheese Sandwiches

1 Preheat oven to 350°F. Arrange tomatoes, cut sides down, in two shallow baking pans. Roast on separate oven racks for 30 minutes, rearranging pans halfway through roasting time. Remove from oven; let stand until cool enough to handle. Using your fingers, lift skins from tomatoes and discard skins (some skins may remain on tomatoes); set tomatoes aside.

2 In a large saucepan cook onion, carrot, celery, and garlic in hot oil about 4 minutes or until onion is tender, stirring occasionally. Add tomatoes and any liquid from baking pans, the chicken stock, thyme, and rosemary. Bring to boiling; reduce heat. Simmer, covered, for 5 minutes. Remove from heat; cool slightly.

3 Transfer half of the tomato mixture to a food processor or blender. Cover and process or blend until smooth. Repeat with the remaining tomato mixture. Return all to the saucepan. Stir in the 1 tablespoon basil, the salt, and pepper. Stir in the 2 tablespoons yogurt. Heat through.

4 To serve, ladle soup into bowls. Spoon additional yogurt onto individual servings. If desired, sprinkle with additional fresh basil. Serve soup with Grilled Cheese Sandwiches.

nutrition facts per serving: 213 cal., 8 g total fat (3 g sat. fat), 12 mg chol., 466 mg sodium, 29 g carb. (8 g fiber, 13 g sugars), 12 g pro. exchanges: 3 vegetable, 0.5 starch, 1 medium-fat meat, 0.5 fat.

grilled cheese sandwiches: Coat one side of each of 4 slices reduced-calorie whole wheat bread with nonstick cooking spray. Lay slices of the bread, coated sides down, on a sheet of waxed paper. Sprinkle 2 of the bread slices with ¼ cup shredded reduced-fat cheddar cheese (1 ounce) and ¼ cup shredded American cheese (1 ounce), dividing cheese evenly. Top with the remaining 2 bread slices, coated sides up. Heat a griddle or large skillet over medium heat. Place sandwiches on hot griddle or skillet; cook about 6 minutes or until bread is golden brown and cheese is melted, turning once halfway through cooking time. Cut sandwiches into quarters to serve.

Serve this fresh, flavorful chilled soup as a sit-down first course for a summer gathering. If you have any leftovers, enjoy them with a salad for lunch the next day.

5g
CARB. PER
SERVING

avocado soup

prep: 20 minutes chill: 1 hour
makes: 6 servings (¾ cup each)

2   small ripe avocados, halved, seeded, peeled, and cut up
½   cup peeled, seeded, and chopped cucumber
⅓   cup chopped onion
¼   cup shredded carrot
1   clove garlic, minced
1   14.5-ounce can reduced-sodium chicken broth
1½ cups water
    Several dashes bottled hot pepper sauce
⅛   teaspoon salt
½   teaspoon paprika
⅓   cup refrigerated fresh salsa
    Snipped fresh cilantro

1 In a blender or food processor combine avocados, cucumber, onion, carrot, garlic, and the broth. Cover; process until almost smooth.

2 Add the water, hot pepper sauce, and salt. Cover; process until smooth. Pour into a bowl. Cover surface of the soup with plastic wrap. Chill for 1 to 24 hours.

3 To serve, ladle soup into chilled bowls or cups. Sprinkle individual servings with paprika and top with salsa and snipped cilantro.

nutrition facts per serving: 64 cal., 5 g total fat (1 g sat. fat), 0 mg chol., 217 mg sodium, 5 g carb. (2 g fiber, 1 g sugars), 2 g pro. exchanges: 1 vegetable, 1 carb., 1 fat.

The colder, the better for this refreshing soup. To get it chilled more quickly, start with a cold cantaloupe.

green tea and honeyed cantaloupe soup

22g
CARB. PER SERVING

prep: 25 minutes **chill:** 2 hours
makes: 6 servings (¾ cup each)

¾ cup cold water
1 green tea bag
6 cups cubed cantaloupe (about 1 medium)
¾ cup plain fat-free yogurt
¼ cup apricot nectar
1 tablespoon grated fresh ginger
1 tablespoon honey
1 teaspoon lime juice
6 tablespoons plain fat-free yogurt
   Finely shredded lime peel

1 In a small saucepan bring the water just to boiling. Remove from heat. Add tea bag to hot liquid. Steep tea for 2 minutes. Remove and discard tea bag.

2 In a food processor or blender combine half of the cantaloupe, half of the ¾ cup yogurt, and half each of the apricot nectar, ginger, honey, lime juice, and brewed tea. Cover and process or blend until smooth. Transfer to a large bowl. Repeat with the remaining half of the ingredients. Stir into processed mixture in bowl. Cover and chill soup in the refrigerator for at least 2 hours.

3 To serve, ladle soup into chilled bowls. Garnish individual servings with 1 tablespoon yogurt and a lime peel each.

nutrition facts per serving: 99 cal., 0 g total fat, 1 mg chol., 63 mg sodium, 22 g carb (2 g fiber, 21 g sugars), 4 g pro.
exchanges: 1.5 fruit, 0.5 lean meat.

Whether you're packing a lunch to enjoy at work or looking for quick, satisfying ways to feed the family, sandwiches and wraps hit the spot for so many meals. We'll show you how to build them with great ingredients—and your health—in mind.

sensational

sand

flax-crusted tuna burgers,
page 168

151

wiches
&wraps

*These wedges are too stuffed to pick up and eat, so serve
them with knives and forks.*

32g
CARB. PER
SERVING

mediterranean chicken pita sandwiches

start to finish: 30 minutes
makes: 4 servings (1 sandwich each)

sensational sandwiches & wraps

1   cup chopped cooked
    chicken breast
½   of a 15-ounce can
    no-salt-added
    organic garbanzo
    beans (chickpeas),
    rinsed and drained
    (about ¾ cup)
½   cup diced tomato
¼   cup thinly sliced red
    onion
¼   cup crumbled
    reduced-fat feta
    cheese
⅓   cup plain low-fat
    yogurt
1   tablespoon snipped
    fresh mint
1   clove garlic, minced
¼   teaspoon ground
    cumin
¼   teaspoon cracked
    black pepper
⅛   teaspoon salt
2   whole wheat pita
    bread rounds
½   of a medium
    cucumber, thinly
    sliced

1 In a large bowl toss together chicken,
beans, tomato, red onion, and feta cheese.
In a small bowl combine yogurt, mint, garlic,
cumin, pepper, and salt. Spoon yogurt mixture
over chicken mixture; toss to combine evenly.

2 To serve, spoon chicken mixture over
1 pita bread round. Top with cucumber
slices and the other pita bread round. Cut
into four wedge-shape sandwiches.

nutrition facts per serving: 242 cal., 4 g total fat
(1 g sat. fat), 33 mg chol., 416 mg sodium, 32 g carb. (5 g fiber,
3 g sugars), 20 g pro. exchanges: 2 starch, 2 lean meat.

Tender butterhead lettuce leaves are just right to use for wraps. Their natural cup shape cradles the filling.

peanut-ginger lettuce wraps

12g CARB. PER SERVING

start to finish: 20 minutes
makes: 4 servings (3 wraps each)

2 cups chopped cooked chicken breast

2 cups shredded cabbage with carrot (coleslaw mix)

1 medium carrot, cut up

2 green onions, cut up

2 tablespoons unsalted peanuts

1 teaspoon minced fresh ginger

⅓ cup bottled light Asian salad dressing

⅓ cup drained canned crushed pineapple

12 leaves butterhead (Boston or Bibb) or green leaf lettuce

1 In a food processor combine about half of the chicken, coleslaw mix, carrot, green onions, peanuts, and ginger; cover and process with several on/off turns until finely chopped. Transfer to a large bowl. Repeat with remaining chicken, coleslaw mix, carrot, green onions, peanuts, and ginger. Add salad dressing and pineapple to mixture; stir to combine well.

2 Spoon about ¼ cup of the chicken mixture onto each lettuce leaf; roll up.

nutrition facts per serving: 221 cal., 8 g total fat (2 g sat. fat), 60 mg chol., 267 mg sodium, 12 g carb. (2 g fiber, 8 g sugars), 24 g pro. exchanges: 1 vegetable, 0.5 carb., 3 lean meat, 0.5 fat.

Look for oval-shape flatbread wraps in the bread section or near the deli meats in the grocery store.

35g CARB. PER SERVING

chicken and black bean pesto wraps

prep: 20 minutes cook: 4 minutes
makes: 4 servings (1 wrap each)

1   15-ounce can no-salt-added black beans, rinsed and drained
½   cup loosely packed cilantro leaves
¼   cup chopped onion
3   tablespoons lime juice
1   teaspoon chili powder
2   cloves garlic, minced
¼   teaspoon crushed red pepper
⅛   teaspoon salt
12 ounces skinless, boneless chicken breast halves, cut into strips
½   teaspoon dried oregano, crushed
⅛   teaspoon salt
2   teaspoons olive oil
4   multigrain flatbread wraps
2   cups shredded fresh spinach
1   small red sweet pepper, cut into bite-size strips

1 In a medium bowl combine beans, cilantro, onion, 1 tablespoon of the lime juice, ½ teaspoon of the chili powder, the garlic, crushed red pepper, and ⅛ teaspoon salt. Mash with a potato masher until almost smooth. Set aside.

2 In a medium bowl toss chicken breast strips with the remaining chili powder, the oregano, and remaining ⅛ teaspoon salt to coat. In a large nonstick skillet cook chicken in hot oil over medium-high heat for 4 to 5 minutes or until chicken is no longer pink. Remove from heat and stir in the remaining 2 tablespoons lime juice.

3 To assemble wraps, spread bean mixture evenly on wraps. Top with spinach, sweet pepper strips, and chicken. Roll up. Serve immediately.

nutrition facts per serving: 311 cal., 7 g total fat (1 g sat. fat), 54 mg chol., 561 mg sodium, 35 g carb. (14 g fiber, 2 g sugars), 33 g pro. exchanges: 1 vegetable, 1.5 starch, 4 lean meat.

When cooked, a spiced-up orange juice and soy mixture creates an amber glaze on the chicken.

orange-soy chicken sandwiches

start to finish: 30 minutes
makes: 4 servings (1 sandwich each)

½ teaspoon finely shredded orange peel
⅓ cup orange juice
1 tablespoon low-sodium soy sauce
1 clove garlic, minced
1 teaspoon snipped fresh thyme
½ teaspoon paprika
¼ teaspoon black pepper
¼ teaspoon crushed red pepper
2 8-ounce skinless, boneless chicken breast halves
2 teaspoons olive oil
1 tablespoon mango chutney
3 tablespoons light mayonnaise
4 multigrain sandwich thins, toasted
2 cups loosely packed watercress

1 In a small bowl stir together orange peel, orange juice, soy sauce, garlic, thyme, paprika, black pepper, and crushed red pepper; set aside.

2 Cut each chicken breast half crosswise in half. Place each piece between two pieces of plastic wrap. Using the flat side of a meat mallet, pound the chicken lightly to about ¼ inch thick. Remove plastic wrap.

3 In an extra-large nonstick skillet heat the oil over medium-high heat. Cook chicken in hot oil for 4 minutes, turning once. Carefully add orange juice mixture to skillet. Simmer for 3 minutes or until liquid reduces to a glaze, turning to coat chicken.

4 Place chutney in a small bowl; snip any large pieces of fruit. Stir in mayonnaise. To assemble sandwiches, spread mayonnaise mixture on cut sides of toasted sandwich thins. For each sandwich, place ½ cup of the watercress and a chicken portion on bottom half of sandwich thin. Add sandwich thin top, spread side down.

nutrition facts per serving: 272 cal., 9 g total fat (1 g sat. fat), 51 mg chol., 564 mg sodium, 30 g carb. (5 g fiber, 7 g sugars), 21 g pro. exchanges: 0.5 fruit, 1.5 starch, 3 lean meat.

38g
CARB. PER
SERVING

If you have extra crunchy slaw, serve it on the side.

chicken "brats" with apple slaw

prep: 10 minutes cook: 15 minutes
makes: 5 servings (1 sausage with bun and ⅓ cup slaw each)

1 tablespoon spicy
   brown mustard
1 tablespoon maple
   syrup
1 cup finely shredded
   napa cabbage
1 small Granny Smith
   apple, cored and cut
   into thin strips or
   coarsely shredded
¼ cup thin wedges of
   red onion
1 tablespoon cider
   vinegar
1 tablespoon olive oil
   Nonstick cooking
   spray
1 12-ounce package
   cooked chicken
   apple sausages (5)
5 whole wheat hot dog
   buns

1 In a small bowl combine mustard and
maple syrup; set aside.

2 In a medium bowl combine cabbage,
apple, and red onion. In a small bowl
whisk the vinegar, olive oil, and 1 teaspoon
of the mustard mixture to blend. Drizzle over
cabbage mixture and toss to coat.

3 Preheat a grill pan or griddle over
medium heat. Add sausages and cook
for 15 to 18 minutes or until heated through,
turning occasionally.

4 Serve sausages on buns. Top with
remaining mustard mixture and
apple slaw.

nutrition facts per serving: 321 cal., 11 g total fat
(3 g sat. fat), 49 mg chol., 661 mg sodium, 38 g carb. (2 g fiber,
15 g sugars), 16 g pro. exchanges: 2.5 starch, 1 medium-fat
meat, 1 fat.

Basil pesto is a pungent, pastelike sauce made with fresh basil, garlic, olive oil, pine nuts, and Parmesan cheese. Look for it in the pasta aisle or in the refrigerator case.

28g
CARB. PER SERVING

grilled greek chicken sandwiches

start to finish: 35 minutes
makes: 4 servings (1 sandwich each)

4   ½-inch slices red onion
1   large red sweet
    pepper, quartered
    Nonstick cooking spray
2   5- to 6-ounce
    skinless, boneless
    chicken breast
    halves, cut in half
    horizontally∗
4   thin multigrain
    sandwich rounds,
    split
2   tablespoons basil
    pesto
2   tablespoons pitted
    Kalamata olives
    or black olives,
    chopped
⅓   cup shredded
    reduced-fat
    mozzarella cheese
¼   cup crumbled
    reduced-fat feta
    cheese

1 Heat a grill pan or an extra-large nonstick skillet over medium heat. Lightly coat onion and sweet pepper with cooking spray; add to hot grill pan or skillet. Cook for 6 to 8 minutes or until tender, turning once. Remove from skillet. Lightly coat chicken with cooking spray; add to hot grill pan or skillet. Cook for 3 to 5 minutes or until no longer pink, turning once. Remove chicken from skillet; if desired, using two forks, pull chicken apart into coarse shreds. Cut the pepper quarters into bite-size strips.

2 To assemble sandwiches, spread cut sides of sandwich rounds with pesto. Sprinkle sandwich round bottoms with olives. Place grilled onion slices on olives. Top with pepper strips. Place chicken over peppers. Sprinkle with mozzarella cheese and feta cheese. Top with sandwich round tops, cut sides down. Lightly coat outsides of sandwiches with cooking spray.

3 Place the grill pan or skillet over medium-low heat. Add sandwiches in batches if necessary. Place a heavy skillet on sandwiches. Cook over medium-low heat for 3 to 4 minutes or until sandwich bottoms are toasted. Carefully remove top skillet (skillet may be hot). Turn sandwiches over; top again with skillet. Cook for 3 to 4 minutes more or until bread is toasted and cheese is melted. Cut in half to serve.

nutrition facts per serving: 296 cal., 10 g total fat (2 g sat. fat), 51 mg chol., 548 mg sodium, 28 g carb. (6 g fiber, 4 g sugars), 26 g pro. exchanges: 1 vegetable, 1.5 starch, 3 lean meat, 0.5 fat.

∗test kitchen tip: If your supermarket sells chicken cutlets, purchase four (weighing 10 to 12 ounces total) to use in place of the halved chicken breasts.

To evenly toast the cumin seeds, gently shake the skillet to keep them moving while over the heat.

indian-spiced turkey kabob pitas

35g CARB. PER SERVING

prep: 25 minutes **grill:** 8 minutes
makes: 4 servings (1 pita round, 1 tablespoon yogurt, ½ cup cucumber mixture, and about 3 ounces turkey each)

4	8- to 10-inch bamboo skewers
1	teaspoon whole cumin seeds
1	cup shredded cucumber (1 small)
⅓	cup seeded and chopped roma tomato (1 small)
¼	cup slivered red onion
¼	cup shredded radishes
¼	cup snipped fresh cilantro
¼	teaspoon black pepper
1	pound turkey breast, cut into 1-inch cubes
1	recipe Curry Blend
¼	cup plain fat-free Greek yogurt
4	2-ounce whole wheat pita bread rounds

1 Soak bamboo skewers in water for at least 30 minutes before using on the grill.

2 In a small dry skillet toast cumin seeds over medium heat for 1 minute or until fragrant. Transfer to a medium bowl. Add cucumber, tomato, red onion, radishes, cilantro, and black pepper. Stir to combine. Set aside.

3 In another medium bowl combine turkey breast cubes and Curry Blend. Stir to coat turkey cubes with seasonings. Thread turkey cubes evenly onto skewers. For a charcoal grill, grill kabobs on the grill rack directly over medium coals. Grill, uncovered, for 8 to 12 minutes or until turkey is no longer pink (170°F), turning kabobs occasionally while grilling. (For a gas grill, preheat grill. Reduce heat to medium. Place kabobs on grill rack over heat. Cover and grill as directed.)

4 Remove turkey from skewers. To serve, spread Greek yogurt evenly on pita rounds. Using a slotted spoon, place cucumber mixture on top of yogurt. Top with grilled turkey.

nutrition facts per serving: 322 cal., 5 g total fat (1 g sat. fat), 70 mg chol., 442 mg sodium, 35 g carb. (5 g fiber, 2 g sugars), 35 g pro. **exchanges:** 2 starch, 4 lean meat.

curry blend: In a small bowl stir together 2 teaspoons olive oil, 1 teaspoon curry powder, ½ teaspoon ground cumin, ½ teaspoon ground turmeric, ½ teaspoon ground coriander, ¼ teaspoon ground ginger, ⅛ teaspoon salt, and ⅛ teaspoon cayenne pepper.

For easy slicing, freeze the steak for 30 minutes and then cut with a sharp knife.

cheesesteak sandwiches

prep: 20 minutes cook: 12 minutes broil: 2 minutes
makes: 6 servings (1 portion each)

4 teaspoons canola oil
1 pound boneless beef sirloin steak, trimmed and cut into thin strips
¼ teaspoon black pepper
⅛ teaspoon salt
1 large portobello mushroom, stems and gills removed, cut into thin strips
1 large yellow sweet pepper, cut into thin strips
1 medium fresh poblano chile pepper, seeded and cut into thin strips (see tip, *page 165*)
1 medium onion, halved and thinly sliced
2 cloves garlic, minced
1 14- to 16-ounce loaf French bread
1 cup shredded reduced-fat Monterey Jack cheese (4 ounces)

1 In an extra-large nonstick skillet heat 2 teaspoons of the oil over medium-high heat. Add beef strips; sprinkle with black pepper and salt. Cook for 4 to 6 minutes or just until beef is slightly pink in the center, stirring frequently. Remove beef from skillet; cover and set aside.

2 In the same skillet combine the remaining 2 teaspoons oil, the mushroom strips, sweet pepper, chile pepper, onion, and garlic. Cook for 8 to 10 minutes or until vegetables are tender, stirring occasionally.

3 Meanwhile, preheat broiler. Split bread loaf in half horizontally. Scoop out the soft centers of the top and bottom of the loaf, leaving about a ½-inch shell. (Save soft bread centers for another use.) Place bread halves, cut sides up, on a large baking sheet.

4 Broil bread 5 to 6 inches from the heat for 1 to 2 minutes or until toasted. Spoon vegetable mixture into bottom half of the loaf. Top with steak strips and cheese. Remove loaf top from the baking sheet. Broil filled bottom half of loaf for 1 to 2 minutes or until cheese is melted. Place loaf top over filling. To serve, cut crosswise into six portions.

nutrition facts per serving: 348 cal., 11 g total fat (4 g sat. fat), 45 mg chol., 562 mg sodium, 34 g carb. (2 g fiber, 3 g sugars), 28 g pro. exchanges: 1 vegetable, 2 starch, 3 lean meat, 0.5 fat.

Refrigerated Italian-style turkey meatballs take the work out of this favorite—and help lower the calories and fat, too.

italian meatball rolls

36g
CARB. PER
SERVING

prep: 15 minutes   cook: 12 minutes   broil: 2 minutes
makes: 4 servings (1 sandwich each)

Nonstick cooking spray
2½   cups thinly sliced cremini mushrooms
1   medium onion, chopped (½ cup)
2   cloves garlic, minced
1   8-ounce can no-salt-added tomato sauce
2   tablespoons balsamic vinegar
½   teaspoon dried rosemary, crushed
½   teaspoon dried oregano, crushed
8   ounces refrigerated Italian-style cooked turkey meatballs (8 meatballs), halved
4   whole wheat hot dog buns
½   cup shredded part-skim mozzarella cheese (2 ounces)
Snipped fresh oregano (optional)

1 Preheat broiler. Coat an unheated large nonstick skillet with cooking spray; preheat over medium heat. Add mushrooms, onion, and garlic to hot skillet; cook for 5 to 10 minutes or until tender, stirring occasionally. Add tomato sauce, balsamic vinegar, rosemary, and the dried oregano. Bring to boiling; reduce heat. Simmer, covered, for 2 minutes. Stir in meatballs. Cook about 5 minutes more or until meatballs are heated through.

2 Meanwhile, open buns so they lie flat and place on a baking sheet, cut sides up. Broil 4 to 5 inches from the heat about 1 minute or until lightly toasted. Divide meatball mixture among buns. Sprinkle with cheese. Broil for 1 to 2 minutes more or until cheese melts. If desired, sprinkle with fresh oregano.

nutrition facts per serving: 344 cal., 12 g total fat (4 g sat. fat), 70 mg chol., 644 mg sodium, 36 g carb. (4 g fiber, 10 g sugars), 21 g pro. exchanges: 1 vegetable, 2 starch, 2 medium-fat meat.

If you use deli-style roast beef, make sure it is low-sodium.

roast beef panini

prep: 25 minutes cook: 3 minutes
makes: 4 servings (1 sandwich each)

32g
CARB. PER
SERVING

Nonstick cooking
   spray
8 slices marble rye, rye,
   or pumpernickel
   bread
1 recipe Horseradish
   Spread
8 ounces leftover
   cooked roast beef,
   sliced
1 cup baby arugula or
   watercress
2 slices Havarti cheese,
   halved (about
   1½ ounces total)
¼ cup thinly sliced red
   onion

1 Lightly coat an unheated panini sandwich maker or grill pan with cooking spray. Preheat panini maker according to manufacturer's directions or grill pan over medium heat.

2 Meanwhile, spread Horseradish Spread on one side of the bread slices. On half of the slices place roast beef, arugula, cheese, and red onion. Top with remaining bread slices, spread sides down.

3 Place sandwiches on panini maker or grill pan, in batches if necessary. If using panini maker, close lid and grill for 2 to 3 minutes or until bread is toasted. (If using grill pan, place a heavy skillet on top of sandwiches. Cook for 1 to 2 minutes or until bottoms are toasted. Using hot pads, carefully remove top skillet. Turn sandwiches and top again with skillet. Cook for 1 to 2 minutes more or until bread is toasted.)

nutrition facts per serving: 333 cal., 11 g total fat (4 g sat. fat), 60 mg chol., 615 mg sodium, 32 g carb. (4 g fiber, 1 g sugars), 24 g pro. exchanges: 2 starch, 2.5 lean meat, 1 fat.

horseradish spread: In a small bowl combine 2 tablespoons light mayonnaise, 1 tablespoon prepared horseradish, 1 teaspoon Dijon-style mustard, and ⅛ teaspoon caraway seeds.

21g
CARB. PER
SERVING

If you have a bag of shredded coleslaw mix (cabbage and carrot) on hand, try it instead of the broccoli slaw mix.

barbecue beef wrap

start to finish: 10 minutes
makes: 1 serving (1 wrap)

2   ounces leftover roast
    beef, shredded
    (⅓ cup)
1   7- to 8-inch whole
    wheat flour tortilla
1   tablespoon bottled
    barbecue sauce
1   tablespoon shredded
    Monterey Jack
    cheese
2   tablespoons packaged
    shredded broccoli
    (broccoli slaw mix)

Arrange beef on the tortilla. Drizzle with barbecue sauce and top with cheese and broccoli; roll up. Serve immediately or wrap tightly in plastic wrap and chill for up to 24 hours.

nutrition facts per serving: 307 cal., 12 g total fat (5 g sat. fat), 51 mg chol., 534 mg sodium, 21 g carb. (10 g fiber, 5 g sugars), 25 g pro. exchanges: 1 starch, 3 lean meat, 1.5 fat.

to tote: Assemble beef wrap the night before, wrap in plastic wrap, and chill. Transport in an insulated lunch box with ice packs; refrigerate within 1 hour. Hold in the refrigerator for up to 5 hours.

A crisp vegetable combo helps tame the fiery heat of the jalapeño.
If you like heat, leave the seeds in the jalapeño.

banh mi vietnamese sandwiches

26g
CARB. PER
SERVING

prep: 25 minutes cook: 4 minutes
makes: 6 servings (1 portion each)

12 ounces pork
      tenderloin
2   tablespoons Asian
      sweet chili sauce
1   tablespoon reduced-
      sodium soy sauce
1   small cucumber,
      seeded and cut into
      thin strips
1   small red sweet
      pepper, cut into thin
      strips
1   medium carrot,
      shredded
¼   cup sliced green
      onions (2)
¼   cup bottled low-fat
      sesame ginger
      salad dressing
1   tablespoon lime juice
1   10-ounce loaf whole
      grain baguette-style
      French bread, split
      horizontally
¼   cup fresh cilantro
      leaves
1   fresh jalapeño chile
      pepper, seeded and
      thinly sliced*

1 Trim fat from pork. Cut pork crosswise into ½-inch slices. Press each piece with the palm of your hand to make an even thickness. In a small bowl combine chili sauce and soy sauce. Brush sauce mixture onto pork. In a greased grill pan or extra-large skillet cook pork over medium-high heat for 4 to 6 minutes or until slightly pink in center and juices run clear, turning once.

2 In a large bowl combine cucumber, sweet pepper, carrot, green onions, salad dressing, and lime juice.

3 Place pork slices on the bottom half of the baguette. Top with vegetable mixture, cilantro, jalapeño slices, and top half of baguette. Cut into six portions to serve.

nutrition facts per serving: 220 cal., 4 g total fat (0 g sat. fat), 37 mg chol., 481 mg sodium, 26 g carb. (6 g fiber, 4 g sugars), 19 g pro. exchanges: 0.5 vegetable, 1.5 starch, 2 lean meat.

✳test kitchen tip: Because chile peppers contain volatile oils that can burn your skin and eyes, avoid direct contact with chiles as much as possible. When working with chile peppers, wear plastic or rubber gloves. If your bare hands do touch the chile peppers, wash your hands and nails well with soap and warm water.

31g
CARB. PER SERVING

sensational sandwiches & wraps

Serve the crunchy slaw on top of the meat for a meal in a bun or serve it alongside for a salad and sandwich lunch.

pork tenderloin sandwiches

prep: 25 minutes chill: 2 hours cook: 8 minutes
makes: 4 servings (3 ounces pork, 1 bun, and ½ cup broccoli slaw each)

12 ounces pork tenderloin
2 tablespoons flour
¼ teaspoon salt
¼ teaspoon onion powder or garlic powder
¼ teaspoon cayenne pepper
¼ teaspoon black pepper
2 tablespoons vegetable oil
4 whole wheat hamburger buns, split and toasted
Ketchup, yellow mustard, and/or pickles (optional)
1 recipe Broccoli Slaw

1 Cut pork crosswise into four pieces. Place one pork piece between two pieces of clear plastic wrap. Pound lightly with the flat side of a meat mallet, working from center to edges until ¼ inch thick. Remove plastic wrap. Repeat with remaining pork pieces.

2 In a shallow dish combine flour, salt, onion powder, cayenne pepper, and black pepper. Dip pork into the flour mixture, turning to coat. In an extra-large skillet heat oil over medium heat. Add pork; cook for 8 to 10 minutes or until no pink remains and juices run clear, turning once. (If all the pork slices won't fit in the skillet, cook in two batches, adding additional oil if necessary.)

3 Place pork on buns. If desired, top with ketchup, mustard, and/or pickles. Serve with Broccoli Slaw.

nutrition facts per serving: 310 cal., 10 g total fat (1 g sat. fat), 55 mg chol., 560 mg sodium, 31 g carb. (3 g fiber, 10 g sugars), 23 g pro. exchanges: 0.5 vegetable, 2 starch, 2.5 lean meat, 1 fat.

broccoli slaw: In a screw-top jar combine 2 tablespoons vinegar, 1 tablespoon honey, ¼ teaspoon salt, ⅛ to ¼ teaspoon black pepper, and, if desired, several dashes bottled hot pepper sauce. Cover and shake well. In a medium bowl combine 2 cups packaged shredded broccoli (broccoli slaw mix), 2 tablespoons thinly sliced green onion, and 1 tablespoon snipped fresh parsley. Pour vinegar mixture over vegetable mixture, tossing to coat. Cover and chill for 2 to 24 hours before serving.

Whole grain French bread, low-sugar apricot preserves, lower-sodium ham, fresh pear, arugula, and goat cheese add up to one scrumptious sandwich. It's a cut above any melt you've ever had!

hot ham and pear melts

36g
CARB. PER
SERVING

prep: 15 minutes bake: 10 minutes
makes: 4 servings (1 sandwich each)

1   10- to 12-ounce whole
    grain baguette
2   tablespoons lower-
    sugar apricot
    preserves
2   cups arugula or fresh
    spinach
1   medium pear,
    quartered, cored,
    and thinly sliced
6   ounces thinly sliced
    lower-sodium
    cooked ham
1   4-ounce package goat
    cheese (chèvre),
    softened
1   teaspoon snipped
    fresh chives
    Nonstick cooking
    spray

1 Preheat oven to 350°F. Cut baguette crosswise into four portions. Split each portion in half horizontally. Scoop out the soft centers of tops and bottoms of baguette portions, leaving about a ½-inch shell. (Save soft bread centers for another use.)

2 Spread preserves on cut sides of bottom halves of baguette portions. Top with half of the arugula, the pear slices, ham, and the remaining arugula. In a small bowl stir together goat cheese and chives; spread on cut sides of the top halves of the baguette portions. Place over arugula, cheese sides down. Lightly coat tops and bottoms of sandwiches with cooking spray.

3 Place sandwiches in a shallow baking pan. Cover with foil. Bake for 10 to 15 minutes or until heated through. Serve warm.

nutrition facts per serving: 300 cal., 10 g total fat (5 g sat. fat), 32 mg chol., 647 mg sodium, 36 g carb. (3 g fiber, 10 g sugars), 16 g pro. exchanges: 0.5 vegetable, 0.5 fruit, 1.5 starch, 2 medium-fat meat.

23g
CARB. PER SERVING

sensational sandwiches & wraps

A combo of flaxseed meal and flaxseed makes a crunchy coating on these burgers. Pictured on page 151.

flax-crusted tuna burgers

prep: 20 minutes cook: 10 minutes
makes: 4 servings (1 tuna patty, ½ sandwich thin, and ¼ of the avocado mixture [about 2½ tablespoons])

1   pound fresh or frozen skinless tuna fillets
1   egg white
¼   cup dry whole wheat bread crumbs
1   tablespoon snipped fresh tarragon
¼   teaspoon salt
¼   teaspoon black pepper
3   tablespoons flaxseed meal
1   tablespoon flaxseeds
    Nonstick cooking spray
1   medium avocado, halved, seeded, and peeled
2   tablespoons light mayonnaise
½   teaspoon finely shredded lemon peel
1   tablespoon lemon juice
1   clove garlic, minced
⅛   teaspoon salt
2   whole grain or whole wheat sandwich thins, split and toasted
1   cup fresh spinach leaves
4   slices tomato

1 Thaw tuna, if frozen. Rinse tuna; pat dry with paper towels. Finely chop tuna and set aside. In a medium bowl beat egg white with a fork. Stir in bread crumbs, tarragon, the ¼ teaspoon salt, and ⅛ teaspoon of the pepper. Add tuna; stir gently to combine. Shape mixture into four ½-inch-thick patties, using damp hands if necessary.

2 In a shallow dish combine the flaxseed meal and flaxseeds. Dip tuna patties into flaxseed mixture, turning to coat evenly.

3 Coat a large nonstick skillet or nonstick griddle with cooking spray. Heat over medium heat. Add tuna patties; cook for 10 to 12 minutes or until an instant-read thermometer inserted into sides of patties registers 160°F, turning once halfway through cooking time.

4 Meanwhile, in a medium bowl use a potato masher or fork to coarsely mash avocado. Add mayonnaise, lemon peel, lemon juice, garlic, the ⅛ teaspoon salt, and the remaining ⅛ teaspoon pepper. Continue to mash until mixture is well mixed but still slightly chunky.

5 To serve, place one sandwich thin half, cut side up, on each of four serving plates. Top with spinach leaves and tomato slices. Top each with a cooked tuna patty. Spoon one-fourth of the avocado mixture over each patty.

nutrition facts per serving: 332 cal., 12 g total fat (1 g sat. fat), 47 mg chol., 531 mg sodium, 23 g carb. (8 g fiber, 3 g sugars), 35 g pro. exchanges: 1 vegetable, 1 starch, 4 lean meat, 1 fat.

To store fresh ginger, wrap the unpeeled piece in freezer wrap and place it in the freezer—it will keep indefinitely.

asian tuna wraps

20g CARB. PER SERVING

start to finish: 15 minutes
makes: 4 servings (1 wrap each)

- 2 6-ounce cans very low–sodium solid white tuna (water pack), drained and broken into chunks
- 3 tablespoons bottled sesame-ginger salad dressing
- ¼ cup light mayonnaise
- 1 teaspoon minced garlic
- ½ teaspoon minced fresh ginger
- 4 8-inch whole wheat low-carb flour tortillas
- 2 cups shredded bok choy*
- 1 medium red sweet pepper, thinly sliced
- ½ cup jicama, cut into matchstick-size pieces

In a large bowl stir together tuna, salad dressing, 2 tablespoons of the mayonnaise, the garlic, and ginger. Spread remaining mayonnaise over one side of each of the tortillas. Divide bok choy, sweet pepper, and jicama among wraps. Top with tuna mixture and roll up.

nutrition facts per serving: 267 cal., 11 g total fat (1 g sat. fat), 43 mg chol., 525 mg sodium, 20 g carb. (10 g fiber, 5 g sugars), 22 g pro. exchanges: 1 vegetable, 1 starch, 3 lean meat, 0.5 fat.

✻test kitchen tip: If you have napa cabbage in your fridge, you can use it instead of the bok choy.

To keep the fish from sticking, be sure to grease the grill rack with vegetable oil before placing it over the hot coals.

20g
CARB. PER
SERVING

fish tacos with jalapeño slaw

prep: 20 minutes grill: 4 minutes
makes: 4 servings (1 taco and ⅔ cup slaw each)

1 pound fresh or frozen
   skinless cod, tilapia,
   or other fish fillets,
   about ½ inch thick
1 recipe Jalapeño Slaw
½ teaspoon ground
   cumin
¼ teaspoon ground
   ancho chile pepper
   or cayenne pepper
   Dash salt
4 8-inch whole grain
   flour tortillas
   Peach or mango salsa
   (optional)
   Lime wedges
   (optional)

1 Thaw fish, if frozen. Rinse fish; pat dry with paper towels. Set aside. Prepare Jalapeño Slaw; cover and chill.

2 In a small bowl combine cumin, ground ancho chile pepper, and salt; sprinkle evenly over one side of each fish fillet.

3 Stack tortillas and wrap in heavy foil. For a charcoal grill, place fish and tortilla stack on the greased grill rack directly over medium coals. Grill, uncovered, for 4 to 6 minutes or until fish flakes easily when tested with a fork and tortillas are heated through, turning fish and tortilla stack once. (For a gas grill, preheat grill. Reduce heat to medium. Place fish and tortilla stack on greased grill rack over heat. Cover and grill as directed.)

4 To serve, cut fish into four serving-size pieces. Divide Jalapeño Slaw among tortillas and top with fish. If desired, serve with salsa and lime wedges.

nutrition facts per serving: 304 cal., 11 g total fat (2 g sat. fat), 48 mg chol., 467 mg sodium, 20 g carb. (11 g fiber, 3 g sugars), 29 g pro. exchanges: 1 vegetable, 1 starch, 3.5 lean meat, 1 fat.

jalapeño slaw: In a bowl combine 2½ cups packaged shredded cabbage with carrot (coleslaw mix); ¼ cup thinly sliced, halved red onion; and 1 small fresh jalapeño chile pepper, seeded and finely chopped (see tip, *page 165*); set aside. In a small bowl whisk together 2 tablespoons lime juice, 2 tablespoons orange juice, 2 tablespoons olive oil, ½ teaspoon ground cumin, and dash salt. Pour lime juice mixture over cabbage mixture. Toss to coat. Cover and chill for up to 6 hours.

This trendy sandwich starring salmon all decked out with a crunchy coffee-spice coating would be a hit at an upscale restaurant.

coffee-rubbed salmon sandwiches

prep: 20 minutes cook: 5 minutes
makes: 4 servings (1 sandwich each)

¼ cup light sour cream
1 tablespoon snipped fresh parsley
2 teaspoons cider vinegar
1 teaspoon prepared horseradish
1 teaspoon instant espresso coffee powder
1 teaspoon dried ancho chile powder
½ teaspoon packed brown sugar*
¼ teaspoon dry mustard
¼ teaspoon ground cumin
⅛ teaspoon cayenne pepper
1 pound skinless salmon fillets
2 teaspoons olive oil
4 whole wheat hamburger buns, toasted
2 cups baby salad greens
8 thin red onion rings

1 In a small bowl stir together the sour cream, parsley, vinegar, and horseradish. Set aside.

2 In another small bowl stir together espresso powder, chile powder, brown sugar, mustard, cumin, and cayenne pepper. Cut salmon into four equal pieces. Sprinkle evenly with spice mixture; rub mixture into salmon with your fingers.

3 In a large nonstick skillet heat oil over medium heat. Cook salmon in hot oil for 5 to 7 minutes or until fish begins to flake when tested with a fork.

4 Top bottom halves of toasted buns with salad greens, salmon pieces, and onion rings. Spoon sauce over salmon and onion rings. Add top halves of buns.

nutrition facts per serving: 363 cal., 12 g total fat (2 g sat. fat), 67 mg chol., 347 mg sodium, 33 g carb. (4 g fiber, 8 g sugars), 29 g pro. exchanges: 2 starch, 3.5 lean meat, 1 fat.

*sugar substitute: We do not recommend using a sugar substitute for this recipe.

Take a bite of this sandwich and you'll discover sassy Cajun-spiced shrimp enhanced by a cool and creamy veggie spread. Not only that, the combo boasts 73 percent of the daily recommended amount for vitamin A and 105 percent for vitamin C.

22g CARB. PER SERVING

shrimp po'boys

start to finish: 30 minutes

makes: 4 servings (1 sandwich each)

1¼   pounds fresh or frozen large shrimp in shells

⅓   cup tub-style light cream cheese, softened

1   tablespoon fat-free milk

1   stalk celery, finely chopped (½ cup)

½   cup jarred roasted red sweet peppers, drained and chopped

2   green onions, thinly sliced

1   teaspoon Cajun seasoning

2   teaspoons canola oil

4   ½-inch slices French bread, toasted

3   cups torn or shredded romaine lettuce

Snipped fresh parsley (optional)

1 Thaw shrimp, if frozen. Peel and devein shrimp. Rinse shrimp; pat dry with paper towels. Set aside. In a small bowl combine cream cheese and milk, stirring until smooth. Stir in celery, roasted red peppers, and green onions; set aside.

2 In a medium bowl toss shrimp with Cajun seasoning to coat. In a large nonstick skillet heat oil over medium-high heat. Add shrimp; cook and stir for 3 to 4 minutes or until opaque. Remove from heat.

3 Divide bread slices among four serving plates. Top with cream cheese mixture, lettuce, and shrimp. If desired, sprinkle with snipped parsley.

nutrition facts per serving: 280 cal., 8 g total fat (3 g sat. fat), 182 mg chol., 486 mg sodium, 22 g carb. (2 g fiber, 3 g sugars), 29 g pro. exchanges: 1 vegetable, 1 starch, 3.5 lean meat, 0.5 fat.

Some goat cheese is creamier than others, so if it doesn't crumble very well, use a spoon to drop small bits of cheese over the bread.

goat cheese and prosciutto panini

30g
CARB. PER SERVING

prep: 15 minutes cook: 4 minutes stand: 5 minutes
makes: 4 servings (1 sandwich each)

1   12-ounce loaf whole grain Italian bread
    Nonstick cooking spray
2   ounces goat cheese (chèvre), crumbled
½   cup fresh basil leaves
2   medium tomatoes, sliced
2   ounces thinly sliced prosciutto
2   cups arugula leaves
1   tablespoon balsamic vinegar (optional)
    Grapes (optional)

1 Cut the bread in half lengthwise. Hollow out top and bottom halves of bread, leaving a ½-inch-thick shell. Reserve removed bread for another use. (There should be about 4 ounces of bread removed.)

2 Lightly coat outsides of the bread halves with cooking spray. Sprinkle goat cheese over the cut side of the bread bottom. Top evenly with the basil, tomatoes, prosciutto, and arugula. If desired, drizzle with balsamic vinegar. Cover with loaf top.

3 Coat a large nonstick skillet with cooking spray; preheat over medium heat. Place loaf in skillet. Place another skillet on top of the loaf, pressing gently to flatten loaf slightly. Cook for 2½ minutes on one side; turn and cook for 2 to 2½ minutes more or until bread is beginning to brown.

4 Remove from skillet. Let stand on cutting board for 5 minutes. Use a serrated knife to slice loaf into four equal sandwiches. Serve sandwiches warm or at room temperature. If desired, serve with grapes.

nutrition facts per serving: 253 cal., 10 g total fat (3 g sat. fat), 11 mg chol., 606 mg sodium, 30 g carb. (5 g fiber, 8 g sugars), 13 g pro. exchanges: 2 starch, 1 medium-fat meat, 0.5 fat.

39g
CARB. PER
SERVING

Make a mock aïoli by stirring fresh garlic into light mayonnaise.
The zesty spread complements hot-off-the-grill vegetables perfectly.

grilled veggie sandwiches

start to finish: 25 minutes
makes: 4 servings (1 sandwich each)

1   small eggplant, sliced
    1 inch thick
1   4-inch portobello
    mushroom, stem
    removed
1   medium yellow
    or green sweet
    pepper, halved
1   tablespoon olive oil
¼   teaspoon black
    pepper
⅛   teaspoon salt
2   tablespoons light
    mayonnaise
2   cloves garlic, minced
4   2-ounce whole wheat
    rolls, split and
    toasted

1 Brush eggplant, mushroom, and sweet pepper with olive oil and sprinkle with black pepper and salt. For a charcoal grill, place the vegetables on the grill rack directly over medium coals. Grill, uncovered, for 10 to 12 minutes or until vegetables are just tender, turning once halfway through grilling. Transfer vegetables to a cutting board and cut into ½-inch slices. (For a gas grill, preheat grill. Reduce heat to medium. Place vegetables on grill rack over heat. Cover and grill as directed.)

2 Meanwhile, in a small bowl combine mayonnaise and garlic. Spread mayonnaise mixture over cut sides of rolls. Fill rolls with grilled vegetables.

nutrition facts per serving: 247 cal., 9 g total fat (1 g sat. fat), 3 mg chol., 353 mg sodium, 39 g carb. (8 g fiber, 9 g sugars), 7 g pro. exchanges: 1 vegetable, 2 starch, 1.5 fat.

27g CARB. PER SERVING

If you are a fan of colorful heirloom tomatoes, pick some up at the farmer's market and use in place of the romas.

fresh tomato sandwiches

prep: 15 minutes bake: 10 minutes

makes: 2 servings (2 bagel halves each)

2 whole wheat bagel thins

⅓ cup shredded part-skim mozzarella cheese

¼ cup part-skim ricotta cheese

1 tablespoon light mayonnaise

1 teaspoon snipped fresh dill or ¼ teaspoon dried dill weed

2 to 3 roma tomatoes, sliced

¼ cup red onion cut into thin wedges and separated into pieces
Dash garlic powder

2 teaspoons grated Parmesan cheese
Fresh dill (optional)

1 Split and lightly toast bagel thins. Place bagel thins, cut sides up, on a baking sheet. Preheat oven to 350°F.

2 In a small bowl combine mozzarella, ricotta, mayonnaise, and dill. Spread mixture on bagel thins.

3 Layer tomato slices and onion pieces on bagel thins. Sprinkle lightly with garlic powder. Sprinkle ½ teaspoon of the Parmesan cheese over each bagel thin half.

4 Bake for 10 to 15 minutes or until mayonnaise mixture is melted and Parmesan is lightly browned. If desired, garnish with additional fresh dill.

nutrition facts per serving: 248 cal., 11 g total fat (5 g sat. fat), 27 mg chol., 423 mg sodium, 27 g carb. (6 g fiber, 6 g sugars), 16 g pro. exchanges: 1 vegetable, 1.5 starch, 1.5 lean meat, 1 fat.

This makes a big batch, so if you wish to store some, place it in an airtight container and refrigerate for up to 1 week or freeze for up to 3 months.

lentil sloppy joes

prep: 15 minutes cook: 8 to 10 hours (low) or 4 to 5 hours (high)
makes: 16 servings (½ cup lentil mixture and 1 bun each)

43g
CARB. PER
SERVING

2 cups lentils, rinsed and drained
1 large green sweet pepper, chopped (1¼ cups)
2 medium carrots, shredded (1 cup)
¾ cup chopped onion
1 cup reduced-sodium hot-style vegetable juice
¼ cup no-salt-added tomato paste
1 4-ounce can diced green chiles, undrained
1 tablespoon reduced-sodium Worcestershire sauce
2 teaspoons chili powder
1 teaspoon cider vinegar
2 cloves garlic, minced
3 cups water
½ cup reduced-sodium ketchup
2 tablespoons packed brown sugar*
16 whole wheat hamburger buns, split and toasted
Shredded carrot (optional)

1 In a 3½- or 4-quart slow cooker combine lentils, sweet pepper, carrots, onion, vegetable juice, tomato paste, chiles, Worcestershire sauce, chili powder, vinegar, garlic, and water.

2 Cover and cook on low-heat setting for 8 to 10 hours or on high-heat setting for 4 to 5 hours.

3 Before serving, stir in ketchup and brown sugar. Serve lentil mixture on toasted buns. If desired, top each serving with shredded carrot.

nutrition facts per serving: 228 cal., 1 g total fat (0 g sat. fat), 0 mg chol., 265 mg sodium, 43 g carb. (10 g fiber, 10 g sugars), 11 g pro. exchanges: 2.5 starch, 0.5 lean meat.

nutrition facts per serving with substitute: Same as original, except 221 cal., 42 g carb. (9 g sugars).

*sugar substitutes: Choose from Sweet'N Low Brown or Sugar Twin Granulated Brown. Follow package directions to use product amount equivalent to 2 tablespoons brown sugar

Fire up the grill for some irresistible burgers, chops, and steaks and fascinating chicken and seafood dishes. And make room on the plate for more good things! Nearly every recipe comes with a fresh, vibrant accompaniment that rounds out the meal stylishly and healthfully.

sizzlin'

grilled favo

pork chops with jalapeño-peach chutney,
page 188

rites

If you use wooden skewers, soak them in water for 30 minutes before adding food.

12g CARB. PER SERVING

greek beef kabobs with cucumber salad

prep: 45 minutes grill: 10 minutes
makes: 4 servings (1 skewer and ¾ cup salad each)

2 tablespoons balsamic vinegar
2 teaspoons olive oil
2 teaspoons finely shredded lemon peel
1 teaspoon dried oregano, crushed
2 cloves garlic, minced
¼ teaspoon salt
¼ teaspoon black pepper
1 pound beef top sirloin steak
1 large red sweet pepper, cut into 1½-inch pieces
1 medium onion, halved crosswise and cut into wedges
1 recipe Cucumber Salad

1 In a shallow dish whisk together vinegar, oil, lemon peel, oregano, garlic, salt, and black pepper. Trim fat from meat. Cut meat into 1½-inch pieces. Add meat, sweet pepper, and onion to vinegar mixture; toss. On four 10-inch skewers alternately thread meat, sweet pepper, and onion.

2 For a charcoal grill, place kabobs on the grill rack directly over medium coals. Grill, uncovered, for 10 to 12 minutes or until meat reaches desired doneness, turning once halfway through grilling. (For a gas grill, preheat grill. Reduce heat to medium. Place kabobs on grill rack over heat. Cover and grill as directed.) Serve with Cucumber Salad.

nutrition facts per serving: 278 cal., 12 g total fat (4 g sat. fat), 63 mg chol., 373 mg sodium, 12 g carb. (2 g fiber, 6 g sugars), 28 g pro. exchanges: 1.5 vegetable, 0.5 carb., 3.5 lean meat, 1 fat.

cucumber salad: In a medium bowl stir together ½ cup plain fat-free Greek yogurt; 2 cloves garlic, minced; ½ teaspoon finely shredded lemon peel; ½ teaspoon dried dill weed; ¼ teaspoon salt; and dash cayenne pepper. Stir in 3 cups thinly sliced cucumber (1 large) and ½ cup thinly slivered red onion.

If desired, substitute 1 to 2 teaspoons of your favorite Southwest seasoning blend for the chili powder, cumin, garlic powder, black pepper, and salt.

southwest flank steak

prep: 20 minutes   grill: 17 minutes   stand: 5 minutes
makes: 4 servings (4 ounces cooked beef, ¼ cup salsa, and 1 tablespoon queso fresco each)

3g
CARB. PER
SERVING

4 medium tomatillos, husked, rinsed, and coarsely chopped
¼ cup snipped fresh cilantro
1 medium fresh jalapeño chile pepper, seeded and finely chopped (see tip, *page 188*)
1 clove garlic, minced
⅛ teaspoon salt
1 1¼- to 1½-pound beef flank steak, cut 1 inch thick
1 teaspoon chili powder
¼ teaspoon ground cumin
¼ teaspoon garlic powder
¼ teaspoon black pepper
⅛ teaspoon salt
¼ cup crumbled queso fresco or shredded Monterey Jack cheese (1 ounce) (optional)

1 For tomatillo salsa, in a food processor combine tomatillos, cilantro, jalapeño, garlic, and ⅛ teaspoon salt. Cover and process with several on/off turns until mixture is chopped. Set aside.

2 Trim fat from steak. Score both sides of steak in a diamond pattern; set aside. In a small bowl stir together chili powder, cumin, garlic powder, black pepper, and ⅛ teaspoon salt. Sprinkle evenly over both sides of steak.

3 For a charcoal grill, place steak on the grill rack directly over medium coals. Grill, uncovered, for 17 to 21 minutes for medium (160°F), turning once halfway through grilling. (For a gas grill, preheat grill. Reduce heat to medium. Place steak on grill rack over heat. Cover and grill as directed.)

4 Transfer steak to a cutting board. Cover loosely with foil; let stand for 5 minutes. Thinly slice steak diagonally across the grain. Serve with tomatillo salsa. If desired, sprinkle with queso fresco.

nutrition facts per serving: 243 cal., 11 g total fat (4 g sat. fat), 57 mg chol., 231 mg sodium, 3 g carb. (1 g fiber, 2 g sugars), 31 g pro. exchanges: 0.5 vegetable, 4 lean meat, 1 fat.

13g
CARB. PER
SERVING

sizzlin' grilled favorites

Most flank steaks weigh 2 pounds. If you buy a 2-pound flank steak for this recipe, cut it in half and freeze the extra pound for later.

chipotle-marinated flank steak

prep: 20 minutes   marinate: 2 hours   grill: 17 minutes   stand: 5 minutes
makes: 4 servings (4 ounces steak, 1 tomato, and ¼ cup grilled onions each)

¼ cup red wine vinegar
1 tablespoon olive oil
2 canned chipotle peppers in adobo sauce, chopped (see tip, *page 188*)
2 teaspoons pure maple syrup
1 teaspoon dried oregano, crushed
1 clove garlic, minced
¼ teaspoon black pepper
1 pound beef flank steak, trimmed
1 medium sweet onion, cut into ¼-inch slices
4 medium roma tomatoes, halved lengthwise
Nonstick cooking spray

1 For marinade, in a small bowl stir together the vinegar, olive oil, chipotle pepper, maple syrup, oregano, garlic, and black pepper; set aside. Score both sides of steak in a diamond pattern with shallow diagonal cuts at 1-inch intervals. Place steak in a large resealable plastic bag set in a shallow dish. Pour marinade over steak in bag; seal bag. Turn to coat steak. Marinate in the refrigerator for 2 to 4 hours, turning bag occasionally.

2 Drain steak, discarding marinade. Lightly coat onion slices and tomato halves with cooking spray. For a gas or charcoal grill, place steak on the grill rack directly over medium heat. Grill, covered, for 17 to 21 minutes for medium (160°F), turning once halfway through grilling. Grill onion slices and tomato halves for 4 to 6 minutes or until charred and tender, turning once halfway through grilling. Let steak stand for 5 minutes. Thinly slice steak diagonally across the grain into bite-size pieces. Cut onion slices in half.

3 Serve steak with onions and tomato halves. If desired, sprinkle with *snipped fresh cilantro* and serve with *lime wedges*.

nutrition facts per serving: 244 cal., 10 g total fat (3 g sat. fat), 75 mg chol., 78 mg sodium, 13 g carb. (3 g fiber), 7 g sugars), 25 g pro. exchanges: 2 vegetable, 3 lean meat, 1 fat.

For bread crumbs, cut a slice of bread into ½-inch cubes. Bake at 300°F in a single layer for 10 to 15 minutes or until golden, stirring once or twice. Cool; process the cubes in a food processor. Measure the amount needed.

stuffed steak pinwheels

4 g
CARB. PER
SERVING

prep: 30 minutes grill: 12 minutes
makes: 6 servings (2 pinwheels each)

8   slices turkey bacon
1   1- to 1¼-pound beef
      flank steak
¾   teaspoon lemon-
      pepper seasoning
1   10-ounce package
      frozen chopped
      spinach, thawed
      and well drained
⅓   cup crumbled
      reduced-fat feta
      cheese
2   tablespoons fine dry
      bread crumbs
½   teaspoon dried
      thyme, crushed
      Fresh thyme sprigs
      (optional)
      Grilled cherry
      tomatoes and/
      or halved small
      tomatoes (optional)

* test kitchen tip: If using wooden skewers, soak them in enough water to cover for at least 30 minutes before using.

1 In a large skillet cook bacon over medium heat just until browned but not crisp. Drain bacon on paper towels.

2 Trim fat from steak. Score both sides of steak in a diamond pattern by making shallow diagonal cuts at 1-inch intervals. Cut steak in half lengthwise. Place each portion of steak between two pieces of plastic wrap. Working from the center to edges, pound lightly with the flat side of a meat mallet into 10×6-inch rectangles. Remove plastic wrap. Sprinkle steaks with ½ teaspoon of the lemon-pepper seasoning. Arrange bacon slices lengthwise on steaks.

3 For stuffing, in a medium bowl combine spinach, feta cheese, bread crumbs, thyme, and the remaining ¼ teaspoon lemon-pepper seasoning. Spread stuffing over bacon. Starting from a short side, roll up each steak into a spiral. Secure with wooden toothpicks at 1-inch intervals, starting ½ inch from one end. Cutting between the toothpicks, slice each roll into six 1-inch pinwheels. On each of six 6-inch skewers* thread two pinwheels.

4 For a charcoal grill, place skewers on rack directly over medium coals. Grill, uncovered, 12 to 14 minutes for medium (160°F), turning once halfway through grilling. (For a gas grill, preheat grill. Reduce heat to medium. Place skewers on grill rack over heat. Cover and grill as directed.)

5 To serve, remove pinwheels from skewers; discard toothpicks. If desired, garnish pinwheels with fresh thyme sprigs and serve with grilled cherry tomatoes and/or halved small tomatoes.

nutrition facts per serving: 206 cal., 10 g total fat (4 g sat. fat), 53 mg chol., 578 mg sodium, 4 g carb. (2 g fiber, 1 g sugars), 22 g pro. exchanges: 3 lean meat, 1.5 fat.

Ancho chiles are the dried version of poblano peppers; the ground ancho powder will bring mild to medium-hot spicy appeal to the steak.

coffee-rubbed beef with red-eye beans

24g
CARB. PER SERVING

prep: 20 minutes grill: 8 minutes stand: 5 minutes
makes: 4 servings (1 steak and ⅓ cup beans each)

2   teaspoons ground ancho chile pepper
2   teaspoons instant espresso coffee powder
1   teaspoon paprika
1   teaspoon dry mustard
1   teaspoon packed brown sugar *
1   teaspoon dried oregano, crushed
½   teaspoon black pepper
¼   teaspoon ground cumin
¼   teaspoon salt
1   pound beef shoulder petite tenders
    Nonstick cooking spray
1   recipe Red-Eye Beans
¼   cup finely chopped red onion

1 In a small bowl stir together the ancho chile pepper, espresso powder, paprika, mustard, brown sugar, oregano, black pepper, cumin, and salt. Trim fat from meat. Lightly coat meat with cooking spray. Sprinkle meat evenly with spice mixture, rubbing it in with your fingers.

2 For a gas or charcoal grill, place beef tenders on the grill rack directly over medium heat. Grill, covered, to desired doneness, turning once halfway through grilling. Allow 8 to 12 minutes for medium rare (145°F) or 10 to 15 minutes for medium (160°F). Let tenders stand for 5 minutes. Slice tenders. Spoon Red-Eye Beans into four shallow dishes. Place beef slices on top of beans and sprinkle with red onion.

nutrition facts per serving: 294 cal., 9 g total fat (3 g sat. fat), 65 mg chol., 553 mg sodium, 24 g carb. (5 g fiber, 7 g sugars), 28 g pro. exchanges: 1.5 starch, 3.5 lean meat, 0.5 fat.

nutrition facts per serving with substitute: Same as original, except 292 cal., 552 mg sodium, 23 g carb.

*sugar substitutes: Choose from Splenda Brown Sugar Blend or Sugar Twin Granulated Brown. Follow package directions to use product amount equivalent to 1 teaspoon brown sugar.

red-eye beans: In a small saucepan cook ¼ cup chopped onion and 1 clove garlic, minced, in 1 teaspoon hot canola oil over medium heat for 4 to 6 minutes or until tender. Stir in one 15-ounce can no-salt-added pinto beans, rinsed and drained; ½ cup water; 1 tablespoon molasses; 2 teaspoons reduced-sodium Worcestershire sauce; 1 teaspoon instant espresso coffee powder; 1 teaspoon ground ancho chile pepper; ½ teaspoon ground cumin; ¼ teaspoon black pepper; and ⅛ teaspoon salt. Bring to boiling; reduce heat. Simmer, covered, for 15 minutes to blend flavors, stirring occasionally.

Jamaican jerk seasoning is a blend of spices that can include allspice, thyme, clove, ginger, cinnamon, onion, chile peppers, sugar, and salt. Use this jazzy mix with grilled fish and chicken, too.

jerk-seasoned beef skewers

prep: 25 minutes marinate: 4 hours grill: 8 minutes
makes: 4 servings (2 skewers each)

14g CARB. PER SERVING

¼ cup snipped fresh cilantro
¼ cup rice vinegar
¼ cup orange juice
2 tablespoons canola oil
2 cloves garlic, minced
2 teaspoons Jamaican jerk seasoning
1 pound boneless beef sirloin steak, trimmed of fat and cut into 1-inch cubes
2 small green sweet peppers, cut into 2-inch pieces
1 medium onion, cut into thin wedges
2 medium oranges, cut into 8 wedges each

1 For marinade, in a small bowl whisk together cilantro, vinegar, orange juice, oil, garlic, and jerk seasoning. Pour mixture into a large resealable plastic bag set in a deep bowl. Add beef, pepper pieces, and onion wedges. Seal bag; turn to coat meat. Marinate in refrigerator for 4 to 6 hours, turning occasionally.

2 Drain meat and vegetables, discarding marinade. On eight 10- to 12-inch skewers* alternately thread beef, pepper pieces, onion wedges, and orange wedges, leaving ¼ inch space between pieces.

3 For a charcoal grill, place kabobs on the grill rack directly over medium coals. Grill, uncovered, for 8 to 10 minutes or until beef pieces are slightly pink in the center, turning occasionally. (For a gas grill, preheat grill. Reduce heat to medium. Place kabobs on grill rack over heat. Cover and grill as directed.)

nutrition facts per serving: 242 cal., 9 g total fat (2 g sat. fat), 53 mg chol., 144 mg sodium, 14 g carb. (3 g fiber, 9 g sugars), 26 g pro. exchanges: 1 vegetable, 0.5 fruit, 3.5 lean meat, 1 fat.

✳ test kitchen tip: If using wooden skewers, soak them in enough water to cover for at least 30 minutes before using.

The pomegranate juice adds a deep, fruity-tart flavor to the marinade and the glaze. The fruit's seeds bring color, sparkle, and crunch to the salad.

30g CARB. PER SERVING

glazed pork chops with spinach-pom salad

prep: 25 minutes marinate: 6 hours cook: 15 minutes grill: 8 minutes
makes: 4 servings (1 pork chop and 1 cup salad each)

- 4 pork loin chops with bone, cut ¾ inch thick (about 1½ pounds)
- 2 cups pomegranate or cranberry juice
- 1 small red onion, finely chopped (½ cup)
- ¼ cup orange juice or port wine
- 1 tablespoon Dijon-style mustard
- 2 teaspoons grated fresh ginger
- 2 cloves garlic, minced
- ½ teaspoon ground nutmeg
- ¼ teaspoon black pepper
- 1 recipe Spinach-Pom Salad

1 Trim fat from chops. Place chops in a large resealable plastic bag set in a shallow dish. For marinade, in a medium bowl stir together pomegranate juice, onion, orange juice, mustard, ginger, garlic, nutmeg, and pepper. Reserve 1 cup of the marinade; cover and refrigerate until needed. Pour remaining marinade over chops in bag; seal bag. Marinate in the refrigerator for 6 to 24 hours, turning bag occasionally. Drain chops, discarding marinade.

2 For glaze, place reserved 1 cup marinade in a small saucepan. Bring to boiling. Boil, uncovered, for 15 to 18 minutes or until reduced to ¼ cup. Remove from heat.

3 For a charcoal grill, place chops on the grill rack directly over medium coals. Grill, uncovered, for 8 to 9 minutes or until chops are slightly pink in the center (145°F), turning once and brushing both sides with glaze halfway through grilling. (For a gas grill, preheat grill. Reduce heat to medium. Place chops on grill rack over heat. Cover and grill as directed.)

4 Brush pork chops with reduced glaze and serve with Spinach-Pom Salad.

nutrition facts per serving: 360 cal., 8 g total fat (2 g sat. fat), 117 mg chol., 343 mg sodium, 30 g carb. (2 g fiber, 22 g sugars), 40 g pro. exchanges: 1.5 vegetable, 1 fruit, 0.5 carb., 5 lean meat.

spinach-pom salad: In a large bowl combine 4 cups fresh baby spinach; 1 small cucumber, peeled if desired and thinly sliced; and ¼ cup slivered red onion. Toss with 3 tablespoons bottled reduced-fat raspberry vinaigrette. Top with ⅓ cup pomegranate seeds.

Most grocery stores sell peeled and cored fresh pineapple. Look for it in the produce section by other cut-up fruit.

grilled pork and pineapple

27 g
CARB. PER SERVING

start to finish: 20 minutes

makes: 4 servings (1 pork chop, about 2 pineapple slices, and about 3 tablespoons yogurt mixture each)

4	¾-inch-thick boneless top loin pork chops (about 1¼ pounds total)
¼	teaspoon salt
¼	teaspoon black pepper
1	fresh pineapple, peeled and cored
1	6-ounce carton plain fat-free yogurt
⅓	cup low-sugar orange marmalade
1	tablespoon snipped fresh thyme

1 Sprinkle both sides of pork with the salt and pepper. Cut pineapple crosswise into ½-inch-thick slices; set aside. Combine yogurt and 2 tablespoons of the marmalade; set aside.

2 For a charcoal grill, place chops on the grill rack directly over medium coals. Grill, uncovered, for 4 minutes. Turn; add pineapple to grill. Brush chops and pineapple with remaining marmalade. Grill for 3 to 5 minutes more or until an instant-read thermometer inserted in pork registers 145°F and pineapple has light grill marks, turning pineapple once. Let pork rest for 3 minutes. (For a gas grill, preheat grill. Reduce heat to medium. Place chops on grill rack. Cover and grill as directed.)

3 Arrange pineapple and chops on serving plates. Spoon yogurt mixture over chops and pineapple; sprinkle with fresh thyme.

nutrition facts per serving: 263 cal., 4 g total fat (1 g sat. fat), 78 mg chol., 231 mg sodium, 27 g carb. (2 g fiber, 21 g sugars), 29 g pro. exchanges: 1 fruit, 1 carb., 4 lean meat.

If you can't find shallots, substitute ¼ cup finely chopped yellow or white onion and 1 finely chopped garlic clove. Pictured on page 179.

pork chops with jalapeño-peach chutney

13g CARB. PER SERVING

prep: 20 minutes   cook: 13 minutes   grill: 7 minutes
makes: 4 servings (5¼ ounces pork and ½ cup chutney each)

¼   cup finely chopped shallot
1   teaspoon canola oil
2   cups chopped peeled fresh or frozen peaches
⅓   cup finely chopped red sweet pepper
1   to 2 tablespoons finely chopped fresh jalapeño chile pepper*
1   tablespoon cider vinegar
2   teaspoons packed brown sugar
⅛   teaspoon ground cinnamon
2   tablespoons snipped fresh cilantro
1   teaspoon chili powder
1   teaspoon dried oregano, crushed
½   teaspoon dried sage, crushed
¼   teaspoon ground cumin
¼   teaspoon granulated garlic
¼   teaspoon salt
¼   teaspoon black pepper
4   boneless pork loin chops, cut 1 inch thick (1½ pounds total)
    Nonstick cooking spray

1 For chutney, in a medium saucepan cook shallot in hot oil over medium heat for 3 to 5 minutes or until tender. Stir in peaches, sweet pepper, jalapeño pepper, vinegar, brown sugar, and cinnamon. Cook about 10 minutes or until peaches are tender and chutney has thickened. Stir in cilantro. Set aside.

2 In a small bowl stir together chili powder, oregano, sage, cumin, garlic, salt, and black pepper. Trim fat from chops. Lightly coat chops with cooking spray. Sprinkle chops evenly with spice mixture and rub in with your fingers.

3 For a gas or charcoal grill, place chops on the grill rack directly over medium heat. Grill, covered, for 7 to 9 minutes or until chops are slightly pink in center and juices run clear (145°F), turning once halfway through grilling. Serve chops with chutney.

nutrition facts per serving: 297 cal., 10 g total fat (3 g sat. fat), 95 mg chol., 261 mg sodium, 13 g carb. (2 g fiber, 10 g sugars), 38 g pro. exchanges: 1 fruit, 5.5 lean meat.

*test kitchen tip: Because chile peppers contain volatile oils that can burn your skin and eyes, avoid direct contact with them as much as possible. When working with chile peppers, wear plastic or rubber gloves. If your bare hands do touch the peppers, wash your hands and nails well with soap and warm water.

Apricot and pork taste great together, and the ginger, soy sauce, and red pepper add a little kick to the dish.

apricot-ginger glazed pork tenderloin

34g
CARB. PER
SERVING

prep: 20 minutes cook: 40 minutes grill: 25 minutes stand: 10 minutes
makes: 4 servings (3½ ounces cooked pork and ¾ cup rice pilaf each)

¾ cup uncooked brown rice
2 cloves garlic, minced
2 teaspoons olive oil
1½ cups reduced-sodium chicken broth or water
1 medium carrot, chopped (½ cup)
2 tablespoons low-sugar apricot preserves
1 teaspoon grated fresh ginger
1 teaspoon reduced-sodium soy sauce
¼ teaspoon crushed red pepper
1 1-pound pork tenderloin
½ cup halved snow pea pods
¼ cup thinly sliced green onions (2)

1 For rice pilaf, in a medium saucepan cook and stir rice and 1 clove of the garlic in olive oil over medium heat for 3 minutes. Carefully stir in broth and carrot. Bring to boiling; reduce heat. Cover and simmer for 40 to 45 minutes or until rice is tender and liquid is absorbed.

2 Meanwhile, for glaze, finely snip any large pieces of preserves. In a small bowl stir together preserves, ginger, soy sauce, the remaining clove garlic, and crushed red pepper. Divide mixture in half.

3 For a charcoal grill, arrange hot coals around a drip pan. Test for medium-hot heat above the pan. Place tenderloin on the greased grill rack over drip pan. Cover and grill for 25 to 30 minutes or until an instant-read thermometer inserted in center of tenderloin registers 145°F, turning tenderloin and brushing occasionally with half of the glaze. (For a gas grill, preheat grill. Reduce heat to medium-high. Adjust for indirect cooking. Place tenderloin on greased grill rack over burner that is turned off. Cover and grill as directed).

4 Transfer tenderloin to a cutting board. Cover loosely with foil. Let stand for 5 minutes before slicing. Stir pea pods into hot rice mixture; cover and let stand for 5 minutes.

5 To serve, top slices of pork with remaining glaze. Serve with rice pilaf. Sprinkle with green onions.

nutrition facts per serving: 307 cal., 6 g total fat (1 g sat. fat), 74 mg chol., 337 mg sodium, 34 g carb (2 g fiber, 5 g sugars), 28 g pro. exchanges: 2 starch, 3.5 lean meat.

You'll love the combination of sweet red peppers and warm, spicy flavor notes. The romaine lettuce provides contrasting color and crunch.

26g CARB. PER SERVING

peppered pork burgers

prep: 20 minutes grill: 10 minutes
makes: 4 servings (1 burger each)

1   recipe Honey-
    Mustard Spread
12 ounces lean ground
    pork∗
½   teaspoon black
    pepper
½   teaspoon paprika
¼   teaspoon garlic
    powder
¼   teaspoon ground
    cumin
⅛   teaspoon salt
4   whole wheat
    hamburger buns,
    split and toasted
2   romaine lettuce
    leaves, halved
¾   cup bottled roasted
    red sweet peppers,
    drained and divided
    into large pieces

1 Prepare Honey-Mustard Spread; cover and chill. In a medium bowl combine pork, black pepper, paprika, garlic powder, cumin, and salt. Shape into four ½-inch-thick patties.

2 For a charcoal grill, place patties on the grill rack directly over medium coals. Grill, uncovered, for 10 to 12 minutes or until an instant-read thermometer inserted into side of each patty registers 160°F, turning patties once halfway through grilling. (For a gas grill, preheat grill. Reduce heat to medium. Place patties on the grill rack over heat. Cover and grill as directed.)

3 To assemble, spread Honey-Mustard Spread on cut sides of bun tops. Place lettuce leaves, grilled burgers, and roasted red peppers on bun bottoms. Add bun tops, spread sides down.

nutrition facts per serving: 272 cal., 8 g total fat (2 g sat. fat), 63 mg chol., 510 mg sodium, 26 g carb. (3 g fiber, 6 g sugars), 23 g pro. exchanges: 2 starch, 2.5 lean meat, 0.5 fat.

∗test kitchen tip: Instead of purchasing ground pork, which can be high in fat, buy a whole piece of lean pork loin and grind it in a food processor.

honey-mustard spread: In a small bowl combine 3 tablespoons light mayonnaise, 1 tablespoon Dijon-style mustard, and 1 teaspoon honey.

Not a fan of lamb? Try the spice mixture on beef kabobs, using beef tenderloin roast, cut into 1½-inch pieces, instead of lamb roast.

southwestern grilled lamb kabobs

34g
CARB. PER SERVING

prep: 30 minutes grill: 10 minutes
makes: 4 servings (1 kabob, ½ cup rice, and ⅓ cup sauce each)

1	tablespoon ground ancho chile pepper
1½	teaspoons ground cumin
1	teaspoon olive oil
½	teaspoon garlic powder
½	teaspoon onion powder
¼	teaspoon salt
¼	teaspoon black pepper
1¼	pounds boneless lamb sirloin roast
2	cups hot cooked brown rice
1	recipe Southwest Tomato Sauce
	Snipped fresh cilantro

1 In a medium bowl stir together the ground ancho chile pepper, cumin, olive oil, garlic powder, onion powder, salt, and black pepper; set aside. Trim fat from meat. Cut meat into 1¼- to 1½-inch pieces. Place meat in bowl with spice mixture; stir to coat. Thread meat onto four 10-inch skewers,✳ leaving a ¼-inch space between pieces. Set aside.

2 For gas or charcoal grill, place kabobs on the grill rack directly over medium heat. Grill, covered, for 10 to 12 minutes or until meat reaches desired doneness, turning once halfway through grilling. Divide rice among four serving plates and spoon tomato sauce over rice. Sprinkle with cilantro. Place one kabob on each serving plate.

nutrition facts per serving: 327 cal., 10 g total fat (3 g sat. fat), 67 mg chol., 354 mg sodium, 34 g carb. (5 g fiber, 6 g sugars), 27 g pro. exchanges: 1 vegetable, 2 starch, 3 lean meat, 0.5 fat.

✳test kitchen tip: If using wooden skewers, soak them in enough water to cover for at least 30 minutes before using.

southwest tomato sauce: In a large saucepan cook ½ cup chopped onion and 1 clove garlic, minced, in 1 teaspoon hot olive oil over medium heat for 4 to 6 minutes or until tender, stirring occasionally. Stir in one 14.5- to 15-ounce can crushed tomatoes, undrained; ½ teaspoon ground ancho chile pepper; ½ teaspoon dried oregano, crushed; ¼ teaspoon ground cumin; ¼ teaspoon dried thyme, crushed; and ¼ teaspoon black pepper. Bring to boiling; reduce heat. Simmer, uncovered, for 8 to 10 minutes or until slightly thickened. Process sauce with an immersion blender or cool slightly and process in a blender until smooth. Keep warm.

In France, chèvre refers to any goat cheese. In the U.S., it sometimes refers specifically to a soft, spreadable goat cheese that has not been aged long enough to develop a rind.

8 g
CARB. PER
SERVING

artichoke-chèvre chicken breasts

prep: 25 minutes **marinate:** 2 hours **grill:** 10 minutes
makes: 4 servings (1 chicken breast and ⅓ cup artichoke mixture each)

½ cup loosely packed fresh basil leaves
2 cloves garlic, coarsely chopped
2 tablespoons white wine vinegar or white balsamic vinegar
1 tablespoon olive oil
¼ teaspoon black pepper
⅛ teaspoon salt
4 5-ounce skinless, boneless chicken breast halves
¼ cup finely chopped shallot
2 cloves garlic, minced
1 teaspoon olive oil
1 14-ounce can artichoke hearts, drained and coarsely chopped
½ cup reduced-sodium chicken broth
2 tablespoons snipped dried tomatoes (not oil-packed)
2 ounces goat cheese (chèvre)
2 tablespoons snipped fresh basil

1 For marinade, in a blender or food processor combine the ½ cup basil, 2 cloves garlic, the vinegar, the 1 tablespoon olive oil, the pepper, and salt. Cover and blend or process until almost smooth. Place chicken breasts in a large resealable plastic bag set in a shallow dish. Pour marinade over chicken in bag; seal bag. Turn to coat chicken. Marinate in the refrigerator for 2 to 4 hours, turning bag occasionally.

2 In a large nonstick skillet cook shallot and 2 cloves garlic in the 1 teaspoon hot oil over medium heat for 3 to 5 minutes or until tender, stirring occasionally. Stir in artichoke hearts, chicken broth, and tomatoes. Simmer for 2 minutes or until most of the liquid is evaporated. Stir in half of the goat cheese and 1 tablespoon of the snipped basil; keep warm.

3 Drain chicken, discarding marinade. For a charcoal grill, place chicken on the grill rack directly over medium coals. Grill, uncovered, for 10 to 12 minutes or until chicken is no longer pink (170°F), turning once halfway through grilling. (For a gas grill, preheat grill. Reduce heat to medium. Place chicken on grill rack over heat. Cover and grill as directed.) Serve chicken with artichoke mixture. Sprinkle the remaining goat cheese and remaining 1 tablespoon snipped basil over the chicken.

nutrition facts per serving: 277 cal., 11 g total fat (4 g sat. fat), 97 mg chol., 562 mg sodium, 8 g carb. (2 g fiber, 3 g sugars), 35 g pro. exchanges: 1.5 vegetable, 4 lean meat, 1 fat.

Keep cayenne pepper, paprika, and other red spices in the refrigerator to help them stay fresh. Most other spices can be stored in a cool, dark, dry place up to 6 months.

42g CARB. PER SERVING

tandoori chicken thighs

prep: 20 minutes marinate: 12 hours grill: 20 minutes
makes: 4 servings (1 chicken thigh and about ⅔ cup couscous each)

½ cup plain fat-free yogurt

1 teaspoon finely shredded lemon peel

2 tablespoons lemon juice

2 tablespoons snipped fresh cilantro

1 teaspoon paprika

1 teaspoon grated fresh ginger

2 cloves garlic, minced

½ teaspoon ground cumin

½ teaspoon ground turmeric

¼ teaspoon ground cardamom

⅛ teaspoon cayenne pepper

4 skinless, boneless chicken thighs (about 1 pound total)

1 recipe Lemon Couscous

1 For sauce, in a shallow dish stir together yogurt, lemon peel, lemon juice, cilantro, paprika, ginger, garlic, cumin, turmeric, cardamom, and cayenne pepper. Reserve ¼ cup of the mixture; cover and chill until serving time. Add chicken to the remaining mixture; turn to coat. Cover and marinate chicken in the refrigerator for 12 to 24 hours.

2 For a charcoal grill, place chicken on the grill rack directly over medium coals. Grill, uncovered, for 20 to 25 minutes or until no longer pink (180°F), turning once halfway through grilling. (For a gas grill, preheat grill. Reduce heat to medium. Place chicken on grill rack over heat. Cover and grill as directed.) Serve with reserved sauce and Lemon Couscous.

nutrition facts per serving: 358 cal., 8 g total fat (1 g sat. fat), 94 mg chol., 264 mg sodium, 42 g carb. (7 g fiber, 6 g sugars), 31 g pro. exchanges: 2.5 starch, 4 lean meat.

lemon couscous: In a medium saucepan cook ¾ cup whole wheat couscous according to package directions, omitting any salt or oil. Stir in 2 tablespoons snipped fresh cilantro; 2 tablespoons pine nuts, toasted; 2 tablespoons dried currants; 2 teaspoons finely shredded lemon peel; 1 clove garlic, minced; and ¼ teaspoon salt.

You can substitute 2 cups chopped frozen unsweetened peach slices, thawed, for the fresh peaches if you like. However, if you do, don't grill the frozen slices.

chipotle chicken with peach salsa

10 g
CARB. PER SERVING

prep: 15 minutes   marinate: 30 minutes   grill: 12 minutes
makes: 4 servings (4 ounces cooked chicken and ½ cup salsa each)

2 teaspoons finely chopped canned chipotle peppers in adobo sauce

1 teaspoon adobo sauce from chipotle peppers

½ teaspoon ground cumin

⅛ teaspoon salt

1 to 1¼ pounds skinless, boneless chicken breast halves

2 peaches, halved and pitted
Nonstick cooking spray

¼ cup finely chopped red onion

¼ cup snipped fresh cilantro

3 tablespoons lime juice

1 tablespoon finely chopped fresh jalapeño chile pepper (see tip, *page 188*)

1 clove garlic, minced

1 In a shallow dish stir together chipotle peppers, adobo sauce, cumin, and salt. Add chicken, turning to coat. Cover and marinate in the refrigerator for 30 to 60 minutes.

2 For a charcoal grill, place chicken on the greased grill rack directly over medium coals. Grill, uncovered, for 12 to 15 minutes or until no longer pink (170°F), turning once halfway through grilling. (For a gas grill, preheat grill. Reduce heat to medium. Place chicken on greased grill rack over heat. Cover and grill as directed.) Coat both sides of peach halves with cooking spray. Add peach halves to grill rack with chicken; grill for 6 to 8 minutes or until tender and slightly charred, turning once.

3 For peach salsa, chop grilled peaches. In a medium bowl combine peaches, red onion, cilantro, lime juice, chopped jalapeño, and garlic. Remove chicken from grill; slice chicken. Serve chicken with peach salsa.

nutrition facts per serving: 171 cal., 3 g total fat (1 g sat. fat), 73 mg chol., 225 mg sodium, 10 g carb. (2 g fiber, 7 g sugars), 25 g pro. exchanges: 0.5 fruit, 3.5 lean meat.

14g CARB. PER SERVING

Brussels sprouts are not generally thought of as crowd-pleasers, but you may be surprised at how fast these get gobbled up. Grilling them brings out fascinating nutty flavors.

kickin' lemon chicken

prep: 30 minutes marinate: 30 minutes cook: 10 minutes grill: 12 minutes
makes: 4 servings (1 chicken breast, 4 ounces Brussels sprouts, and 5 tomatoes each)

2 teaspoons finely shredded lemon peel
¾ cup lemon juice
1 tablespoon olive oil
4 cloves garlic, minced
½ to 1 teaspoon crushed red pepper
¼ teaspoon salt
4 4- to 5-ounce skinless, boneless chicken breast halves
1 pound Brussels sprouts, trimmed
20 cherry tomatoes

1 For marinade, in a small bowl whisk together the lemon peel, lemon juice, olive oil, garlic, crushed red pepper, and salt. Reserve ¼ cup of the marinade. Place chicken breasts in a large resealable plastic bag set in a shallow dish. Pour remaining marinade over chicken in bag; seal bag. Turn to coat chicken. Marinate in the refrigerator for 30 minutes, turning bag once.

2 Meanwhile, place Brussels sprouts in a steamer basket. Place basket in a Dutch oven over 1 inch of boiling water. Steam, covered, for 10 to 12 minutes or until tender. Immediately transfer Brussels sprouts to ice water to cool. Drain well.

3 Drain chicken, discarding marinade. Thread Brussels sprouts and tomatoes on four 12-inch skewers.✱ Brush skewers with some of the reserved ¼ cup marinade.

4 For a charcoal grill, place chicken on the grill rack directly over medium coals. Grill, uncovered, for 12 to 15 minutes or until chicken is no longer pink (170°F), turning once halfway through grilling. Grill the vegetable skewers for 10 to 12 minutes or until Brussels sprouts are browned, turning skewers occasionally and brushing with reserved marinade once halfway through grilling. (For a gas grill, preheat grill. Reduce heat to medium. Place chicken and vegetable skewers on grill rack over heat. Cover and grill as directed.) Serve chicken with vegetable skewers.

nutrition facts per serving: 234 cal., 5 g total fat (1 g sat. fat), 91 mg chol., 236 mg sodium, 14 g carb. (5 g fiber, 5 g sugars), 34 g pro. exchanges: 3 vegetable, 4 lean meat.

✱test kitchen tip: If using wooden skewers, soak them in enough water to cover for at least 30 minutes before using.

Rich in vitamin C and antioxidants, artichoke hearts lend a touch of sophistication and wonderful flavor to this veggie- and cheese-stuffed chicken.

mediterranean stuffed chicken

2g
CARB. PER
SERVING

prep: 20 minutes cook: 12 minutes
makes: 4 servings (1 breast half each)

4   skinless, boneless chicken breast halves (1 to 1½ pounds total)
¼   cup crumbled reduced-fat feta cheese (1 ounce)
¼   cup finely chopped, drained bottled marinated artichoke hearts
2   tablespoons finely chopped, drained bottled roasted red sweet peppers
2   tablespoons thinly sliced green onion (1)
2   teaspoons snipped fresh oregano or ½ teaspoon dried oregano, crushed
⅛   teaspoon black pepper
     Nonstick cooking spray

1 Using a sharp knife, cut a pocket in each chicken breast half by cutting horizontally through the thickest portion to, but not through, the opposite side. Set aside.

2 In a small bowl combine feta, artichoke hearts, roasted peppers, green onions, and oregano. Spoon evenly into pockets in chicken breasts. If necessary, secure openings with wooden toothpicks. Sprinkle chicken with the black pepper.

3 For a charcoal grill, grill chicken on the rack of an uncovered grill directly over medium coals for 12 to 15 minutes or until chicken is no longer pink (170°F), turning once halfway through grilling. (For a gas grill, preheat grill. Reduce heat to medium. Place chicken on grill rack over heat. Cover and grill as directed.)

nutrition facts per serving: 171 cal., 5 g total fat (2 g sat. fat), 68 mg chol., 226 mg sodium, 2 g carb. (0 g fiber, 3 g sugars), 28 g pro. exchanges: 4 lean meat, 1 fat.

stove-top directions: Coat an unheated large nonstick skillet with cooking spray. Preheat skillet over medium heat. Add chicken. Cook for 12 to 14 minutes or until no longer pink (170°F), turning once.

22g
CARB. PER
SERVING

Be sure to use only the reserved marinade to flavor the cantaloupe. The marinade that has come into contact with the raw meat must be discarded.

lime-marinated turkey

prep: 10 minutes marinate: 4 hours grill: 12 minutes
makes: 4 servings (4 ounces turkey and 1 cup cantaloupe each)

2 turkey breast tenderloins (1 to 1½ pounds total)
¼ cup finely snipped fresh mint
2 teaspoons finely shredded lime peel
¼ cup lime juice
3 tablespoons orange juice
1 tablespoon olive oil
1 tablespoon honey
¼ teaspoon salt
¼ teaspoon black pepper
4 cups cut-up cantaloupe
  Lime wedges
  Fresh mint sprigs (optional)

1 Cut each turkey tenderloin in half horizontally to make four steaks. Place turkey steaks in a resealable plastic bag set in a shallow dish. For marinade, in a bowl whisk together mint, lime peel, lime juice, orange juice, olive oil, honey, salt, and pepper. Reserve 2 tablespoons marinade; cover and chill. Pour remaining marinade over turkey in bag; seal bag. Marinate in the refrigerator for 4 to 6 hours, turning bag occasionally.

2 Drain turkey, discarding marinade. For a charcoal grill, place turkey on the grill rack directly over medium coals. Grill, uncovered, for 12 to 15 minutes or until no longer pink (170°F), turning once halfway through grilling. (For a gas grill, preheat grill. Reduce heat to medium. Place turkey on grill rack over heat. Cover and grill as directed.)

3 Meanwhile, place cantaloupe in a bowl. Drizzle the 2 tablespoons reserved marinade over cantaloupe and toss to coat. Serve turkey with cantaloupe and lime wedges. If desired, garnish with fresh mint sprigs.

nutrition facts per serving: 242 cal., 5 g total fat (1 g sat. fat), 70 mg chol., 230 mg sodium, 22 g carb. (2 g fiber, 18 g sugars), 30 g pro. exchanges: 1 fruit, 0.5 carb., 4 lean meat.

Sweet plums and salty bacon help the flavors really take off! If your plums are already ripe when you buy them, refrigerate them to help slow down further ripening.

plum-delicious bacon-wrapped turkey tenderloins

 11g
CARB. PER SERVING

prep: 20 minutes cook: 10 minutes grill: 12 minutes
makes: 6 servings (2 turkey pieces and ⅓ cup plum mixture each)

1 teaspoon ground coriander
1 teaspoon ground cumin
1 teaspoon black pepper
½ teaspoon salt
3 turkey breast tenderloins (2 to 2½ pounds total)
12 slices turkey bacon, cooked just until browned but not crisp
3 medium plums, pitted and sliced
¼ cup grape spreadable fruit
1 tablespoon cider vinegar
   Grilled Asparagus (optional)

1 In a small bowl combine coriander, cumin, pepper, and salt; sprinkle mixture lightly on both sides of turkey tenderloins. Cut each tenderloin crosswise into quarters to make 12 total pieces. Wrap each turkey piece with a slice of bacon and secure with a wooden toothpick.

2 For a charcoal grill, place turkey on the rack directly over medium coals. Grill, uncovered, 12 to 15 minutes or until turkey is no longer pink (170°F), turning halfway through grilling. (For a gas grill, preheat grill. Reduce heat to medium. Place turkey on grill rack over heat. Cover and grill as directed.)

3 Meanwhile, in a medium saucepan, combine plum slices, spreadable fruit, and vinegar. Bring to boiling over medium heat, stirring frequently. Reduce heat; simmer, uncovered, 4 to 6 minutes or until plums are tender. Serve plums over turkey pieces. If desired, serve with grilled asparagus.

nutrition facts per serving: 283 cal., 6 g total fat (2 g sat. fat), 124 mg chol., 629 mg sodium, 11 g carb. (1 g fiber, 10 g sugars), 42 g pro. exchanges: 1 carb., 5.5 lean meat.

grilled asparagus: For a charcoal grill, place asparagus spears on rack directly over medium coals. Grill, uncovered, 3 to 5 minutes or until tender and starting to brown, turning once. (For a gas grill, preheat grill. Reduce heat to medium. Place asparagus on grill rack over heat. Cover and grill as directed.)

The best way to thaw frozen shrimp is in the refrigerator. For a quicker option, microwave on the defrost setting until pliable but still icy. For food safety, shrimp thawed in the microwave must be cooked immediately.

skewered shrimp and tomato linguine

start to finish: 40 minutes
makes: 4 servings (1¼ cups each)

40g
CARB. PER
SERVING

201

12	ounces fresh or frozen large shrimp in shells
24	red and/or yellow cherry or grape tomatoes
1	tablespoon olive oil
1	clove garlic, minced
¼	teaspoon black pepper
⅛	teaspoon salt
6	ounces dried whole grain linguine
1	tablespoon butter
1	tablespoon lemon juice
4	cups torn baby arugula or packaged baby spinach
1	tablespoon snipped fresh oregano
¼	cup finely shredded Parmesan cheese
	Freshly cracked black pepper
	Lemon wedges (optional)

1 Thaw shrimp, if frozen. Peel and devein shrimp. Rinse shrimp; pat dry with paper towels. On four 10-inch metal skewers✱ thread shrimp and tomatoes. In a small bowl whisk together the olive oil, garlic, ¼ teaspoon pepper, and salt. Brush over shrimp and tomatoes on skewers.

2 For a charcoal grill, place skewers on the grill rack directly over medium-hot coals. Grill, uncovered, for 5 to 8 minutes or until shrimp turn opaque, turning once halfway through grilling. (For a gas grill, preheat grill. Reduce heat to medium-hot. Place skewers on grill rack over heat. Cover and grill as directed.)

3 Meanwhile, prepare linguine according to package directions. Drain, reserving ⅓ cup cooking water. Return pasta to saucepan. Add butter and lemon juice. Toss to combine. Add the reserved cooking water, the grilled shrimp and tomatoes, arugula, and oregano. Toss to combine. Sprinkle with Parmesan cheese and cracked black pepper. If desired, serve with lemon wedges.

nutrition facts per serving: 321 cal., 10 g total fat (3 g sat. fat), 118 mg chol., 603 mg sodium, 40 g carb. (7 g fiber, 5 g sugars), 20 g pro. exchanges: 1.5 vegetable, 2 starch, 2 lean meat, 1 fat.

✱test kitchen tip: If using wooden skewers, soak them in enough water to cover for at least 30 minutes before using.

8 g
CARB. PER
SERVING

*If you're out of chili powder, use a
dash of bottled hot pepper sauce plus
equal measures of dried oregano and
ground cumin.*

lemon-chili shrimp skewers

prep: 30 minutes grill: 5 minutes
makes: 4 servings (2 skewers each)

1   pound fresh or frozen
    large shrimp
2   green onions, cut into
    1½-inch pieces
16 cherry tomatoes
1   medium green sweet
    pepper, cut into
    1½-inch pieces
⅓   cup reduced-sugar
    ketchup
2   tablespoons lemon
    juice
1   teaspoon chili
    powder
1   clove garlic, minced
    Hot cooked rice
    (optional)

1 Thaw shrimp, if frozen. Peel and devein
shrimp; rinse and pat dry. On eight 10-inch
skewers✷ alternately thread shrimp, green
onions, tomatoes, and pepper.

2 For sauce, in a small bowl stir together
ketchup, lemon juice, chili powder, and
garlic. Brush shrimp and vegetables with half
of the sauce.

3 For a charcoal grill, place skewers on
the greased grill rack directly over
medium-hot coals. Grill, uncovered, for
5 to 8 minutes or until shrimp turn opaque,
turning once and brushing with remaining
sauce halfway through grilling. (For a gas grill,
preheat grill. Reduce heat to medium-high.
Place skewers on greased grill rack over heat.
Cover and grill as directed.) If desired, serve
over hot cooked rice.

nutrition facts per serving: 152 cal., 2 g total fat
(0 g sat. fat), 172 mg chol., 411 mg sodium, 8 g carb. (2 g fiber,
4 g sugars), 24 g pro. exchanges: 1 vegetable, 3 lean meat.

✷test kitchen tip: If using wooden skewers,
soak them in enough water to cover for at least
30 minutes before using.

Generally, deep-color greens have more vitamins and fiber than light-color greens. That means the emerald green kale in this recipe is a nutritional winner!

salmon with kale sauté

prep: 25 minutes   grill: 8 minutes   cook: 10 minutes
makes: 4 servings (1 salmon fillet and about 1½ cups kale each)

4	5-ounce fresh or frozen skinless salmon fillets, about 1 inch thick
1	teaspoon dried thyme, crushed
½	teaspoon garlic powder
¼	teaspoon salt
¼	teaspoon cayenne pepper
1	teaspoon olive oil
1	medium shallot, finely chopped (2 tablespoons)
1	clove garlic, minced
12	ounces fresh kale, torn and stems discarded
1	teaspoon finely shredded lemon peel
⅛	teaspoon salt Lemon wedges

1 Thaw fish, if frozen. Rinse fish; pat dry with paper towels. Set aside. In a small bowl stir together the thyme, garlic powder, the ¼ teaspoon salt, and the cayenne pepper. Sprinkle tops of fillets evenly with seasoning mixture.

2 For a charcoal grill, place fish on the greased grill rack directly over medium coals. Grill, uncovered, for 8 to 12 minutes or until fish begins to flake when tested with a fork, turning fish once halfway through grilling. (For a gas grill, preheat grill. Reduce heat to medium. Place fish on greased grill rack over heat. Cover and grill as directed.) Cover fish to keep warm.

3 In a Dutch oven cook shallot and garlic in hot oil over medium heat for 2 to 4 minutes or until tender. Add kale and lemon peel. Cover and cook for 2 minutes. Uncover and cook for 6 to 8 minutes more or just until kale is beginning to wilt, turning with long-handled tongs to cook. Sprinkle with the ⅛ teaspoon salt. Serve salmon with kale and lemon wedges.

nutrition facts per serving: 357 cal., 21 g total fat (5 g sat. fat), 78 mg chol., 340 mg sodium, 11 g carb. (2 g fiber, 2 g sugars), 32 g pro. exchanges: 2 vegetable, 4 medium-fat meat.

Fennel brings a faint licorice taste, and basil adds fresh minty-clove flavors to this delightfully aromatic dish.

tuscan tuna with tomato salad

prep: 15 minutes grill: 6 minutes
makes: 4 servings (1 tuna steak and ½ cup tomato salad each)

4   5- to 6-ounce fresh or
    frozen tuna steaks,
    about 1 inch thick
3   teaspoons white
    wine vinegar
1   teaspoon olive oil
½   teaspoon dried Italian
    seasoning, crushed
¼   teaspoon salt
¼   teaspoon black
    pepper
2   medium tomatoes,
    seeded and
    chopped (1 cup)
½   cup thinly sliced
    fennel bulb
¼   cup snipped fresh
    basil
1   medium shallot,
    halved and thinly
    sliced
1   clove garlic, minced
¼   teaspoon black
    pepper
1   tablespoon pine
    nuts, toasted and
    chopped*
1   tablespoon finely
    shredded Parmesan
    cheese

1 Thaw fish, if frozen. Rinse fish; pat dry with paper towels. Set aside. In a small bowl stir together 1 teaspoon of the vinegar, the olive oil, Italian seasoning, salt, and ¼ teaspoon pepper. Brush on both sides of tuna steaks. Set aside.

2 For tomato salad, in a medium bowl stir together tomatoes, fennel, basil, shallot, garlic, the remaining 2 teaspoons vinegar, and ¼ teaspoon pepper. Set aside.

3 For a charcoal grill, place fish on the greased grill rack directly over medium coals. Grill, uncovered, for 6 to 8 minutes or until fish begins to flake when tested with a fork, turning fish once halfway through grilling. (For a gas grill, preheat grill. Reduce heat to medium. Place fish on a greased grill rack over heat. Cover and grill as directed.)

4 Serve tuna with tomato salad. Sprinkle with pine nuts and Parmesan cheese.

nutrition facts per serving: 255 cal., 10 g total fat (2 g sat. fat), 55 mg chol., 232 mg sodium, 5 g carb. (1 g fiber, 2 g sugars), 35 g pro. exchanges: 0.5 vegetable, 5 lean meat, 0.5 fat.

*test kitchen tip: Toast pine nuts in a dry skillet over medium heat, shaking the skillet frequently to prevent burning.

Place any leftover ginger, unpeeled, in a freezer bag. It freezes well, and you can peel and grate the frozen root as needed.

plank-grilled tuna steaks

prep: 20 minutes   marinate: 1 hour   soak: 30 minutes   grill: 14 minutes
makes: 4 servings (1 tuna steak and 2 baby bok choy halves each)

4   5- to 6-ounce fresh or
      frozen tuna steaks,
      about 1 inch thick
2   tablespoons rice
      vinegar
2   tablespoons finely
      chopped green
      onion
½   teaspoon finely
      shredded lime peel
1   tablespoon lime juice
1   tablespoon grated
      fresh ginger
1   tablespoon toasted
      sesame oil
1   tablespoon snipped
      fresh cilantro
2   teaspoons reduced-
      sodium soy sauce
1   clove garlic, minced
¼   teaspoon salt
¼   teaspoon crushed
      red pepper
1   cedar grilling plank
      (about 14×6 inches)
4   bunches baby bok
      choy
2   teaspoons toasted
      sesame seeds

1 Thaw fish, if frozen. Rinse fish; pat dry with paper towels. In a shallow dish whisk together the rice vinegar, green onion, lime peel, lime juice, ginger, sesame oil, cilantro, soy sauce, garlic, salt, and crushed red pepper. Reserve ¼ cup of the marinade; set aside. Add the tuna steaks to the dish, turning to coat. Cover and marinate in the refrigerator for 1 hour, turning steaks once. Meanwhile, soak the cedar plank in water for at least 30 minutes.

2 Drain and discard marinade from fish. Remove cedar plank from water. Cut bok choy bunches in halves lengthwise; set aside.

3 For a charcoal grill, place the cedar plank on the grill rack directly over medium-hot coals. Cover and grill for 3 minutes or until it begins to crackle and smoke. Turn plank over. Place tuna steaks on plank. Cover and grill for 12 to 15 minutes or until tuna begins to flake when tested with a fork (fish will be slightly pink in the center). Do not turn tuna. Grill bok choy on grill rack directly over coals for 2 to 3 minutes or until wilted, turning once. (For a gas grill, preheat grill. Reduce heat to medium-hot. Place plank on grill rack over heat. Cover and grill as directed.) Drizzle the bok choy with the reserved marinade mixture. Sprinkle bok choy and tuna with sesame seeds.

nutrition facts per serving: 213 cal., 5 g total fat (1 g sat. fat), 55 mg chol., 362 mg sodium, 4 g carb. (1 g fiber, 1 g sugars), 36 g pro. exchanges: 0.5 vegetable, 5 lean meat.

Many Thai dishes bring a fascinating blend of salty, sour, sweet, and spicy flavors. This recipe is a tantalizing example.

9 g
CARB. PER SERVING

thai sole in foil

prep: 15 minutes grill: 10 minutes
makes: 4 servings (1 foil packet each)

4   4-ounce fresh or frozen sole fillets
2   tablespoons rice vinegar
1   tablespoon reduced-sodium soy sauce
1   teaspoon honey
1   teaspoon toasted sesame oil
½   to 1 teaspoon Asian chili sauce (sriracha sauce)
¼   teaspoon ground ginger
8   ounces fresh haricots verts (young green beans), trimmed
1   small red sweet pepper, cut into thin strips (½ cup)
¼   cup sliced green onions, sliced (2)
2   tablespoons chopped cashews

1 Thaw fish, if frozen. Rinse fish; pat dry with paper towels. Set aside. In a small bowl whisk together vinegar, soy sauce, honey, sesame oil, chili sauce, and ginger; set aside.

2 Cut four 14-inch square pieces of heavy-duty foil. In the center of each square arrange haricots verts and sweet pepper strips. Top with fish fillets. Drizzle vinegar mixture over fish. Fold foil over fish, making a double fold in the center and on the ends to close tightly.

3 For a charcoal or gas grill, place foil packets on the grill rack directly over medium coals or heat. Grill, covered, for 10 to 15 minutes or until fish turns opaque. Carefully open packets. Garnish with sliced green onions and cashews.

nutrition facts per serving: 162 cal., 4 g total fat (1 g sat. fat), 52 mg chol., 251 mg sodium, 9 g carb. (2 g fiber, 5 g sugars), 21 g pro. exchanges: 1 vegetable, 3 lean meat.

Delightfully nutty and chewy, farro is packed with protein, fiber, magnesium, and vitamins A, B, C, and E.

grilled vegetables and farro

prep: 20 minutes   grill: 10 minutes   stand: 30 minutes
makes: 6 servings (1 cup each)

2½   cups reduced-sodium chicken broth
1¼   cups pearled farro, rinsed and drained
⅔   cup lemon juice
3   tablespoons olive oil
½   teaspoon black pepper
1   Japanese eggplant (about 6 ounces), halved lengthwise
1   small zucchini or yellow summer squash, halved lengthwise
1   large portobello mushroom, stem removed
1   medium red sweet pepper, quartered
½   cup snipped fresh parsley
⅓   cup slivered red onion
2   tablespoons snipped fresh mint
2   tablespoons crumbled reduced-fat feta cheese

1 In a medium saucepan bring the broth to boiling. Stir in farro. Return to boiling; reduce heat. Simmer, uncovered, about 20 minutes or until farro is tender and most of the broth is absorbed. Drain any excess broth.

2 Meanwhile, in a small bowl stir together the lemon juice, olive oil, and black pepper. Brush eggplant, zucchini, mushroom, and sweet pepper lightly with lemon juice mixture. Set remaining lemon juice mixture aside.

3 For a gas or charcoal grill, place the vegetables on the grill rack directly over medium heat. Grill, covered, allowing 5 to 6 minutes for zucchini, 8 to 10 minutes for eggplant and sweet pepper, and 10 to 12 minutes for mushroom or just until tender, turning once halfway through grilling.

4 Wrap sweet pepper in foil and let stand for 15 minutes. Peel and remove charred skin from pepper. Coarsely chop pepper and remaining vegetables. In a large bowl combine vegetables, farro, parsley, onion, mint, and the remaining lemon juice mixture. Toss to combine. Let stand for 30 minutes to 1 hour before serving. Sprinkle with feta cheese.

nutrition facts per serving: 249 cal., 8 g total fat (1 g sat. fat), 1 mg chol., 304 mg sodium, 36 g carb. (5 g fiber, 4 g sugars), 10 g pro. exchanges: 1 vegetable, 2 starch, 1 fat.

✱test kitchen tip: As a side dish, serve ½-cup portions of the vegetable-farro mixture.

chile-lime catfish with corn sauté,
page 234

everyday

din

Quesadillas, mac and cheese, walking tacos, and casseroles galore—those are just some of the slimmed-down yet gratifying weeknight dishes you'll find here. Looking for something a little more refined? Check out recipes for herbed fish, dilled shrimp, saucy chicken, and more.

ners

Strip steaks—also known as boneless beef top loin steaks—go by a variety of names from coast to coast. Depending on your region, they might be labeled New York Strip, Kansas City Strip, or shell steaks.

29g
CARB. PER
SERVING

strip steak with mushroom-mustard sauce

prep: 25 minutes cook: 17 minutes
makes: 4 servings (3½ ounces beef, ½ cup sauce, and ½ cup potatoes each)

2   8- to 10-ounce boneless beef top loin steaks, cut about ¾ inch thick
¼   teaspoon black pepper
⅛   teaspoon salt
1   tablespoon canola oil
¼   cup dry white wine or reduced-sodium chicken broth
8   ounces sliced fresh mushrooms
1   medium onion, chopped
2   tablespoons Dijon-style mustard
1   clove garlic, minced
1   cup reduced-sodium chicken broth
¼   cup reduced-sodium chicken broth
2   tablespoons flour
1   recipe Garlic Mashed Potatoes

1 Sprinkle steaks with the pepper and salt. In a large skillet heat oil over medium-high heat. Add steaks. Cook for 10 to 12 minutes or until medium rare (145°F), turning once halfway through cooking time.

2 Remove from heat. Remove steaks from skillet; cover and keep warm. Carefully add wine to the skillet. Return to medium-high heat. Cook and stir, scraping up any browned bits from the bottom of the pan. Add mushrooms, onion, mustard, and garlic to pan. Cook and stir for 5 minutes or until mushrooms are tender. Add the 1 cup broth; bring to boiling.

3 Meanwhile, in a small bowl combine the ¼ cup broth and flour. Stir broth mixture into mushroom mixture. Return to boiling. Cook and stir for 2 minutes or until thickened and bubbly.

4 To serve, cut steaks in half crosswise, making four servings. Serve steaks with mushroom sauce over Garlic Mashed Potatoes.

nutrition facts per serving: 321 cal., 10 g total fat (3 g sat. fat), 45 mg chol., 576 mg sodium, 29 g carb. (3 g fiber, 4 g sugars), 25 g pro. exchanges: 1 vegetable, 1.5 starch, 3 lean meat, 1 fat.

garlic mashed potatoes: Peel and cut 1 pound russet potatoes into 2-inch pieces. In a medium saucepan cook potatoes, covered, in a small amount of boiling water for 20 to 25 minutes or until tender; drain. Mash with a potato masher or an electric mixer on low speed. Beat in 2 teaspoons butter; 2 cloves garlic, minced; ¼ teaspoon ground white pepper; and ⅛ teaspoon salt. Using ¼ to ⅓ cup fat-free milk, gradually beat in enough milk to make potatoes light and fluffy. Sprinkle with 1 tablespoon snipped fresh chives.

Also known as buckwheat groats, kasha is a fiber-rich, nutty-flavor grain common in Eastern Europe. Find it in the international section of the supermarket or in health food stores.

beef medallions with kasha pilaf

32g
CARB. PER SERVING

start to finish: 35 minutes
makes: 4 servings (3 slices meat and ¾ cup pilaf each)

1½   cups water
⅔   cup toasted buckwheat groats (kasha)
2   tablespoons olive oil
½   cup chopped red onion (1 medium)
2   large cloves garlic, minced
¼   cup dried cherries
¼   cup coarsely snipped fresh basil
1   tablespoon balsamic vinegar
½   teaspoon salt
1   pound beef shoulder petite tenders
¼   teaspoon Montreal steak seasoning
⅓   cup sliced almonds, toasted

1 In a medium saucepan bring the water to boiling. Stir in buckwheat groats; reduce heat. Simmer, covered, for 5 to 7 minutes or until the water is absorbed (you should have about 2 cups of cooked groats). Set aside.

2 In a large nonstick skillet heat 1 teaspoon of the oil over medium-high heat. Add onion and garlic; cook and stir for 2 to 3 minutes or just until onion begins to soften.

3 Drain cooked groats if necessary. Add onion mixture to the cooked groats. Stir in 4 teaspoons of the remaining oil, the cherries, basil, vinegar, and salt. Let stand at room temperature while preparing the beef.

4 Meanwhile, cut beef crosswise into 12 slices, each about 1 inch thick. Add the remaining 1 teaspoon oil to the same skillet; heat over medium heat. Evenly sprinkle beef pieces with Montreal seasoning. Cook beef pieces in hot oil about 6 minutes or until medium rare (145°F), turning once halfway through cooking time. Serve beef pieces over groats mixture. Sprinkle with almonds.

nutrition facts per serving: 358 cal., 19 g total fat (4 g sat. fat), 65 mg chol., 407 mg sodium, 32 g carb. (5 g fiber, 8 g sugars), 29 g pro. exchanges: 2 starch, 3 lean meat, 1.5 fat.

30g
CARB. PER
SERVING

For a change of pace and to add extra nutrients, this slimmed-down stir-fry is served over multigrain pasta instead of rice.

sweet asian beef stir-fry

start to finish: 40 minutes

makes: 4 servings (1 cup beef stir-fry and ½ cup cooked spaghetti each)

3   tablespoons low-sugar orange marmalade

2   tablespoons light teriyaki sauce

2   tablespoons water

1   tablespoon grated fresh ginger

¼   to ½ teaspoon crushed red pepper

3   ounces dried multigrain spaghetti or soba (buckwheat noodles)
     Nonstick cooking spray

2   cups small broccoli florets

½   of a small red onion, cut into thin wedges

1   cup packaged julienned carrots or 2 carrots, cut into thin bite-size strips

2   teaspoons canola oil

12   ounces boneless beef top sirloin steak, cut into thin bite-size strips✳

3   cups shredded napa cabbage

1   teaspoon sesame seeds, toasted (optional)

✳test kitchen tip: For easier slicing, partially freeze the steak before cutting it.

1 For sauce, in a small bowl combine marmalade, teriyaki sauce, the water, ginger, and crushed red pepper; set aside. Cook spaghetti according to package directions.

2 Meanwhile, coat an unheated large nonstick skillet or wok with cooking spray. Preheat over medium-high heat. Add broccoli and red onion to hot skillet. Cover and cook for 3 minutes, stirring occasionally. Add carrots; cover and cook for 3 to 4 minutes more or until vegetables are crisp-tender, stirring occasionally. Remove vegetables from skillet.

3 Add oil to the same skillet. Add beef strips. Stir-fry over medium-high heat for 3 to 5 minutes or until beef is slightly pink in center. Return vegetables to skillet along with sauce and cabbage. Cook and stir for 1 to 2 minutes or until heated through and cabbage is just wilted. Serve immediately over the hot cooked spaghetti. If desired, sprinkle with sesame seeds.

nutrition facts per serving: 279 cal., 6 g total fat (2 g sat. fat), 36 mg chol., 259 mg sodium, 30 g carb. (5 g fiber, 8 g sugars), 25 g pro. exchanges: 2 vegetable, 1 starch, 2.5 lean meat, 1 fat.

Who doesn't love a biscuit-topped casserole? More veggies and less fat means you can enjoy this one without the dreaded side serving of guilt!

beef and vegetable biscuit bake

prep: 25 minutes   roast: 20 minutes   bake: 12 minutes
makes: 5 servings (1 cup meat-vegetable mixture and 1 biscuit each)

34g
CARB. PER
SERVING

Nonstick cooking
   spray
12 ounces fresh Brussels
   sprouts, halved
2½ cups sliced carrots
2 teaspoons olive oil
1 teaspoon dried
   thyme, crushed
¼ teaspoon black
   pepper
8 ounces extra-lean
   ground beef
½ cup chopped onion
5 teaspoons butter
3 tablespoons flour
¼ teaspoon salt
1 cup fat-free milk
¾ cup water
4 ounces fresh
   mushrooms,
   chopped
½ of a 12-ounce package
   refrigerated biscuits
   (5), such as Pillsbury
   Grands! Jr. brand

1 Preheat oven to 425°F. Coat a 2-quart square or oval baking dish with cooking spray. Line a 15×10×1-inch baking pan with foil. Place Brussels sprouts and carrots on the foil-lined baking pan. In a small bowl combine oil, thyme, and pepper. Drizzle over vegetables; toss to coat. Spread vegetables in a single layer on baking pan. Roast, uncovered, 20 to 25 minutes or until vegetables are browned and tender, stirring once.

2 Meanwhile, in a large skillet cook meat and onion over medium heat until meat is browned and onion is tender, using a wooden spoon to break up meat as it cooks. Remove from skillet; drain. Set aside.

3 In the same large skillet melt butter over medium heat. In a bowl combine flour and salt; carefully add about half of the flour mixture to the milk, whisking until smooth. Add the remaining flour mixture to melted butter, whisking until well mixed. Add the milk mixture and the water all at once to butter mixture in skillet. Cook and stir until thickened and bubbly; cook and stir 2 minutes more. Stir in mushrooms, roasted vegetables, and cooked meat mixture; heat through.

4 Spoon meat-vegetable mixture into prepared 2-quart baking dish. Top with biscuits. Bake for 12 to 15 minutes or until biscuits are golden brown and casserole is bubbly.

nutrition facts per serving: 309 cal., 12 g total fat (5 g sat. fat), 39 mg chol., 621 mg sodium, 34 g carb. (5 g fiber, 10 g sugars), 17 g pro. exchanges: 2 vegetable, 1.5 starch, 2 lean meat, 1 fat.

If you're new to goat cheese, give it a try. A little goes a long way to add richness and a flavorful tang to recipes.

beef and red pepper angel hair pasta

start to finish: 35 minutes
makes: 4 servings (¾ cup pasta, ¼ cup vegetable mixture, ½ cup meat mixture, and ½ tablespoon parsley each)

10	ounces beef sirloin steak or boneless beef top round steak
½	teaspoon salt
½	teaspoon black pepper
4	teaspoons canola oil
1	medium red sweet pepper, seeded and chopped
1	medium onion, chopped
1	medium tomato, seeded and chopped
½	cup shredded, peeled sweet potato
3	cloves garlic, minced
1	ounce goat cheese (chèvre), cut into small pieces
5	ounces whole grain angel hair pasta or angel hair pasta
4	medium green onions, thinly sliced
2	tablespoons fresh parsley leaves (optional)

1 Trim fat from beef. Thinly slice beef across the grain into bite-size strips; sprinkle with ¼ teaspoon each of the salt and pepper. Set aside.

2 For sauce, in a large nonstick skillet heat 2 teaspoons of the oil over medium heat. Add sweet pepper, onion, tomato, sweet potato, garlic, and remaining ¼ teaspoon salt and black pepper to skillet. Cook, stirring frequently, for 10 to 15 minutes or until vegetables are very tender. Transfer mixture to a food processor. Pulse several times or until mixture is finely chopped but not smooth. Stir in goat cheese.

3 Meanwhile, prepare pasta according to package directions; drain. Return pasta to saucepan. Add pepper mixture to pasta; toss to mix.

4 In the large nonstick skillet heat remaining 2 teaspoons oil over medium-high heat. Add steak strips and green onions to hot skillet. Cook for 3 to 5 minutes or until steak is browned, stirring occasionally.

5 To serve, arrange pasta in shallow bowls. Top with beef mixture and, if desired, sprinkle with fresh parsley leaves.

nutrition facts per serving: 335 cal., 11 g total fat (3 g sat. fat), 55 mg chol., 405 mg sodium, 34 g carb. 5 g fiber, 5 g sugars), 26 g pro. exchanges: 2 vegetable, 1.5 starch, 2.5 lean meat, 1 fat.

Spaghetti squash serves as a low-calorie option to pasta in this flavor-charged chili dish.

spaghetti squash with chili

prep: 20 minutes bake: 45 minutes cook: 10 minutes
makes: 4 servings (1 cup chili and ½ cup spaghetti squash each)

Nonstick cooking
  spray
1 2-pound spaghetti
  squash
1 pound extra-lean
  ground beef
½ cup chopped onion
  (1 medium)
1 clove garlic, minced
1 14.5-ounce can diced
  tomatoes and green
  chiles, undrained
1 15-ounce can no-salt-
  added corn, drained
1 8-ounce can no-salt-
  added tomato sauce
2 tablespoons no-salt-
  added tomato paste
2 teaspoons chili
  powder
½ teaspoon dried
  oregano, crushed
  Fresh oregano leaves
  (optional)

1 Preheat oven to 350°F. Line a baking sheet with foil. Coat foil with cooking spray; set aside. Halve the spaghetti squash lengthwise and remove seeds and membranes. Place squash halves, cut sides down, on prepared baking sheet. Bake for 45 to 50 minutes or until tender.✱ Cool slightly. Using a fork, shred and separate the spaghetti squash into strands.

2 Meanwhile, for sauce, in a medium saucepan cook ground beef, onion, and garlic until meat is browned and onion is tender, stirring to break up meat as it cooks. Drain off fat.

3 Stir in tomatoes and green chiles, corn, tomato sauce, tomato paste, chili powder, and dried oregano. Bring to boiling; reduce heat. Simmer, uncovered, about 10 minutes or until desired consistency.

4 Serve meat sauce with spaghetti squash. If desired, sprinkle with fresh oregano.

nutrition facts per serving: 300 cal., 7 g total fat (3 g sat. fat), 70 mg chol., 566 mg sodium, 32 g carb. (8 g fiber, 17 g sugars), 29 g pro. exchanges: 1 vegetable, 1.5 starch, 3.5 lean meat.

✱ test kitchen tip: To cook squash in the microwave, place, cut sides down, in a baking dish with ¼ cup water. Microwave, covered, on 100 percent power (high) about 15 minutes or until tender. Continue as directed.

The Sugar and Spice Rub also makes a great food gift. Present batches in decorative jars and offer this recipe as a serving suggestion.

sautéed pork chops with apples

prep: 20 minutes chill: 1 hour cook: 16 minutes
makes: 4 servings (1 pork chop, ¼ cup cooked apples, and 1 tablespoon broth mixture each)

4   8-ounce bone-in
     center-cut pork
     chops, cut ¾ inch
     thick
2   teaspoons canola oil
1   tablespoon Sugar and
     Spice Rub
1   tablespoon canola oil
¼   cup dry white wine
2   cups thinly sliced
     Granny Smith
     apples
½   cup reduced-sodium
     chicken broth or
     chicken stock
     Fresh thyme sprigs

1 Trim fat from chops. Brush the 2 teaspoons oil over all sides of chops. Sprinkle chops evenly with Sugar and Spice Rub; rub in with your fingers. Cover chops with plastic wrap; chill in refrigerator 1 hour.

2 Preheat a large skillet over medium-high heat 2 minutes. Add the 1 tablespoon oil; swirl to lightly coat skillet. Add chops; cook for 8 to 10 minutes or until golden brown and juices run clear (145°F), turning once. Transfer chops to a warm platter; cover and keep warm.

3 Remove skillet from heat. Slowly add wine to hot skillet, stirring to scrape up any browned bits from bottom of skillet. Return skillet to heat. Add apples, broth, and 1 sprig of thyme. Bring to boiling; reduce heat. Simmer, covered, 3 minutes or just until apples are tender. Using a slotted spoon, transfer apples to a small bowl; cover and keep warm.

4 Bring broth mixture in skillet to boiling. Boil 5 minutes or until liquid is reduced by half. Return chops and apples to skillet; heat through. Garnish with fresh thyme sprigs and serve immediately.

nutrition facts per serving: 297 cal., 12 g total fat (2 g sat. fat), 108 mg chol., 256 mg sodium, 9 g carb. (2 g fiber, 7 g sugars), 35 g pro. exchanges: 0.5 fruit, 5 lean meat, 1 fat.

sugar and spice rub: In a small bowl stir together 2 tablespoons packed brown sugar, 2 teaspoons chili powder, 1½ teaspoons kosher salt, 1½ teaspoons garlic powder, 1½ teaspoons onion powder, 1½ teaspoons ground cumin, ¾ teaspoon cayenne pepper, and ¾ teaspoon black pepper. Store in an airtight container for up to 3 months. Makes about ½ cup.

Although rhubarb's nickname is pie plant, its uses stretch far beyond pies. The tart, acidic stalks lend themselves to savory preparations that pair especially well with pork.

32g
CARB. PER
SERVING

pork rhubarb skillet

start to finish: 30 minutes

makes: 4 servings (1 cup pork mixture and ⅓ cup couscous each)

1 tablespoon vegetable oil
1 pound lean boneless pork, cut into bite-size strips
1 medium onion, cut into thin wedges
1½ cups sliced fresh rhubarb or frozen unsweetened sliced rhubarb, thawed
1 medium cooking apple, cored and sliced
1 cup chicken broth
2 tablespoons packed brown sugar✳
1 tablespoon cornstarch
1 tablespoon snipped fresh sage
½ teaspoon salt
¼ teaspoon black pepper
1⅓ cups hot cooked couscous

1 In an extra-large skillet heat oil over medium-high heat. Add pork to skillet. Cook and stir for 3 to 4 minutes or until browned. Remove pork from skillet.

2 Add onion to skillet. Cook and stir for 2 to 3 minutes or until tender. Add rhubarb and apple; cook for 3 to 4 minutes or until crisp-tender.

3 For sauce, in a small bowl combine broth, brown sugar, cornstarch, sage, salt, and pepper. Add to skillet; cook and stir until thickened and bubbly. Add pork to skillet; heat through. Serve over hot cooked couscous.

nutrition facts per serving: 342 cal., 11 g total fat (3 g sat. fat), 64 mg chol., 565 mg sodium, 32 g carb. (3 g fiber, 13 g sugars), 28 g pro. exchanges: 1 fruit, 1 starch, 3.5 lean meat, 1 fat.

nutrition facts per serving with substitute: Same as original, except 331 cal., 563 mg sodium, 28 g carb. (10 g sugars).

✳ sugar substitute: Choose Splenda Brown Sugar Blend. Follow package directions to use product amount equivalent to 2 tablespoons brown sugar.

Cocoa powder, chipotle chile pepper, cumin, and cinnamon team up to give this corn bread–topped pork pie rich Tex-Mex flavor without adding a lot of carbs, calories, and fat.

mole-style pork pie

prep: 30 minutes   cook: 10 minutes   bake: 30 minutes
makes: 6 servings (1 cup each)

Nonstick cooking
   spray
1 large onion, chopped
   (1 cup)
1 small red sweet
   pepper, chopped
   (½ cup)
4 cloves garlic, minced
1 8-ounce can tomato
   sauce
1 tablespoon
   unsweetened cocoa
   powder
1 to 2 teaspoons
   chopped canned
   chipotle pepper in
   adobo sauce (see
   tip, *page 223*)
½ teaspoon ground
   cumin
¼ teaspoon ground
   cinnamon
4 teaspoons canola oil
1 pound boneless pork
   loin roast, cut into
   ½-inch cubes
2 medium zucchini,
   chopped (about
   3 cups)
¾ cup fat-free milk
½ cup refrigerated or
   frozen egg product,
   thawed, or 2 eggs
½ cup flour
½ cup yellow cornmeal
¼ teaspoon salt

1 Preheat oven to 400°F. Coat an unheated oven-going large skillet with cooking spray. Preheat skillet over medium heat. Add onion, sweet pepper, and garlic; cook about 5 minutes or until just tender, stirring occasionally. Transfer half of the onion mixture to a blender or food processor. Add tomato sauce, cocoa powder, chipotle pepper, cumin, and cinnamon. Cover and blend or process until smooth. Set aside.

2 Add 2 teaspoons of the oil to the remaining onion mixture in skillet. Add pork and zucchini; cook over medium heat for 4 to 6 minutes or until pork is no longer pink and zucchini is just tender, stirring occasionally. Drain off liquid if necessary. Stir in blended sauce; heat to boiling. Spread in an even layer.

3 Meanwhile, in a medium bowl whisk together milk, egg, and the remaining 2 teaspoons oil. Whisk in flour, cornmeal, and salt until smooth. Pour flour mixture evenly over pork mixture in skillet, covering completely.

4 Bake, uncovered, for 30 to 35 minutes or until topping is set and filling bubbles at the edges. Serve immediately.

nutrition facts per serving: 262 cal., 7 g total fat (1 g sat. fat), 48 mg chol., 371 mg sodium, 26 g carb. (3 g fiber, 5 g sugars), 24 g pro. exchanges: 1 vegetable, 1.5 starch, 2.5 lean meat, 0.5 fat.

With their citrusy-mustardy notes, capers are classic in this dish. They're generally packed in a salty brine, so be sure to rinse them well to reduce the sodium.

chicken piccata

10g
CARB. PER
SERVING

prep: 25 minutes cook: 14 minutes
makes: 4 servings (2 chicken pieces and 2 tablespoons sauce each)

⅓ cup flour
¼ teaspoon salt
¼ teaspoon black
   pepper
1 pound skinless,
   boneless chicken
   breast halves
4 teaspoons olive oil
¾ cup reduced-sodium
   chicken broth
⅓ cup dry white wine
   or reduced-sodium
   chicken broth
2 tablespoons lemon
   juice
2 tablespoons capers,
   rinsed and drained
1 tablespoon butter
2 tablespoons finely
   shredded Parmesan
   cheese
2 tablespoons snipped
   fresh Italian
   (flat-leaf) parsley
3 cups steamed fresh
   broccoli rabe
   (optional)

1 In a shallow dish combine flour, salt, and pepper. Cut chicken into eight pieces. Place chicken pieces, one at a time, between two pieces of plastic wrap. Starting from the center, use the flat side of a meat mallet to lightly pound chicken to ⅛-inch thickness. Coat chicken with flour mixture.

2 In an extra-large nonstick skillet heat 2 teaspoons of the olive oil over medium-high heat. Add half of the chicken to the skillet. Cook for 4 minutes or until no longer pink, turning once. Remove from skillet to a serving dish; cover to keep warm while cooking remaining chicken. If necessary, carefully wipe skillet clean with paper towels. Repeat with remaining chicken and oil. Carefully wipe skillet clean with paper towels.

3 Remove skillet from heat. Add chicken broth and wine to the skillet. Return skillet to heat. Bring to boiling; reduce heat. Simmer, uncovered, for 6 to 8 minutes or until reduced to ¼ cup. Stir in lemon juice, capers, and butter. Stir until butter is melted. Spoon sauce over chicken in serving dish. Sprinkle with Parmesan cheese and parsley. If desired, serve with steamed broccoli rabe.

nutrition facts per serving: 266 cal., 11 g total fat (4 g sat. fat), 82 mg chol., 578 mg sodium, 10 g carb. (1 g fiber, 1 g sugars), 27 g pro. exchanges: 0.5 starch, 3.5 lean meat, 1 fat.

Select a pasta that has a whole grain, such as whole wheat flour, listed first in the ingredient listing. This indicates that the product contains more whole grain than any other ingredient.

35g
CARB. PER SERVING

chicken with broccoli pesto pasta

prep: 25 minutes cook: 6 minutes
makes: 4 servings (¾ cup pasta mixture and 4 ounces chicken each)

everyday dinners

6	ounces whole grain medium shell pasta or shell pasta
4	ounces large broccoli florets
	Nonstick cooking spray
1	pound skinless, boneless chicken breast halves, halved horizontally
¼	teaspoon salt
¼	teaspoon black pepper
¼	cup fresh basil leaves
¼	cup shredded Parmesan cheese
4	teaspoons olive oil
2	tablespoons lemon juice
2	tablespoons pistachio nuts
2	tablespoons fat-free ricotta cheese
1	clove garlic

1 In a large saucepan cook pasta according to package directions, adding broccoli to pan for the last 6 minutes of cooking time. Using a slotted spoon, remove broccoli from pasta and transfer broccoli to a food processor. Drain pasta, reserving ⅓ cup pasta water; keep warm.

2 Meanwhile, coat an unheated large skillet with cooking spray. Heat skillet over medium heat. Sprinkle chicken with ⅛ teaspoon each of the salt and pepper. Add chicken to the skillet and cook for 6 to 8 minutes or until chicken is tender and no longer pink, turning once.

3 For broccoli pesto, in a food processor combine cooked broccoli, basil, 3 tablespoons of the Parmesan cheese, the olive oil, lemon juice, pistachios, ricotta cheese, garlic, and remaining ⅛ teaspoon salt and pepper. Process until finely chopped.

4 To serve, toss pasta with broccoli pesto, adding reserved pasta water if necessary. Divide pasta mixture among four serving plates. Slice chicken breasts. Arrange chicken over pasta. Sprinkle with remaining 1 tablespoon Parmesan cheese.

nutrition facts per serving: 381 cal., 12 g total fat (2 g sat. fat), 78 mg chol., 407 mg sodium, 35 g carb. (6 g fiber, 3 g sugars), 34 g pro. exchanges: 0.5 vegetable, 2 starch, 4 lean meat, 1 fat.

Domestic blood oranges are available from December through May. They have a striking crimson flesh and a fascinating sweet-tart taste imbued with subtle hints of raspberry.

spiced chicken with orange salsa

prep: 20 minutes cook: 8 minutes
makes: 4 servings (4 ounces chicken and ⅓ cup salsa each)

2   medium blood oranges or oranges, sectioned and chopped
¼   cup chopped red onion
¼   cup snipped fresh cilantro
2   cloves garlic, minced
½   of a small fresh jalapeño or habanero chile pepper, seeded and minced∗
2   teaspoons red wine vinegar
4   teaspoons canola oil
½   teaspoon coriander seeds, crushed
½   teaspoon cumin seeds, crushed
¼   teaspoon kosher salt
¼   teaspoon cracked black pepper
4   4- to 5-ounce skinless, boneless chicken breast halves (16 to 20 ounces total)

1 For salsa, in a medium bowl combine oranges, red onion, cilantro, garlic, jalapeño pepper, vinegar, and 1 teaspoon of the oil. Set aside.

2 In a small bowl combine coriander seed, cumin seed, kosher salt, and black pepper. Sprinkle mixture over chicken breast halves. Press spice mixture into chicken with your fingers to coat.

3 In a large skillet heat the remaining 3 teaspoons oil over medium heat. Add chicken and cook for 8 to 12 minutes or until chicken is tender and no longer pink (170°F), turning once. Serve chicken breast with orange salsa.

nutrition facts per serving: 242 cal., 8 g total fat (1 g sat. fat), 91 mg chol., 289 mg sodium, 10 g carb. (2 g fiber, 7 g sugars), 31 g pro. exchanges: 0.5 fruit, 4 lean meat, 1 fat.

∗test kitchen tip: Because chile peppers contain volatile oils that can burn your skin and eyes, avoid direct contact with them as much as possible. When working with chile peppers, wear plastic or rubber gloves. If your bare hands do touch the chile peppers, wash your hands and nails well with soap and warm water.

A little like Greek gyros, shawarma is a Middle-Eastern specialty in which meats are grilled on a rotating spit.

chicken shawarma platter

prep: 15 minutes broil: 8 minutes
makes: 4 servings (½ chicken breast, ½ pita bread, ¼ cup lettuce, ¼ tomato, ¼ avocado, and 2 tablespoons sauce each)

½ cup plain nonfat
    yogurt
1   tablespoon tahini
    (sesame seed paste)
½   teaspoon salt
¼   teaspoon finely
    shredded lemon
    peel
¼   teaspoon ground
    allspice
¼   teaspoon black
    pepper
⅛   teaspoon ground
    cardamom
⅛   teaspoon ground
    nutmeg
2   8-ounce skinless,
    boneless chicken
    breast halves,
    halved horizontally
2   pita bread rounds, cut
    in half horizontally
    and heated
1   cup shredded lettuce
1   medium tomato,
    sliced
1   medium avocado,
    halved, seeded,
    peeled, and sliced

1 Preheat broiler. For yogurt sauce, in a small bowl stir together yogurt, tahini, and ¼ teaspoon of the salt; set aside.

2 In a small bowl stir together the lemon peel, remaining ¼ teaspoon salt, allspice, pepper, cardamom, and nutmeg. Sprinkle mixture over chicken breast halves. Rub into chicken to coat all sides evenly.

3 Arrange chicken on the unheated rack of a broiler pan. Place the pan under the broiler so the surface of the chicken is 4 to 5 inches from the heat. Broil 8 to 10 minutes or until chicken is no longer pink and juices run clear, turning once halfway through cooking time.

4 Arrange warm pita halves on a platter. Top with lettuce, tomato, and avocado slices. Top with chicken breast halves and drizzle with yogurt sauce.

nutrition facts per serving: 316 cal., 11 g total fat (2 g sat. fat), 73 mg chol., 613 mg sodium, 25 g carb. (4 g fiber, 4 g sugars), 30 g pro. exchanges: 0.5 vegetable, 1.5 starch, 3 lean meat, 1 fat.

Spraying the coated chicken strips with nonstick cooking spray before baking helps them get irresistibly crisp and browned.

breaded chicken strips and sweet potato fries

35g CARB. PER SERVING

prep: 25 minutes   marinate: 2 hours   bake: 12 minutes
makes: 4 servings (2 chicken strips and 2½ ounces fries each)

1   pound chicken breast tenders
1   cup low-fat buttermilk
    Nonstick cooking spray
1   large sweet potato (12 ounces)
2   tablespoons olive oil
¼   teaspoon garlic powder
¼   teaspoon salt
¼   teaspoon black pepper
2½ cups cornflakes
1   teaspoon garlic powder
1   teaspoon onion powder
1   teaspoon paprika
½   teaspoon black pepper

1 In a large resealable plastic bag combine chicken and buttermilk. Seal bag; turn to coat chicken. Marinate in the refrigerator 2 to 8 hours, turning bag occasionally.

2 Preheat oven to 425°F. Line a large baking sheet with foil. Coat foil with cooking spray.

3 Cut sweet potato lengthwise into ½-inch-thick by ½-inch-wide fries; place in a medium bowl. Drizzle with oil; toss to coat. Sprinkle with the ¼ teaspoon garlic powder, salt, and ¼ teaspoon pepper; toss to coat evenly. Spread fries in a single layer on one side of the prepared baking sheet.

4 Drain chicken, discarding excess buttermilk. In another large plastic bag coarsely crush cornflakes; add the 1 teaspoon garlic powder, the onion powder, paprika, and ½ teaspoon pepper. Seal bag; shake well to combine. Add chicken, one piece at a time, and shake the bag to coat the chicken well.

5 Place chicken on the baking sheet beside the fries. Coat chicken with cooking spray. Bake for 12 to 15 minutes or until chicken is no longer pink (170°F) and fries are browned (turn fries once halfway through cooking).

nutrition facts per serving: 339 cal., 10 g total fat (2 g sat. fat), 73 mg chol., 466 mg sodium, 35 g carb. (4 g fiber, 6 g sugars), 27 g pro. exchanges: 2 starch, 3.5 lean meat, 1 fat.

This recipe features a homemade spice mixture that is the perfect combination of zesty and sweet.

tandoori spiced chicken and rice bake

prep: 45 minutes bake: 1 hour 5 minutes
makes: 4 servings (1 chicken breast half and 1 cup rice mixture each)

Nonstick cooking
   spray
1 tablespoon butter
½ cup coarsely chopped
   onion
½ cup coarsely
   shredded carrot
½ cup chopped red
   sweet pepper
½ of a fresh Anaheim
   chile pepper, seeded
   and chopped (see
   tip, *page 223*)
1 small zucchini,
   halved lengthwise
   and cut into ¼-inch-
   thick slices
2 cloves garlic, thinly
   sliced
1 14.5-ounce can
   reduced-sodium
   chicken broth
⅔ cup uncooked long
   grain brown rice
½ cup water
¼ cup no-salt-added
   tomato paste
1 recipe Tandoori Spice
   Mixture
1½ teaspoons butter
4 4- to 5-ounce skinless,
   boneless chicken
   breast halves
   Snipped fresh cilantro

1 Preheat oven to 350°F. Lightly coat a 2-quart rectangular baking dish with cooking spray.

2 In a large skillet melt the 1 tablespoon butter over medium heat. Add onion, carrot, sweet pepper, and chile pepper; cook and stir 6 minutes. Stir in zucchini and garlic. Cook and stir 3 minutes more. Stir in broth, rice, the water, tomato paste, and 1 tablespoon of the Tandoori Spice Mixture. Bring to boiling; boil 1 minute. Pour rice mixture into prepared dish. Cover tightly with foil. Bake for 45 minutes.

3 Meanwhile, sprinkle remaining Tandoori Spice Mixture evenly over all sides of chicken. Using your fingers, rub spices into the meat. In a large skillet melt the 1½ teaspoons butter over medium-high heat. Cook chicken in hot butter about 4 minutes or just until browned, turning once halfway through cooking. Transfer chicken to a plate; chill in refrigerator until needed.

4 Remove rice mixture from oven and uncover it. Arrange chicken pieces on rice mixture. Replace foil. Bake for 20 to 25 minutes more or until chicken is done (170°F) and rice is tender. To serve, sprinkle with cilantro.

nutrition facts per serving: 344 cal., 9 g total fat (4 g sat. fat), 84 mg chol., 575 mg sodium, 35 g carb. (4 g fiber, 6 g sugars), 30 g pro. exchanges: 1 vegetable, 2 starch, 3.5 lean meat.

tandoori spice mixture: In a small bowl combine 1 teaspoon each yellow curry powder and garam masala; ½ teaspoon each ground ginger, ground cumin, ground coriander, and ground cardamom; and ¼ teaspoon each ground cinnamon, salt, and black pepper.

Get a full serving of veggies in each portion of this creamy, crunchy casserole.

garlic cashew chicken casserole

40g
CARB. PER
SERVING

prep: 35 minutes bake: 24 minutes
makes: 6 servings (1⅓ cups each)

Nonstick cooking
  spray
1 cup reduced-sodium
    chicken broth
¼ cup hoisin sauce
2 tablespoons grated
    fresh ginger
4 teaspoons cornstarch
½ teaspoon crushed red
    pepper
⅛ teaspoon black
    pepper
1 pound skinless,
    boneless chicken
    breast halves, cut
    into 1-inch strips
2 medium onions, cut
    into thin wedges
2 cups sliced bok choy
1 cup sliced celery
1 cup sliced carrots
¾ cup chopped green
    sweet pepper
6 cloves garlic, minced
2 cups cooked brown
    rice
1 cup chow mein
    noodles, coarsely
    broken
½ cup cashews
¼ cup sliced green
    onions (2)

1 Preheat oven to 400°F. Lightly coat a 2-quart rectangular baking dish with cooking spray.

2 For sauce, in a medium bowl whisk together broth, hoisin sauce, ginger, cornstarch, crushed red pepper, and black pepper; set aside.

3 Lightly coat an extra-large skillet with cooking spray; heat over medium-high heat. Add chicken to skillet; cook until lightly browned. Remove from skillet. Add onion wedges, bok choy, celery, carrots, and sweet pepper to the skillet. Cook 3 to 4 minutes or until vegetables start to soften. Add garlic; cook 30 seconds more. Stir in the sauce. Cook and stir about 3 minutes or until sauce is thickened and bubbly. Stir in cooked rice and browned chicken.

4 Spoon chicken mixture into the prepared baking dish. Cover and bake about 20 minutes or until casserole is bubbly and chicken is no longer pink. Sprinkle chow mein noodles and cashews over top. Bake, uncovered, 4 to 5 minutes more or until noodles and cashews are golden brown. Sprinkle with green onions.

nutrition facts per serving: 340 cal., 10 g total fat (2 g sat. fat), 49 mg chol., 480 mg sodium, 40 g carb. (4 g fiber, 8 g sugars), 23 g pro. exchanges: 2 vegetable, 2 starch, 2.5 lean meat.

Be sure that the ground turkey or chicken breast you use is lean and made only of breast meat. Some ground poultry contains dark meat, which contains more fat.

homemade walking tacos

start to finish: 30 minutes

makes: 5 servings (1 package chips, 1½ ounces cooked meat, about ½ cup vegetables, and 1 tablespoon cheese each)

8   ounces uncooked
      lean ground turkey
      breast or chicken
      breast
¼   cup chopped onion
¼   cup chopped red
      sweet pepper
2   teaspoons olive oil
      or canola oil
1   tablespoon reduced-
      sodium taco
      seasoning
1   tablespoon water
⅛   to ¼ teaspoon
      crushed red pepper
      Dash black pepper
5   100-calorie packages
      nacho cheese-flavor
      tortilla chips
1   cup shredded
      romaine lettuce
⅔   cup diced tomato
⅓   cup shredded
      reduced-fat cheddar
      cheese
5   teaspoons light sour
      cream (optional)

1 In a large skillet cook turkey, onion, and sweet pepper in hot oil over medium heat until turkey is no longer pink, using a wooden spoon to break up meat as it cooks. Stir in taco seasoning, the water, crushed red pepper, and black pepper. Cook and stir for 1 minute more.

2 Meanwhile, open the bags of tortilla chips; if desired, gently crush chips. Divide lettuce among the bags. Divide cooked turkey mixture, tomato, and cheese among the bags. If desired, top each with a teaspoon of the sour cream. Use a fork to mix together and eat from the bag.

nutrition facts per serving: 207 cal., 10 g total fat (2 g sat. fat), 28 mg chol., 327 mg sodium, 16 g carb. (1 g fiber, 2 g sugars), 15 g pro. exchanges: 0.5 vegetable, 1 starch, 1.5 lean meat, 1.5 fat.

Using turkey breast, light sour cream, and fat-free cream cheese lowers calories and keeps the fat in check.

creamy turkey and spinach pie

prep: 35 minutes bake: 40 minutes stand: 10 minutes
makes: 8 servings (1 wedge each)

15g
CARB. PER SERVING

Nonstick cooking spray

4 ounces dried multigrain or plain angel hair pasta, broken

1 8-ounce package fat-free cream cheese, softened

¾ cup refrigerated or frozen egg product, thawed, or 3 eggs

½ cup light sour cream

¼ cup snipped fresh basil or 2 teaspoons dried basil, crushed

¼ teaspoon salt

¼ teaspoon garlic powder

¼ teaspoon crushed red pepper

2 cups chopped cooked turkey breast (10 ounces)*

1 10-ounce package frozen chopped spinach, thawed and well drained

1 cup shredded part-skim mozzarella cheese (4 ounces)

⅓ cup chopped bottled roasted red sweet pepper

1 Preheat oven to 350°F. Coat a 9-inch deep-dish pie plate or a 2-quart square baking dish with cooking spray; set aside. Cook pasta according to package directions; drain well.

2 Meanwhile, in a large bowl beat cream cheese with an electric mixer on low to medium speed until smooth. Gradually beat in eggs and sour cream. Stir in basil, salt, garlic powder, and crushed red pepper. Stir in cooked pasta, turkey, spinach, mozzarella cheese, and roasted red pepper. Spread mixture in prepared plate or dish.

3 Bake, uncovered, for 40 to 45 minutes or until edges are slightly puffed and golden and center is heated through. Let stand on a wire rack for 10 minutes before serving. Cut into wedges or rectangles to serve.

nutrition facts per serving: 207 cal., 4 g total fat (2 g sat. fat), 46 mg chol., 488 mg sodium, 15 g carb. (2 g fiber, 2 g sugars), 25 g pro. exchanges: 0.5 vegetable, 1 starch, 3 lean meat.

✻ test kitchen tip: Cook turkey breast tenderloin rather than using purchased cooked turkey breast to keep the sodium down. To cook turkey breast tenderloin, heat water in a skillet to boiling. Cut 1 turkey breast tenderloin in half lengthwise and add to skillet. Return to boiling; reduce heat. Simmer, covered, 10 to 12 minutes or until no longer pink. Drain, cool slightly, and chop. Makes 2 cups.

Gather everyone around the table a few minutes before this dish is done. Serve it the minute it comes out of the oven so that the topping doesn't deflate.

31g CARB. PER SERVING

popover pizza casserole

prep: 35 minutes bake: 30 minutes
makes: 6 servings (1⅓ cups each)

230

everyday dinners

1¼ pounds ground turkey breast or extra-lean ground beef
2 cups sliced fresh mushrooms
1½ cups chopped yellow summer squash
1 cup chopped onion (1 large)
1 cup chopped green sweet pepper (1 large)
1 14- to 15.5-ounce can pizza sauce
1 teaspoon dried Italian seasoning, crushed
½ teaspoon fennel seeds, crushed
1 cup fat-free milk
½ cup refrigerated or frozen egg product, thawed, or 2 eggs
1 tablespoon canola oil
1 cup all-purpose flour*
1 cup shredded reduced-fat mozzarella cheese (4 ounces)
2 tablespoons grated Parmesan cheese

1 Preheat oven to 400°F. In an oven-going large skillet cook turkey, mushrooms, squash, onion, and sweet pepper over medium heat until meat is browned and vegetables are tender, stirring to break up meat as it cooks. Drain off fat. Stir pizza sauce, Italian seasoning, and fennel seeds into meat mixture. Bring to boiling; reduce heat. Simmer, uncovered, for 5 minutes, stirring occasionally. Spread to an even layer.

2 For popover topping, in a medium bowl combine milk, egg, and oil. Beat with an electric mixer on medium speed or whisk for 1 minute. Add flour; beat or whisk about 1 minute more or until smooth.

3 Sprinkle mozzarella cheese over meat mixture in skillet. Pour popover topping evenly over mixture in skillet, covering completely. Sprinkle with Parmesan cheese.

4 Bake, uncovered, for 30 to 35 minutes or until topping is puffed and golden brown. Serve immediately.

nutrition facts per serving: 327 cal., 7 g total fat (2 g sat. fat), 58 mg chol., 611 mg sodium, 31 g carb. (3 g fiber, 7 g sugars), 34 g pro. exchanges: 1 vegetable, 1.5 starch, 4 lean meat.

*test kitchen tip: If desired, substitute ½ cup white whole wheat flour or regular whole wheat flour for ½ cup of the all-purpose flour.

*Our taste panel declared this creamy dish is
"even better than regular tuna casserole."*

tuna and noodles

33g CARB. PER SERVING

prep: 15 minutes stand: 35 minutes microwave: 6 minutes
makes: 4 servings (1 cup each)

1 6.5-ounce package
   light semisoft
   cheese with
   cucumber and dill
   or garlic and herb
4 ounces dried wide
   rice noodles, broken
1½ cups sliced fresh
   mushrooms
1 stalk celery, sliced
   (½ cup)
1 small onion, chopped
   (⅓ cup)
¼ cup water
⅓ cup fat-free milk
3 4.5-ounce cans very
   low–sodium chunk
   white tuna (water
   pack), drained and
   broken into chunks
½ cup cornflakes or
   crushed reduced-
   fat shredded wheat
   crackers

1 Let cheese stand at room temperature
for 30 minutes. Place noodles in a large
bowl. Add enough boiling water to cover by
several inches. Let stand for 5 minutes, stirring
occasionally. Drain and set aside.

2 Meanwhile, in a microwave-safe 2-quart
casserole combine mushrooms, celery,
onion, and the ¼ cup water. Microwave,
covered, on 100 percent power (high) for
3 to 4 minutes or until vegetables are tender,
stirring once halfway through cooking.

3 Add cheese and milk to mushroom
mixture. Stir until well mixed. Stir in
drained noodles and tuna. Microwave,
covered, on 100 percent power (high) for
3 to 4 minutes or until heated through, gently
stirring once halfway through cooking.
Sprinkle with cornflakes.

nutrition facts per serving: 331 cal., 9 g total fat
(5 g sat. fat), 73 mg chol., 454 mg sodium, 33 g carb. (1 g fiber,
4 g sugars), 31 g pro. exchanges: 1 vegetable, 2 starch,
3.5 lean meat.

232

You'll likely have some extra ginger. Add just a touch, finely grated, to a glass of iced tea for a perky low-cal beverage.

8g
CARB. PER
SERVING

pepper-crusted salmon with yogurt-lime sauce

prep: 10 minutes cook: 6 minutes
makes: 4 servings (1 salmon fillet and ¼ cup sauce each)

4   4- to 5-ounce skinless
     salmon fillets
½   teaspoon multi-
     colored peppercorns,
     coarsely crushed
¼   teaspoon salt
2   teaspoons olive oil
¾   cup plain nonfat
     yogurt
1   tablespoon honey
1   tablespoon snipped
     fresh parsley
¼   teaspoon finely
     shredded lime peel
2   teaspoons lime juice
½   teaspoon minced
     fresh ginger
     Lime peel strips and/
     or fresh parsley
     leaves (optional)
12 ounces steamed fresh
     asparagus spears
     (optional)

1 Sprinkle salmon with peppercorns and salt; gently press peppercorns into the salmon. In a large nonstick skillet heat oil over medium-high heat. Add salmon; cook for 3 minutes. Turn; cook for 3 minutes more or until fish flakes easily when tested with a fork.

2 Meanwhile, in a medium bowl combine yogurt, honey, snipped parsley, finely shredded lime peel, lime juice, and ginger.

3 Serve salmon with yogurt-lime sauce. If desired, garnish with lime peel strips and/or parsley leaves and serve with steamed asparagus spears.

nutrition facts per serving: 224 cal., 10 g total fat (1 g sat. fat), 63 mg chol., 232 mg sodium, 8 g carb. (0 g fiber, 8 g sugars), 25 g pro. exchanges: 0.5 starch, 3 lean meat, 1 fat.

Stirring the snipped fresh cilantro into the corn mixture just before serving retains the herb's bright color and flavor. Pictured on page 208.

25g
CARB. PER
SERVING

chile-lime catfish with corn sauté

prep: 25 minutes   cook: 4 minutes per ½-inch thickness
makes: 4 servings (1 piece fish and ½ cup corn mixture each)

4   4- to 5-ounce fresh
     or frozen skinless
     catfish, sole, or
     tilapia fillets
1   tablespoon lime juice
1   teaspoon ground
     ancho chile pepper
     or chili powder
¼   teaspoon salt
2   teaspoons canola oil
2⅔ cups frozen gold and
     white whole kernel
     corn, thawed
¼   cup finely chopped
     red onion
2   teaspoons finely
     chopped seeded
     fresh jalapeño chile
     pepper (see tip,
     page 223)
2   cloves garlic, minced
1   tablespoon snipped
     fresh cilantro
     Lime wedges
     (optional)

1 Thaw fish, if frozen. Rinse fish; pat dry with paper towels. In a small bowl stir together lime juice, ancho chile pepper, and salt. Brush mixture evenly over both sides of each fish fillet. Measure thickness of fish.

2 In a large nonstick skillet heat 1 teaspoon of the oil over medium-high heat. Add fish fillets to hot oil; cook for 4 to 6 minutes per ½-inch thickness or until fish flakes easily when tested with a fork, turning once halfway through cooking. Remove from skillet. Cover to keep warm.

3 In the same skillet cook corn, onion, jalapeño chile pepper, and garlic in the remaining 1 teaspoon oil about 2 minutes or until vegetables are heated through and just starting to soften, stirring occasionally. Remove from heat. Stir in cilantro.

4 To serve, divide corn mixture among four serving plates. Top with fish. If desired, serve with lime wedges.

nutrition facts per serving: 278 cal., 12 g total fat (2 g sat. fat), 53 mg chol., 216 mg sodium, 25 g carb. (3 g fiber, 3 g sugars), 21 g pro. exchanges: 1.5 starch, 2.5 lean meat, 1 fat.

A bit of green onion with a touch of lemon peel and juice turns ordinary mayonnaise into an extraordinary topping for steamed fish.

herbed fish and vegetables with lemon mayo

13g CARB. PER SERVING

prep: 20 minutes cook: 6 minutes
makes: 2 servings (1 piece fish, about ⅔ cup vegetables, and 2 tablespoons Lemon Mayo each)

- 2   6-ounce fresh or frozen skinless flounder, sole, cod, or perch fillets, ½ to ¾ inch thick
- 2   tablespoons assorted snipped fresh herbs (such as parsley, basil, oregano, and thyme)
- 1   cup matchstick-size pieces carrot
- 1   cup matchstick-size pieces zucchini and/ or yellow summer squash
- ½   of a lemon, thinly sliced
- 1   recipe Lemon Mayo

1 Thaw fish, if frozen. Rinse fish; pat dry with paper towels. Using a sharp knife, make shallow bias cuts in the fish fillets, spacing cuts ¾ inch apart. Sprinkle herbs over fillets, tucking into cuts.

2 Place a steamer insert in a large deep saucepan or large deep skillet with a tight-fitting lid. Add water to the saucepan or skillet until just below the steamer insert. Bring water to boiling. Place carrot and squash in the steamer basket. Place fish on top of vegetables. Arrange lemon slices on top of fish. Cover and steam over medium heat for 6 to 8 minutes or until fish flakes easily when tested with a fork, adding more water as needed to maintain steam.

3 To serve, divide fish and vegetables between two serving plates. Serve with Lemon Mayo.

nutrition facts per serving: 270 cal., 10 g total fat (2 g sat. fat), 90 mg chol., 340 mg sodium, 13 g carb. (4 g fiber, 6 g sugars), 34 g pro. exchanges: 1.5 vegetable, 4 lean meat, 1 fat.

lemon mayo: In a small bowl stir together 3 tablespoons light mayonnaise, 1 tablespoon thinly sliced green onion, ¼ teaspoon finely shredded lemon peel, and 1 teaspoon lemon juice.

For recipes that use stir-frying as the cooking technique, cut foods into similar sizes so they cook evenly. Cut thicker foods, such as sea scallops, in half horizontally.

shrimp and scallop vegetable stir-fry

32g
CARB. PER
SERVING

prep: 25 minutes   cook: 5 minutes
makes: 4 servings (1 generous cup stir-fry mixture and ⅓ cup rice each)

everyday dinners

8   ounces fresh or frozen scallops, thawed if frozen
½   cup orange juice
1   tablespoon reduced-sodium soy sauce
2   teaspoons cornstarch
½   teaspoon ground ginger
⅛   teaspoon crushed red pepper
    Canola oil spray
4   cups small broccoli florets (about 8 ounces)
1   large red sweet pepper, cut into strips
2   teaspoons finely shredded fresh ginger
1   large clove garlic, minced
1   cup shiitake mushrooms, stemmed and sliced
6   ounces fresh or frozen medium shrimp, thawed if frozen, peeled and deveined
1⅓   cups hot cooked brown rice

1 Cut scallops in half horizontally to form thin disks. Set aside.

2 In a small bowl combine orange juice, soy sauce, cornstarch, ground ginger, and crushed red pepper.

3 Coat an extra-large nonstick skillet or wok with canola oil spray and heat over high heat until hot. Stir-fry broccoli and sweet pepper 2 minutes or until broccoli is bright green. Add fresh ginger and garlic; stir-fry 15 seconds or until fragrant. Add mushrooms, scallops, shrimp, and orange juice mixture. Cook and stir 3 to 4 minutes or until the scallops and shrimp are opaque and cooked through. Serve immediately over hot cooked rice.

nutrition facts per serving: 215 cal., 2 g total fat (0 g sat. fat), 67 mg chol., 598 mg sodium, 32 g carb. (5 g fiber, 7 g sugars), 18 g pro. exchanges: 1 vegetable, 0.5 fruit, 1 starch, 2 lean meat.

If you happen to have fresh dill, chop 1½ teaspoons and add it to the recipe in the last minute of cooking time.

dilled shrimp with beans and carrots

prep: 25 minutes   cook: 40 minutes
makes: 4 servings (⅓ cup rice and 1 cup shrimp mixture each)

1   pound fresh or frozen large shrimp in shells
1⅓   cups water
⅔   cup regular brown rice
1   tablespoon butter
3   medium carrots, cut into thin julienne strips
8   ounces fresh green beans, trimmed and cut into 1-inch pieces
¼   cup reduced-sodium chicken broth
1   teaspoon finely shredded lemon peel
½   teaspoon dried dill weed

1 Thaw shrimp, if frozen. Peel and devein shrimp, leaving tails intact if desired. Rinse shrimp; pat dry with paper towels. Set aside.

2 In a medium saucepan bring the water and rice to boiling; reduce heat. Simmer, covered, about 40 minutes or until rice is tender and most of the liquid is absorbed.

3 Meanwhile, in a large skillet melt butter over medium heat. Add carrots and green beans; cook and stir for 4 to 5 minutes or until vegetables are crisp-tender. Add broth, shrimp, lemon peel, and dill weed to bean mixture. Cook, uncovered, over medium heat for 3 to 4 minutes or until shrimp are opaque, stirring occasionally.

4 To serve, divide rice among four bowls. Divide shrimp mixture among bowls.

nutrition facts per serving: 298 cal., 6 g total fat (2 g sat. fat), 180 mg chol., 264 mg sodium, 33 g carb. (4 g fiber, 3 g sugars), 27 g pro. exchanges: 1.5 vegetable, 1.5 starch, 2.5 lean meat.

quick dilled shrimp with beans and carrots: Use 12 ounces cooked, peeled shrimp in place of the shrimp in shells. Add with the broth, lemon peel, and dill weed and just heat through. Use one 8.8-ounce pouch cooked brown rice in place of the water and regular brown rice; cook according to package directions. Use 1½ cups purchased julienned carrots in place of the 3 medium carrots.

41g
CARB. PER SERVING

High in fiber and phytonutrients and low in fat and saturated fat, beans are inexpensive, easy-to-enjoy superfoods.

double bean quesadillas

prep: 20 minutes cook: 12 minutes
makes: 4 servings (1 quesadilla, ½ tablespoon salsa, ½ tablespoon green onion, and ½ tablespoon sour cream each)

2   teaspoons olive oil
1   medium onion, chopped
1   teaspoon minced fresh jalapeño chile pepper (see tip, *page 223*)
2   cloves garlic, minced
1   cup canned no-salt-added black beans, rinsed and drained
1   cup canned no-salt-added pinto beans, rinsed and drained
⅓   cup reduced-sodium bottled salsa
1½ teaspoons chili powder
4   7-inch low-carb, high-fiber tortillas such as La Tortilla Factory Smart & Delicious brand
2   ounces Monterey Jack cheese with jalapeño peppers, shredded (½ cup)
Nonstick cooking spray
2   tablespoons reduced-sodium bottled salsa
2   tablespoons sliced green onion (1)
2   tablespoons light sour cream

1 In a large skillet heat olive oil over medium heat. Add onion, jalapeño, and garlic. Cook and stir for 5 to 8 minutes or until tender. Stir in black beans, pinto beans, ⅓ cup salsa, and the chili powder. Heat through, mashing some of the beans slightly with the back of a wooden spoon.

2 Divide bean mixture among tortillas, placing the mixture on half of each tortilla. Sprinkle bean mixture with cheese. Fold tortillas over filling; press down lightly.

3 Coat an unheated extra-large nonstick skillet or griddle with cooking spray. Preheat skillet or griddle over medium-high heat; reduce heat to medium. Cook quesadillas, half at a time, in hot skillet or griddle about 3 to 4 minutes or until tortillas are browned, turning once halfway through cooking. Place quesadillas on a baking sheet; keep warm in a 300°F oven while cooking the remaining quesadillas. Serve with 2 tablespoons salsa, green onions, and sour cream.

nutrition facts per serving: 291 cal., 11 g total fat (3 g sat. fat), 16 mg chol., 491 mg sodium, 41 g carb. (19 g fiber, 3 g sugars), 18 g pro. exchanges: 1 vegetable, 2 starch, 1.5 lean meat, 1 fat.

Cannellini beans (white kidney beans) provide plenty of protein in this vegetarian main dish. Look for them with the other canned beans at the supermarket.

easy pasta and pepper primavera

37g
CARB. PER SERVING

start to finish: 20 minutes
makes: 4 servings (1¼ cups each)

4   ounces dried multigrain spaghetti
2   teaspoons bottled minced garlic or 4 cloves garlic, minced
1   tablespoon olive oil or canola oil
1   16-ounce package frozen peppers and onions mix or sugar snap stir-fry vegetable mix
1   15-ounce can cannellini beans (white kidney beans), rinsed and drained
¼   cup dry white wine or reduced-sodium chicken broth
½   teaspoon finely shredded lemon peel (set aside)
1   tablespoon lemon juice
½   teaspoon dried thyme, crushed
¼   teaspoon salt
¼   teaspoon freshly ground black pepper
¼   teaspoon crushed red pepper
1   tablespoon butter
1   ounce Parmesan cheese, shaved

1 Cook pasta according to package directions.

2 Meanwhile, in a large skillet cook and stir garlic in hot oil over medium heat for 30 seconds. Add frozen vegetables. Cook and stir for 2 minutes. Add beans, wine, lemon juice, thyme, salt, black pepper, and crushed red pepper. Bring to boiling; reduce heat. Cook, uncovered, about 4 minutes or until vegetables are crisp-tender, stirring occasionally. Remove from heat. Stir in butter.

3 Drain pasta. Add pasta to vegetable mixture in skillet. Toss gently to combine.

4 To serve, divide pasta mixture among four shallow bowls. Sprinkle with Parmesan and lemon peel.

nutrition facts per serving: 272 cal., 9 g total fat (3 g sat. fat), 12 mg chol., 410 mg sodium, 37 g carb. (7 g fiber, 5 g sugars), 13 g pro. exchanges: 1 vegetable, 2 starch, 1 lean meat, 1 fat.

Don't tell! Nutrient-rich butternut squash is hidden within this cheesy, kid-pleasing meal.

four-cheese macaroni and cheese

31g CARB. PER SERVING

prep: 30 minutes roast: 40 minutes bake: 25 minutes
makes: 8 servings (¾ cup each)

Nonstick cooking spray
1   pound butternut squash, halved and seeded
8   ounces dried whole grain elbow macaroni (about 2 cups)
4   teaspoons butter
2   tablespoons flour
½   teaspoon salt
⅛   teaspoon ground white pepper
1   cup fat-free milk
2   tablespoons semisoft cheese with garlic and fine herbs
¾   cup shredded part-skim mozzarella cheese (3 ounces)
¾   cup shredded reduced-fat sharp cheddar cheese (3 ounces)
½   cup shredded Muenster cheese (2 ounces)

1 Preheat oven to 375°F. Line a 15×10×1-inch baking pan with parchment paper; set aside. Coat a 2-quart square baking dish with cooking spray; set aside.

2 Coat the cut sides of the butternut squash with cooking spray; place squash halves, cut sides down, on the prepared baking pan. Roast for 40 to 45 minutes or until squash is very tender and cooked through. Remove from oven; let stand until cool enough to handle. Scoop flesh from squash halves; discard skin. Using a potato masher, mash the squash; set aside.

3 Meanwhile, cook pasta according to package directions. Drain well.

4 In a medium saucepan melt butter over medium heat. Whisk in flour, salt, and white pepper until combined. Add milk, whisking until smooth. Cook and stir until thickened and bubbly. Add semisoft cheese; whisk until cheese is melted. Stir in mashed squash. Add cooked pasta; stir until coated.

5 Place half of the pasta mixture in the prepared baking dish. Evenly sprinkle half of the mozzarella cheese and half of the cheddar cheese on top of the pasta. Arrange half of the Muenster cheese over all. Repeat layers. Bake about 25 minutes or until cheese is golden brown.

nutrition facts per serving: 266 cal., 11 g total fat (6 g sat. fat), 26 mg chol., 402 mg sodium, 31 g carb. (4 g fiber, 4 g sugars), 13 g pro. exchanges: 2 starch, 1 medium-fat meat, 1 fat.

Fresh, flavorful ingredients transform ground meat substitute into a tasty taco filling.

vegetarian citrus-corn tacos

47g
CARB. PER
SERVING

start to finish: 30 minutes
makes: 4 servings (2 tacos each)

½ cup orange juice
¼ cup snipped fresh
   cilantro
1 teaspoon finely
   shredded lime peel
2 tablespoons lime juice
1 fresh jalapeño chile
   pepper, seeded and
   finely chopped∗
3 cloves garlic, minced
1½ teaspoons cornstarch
⅛ teaspoon salt
⅛ teaspoon black pepper
2 teaspoons cooking oil
1 medium red sweet
   pepper, cut into thin
   strips
1 12-ounce package
   frozen cooked and
   crumbled ground
   meat substitute
   (soy protein)
1 cup frozen whole
   kernel corn
8 6-inch corn tortillas
½ cup light sour cream

1 For sauce, in a small bowl combine orange juice, cilantro, lime peel, lime juice, jalapeño pepper, garlic, cornstarch, salt, and black pepper. Set aside.

2 In a large nonstick skillet heat oil over medium-high heat. Add sweet pepper strips; cook and stir until crisp-tender. Remove sweet pepper strips.

3 Add soy protein crumbles to skillet. Cook, stirring occasionally, for 3 to 4 minutes or until heated through. Stir in corn. Stir sauce; add to skillet. Cook and stir until thickened and bubbly. Reduce heat; cook and stir for 2 minutes more. Return sweet pepper strips to skillet; stir to combine.

4 Wrap tortillas in microwave-safe paper towels. Microwave on 100 percent power (high) for 45 to 60 seconds or until warm. Divide the pepper mixture among tortillas and top with sour cream. Fold the tortillas over the filling.

nutrition facts per serving: 361 cal., 11 g total fat (2 g sat. fat), 8 mg chol., 490 mg sodium, 47 g carb. (10 g fiber, 6 g sugars), 21 g pro. exchanges: 3 starch, 2 lean meat, 1 fat.

∗test kitchen tip: Because chile peppers contain volatile oils that can burn your skin and eyes, avoid direct contact with them as much as possible. When working with chile peppers, wear plastic or rubber gloves. If your bare hands do touch the peppers, wash your hands and nails well with soap and warm water.

easy

slow
cooker
sup

pork tenderloin with sweet-spiced onions, *page 258*

You already love your slow cooker for its fix-now/savor-later ease. Now you'll love it for the healthful meals it can bring to your table. Enjoy soups, stews, roasts, and other long-simmering entrées that are as tasty as they are easy to prepare.

pers

22g
CARB. PER
SERVING

Thickening the sauce with cornstarch plumps up the sauce without the need for added fat.

beef stroganoff

prep: 30 minutes cook: 8 to 10 hours (low) or 4 to 5 hours (high) + 30 minutes (high)
makes: 6 servings (¾ cup meat mixture and ⅓ cup noodles each)

1½   pounds beef stew
       meat
2   teaspoons vegetable
       oil
2   cups sliced fresh
       mushrooms
1   medium onion,
       chopped
2   cloves garlic, minced
½   teaspoon dried
       oregano, crushed
½   teaspoon salt
¼   teaspoon dried
       thyme, crushed
¼   teaspoon black
       pepper
1   bay leaf
1   14.5-ounce can lower-
       sodium beef broth
⅓   cup dry sherry or
       lower-sodium beef
       broth
1   8-ounce carton light
       sour cream
2   tablespoons
       cornstarch
2   cups hot cooked
       noodles
       Snipped fresh parsley
       (optional)

1 Trim fat from beef. Cut beef into 1-inch pieces. In a large skillet cook beef, half at a time, in hot oil over medium heat until browned. Drain off fat.

2 In a 3½- or 4-quart slow cooker place mushrooms, onion, garlic, oregano, salt, thyme, pepper, and bay leaf. Add beef. Pour broth and sherry over all.

3 Cover and cook on low-heat setting for 8 to 10 hours or on high-heat setting for 4 to 5 hours. Discard bay leaf.

4 If using low-heat setting, turn to high-heat setting. In a medium bowl combine sour cream and cornstarch. Gradually whisk about 1 cup of the hot cooking liquid into sour cream mixture. Stir sour cream mixture into cooker. Cover and cook about 30 minutes more or until thickened. Serve over hot cooked noodles. If desired, sprinkle each serving with parsley.

nutrition facts per serving: 342 cal., 12 g total fat (4 g sat. fat), 89 mg chol., 441 mg sodium, 22 g carb. (1 g fiber, 4 g sugars), 32 g pro. exchanges: 1 vegetable, 1 starch, 4 lean meat, 1 fat.

German mustard, pickles, and a touch of cloves give this pot roast its distinctly German flavors.

german-style beef roast

30g CARB. PER SERVING

prep: 25 minutes cook: 10 to 11 hours (low) or 5 to 5½ hours (high)
makes: 8 servings (4 ounces meat, ½ cup spaetzle, and ⅔ cup sauce each)

1   2½- to 3-pound boneless beef chuck pot roast
2   teaspoons vegetable oil
4   medium carrots, sliced (2 cups)
2   large onions, chopped (2 cups)
2   stalks celery, sliced (1 cup)
½   cup chopped kosher-style dill pickles
½   cup dry red wine or lower-sodium beef broth
3   tablespoons German-style mustard
½   teaspoon coarsely ground black pepper
¼   teaspoon ground cloves
2   bay leaves
2   tablespoons flour
2   tablespoons dry red wine or lower-sodium beef broth
4   cups hot cooked spaetzle or noodles
    Fresh chopped parsley (optional)

1 Trim fat from roast. If necessary, cut roast to fit in a 3½- or 4-quart slow cooker. In a large nonstick skillet brown the roast on all sides in hot oil.

2 Meanwhile, in the cooker combine carrots, onions, celery, and pickles. Add roast. Combine the ½ cup red wine, the mustard, pepper, cloves, and bay leaves. Pour over all in cooker.

3 Cover and cook on low-heat setting for 10 to 11 hours or on high-heat setting for 5 to 5½ hours.

4 Transfer meat to a serving platter; cover. For sauce, transfer vegetables and cooking liquid to a 2-quart saucepan. Skim off fat. Discard bay leaves. In a small bowl stir together flour and the 2 tablespoons red wine. Stir into mixture in saucepan. Cook and stir over medium heat until thickened and bubbly; cook and stir for 1 minute more. Slice meat. Serve meat and vegetables with sauce and spaetzle. If desired, sprinkle with fresh chopped parsley.

nutrition facts per serving: 358 cal., 7 g total fat (2 g sat. fat), 106 mg chol., 592 mg sodium, 30 g carb. (3 g fiber, 5 g sugars), 36 g pro. exchanges: 0.5 vegetable, 2 starch, 4 lean meat.

Popular throughout France, persillade *is a mix of minced garlic and parsley. We've tweaked the tradition, adding a South of France angle with olives and lemon.*

8g
CARB. PER
SERVING

mediterranean beef roast

prep: 15 minutes cook: 10 hours (low)

makes: 6 servings (3 ounces cooked meat and about 1 tablespoon persillade each)

1   2-pound beef chuck
    roast
30 cloves garlic, peeled
    (about 2½ heads)
¼   cup snipped dried
    tomatoes (not
    oil-packed)
½   cup beef broth
2   tablespoons balsamic
    vinegar
1   teaspoon dried Italian
    seasoning, crushed
¼   teaspoon black
    pepper
1   recipe Olive
    Persillade
    Lemon wedges
    (optional)

1 Trim fat from roast. Place garlic cloves and dried tomatoes in a 3½- or 4-quart slow cooker. Top with roast. Pour broth over all in cooker. Sprinkle roast with vinegar, Italian seasoning, and pepper.

2 Cover and cook on low-heat setting for 10 hours. Remove roast from cooker. Using two forks, shred roast or slice the meat. Sprinkle with Olive Persillade. If desired, garnish with lemon wedges.

nutrition facts per serving: 240 cal., 7 g total fat (2 g sat. fat), 67 mg chol., 262 mg sodium, 8 g carb. (1 g fiber, 2 g sugars), 35 g pro. exchanges: 1 vegetable, 4 lean meat, 1 fat.

olive persillade: In a small bowl stir together ¼ cup snipped fresh parsley, 1 to 2 tablespoons chopped pitted Kalamata olives, and 1 teaspoon finely shredded lemon peel.

For succulent results, beef brisket is best cooked "low and slow"—on low heat and for a lengthy cooking time. That's why no high-heat option is given with this recipe.

layered brisket dinner

prep: 20 minutes cook: 10 to 12 hours (low)
makes: 8 servings (⅔ cup meat, about ½ cup vegetables, and 1 tablespoon sauce each)

1	3-pound fresh beef brisket
1	tablespoon Dijon-style mustard
1	tablespoon Worcestershire sauce
1	tablespoon balsamic vinegar
¼	teaspoon black pepper
1	pound baby red or yellow potatoes, halved if large
1	8-ounce package baby carrots (2 cups)
1	small onion, cut into wedges
2	teaspoons olive oil
½	teaspoon dried Italian seasoning, crushed
¼	teaspoon salt
¼	teaspoon black pepper
1	recipe Tangy Mustard Sauce

1 Trim fat from brisket. Place brisket in a 5- to 6-quart slow cooker. In a small bowl stir together the mustard, Worcestershire sauce, vinegar, and ¼ teaspoon pepper. Pour over brisket, turning brisket to coat both sides.

2 On a 20×18-inch sheet of heavy foil place potatoes, carrots, and onion. Drizzle with olive oil and sprinkle with Italian seasoning, salt, and ¼ teaspoon pepper. Bring up long sides of foil and fold to seal. Roll up short sides of foil to enclose vegetables. If necessary, manipulate foil packet to fit in cooker, making sure the brisket is completely covered with the foil packet.

3 Cover and cook on low-heat setting for 10 to 12 hours.

4 Remove foil packet and brisket from cooker. Using two forks, shred brisket or slice the meat. Carefully open the foil packet to avoid getting burned by escaping steam. Serve meat and vegetables with Tangy Mustard Sauce.

nutrition facts per serving: 273 cal., 11 g total fat (4 g sat. fat), 78 mg chol., 289 mg sodium, 14 g carb. (2 g fiber, 3 g sugars), 27 g pro. exchanges: 1 starch, 3.5 lean meat, 1 fat.

tangy mustard sauce: In a small bowl combine ½ cup light sour cream; 1½ teaspoons Dijon-style mustard; ½ teaspoon dried Italian seasoning, crushed; and ½ teaspoon snipped fresh thyme (optional). Chill sauce in refrigerator. Before serving, sprinkle with additional snipped fresh thyme if desired.

*This soup allows you to savor all the flavors you love about
a meaty, red-sauced pasta—without an overload of pasta.*

spaghetti lover's soup

prep: 25 minutes cook: 8 to 10 hours (low) or 4 to 5 hours (high)
+ 15 to 20 minutes (high)
makes: 6 servings (1 cup each)

1   pound lean ground
    beef
1   medium onion,
    chopped (½ cup)
1   medium green sweet
    pepper, chopped
    (½ cup)
1   stalk celery, chopped
    (½ cup)
1   medium carrot,
    chopped (½ cup)
2   cloves garlic, minced
2   14.5-ounce can
    no-salt-added
    diced tomatoes,
    undrained
1   14-ounce jar
    spaghetti sauce
1   cup water
1   tablespoon quick-
    cooking tapioca,
    crushed
½   teaspoon dried Italian
    seasoning, crushed
¼   teaspoon salt
¼   teaspoon black
    pepper
⅛   teaspoon cayenne
    pepper
2   ounces dried
    spaghetti, broken
    into 2- to 3-inch
    pieces

1 In a large skillet cook ground beef, onion,
sweet pepper, celery, carrot, and garlic
over medium heat until meat is browned and
vegetables are tender. Drain off fat. Transfer
meat mixture to a 3½- or 4-quart slow cooker.
Stir in tomatoes, spaghetti sauce, the water,
tapioca, Italian seasoning, salt, black pepper,
and cayenne pepper.

2 Cover and cook on low-heat setting for
8 to 10 hours or on high-heat setting for
4 to 5 hours.

3 If using low-heat setting, turn to high-
heat setting. Stir in spaghetti. Cover and
cook for 15 to 20 minutes more or until pasta
is tender.

nutrition facts per serving: 252 cal., 8 g total fat
(3 g sat. fat), 49 mg chol., 529 mg sodium, 27 g carb. (5 g fiber,
12 g sugars), 19 g pro. exchanges: 2 vegetable, 1 starch,
2 lean meat, 0.5 fat.

Browning the meat before simmering it adds enticing color and flavor and also makes draining off unwanted fat easy.

stuffed pepper soup

prep: 25 minutes cook: 8 to 10 hours (low) or 4 to 5 hours (high) + 30 minutes (high)
makes: 8 servings (1¼ cups each)

22g
CARB. PER
SERVING

1 pound lean ground beef
1 large onion, chopped (1 cup)
1 medium red sweet pepper, chopped (½ cup)
1 medium orange sweet pepper, chopped (½ cup)
1 medium green sweet pepper, chopped (½ cup)
2 cloves garlic, minced
4 cups lower-sodium beef broth
2 cups water
1 14.5-ounce can diced tomatoes, undrained
½ teaspoon black pepper
½ teaspoon chili powder
½ teaspoon smoked paprika
¾ cup uncooked instant brown rice
½ cup finely shredded Colby and Monterey Jack cheese (2 ounces)

1 In a large skillet cook beef, onion, sweet peppers, and garlic over medium heat until meat is browned and vegetables are tender. Drain off fat.

2 In a 4- to 5-quart slow cooker combine beef-vegetable mixture, broth, the water, tomatoes, black pepper, chili powder, and smoked paprika.

3 Cover and cook on low-heat setting for 8 to 10 hours or on high-heat setting for 4 to 5 hours. If using low-heat setting, turn to high-heat setting. Stir in rice. Cover and cook for 30 minutes more or until heated through. Sprinkle each serving with cheese.

nutrition facts per serving: 218 cal., 7 g total fat (3 g sat. fat), 37 mg chol., 405 mg sodium, 22 g carb. (2 g fiber, 4 g sugars), 17 g pro. exchanges: 1 vegetable, 1 starch, 2 lean meat, 0.5 fat.

When shredding the lemon peel, be sure not to include any of the pith (the white part of the rind). It could bring too much bitterness to the sauce.

meatballs with sweet lemon glaze

33g CARB. PER SERVING

prep: 25 minutes **cook:** 4 hours (low) or 2 hours (high) + 10 minutes (high)
makes: 4 servings (8 meatballs, ¾ cup steamed pea pods, and about 3 tablespoons sauce each)

½ cup finely chopped green onions (4)
¼ cup quick-cooking rolled oats
¼ cup refrigerated or frozen egg product, thawed
3 teaspoons finely shredded lemon peel
¼ teaspoon crushed red pepper
¼ teaspoon salt
1 pound 93 percent lean ground beef, ground pork, or ground turkey
   Nonstick cooking spray
½ cup apricot spreadable fruit
¼ cup water
2 tablespoons reduced-sodium soy sauce
2 tablespoons lemon juice
2 teaspoons cornstarch
4 cups fresh snow pea pods, steamed*
   Freshly ground black pepper (optional)
   Lemon wedges (optional)

1 In a large bowl combine green onions, oats, egg, 2 teaspoons of the lemon peel, the crushed red pepper, and salt. Add ground beef; mix well. Form into 1-inch meatballs.

2 Lightly coat an unheated large nonstick skillet with cooking spray; heat over medium-high heat until hot. Brown meatballs in skillet, turning occasionally. Meanwhile, in a small bowl combine spreadable fruit, the water, 1 tablespoon of the soy sauce, and 1 tablespoon of the lemon juice. Lightly coat an unheated 1½- or 2-quart slow cooker with cooking spray. Add meatballs to cooker and pour the fruit spread mixture over all in cooker.

3 Cover and cook on low-heat setting for 4 hours or on high-heat setting for 2 hours.

4 Using a slotted spoon, transfer the meatballs to a plate. In a small bowl whisk together the remaining 1 tablespoon soy sauce, 1 tablespoon lemon juice, the cornstarch, and remaining 1 teaspoon lemon peel. Whisk into the cooking liquid in slow cooker. Gently fold in the meatballs.

5 If using low-heat setting, turn to high-heat setting. Cover and cook about 10 minutes more or until thoroughly heated and sauce is slightly thickened. Stir in snow peas. If desired, sprinkle with black pepper and serve with lemon wedges.

nutrition facts per serving: 332 cal., 9 g total fat (3 g sat. fat), 61 mg chol., 511 mg sodium, 33 g carb. (3 g fiber, 20 g sugars), 29 g pro. exchanges: 1 vegetable, 1 fruit, 1 starch, 1 lean meat.

＊test kitchen tip: To steam snow pea pods, place a steamer basket in a saucepan. Add water to just below the bottom of the basket. Bring water to boiling. Add pea pods to steamer basket. Cover and reduce heat. Steam for 2 to 4 minutes or until desired doneness.

Like spinach, chard is a storehouse of vitamins and phytonutrients. To prep, simply chop the leaves and sauté in a little olive oil until lightly wilted.

16g
CARB. PER
SERVING

steak with tuscan tomato sauce

prep: 25 minutes   cook: 8 to 10 hours (low) or 4 to 5 hours (high)
makes: 4 servings (3 ounces meat and about ⅓ cup sauce each)

1   pound boneless beef round steak, cut 1 inch thick
1   tablespoon vegetable oil
1   medium onion, sliced (½ cup)
2   tablespoons quick-cooking tapioca, crushed
1   teaspoon dried thyme, crushed
¼   teaspoon black pepper
1   14.5-ounce can diced tomatoes with basil, garlic, and oregano, undrained
2   cups hot cooked red chard, noodles, or brown rice (optional)

1 Trim fat from steak. In a large skillet brown steak on all sides in hot oil over medium heat. Drain off fat.

2 Place onion in a 3½- or 4-quart slow cooker. Sprinkle with tapioca, dried thyme, and pepper. Pour tomatoes over onion in cooker. Place steak on mixture in cooker.

3 Cover and cook on low-heat setting for 8 to 10 hours or on high-heat setting for 4 to 5 hours.

4 Transfer meat to a cutting board. Slice meat; serve with cooking sauce and, if desired, hot cooked chard, noodles, or rice.

nutrition facts per serving: 230 cal., 6 g total fat (1 g sat. fat), 49 mg chol., 595 mg sodium, 16 g carb. (1 g fiber, 7 g sugars), 28 g pro. exchanges: 1 vegetable, 0.5 starch, 2.5 lean meat.

No need to cook the spinach; it will wilt from the heat of the stew. The green color adds a lovely sparkle to the plate.

greek lamb with spinach and orzo

28g
CARB. PER SERVING

prep: 25 minutes cook: 8 to 10 hours (low) or 4 to 5 hours (high)
makes: 10 servings (1 cup lamb mixture, 1 cup spinach, and 1½ tablespoons cheese each)

1	tablespoon dried oregano, crushed
1	tablespoon finely shredded lemon peel
4	cloves garlic, minced
½	teaspoon salt
3	pounds lamb stew meat
¼	cup lemon juice
12	ounces dried orzo (2 cups dried)
1	10-ounce package fresh spinach, chopped
1	cup crumbled reduced-fat feta cheese (4 ounces)
	Lemon wedges

1 In a small bowl stir together oregano, lemon peel, garlic, and salt. Sprinkle oregano mixture evenly over lamb; rub in with your fingers. Place lamb in a 3½- or 4-quart slow cooker. Sprinkle lamb with lemon juice.

2 Cover and cook on low-heat setting for 8 to 10 hours or on high-heat setting for 4 to 5 hours.

3 Meanwhile, cook orzo according to package directions; drain. Stir cooked orzo into meat mixture in cooker. Place spinach on a large serving platter. Spoon lamb mixture over spinach. Sprinkle with feta cheese. Serve with lemon wedges.

nutrition facts per serving: 347 cal., 10 g total fat (4 g sat. fat), 92 mg chol., 417 mg sodium, 28 g carb. (2 g fiber, 1 g sugars), 36 g pro. exchanges: 1 vegetable, 1.5 starch, 4 lean meat.

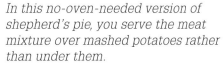

*In this no-oven-needed version of
shepherd's pie, you serve the meat
mixture over mashed potatoes rather
than under them.*

43g
CARB. PER
SERVING

lamb-lentil shepherd's pie

prep: 20 minutes   cook: 6 to 8 hours (low) or 3 to 4 hours (high)
makes: 8 servings (1 cup meat mixture and ⅓ cup potatoes each)

1   pound lean ground
    lamb or beef
1   large onion, chopped
    (1 cup)
1   16-ounce package
    frozen mixed
    vegetables
1   14.5-ounce can lower-
    sodium beef broth
1   14.5-ounce can no-
    salt-added diced
    tomatoes with basil,
    garlic, and oregano,
    undrained
1   10.75-ounce can
    reduced-fat and
    reduced-sodium
    condensed tomato
    soup
1   cup dry brown lentils,
    rinsed and drained
¼   teaspoon crushed
    red pepper
2⅔ cups prepared
    mashed potatoes

1 In a large skillet cook ground lamb and onion until meat is browned and onion is tender; drain off fat.

2 In a 3½- or 4-quart slow cooker combine meat mixture, frozen vegetables, broth, tomatoes, tomato soup, lentils, and crushed red pepper.

3 Cover and cook on low-heat setting for 6 to 8 hours or on high-heat setting for 3 to 4 hours. Serve meat and lentil mixture over potatoes.

nutrition facts per serving: 317 cal., 6 g total fat
(2 g sat. fat), 36 mg chol., 429 mg sodium, 43 g carb. (14 g fiber,
8 g sugars), 24 g pro. exchanges: 0.5 vegetable, 2.5 carb.,
2 lean meat.

The flavor of paprika is released during cooking. When paprika is sprinkled onto foods just before serving, you'll get the red color but not much additional flavor.

hungarian pork goulash

prep: 30 minutes   cook: 5 to 6 hours (low) or 2½ to 3 hours (high) + 30 minutes (high)
makes: 6 servings (1¼ cups each)

1   1½- to 2-pound pork sirloin roast
1   tablespoon Hungarian paprika or Spanish paprika
1   teaspoon caraway seeds, crushed
½   teaspoon garlic powder
½   teaspoon black pepper
¼   teaspoon salt
1   tablespoon canola oil
2   stalks celery, thinly sliced (1 cup)
2   medium carrots, thinly sliced (1 cup)
2   medium parsnips, halved lengthwise if large and thinly sliced (1 cup)
1   large onion, chopped (1 cup)
1   14.5-ounce can no-salt-added diced tomatoes, undrained
½   cup water
4   ounces dried wide whole grain noodles (2 cups dried)
6   tablespoons light sour cream
    Paprika (optional)

1 Trim fat from roast. Cut roast into 2-inch cubes. In a large bowl combine paprika, caraway seeds, garlic powder, pepper, and salt. Add pork cubes and toss to coat. In a large skillet cook pork, half at a time, in hot oil over medium heat until browned, turning occasionally. Transfer pork to a 3½- or 4-quart slow cooker. Add celery, carrots, parsnips, onion, and tomatoes. Pour the water over all in cooker.

2 Cover and cook on low-heat setting for 5 to 6 hours or on high-heat setting for 2½ to 3 hours.

3 If using low-heat setting, turn to high-heat setting. Stir noodles into pork mixture in cooker. Cover and cook on high-heat setting for 30 minutes more or until noodles are tender, stirring once halfway through cooking. Top each serving with 1 tablespoon sour cream. If desired, sprinkle servings with paprika.

nutrition facts per serving: 285 cal., 9 g total fat (2 g sat. fat), 82 mg chol., 234 mg sodium, 24 g carb. (5 g fiber, 6 g sugars), 28 g pro. exchanges: 2 vegetable, 1 starch, 3 lean meat, 1 fat.

For more nutrients and a satisfying nutty flavor, consider substituting multigrain pasta or whole wheat pasta for regular pasta in your other pasta recipes.

35g CARB. PER SERVING

cajun-style pork and shrimp pasta

prep: 30 minutes   cook: 6 to 7 hours (low) or 3 to 3½ hours (high)
+ 15 minutes (high)
makes: 8 servings (1½ cups each)

1	1½- to 2-pound pork sirloin roast
½	teaspoon salt
¼	teaspoon black pepper
	Nonstick cooking spray
2	stalks celery, thinly sliced (1 cup)
1	large onion, cut into thin wedges
1	15-ounce can red beans, rinsed and drained
1	14.5-ounce can no-salt-added diced tomatoes, undrained
8	ounces dried multigrain rotini pasta (3¼ cups dried)
1½	tablespoons salt-free Cajun seasoning or Homemade Salt-Free Cajun Seasoning
1	medium green sweet pepper, chopped (¾ cup)
8	ounces frozen cooked peeled and deveined shrimp, thawed
	Snipped fresh cilantro

1 Trim fat from roast. Cut roast into three portions. Sprinkle pork portions with salt and black pepper. Coat an unheated large nonstick skillet with cooking spray; heat over medium heat. Brown roast portions in hot skillet, turning to brown all sides evenly. In a 3½- or 4-quart slow cooker combine celery, onion, beans, and tomatoes. Top with browned pork pieces.

2 Cover and cook on low-heat setting for 6 to 7 hours or on high-heat setting for 3 to 3½ hours.

3 Meanwhile, cook pasta according to package directions, except cook 1 minute less than package directions; drain. Remove meat from cooker; set aside. If using low-heat setting, turn to high-heat setting. Add Cajun seasoning, pasta, and sweet pepper to the cooker. Cover and cook for 15 minutes more. Cut meat into ½- to ¾-inch cubes; stir into pasta mixture along with thawed shrimp. Sprinkle each serving with cilantro.

nutrition facts per serving: 306 cal., 5 g total fat (1 g sat. fat), 109 mg chol., 370 mg sodium, 35 g carb. (6 g fiber, 4 g sugars), 32 g pro. exchanges: 1 vegetable, 2 starch, 3.5 lean meat.

homemade salt-free cajun seasoning: In a small bowl stir together 1 teaspoon onion powder, 1 teaspoon paprika, ¾ teaspoon ground white pepper, ¾ teaspoon garlic powder, ¼ teaspoon cayenne pepper, and ¼ teaspoon black pepper.

Turn to this recipe when you crave something hearty and filling. The bean duo will help you feel especially satisfied.

pork ribs and beans

prep: 20 minutes cook: 8 to 9 hours (low) or 4 to 4½ hours (high)
makes: 6 servings (4½ ounces meat and ⅔ cup bean mixture each)

2 pounds boneless country-style pork ribs

1 teaspoon Italian seasoning, crushed

¾ teaspoon dried rosemary, crushed

¼ teaspoon black pepper

1 medium onion, chopped

1 15- to 19-ounce can white kidney (cannellini) beans, rinsed and drained

1 15-ounce can black beans, rinsed and drained

1 14.5-ounce can no-salt-added diced tomatoes, undrained

¼ cup dry red wine or water

1 Trim fat from meat. Sprinkle meat with Italian seasoning, rosemary, and pepper. Place meat in a 3½- or 4-quart slow cooker. Place onion, beans, and tomatoes on top of meat. Pour wine over all in cooker.

2 Cover and cook on low-heat setting for 8 to 9 hours or on high-heat setting for 4 to 4½ hours.

3 Using a slotted spoon, transfer meat and bean mixture to a serving bowl. Spoon some of the cooking liquid over meat and beans.

nutrition facts per serving: 325 cal., 8 g total fat (3 g sat. fat), 111 mg chol., 415 mg sodium, 24 g carb. (8 g fiber, 3 g sugars), 41 g pro. exchanges: 0.5 vegetable, 1 starch, 5 lean meat.

258

Pork takes well to the flavorings of orange and spice, as you'll see in this fascinating dish. Pictured on page 243.

33g
CARB. PER
SERVING

pork tenderloin with sweet-spiced onions

prep: 25 minutes   cook: 2 hours (low) or 1½ hours (high) + 15 minutes (high)
makes: 4 servings (3 ounces meat, ½ cup couscous mixture, and ¼ cup sauce each)

½ teaspoon coarsely ground black pepper
½ teaspoon ground cinnamon
¼ teaspoon ground allspice
⅛ teaspoon salt
1 pound pork tenderloin
2 teaspoons canola oil
  Nonstick cooking spray
1 large onion, chopped (1 cup)
½ teaspoon finely shredded orange peel (set aside)
¼ cup orange juice
2 tablespoons reduced-sodium soy sauce
2 teaspoons cornstarch
2 teaspoons sugar∗
2 cups hot cooked whole wheat couscous
½ cup frozen peas, thawed
1 ounce sliced almonds, toasted (about ¼ cup)

1 In a small bowl combine pepper, cinnamon, allspice, and salt. Sprinkle evenly over the pork and press onto meat.

2 In a large nonstick skillet heat 1 teaspoon of the oil over medium-high heat. Brown pork in hot oil about 4 minutes, turning occasionally to brown evenly. Lightly coat an unheated 3- or 3½-quart slow cooker with cooking spray. Place pork in cooker. Heat the remaining 1 teaspoon oil in the skillet. Cook onion in skillet about 4 minutes or until browned, stirring frequently. Spoon onion around pork in cooker. Pour orange juice over onion.

3 Cover and cook on low-heat setting for 2 hours or on high-heat setting for 1½ hours or until internal temperature of pork registers 145°F on an instant-read thermometer.

4 Transfer pork to a cutting board; cover to keep warm. If using low-heat setting, turn cooker to high-heat setting. In a small bowl whisk together soy sauce, cornstarch, sugar, and reserved orange peel until cornstarch is completely dissolved. Stir into onion mixture in slow cooker. Cover and cook for 15 minutes more to thicken slightly.

5 To serve, toss couscous with peas and almonds. Slice pork; serve with couscous mixture and sauce.

nutrition facts per serving: 340 cal., 10 g total fat (2 g sat. fat), 71 mg chol., 408 mg sodium, 33 g carb. (4 g fiber, 7 g sugars), 29 g pro. exchanges: 2 starch, 3.5 lean meat.

nutrition facts per serving with substitute: Same as original, except 333 cal., 31 g carb. (6 g sugars).

∗sugar substitutes: Choose from Splenda granular or Sweet'N Low bulk or packets. Follow package directions to use product amount equivalent to 2 teaspoons sugar.

Fresh rosemary, thyme, and sage all freeze well. Just rinse, pat dry, and place in freezer bags.

herbed apricot pork loin roast

prep: 20 minutes cook: 6 to 7 hours (low) or 3 to 3½ hours (high)
stand: 15 minutes
makes: 8 servings (5 ounces meat, ½ apricot, and ¼ cup sauce each)

1 3-pound boneless pork top loin roast
¼ teaspoon salt
¼ teaspoon black pepper
1 10-ounce jar apricot spreadable fruit
⅓ cup finely chopped onion
2 tablespoons Dijon-style mustard
1 tablespoon brandy (optional)
1 teaspoon finely shredded lemon peel
1 teaspoon snipped fresh rosemary or ½ teaspoon dried rosemary, crushed
1 teaspoon snipped fresh sage or ½ teaspoon dried sage, crushed
1 teaspoon snipped fresh thyme or ½ teaspoon dried thyme, crushed
¼ teaspoon black pepper
2 tablespoons cold water
4 teaspoons cornstarch
4 fresh apricots, pitted and quartered
   Fresh thyme, sage, and/or rosemary sprigs (optional)

1 Season pork roast with salt and ¼ teaspoon pepper. Place roast in a 4- to 5-quart slow cooker. In a medium bowl combine spreadable fruit, onion, mustard, brandy (if using), lemon peel, rosemary, sage, thyme, and ¼ teaspoon pepper. Pour mixture over roast in cooker.

2 Cover and cook on low-heat setting for 6 to 7 hours or on high-heat setting for 3 to 3½ hours.

3 Remove roast from cooker, reserving cooking liquid. Cover roast loosely with foil and let stand for 15 minutes before carving.

4 For sauce, in a medium saucepan combine the cold water and cornstarch; carefully stir in liquid from slow cooker. Cook and stir over medium heat until thickened and bubbly; cook and stir for 2 minutes more. Serve pork with sauce and apricots. If desired, garnish with fresh thyme, sage, and/or rosemary sprigs.

nutrition facts per serving: 322 cal., 7 g total fat (2 g sat. fat), 107 mg chol., 247 mg sodium, 24 g carb. (1 g fiber, 18 g sugars), 38 g pro. exchanges: 1.5 carb., 5 lean meat.

Salsa verde gets its green color mainly from tomatillos, a fruit that looks a little like a green tomato but imparts hints of citrus, apple, and herb flavors.

31g
CARB. PER
SERVING

braised pork with salsa verde

prep: 20 minutes cook: 6 to 6 ½ hours (low) or 3 hours (high)
makes: 6 servings (1 cup pork mixture and ½ cup rice each)

1 large onion, cut into thin wedges
1½ pounds boneless pork loin, cut into 1½-inch pieces
2 large tomatoes, coarsely chopped (1⅓ cups)
1 16-ounce jar green salsa (salsa verde)
½ cup reduced-sodium chicken broth
2 cloves garlic, minced
1 teaspoon ground cumin
¼ teaspoon black pepper
3 cups hot cooked brown rice
   Snipped fresh cilantro

1 In a 3½- or 4-quart slow cooker place onion and pork. Top with tomatoes, salsa, broth, garlic, cumin, and pepper.

2 Cover and cook on low-heat setting for 6 to 6½ hours or on high-heat setting for 3 hours. Serve with hot cooked brown rice and top each serving with cilantro.

nutrition facts per serving: 297 cal., 6 g total fat (1 g sat. fat), 78 mg chol., 231 mg sodium, 31 g carb. (3 g fiber, 3 g sugars), 29 g pro. exchanges: 0.5 vegetable, 2 starch, 3 lean meat.

The touch of white wine vinegar brightens and intensifies the flavors of this long-simmering stew.

chicken ragout

prep: 20 minutes cook: 8 to 10 hours (low)
makes: 8 servings (1 cup chicken mixture and about ⅓ cup noodles each)

8 chicken thighs (about
    3½ pounds total),
    skinned
2 14.5-ounce cans
    no-salt-added diced
    tomatoes, drained
3 cups 1-inch carrot
    slices or baby
    carrots
1 large onion, cut into
    wedges (1 cup)
⅓ cup reduced-sodium
    chicken broth
2 tablespoons white
    wine vinegar
1 teaspoon dried
    rosemary, crushed
1 teaspoon dried
    thyme, crushed
¼ teaspoon black
    pepper
8 ounces fresh button
    mushrooms, sliced
1 teaspoon olive oil
3 cups hot cooked
    whole wheat
    noodles
    Snipped fresh parsley
    (optional)

1 Place chicken thighs in a 3½- or 4-quart slow cooker. In a large bowl stir together tomatoes, carrots, onion, broth, vinegar, rosemary, thyme, and pepper. Pour over chicken in cooker.

2 Cover and cook on low-heat setting for 8 to 10 hours.

3 Just before serving, in a large nonstick skillet cook and stir mushrooms in hot oil over medium-high heat for 8 to 10 minutes or until golden. Remove chicken from cooker. Remove chicken from bones; discard bones. Stir chicken and mushrooms into mixture in cooker. Serve chicken mixture over hot cooked noodles. If desired, sprinkle each serving with parsley.

nutrition facts per serving: 234 cal., 4 g total fat (1 g sat. fat), 57 mg chol., 163 mg sodium, 33 g carb. (7 g fiber, 7 g sugars), 20 g pro. exchanges: 1.5 vegetable, 1.5 starch, 2 lean meat.

Veracruz sauce melds hot chile peppers—common in Mexican cooking—with olives, a typical Spanish touch.

chicken veracruz

prep: 25 minutes cook: 10 hours (low)

makes: 6 servings (1 chicken thigh, ¾ cup vegetable mixture, and about 2 tablespoons topping each)

1   **medium onion, cut into wedges**

1   **pound yellow-skin potatoes, cut into 1-inch pieces**

6   **skinless, boneless chicken thighs (about 1¼ pounds total)**

2   **14.5-ounce cans no-salt-added diced tomatoes**

1   **fresh jalapeño chile pepper, seeded and sliced** *

2   **tablespoons Worcestershire sauce**

1   **tablespoon chopped garlic**

1   **teaspoon dried oregano, crushed**

¼   **teaspoon ground cinnamon**

⅛   **teaspoon ground cloves**

1   **recipe Parsley-Olive Topping**

1 Place onion in a 3½- or 4-quart slow cooker. Top with potatoes and chicken thighs. Drain juice from 1 can of tomatoes and discard the juice. In a bowl stir together the drained and undrained tomatoes, the jalapeño pepper, Worcestershire sauce, garlic, oregano, cinnamon, and cloves. Pour over all in cooker.

2 Cover and cook on low-heat setting for 10 hours. Sprinkle Parsley-Olive Topping over individual servings.

nutrition facts per serving: 228 cal., 5 g total fat (1 g sat. fat), 78 mg chol., 287 mg sodium, 25 g carb. (5 g fiber, 9 g sugars), 22 g pro. exchanges: 1 vegetable, 1.5 starch, 2.5 lean meat.

*test kitchen tip: Because chile peppers contain volatile oils that can burn your skin and eyes, avoid direct contact with them as much as possible. When working with chile peppers, wear plastic or rubber gloves. If your bare hands do touch the peppers, wash your hands and nails well with soap and warm water.

parsley-olive topping: In a small bowl stir together ½ cup snipped fresh parsley and ¼ cup chopped pimiento-stuffed green olives.

Quick-cooking tapioca thickens this sauce. Unlike other thickeners, such as flour and cornstarch, it won't break down during the long cooking process.

herbed chicken and mushrooms

prep: 25 minutes cook: 7 to 8 hours (low) or 3½ to 4 hours (high)
makes: 6 servings (2 chicken thighs, ⅔ cup vegetable mixture, and ½ cup cooked noodles each)

5   cups sliced assorted
    fresh mushrooms
    (such as stemmed
    shiitake, button,
    cremini, and oyster)
1   medium onion,
    chopped
1   medium carrot,
    chopped
¼   cup dried tomato
    pieces (not oil-
    packed)
¾   cup reduced-sodium
    chicken broth
¼   cup dry white wine
    or reduced-sodium
    chicken broth
3   tablespoons quick-
    cooking tapioca
1   teaspoon dried
    thyme, crushed
½   teaspoon dried basil,
    crushed
½   teaspoon salt
¼   to ½ teaspoon black
    pepper
12 small chicken thighs
    and/or drumsticks
    (about 3 pounds
    total), skinned
3   cups hot cooked
    whole wheat and/or
    spinach fettuccine
    or linguine
    Small fresh basil
    leaves (optional)

1 In a 4- to 5-quart slow cooker combine mushrooms, onion, carrot, and dried tomato pieces. Add chicken broth and wine. Sprinkle with tapioca, thyme, dried basil, salt, and pepper. Add chicken pieces to cooker.

2 Cover and cook on low-heat setting for 7 to 8 hours or on high-heat setting for 3½ to 4 hours.

3 Transfer chicken and vegetables to a serving platter. Spoon some of the cooking liquid over the top. Serve with hot cooked pasta. If desired, garnish with fresh basil.

nutrition facts per serving: 306 cal., 7 g total fat (2 g sat. fat), 107 mg chol., 415 mg sodium, 29 g carb. (5 g fiber, 4 g sugars), 33 g pro. exchanges: 1 vegetable, 1.5 starch, 4 lean meat.

In a hurry? You'll appreciate that just a handful of ingredients brings so much flavor to the table without a lot of chopping and measuring.

simple hoisin chicken

31g
CARB. PER
SERVING

prep: 15 minutes cook: 4 to 5 hours (low) or 2½ hours (high) + 30 to 45 minutes (high)
makes: 6 servings (2 chicken thighs, ½ cup vegetable mixture, and ⅓ cup rice each)

Nonstick cooking
  spray
12 bone-in chicken
    thighs (3½ to
    4 pounds total),
    skinned
 2 tablespoons quick-
    cooking tapioca
 ⅛ teaspoon salt
 ⅛ teaspoon black
    pepper
 ½ cup bottled hoisin
    sauce
 1 16-ounce package
    frozen broccoli
    stir-fry vegetables
 2 cups hot cooked
    brown rice

1 Coat a 3½- or 4-quart slow cooker
with cooking spray. Place chicken in
the prepared cooker. Sprinkle chicken with
tapioca, salt, and pepper. Pour hoisin sauce
over chicken.

2 Cover and cook on low-heat setting for
4 to 5 hours or on high-heat setting for
2½ hours.

3 If using low-heat setting, turn to high-heat
setting. Stir in frozen vegetables. Cover
and cook for 30 to 45 minutes more or just
until vegetables are tender. Serve over hot
cooked rice.

nutrition facts per serving: 332 cal., 7 g total fat
(2 g sat. fat), 126 mg chol., 524 mg sodium, 31 g carb. (3 g fiber,
8 g sugars), 34 g pro. exchanges: 1 vegetable, 1.5 starch,
4 lean meat, 0.5 fat.

24g CARB. PER SERVING

In Asian cooking, foods cooked in soy sauce are referred to as "red-cooked"—but they usually take on a rich brown color.

chinese red-cooked chicken

prep: 25 minutes cook: 6 to 7 hours (low) or 3 to 3½ hours (high)
makes: 6 servings (4½ ounces meat, ½ cup noodles, and about ¼ cup cooking liquid each)

2½ to 3 pounds chicken drumsticks and/or thighs, skinned
3 whole star anise
2 3-inch-long strips orange peel✳
1 2-inch piece fresh ginger, thinly sliced
3 inches stick cinnamon
2 cloves garlic, smashed
1 teaspoon whole Szechwan peppercorns or black peppercorns
2 green onions, cut into 2-inch pieces
1 cup reduced-sodium chicken broth
2 tablespoons reduced-sodium soy sauce
2 teaspoons packed brown sugar
1 teaspoon dry sherry (optional)
1 8-ounce package Chinese egg noodles
2 tablespoons fresh cilantro leaves

1 Place chicken in a 3½- or 4-quart slow cooker. For the spice bag, place star anise, orange peel, ginger, cinnamon, garlic, and peppercorns in the center of a double-thick 8-inch square of 100-percent-cotton cheesecloth. Gather corners together and tie closed with 100-percent-cotton kitchen string. Add spice bag to slow cooker. Top with green onions. In a bowl combine broth, soy sauce, brown sugar, and, if desired, sherry. Pour over all in cooker.

2 Cover and cook on low-heat setting for 6 to 7 hours or on high-heat setting for 3 to 3½ hours.

3 Meanwhile, cook noodles according to package directions; drain. Remove chicken from cooking liquid. Strain liquid, discarding spice bag and solids; skim off fat. Serve chicken over noodles in shallow bowls. Drizzle chicken and noodles with cooking liquid and garnish with cilantro leaves.

nutrition facts per serving: 244 cal., 4 g total fat (1 g sat. fat), 90 mg chol., 576 mg sodium, 24 g carb. (1 g fiber, 2 g sugars), 26 g pro. exchanges: 1.5 starch, 3 lean meat.

✳test kitchen tip: Use a vegetable peeler to remove 3-inch-long strips of peel from an orange, avoiding the bitter white pith underneath.

Popular in Indian cooking, chutney is a condiment made of fruits, spices, vinegar, and sugar. Another time, use the chutney to dress up roasted pork or chicken.

mango-chutney chicken

48g CARB. PER SERVING

prep: 20 minutes   cook: 6 to 7 hours (low) or 3 to 3½ hours (high)
makes: 4 servings (1 chicken leg, ½ cup sauce, and ⅓ cup rice each)

1	medium onion, cut into wedges
3	pounds meaty chicken pieces (breast halves or whole chicken legs), skinned
⅛	teaspoon black pepper
¼	cup mango chutney
⅓	cup bottled low-calorie barbecue sauce
½	teaspoon curry powder
1⅓	cups hot cooked brown rice
1	mango, finely chopped
	Chopped green onions (optional)

1 Place onion wedges in a 3½- or 4-quart slow cooker. Remove any visible fat from chicken. Place chicken in cooker; sprinkle with pepper. Snip any large pieces of chutney. In a small bowl combine chutney, barbecue sauce, and curry powder. Pour over chicken in cooker.

2 Cover and cook on low-heat setting for 6 to 7 hours or on high-heat setting for 3 to 3½ hours. Remove chicken from cooker. Stir onions and sauce in cooker.

3 Toss rice with chopped mango and, if desired, green onions. Serve onion and sauce mixture over chicken and rice.

nutrition facts per serving: 433 cal., 8 g total fat (2 g sat. fat), 155 mg chol., 419 mg sodium, 48 g carb. (3 g fiber, 26 g sugars), 42 g pro. exchanges: 1 fruit, 1 starch, 1 carb., 5 lean meat.

Celery, onion, and sweet peppers are considered the "holy trinity" of Cajun and Creole cooking; they form a rich, flavorful backdrop for this spirited dish.

chicken and shrimp jambalaya

37g CARB. PER SERVING

prep: 20 minutes   cook: 4½ to 5 ½ hours (low) or 2¼ to 2¾ hours (high) + 30 minutes (high)

makes: 8 servings (1½ cups each)

1 pound skinless, boneless chicken breast halves or thighs
4 stalks celery, thinly sliced (2 cups)
2 large onions, chopped (2 cups)
1 14.5-ounce can no-salt-added diced tomatoes, undrained
1 14.5-ounce can reduced-sodium chicken broth
½ of a 6-ounce can no-salt-added tomato paste (⅓ cup)
1 recipe Homemade Salt-Free Cajun seasoning or 1½ teaspoons salt-free Cajun seasoning
2 cloves garlic, minced
½ teaspoon salt
1½ cups uncooked instant brown rice
¾ cup chopped assorted sweet peppers
8 ounces fresh or frozen peeled and deveined cooked shrimp*
2 tablespoons snipped fresh Italian (flat-leaf) parsley

1 Cut chicken into ¾-inch pieces. In a 3½- or 4-quart slow cooker combine chicken, celery, onions, tomatoes, broth, tomato paste, Homemade Salt-Free Cajun Seasoning, garlic, and salt.

2 Cover and cook on low-heat setting for 4½ to 5½ hours or on high-heat setting for 2¼ to 2¾ hours.

3 If using low-heat setting, turn to high-heat setting. Stir in uncooked rice and sweet peppers. Cover and cook about 30 minutes more or until most of the liquid is absorbed and rice is tender.

4 Before serving, thaw shrimp, if frozen. Stir shrimp and parsley into chicken mixture.

nutrition facts per serving: 266 cal., 2 g total fat (0 g sat. fat), 88 mg chol., 419 mg sodium, 37 g carb. (4 g fiber, 6 g sugars), 24 g pro. exchanges: 3 vegetable, 1.5 starch, 2 lean meat.

✱test kitchen tip: If desired, leave tails on shrimp.

homemade salt-free cajun seasoning: In a small bowl combine ¼ teaspoon ground white pepper, ¼ teaspoon garlic powder, ¼ teaspoon onion powder, ¼ teaspoon paprika, ¼ teaspoon black pepper, and ⅛ to ¼ teaspoon cayenne pepper.

Popular in Spain, paella generally calls on chorizo—a spicy pork sausage. Turkey sausage and hot sauce in this version keep the fat in check.

chicken and shrimp paella

36g
CARB. PER
SERVING

prep: 25 minutes   cook: 8 to 10 hours (low) or 4 to 5 hours (high) + 30 minutes (high)
stand: 10 minutes
makes: 10 servings (1⅓ cups each)

1 medium green sweet pepper, chopped (¾ cup)
1 medium onion, chopped
2 cloves garlic, minced
3 medium tomatoes, chopped
2 cups reduced-sodium chicken broth
1 cup water
2 teaspoons dried oregano, crushed
½ teaspoon salt
½ teaspoon ground turmeric
½ teaspoon black pepper
½ teaspoon bottled hot pepper sauce (optional)
3 pounds chicken thighs and drumsticks, skinned
8 ounces smoked turkey sausage link, halved lengthwise and sliced
2 cups uncooked long grain rice
8 ounces cooked, peeled, and deveined shrimp (tails removed), thawed if frozen
1 cup frozen peas

1 In a 6-quart slow cooker combine sweet pepper, onion, garlic, tomatoes, broth, the water, oregano, salt, turmeric, black pepper, and, if desired, hot pepper sauce. Top with chicken and sausage.

2 Cover and cook on low-heat setting for 8 to 10 hours or on high-heat setting for 4 to 5 hours.

3 If using low-heat setting, turn to high-heat setting. Stir in rice. Cover and cook for 30 to 45 minutes more or until rice is tender. Stir in cooked shrimp and peas. Cover; let stand for 10 minutes.

nutrition facts per serving: 312 cal., 5 g total fat (1 g sat. fat), 121 mg chol., 568 mg sodium, 36 g carb. (2 g fiber, 3 g sugars), 28 g pro. exchanges: 1 vegetable, 2 starch, 3 lean meat.

Shrimp can be a pricey protein option, but the zucchini, sweet red pepper, and acini di pepe help transform a mere 8 ounces into four servings.

32g CARB. PER SERVING

mediterranean shrimp

prep: 25 minutes   cook: 4 hours (low) or 2 hours (high) + 30 minutes (high)
makes: 4 servings (¾ cup shrimp mixture and ½ cup pasta each)

8 ounces fresh or frozen shrimp
Nonstick cooking spray
1 14.5-ounce can no-salt-added diced tomatoes, drained
1 cup sliced zucchini
1 cup red sweet pepper, chopped
½ cup dry white wine or reduced-sodium chicken broth
2 cloves garlic, minced
8 pitted Kalamata olives, chopped
¼ cup chopped fresh basil
1 tablespoon olive oil
1½ teaspoons chopped fresh rosemary or ½ teaspoon dried rosemary, crushed
¼ teaspoon salt
4 ounces dried acini di pepe or whole wheat acini di pepe, cooked according to package directions
2 ounces reduced-fat feta cheese, crumbled

1 Thaw shrimp, if frozen. Peel and devein shrimp; cover and chill until ready to use. Lightly coat an unheated 1½-quart slow cooker with cooking spray. In the slow cooker combine tomatoes, zucchini, sweet pepper, wine, and garlic.

2 Cover and cook on low-heat setting for 4 hours or high-heat setting for 2 hours. (If no heat setting is available, cook for 3 hours.) Stir in the shrimp. If using low-heat setting, turn to high-heat setting. Cover; cook 30 minutes more.

3 Stir in olives, basil, olive oil, rosemary, and salt. Place cooked pasta in a serving bowl and top with shrimp mixture. Sprinkle feta cheese evenly over all.

nutrition facts per serving: 301 cal., 8 g total fat (2 g sat. fat), 90 mg chol., 572 mg sodium, 32 g carb. (4 g fiber, 6 g sugars), 20 g pro. exchanges: 2 vegetable, 1.5 starch, 2 lean meat, 1 fat.

Dig in! Not only does bulgur add a tender, chewy texture and earthy flavor, it also brings fiber, iron, phosphorus, zinc, and other nutrients to the plate.

smoked turkey and bulgur

17g
CARB. PER SERVING

prep: 20 minutes   cook: 3 hours (low)
makes: 8 servings (1 cup each)

Nonstick cooking
    spray
1 large onion, chopped
    (1 cup)
1 medium green sweet
    pepper, cut into
    1-inch pieces (1 cup)
1 stalk celery, sliced
    (½ cup)
1½ cups water
1 medium smoked
    turkey drumstick,
    skin and bone
    removed and meat
    chopped (about
    4 cups)
1 cup uncooked bulgur
¼ teaspoon black pepper
1 medium zucchini,
    coarsely chopped
    (1½ cups)
1 tablespoon snipped
    fresh sage

1 Coat an unheated 4-quart slow cooker with cooking spray. Place onion, sweet pepper, and celery in the prepared cooker. Stir in the water, turkey, bulgur, and black pepper.

2 Cover and cook on low-heat setting for 2½ hours. Stir in zucchini and snipped sage. Cover and cook for 30 minutes more.

nutrition facts per serving: 216 cal., 7 g total fat (2 g sat. fat), 57 mg chol., 684 mg sodium, 17 g carb. (4 g fiber, 2 g sugars), 22 g pro. exchanges: 0.5 vegetable, 1 starch, 2.5 lean meat, 0.5 fat.

Lemon juice and fresh ginger provide a bright, fresh contrast to the deeply nutty sesame oil and seeds.

3g
CARB. PER SERVING

sesame turkey

prep: 15 minutes cook: 5 to 6 hours (low) or 2½ to 3 hours (high)
makes: 8 servings (4 ounces meat and about 3 tablespoons sauce each)

3 pounds turkey breast
  tenderloins
¼ teaspoon black pepper
⅛ teaspoon cayenne
  pepper
¼ cup reduced-sodium
  chicken broth
¼ cup reduced-sodium
  soy sauce
4 teaspoons grated
  fresh ginger
1 tablespoon lemon
  juice
1 tablespoon toasted
  sesame oil
2 cloves garlic, minced
2 tablespoons
  cornstarch
2 tablespoons cold
  water
2 tablespoons green
  onion slivers
1 tablespoon sesame
  seeds, toasted

1 Place turkey in a 3½- or 4-quart slow cooker. Sprinkle with black pepper and cayenne pepper. In a small bowl combine broth, soy sauce, ginger, lemon juice, sesame oil, and garlic. Pour over turkey in cooker.

2 Cover and cook on low-heat setting for 5 to 6 hours or on high-heat setting for 2½ to 3 hours.

3 Transfer turkey to a serving platter, reserving cooking liquid. Cover turkey to keep warm.

4 For sauce, strain cooking liquid into a small saucepan. In a small bowl combine cornstarch and the cold water. Stir into liquid in saucepan. Cook and stir over medium heat until thickened and bubbly; cook and stir for 2 minutes more. Slice turkey. Spoon sauce over turkey and sprinkle with green onion slivers and sesame seeds.

nutrition facts per serving: 222 cal., 3 g total fat (1 g sat. fat), 112 mg chol., 373 mg sodium, 3 g carb. (0 g fiber, 0 g sugars), 42 g pro. exchanges: 6 lean meat.

When you start with dried black beans instead of canned, you can control the amount of sodium that goes into the dish. Your slow cooker will simmer the dried beans to perfection.

black beans and avocado on quinoa

39g CARB. PER SERVING

prep: 20 minutes **stand:** 1 hour 15 minutes **cook:** 10 hours (low) or 5 hours (high)
makes: 6 servings (½ cup spinach, ⅓ cup quinoa, ⅔ cup bean mixture, and ¼ cup avocado each)

6	ounces dried black beans (¾ cup)
5	cups water
	Nonstick cooking spray
1	large onion, chopped (1 cup)
10	ounces grape tomatoes, halved
1	teaspoon ground cumin
½	cup chopped fresh cilantro
2	tablespoons lime juice
1	tablespoon olive oil
½	teaspoon salt
2	cups cooked quinoa
¼	cup chopped fresh cilantro
1	tablespoon olive oil
¼	teaspoon salt
3	cups fresh spinach or arugula
1	ripe medium avocado, peeled, seeded, and chopped
1	medium lime, cut into six wedges

1 Rinse beans; drain. In a large saucepan combine beans and 3 cups of the water. Bring to boiling; reduce heat. Simmer, uncovered, for 10 minutes. Remove from heat. Cover and let stand for 1 hour. Drain and rinse beans.

2 Lightly coat an unheated 3- or 3½-quart slow cooker with cooking spray. Place beans in cooker. Stir in the remaining 2 cups water, the onion, half of the tomatoes, and the cumin.

3 Cover and cook on low-heat setting for 10 hours or on high-heat setting for 5 hours or until beans are soft. Stir in the remaining tomatoes, the ½ cup cilantro, the lime juice, 1 tablespoon oil, and the ½ teaspoon salt. Let stand at least 15 minutes to develop flavors.

4 Before serving, toss the quinoa with the ¼ cup cilantro, 1 tablespoon oil, and the ¼ teaspoon salt. Divide spinach among six serving plates. Spoon the quinoa mixture over the spinach. Spoon bean mixture over the quinoa. Top with avocado and serve with lime wedges.

nutrition facts per serving: 277 cal., 10 g total fat (1 g sat. fat), 0 mg chol., 321 mg sodium, 39 g carb. (9 g fiber, 3 g sugars), 11 g pro. **exchanges:** 1 vegetable, 2 starch, 1 lean meat, 1 fat.

For crisp-tender summer squash, add it to the cooker for the last 20 minutes of cooking. Use that time to prep the salad greens and tomatoes.

40g
CARB. PER
SERVING

lentil taco salad

prep: 20 minutes   cook: 10 to 12 hours (low) + 20 minutes (high)
makes: 8 servings (¾ cup lentil mixture, ¾ cup lettuce, ¼ cup tomato, 1 tablespoon cheese, 1½ tablespoons yogurt, and about ¼ cup chips each)

2   large red and/or green sweet peppers, coarsely chopped (2 cups)
1   large onion, chopped (1 cup)
1   cup dry brown lentils, rinsed and drained
½   cup uncooked regular brown rice
3   cloves garlic, minced
2   teaspoons chili powder
¼   teaspoon salt
2   14.5-ounce cans reduced-sodium chicken or vegetable broth
1   medium yellow summer squash, quartered lengthwise and sliced ½ inch thick (1½ cups)
6   cups mixed salad greens
2   cups chopped tomatoes
½   cup shredded reduced-fat cheddar cheese (2 ounces)
¾   cup plain fat-free Greek yogurt
3   ounces multigrain tortilla chips, broken (about 2 cups)

1 In a 3½- or 4-quart slow cooker combine sweet peppers, onion, lentils, rice, garlic, chili powder, and salt. Pour broth over all in cooker.

2 Cover and cook on low-heat setting for 10 to 12 hours. Turn to high-heat setting. Stir in squash. Cover and cook for 20 minutes more.

3 To serve, arrange salad greens on eight dinner plates. Spoon lentil mixture over greens. Top with tomatoes and sprinkle with cheese. Add a spoonful of yogurt to each serving. Sprinkle with tortilla chips.

nutrition facts per serving: 262 cal., 6 g total fat (1 g sat. fat), 5 mg chol., 446 mg sodium, 40 g carb. (11 g fiber, 7 g sugars), 15 g pro. exchanges: 1 vegetable, 2 starch, 1 lean meat, 0.5 fat.

Enjoy this robust stew filled with tasty vegetables. You won't miss meat.

southwestern sweet potato stew

42g CARB. PER SERVING

prep: 15 minutes cook: 10 to 12 hours (low)
makes: 6 servings (1⅓ cups each)

2 cups lower-sodium vegetable broth
2 cups water
1½ pounds sweet potatoes, peeled and cut into 2-inch pieces
1 medium onion, chopped
2 cloves garlic, minced
1½ teaspoons dried oregano, crushed
1 teaspoon chili powder
½ teaspoon ground cumin
¼ teaspoon salt
1 15-ounce can golden hominy, rinsed and drained
1 15-ounce can no-salt-added black beans, rinsed and drained
1 poblano chile pepper, roasted,✳ seeds removed (optional), and cut into thin strips (see tip, *page 262*)
Snipped fresh cilantro
Lime wedges

1 In a 3½- or 4-quart slow cooker combine vegetable broth, the water, sweet potatoes, onion, garlic, oregano, chili powder, cumin, and salt. Stir in hominy, beans, and poblano pepper.

2 Cover and cook on low-heat setting for 10 to 12 hours.

3 Use a potato masher to coarsely mash the sweet potatoes. Sprinkle servings with snipped cilantro. Serve with lime wedges.

nutrition facts per serving: 202 cal., 1 g total fat (0 g sat. fat), 0 mg chol., 491 mg sodium, 42 g carb. (8 g fiber, 5 g sugars), 7 g pro. exchanges: 2 vegetable, 2 starch.

✳test kitchen tip: To roast a poblano chile pepper, preheat oven to 425°F. Cut pepper in half lengthwise; remove stem, seeds, and membranes. Place pepper halves, cut sides down, on a foil-lined baking sheet. Bake for 15 to 20 minutes or until pepper is charred and very tender. Bring foil up around pepper and fold edges together to enclose. Let stand about 15 minutes or until cool enough to handle. Use a sharp knife to loosen edges of skin; pull off skin in strips and discard.

kung pao chicken,
page 283

restaurant

rem

What will it be tonight—an Asian, Italian, or Mexican dish or a bold barbecue sandwich? If you crave restaurant food, we'll show how to make it better for your health—and easier on your wallet—at home.

akes

Double goodness—a homemade vegetable mixture is both a binder for the meat filling and a sauce to spoon over the shells.

33g CARB. PER SERVING

beefy stuffed shells

prep: 30 minutes bake: 25 minutes
makes: 6 servings (2 filled shells each)

Nonstick cooking
    spray
12 dried jumbo shell
    macaroni
12 ounces extra-lean
    ground beef
1 tablespoon olive oil
1½ cups chopped fresh
    mushrooms
    (4 ounces)
1 cup chopped onion
    (1 large)
½ cup shredded carrot
    (1 medium)
¼ cup chopped celery
4 cloves garlic, minced
½ teaspoon dried Italian
    seasoning, crushed
1 14.5-ounce can no-
    salt-added diced
    tomatoes with basil,
    garlic, and oregano,
    undrained
¼ teaspoon salt
1 cup shredded
    reduced-fat Italian-
    style cheese blend
    (2 ounces)
1 medium tomato,
    chopped

1 Preheat oven to 350°F. Lightly coat a 2-quart square baking dish with cooking spray; set aside. Cook pasta according to package directions; drain. Rinse with cold water; drain again. Set aside.

2 Meanwhile, in a medium skillet cook ground beef until browned, using a wooden spoon to break up meat as it cooks. Drain off fat. Set meat aside.

3 In a large nonstick skillet heat oil over medium heat. Add mushrooms, onion, carrot, celery, garlic, and Italian seasoning; cook for 6 to 8 minutes or until vegetables are tender, stirring frequently. Add diced tomatoes and salt. Cook and stir for 2 minutes more. Remove from heat; cool slightly.

4 Spoon the tomato mixture into a blender or food processor; cover and blend or process until nearly smooth. Set aside ¾ cup of the pureed tomato mixture. Return the remaining pureed tomato mixture to the skillet. Stir cooked meat into tomato mixture in skillet. Spoon a rounded tablespoon of the meat mixture into each pasta shell.

5 Arrange filled pasta shells in the prepared baking dish. Spoon the reserved ¾ cup pureed tomato mixture over the shells.

6 Bake, covered, for 20 minutes. Sprinkle with cheese and fresh tomato. Bake about 5 minutes more or until heated through and cheese is melted.

nutrition facts per serving: 310 cal., 9 g total fat (4 g sat. fat), 45 mg chol., 322 mg sodium, 33 g carb. (6 g fiber, 8 g sugars), 24 g pro. exchanges: 0.5 vegetable, 2 starch, 2.5 lean meat, 1 fat.

Hoisin sauce is the ultimate Asian convenience product—it brings a spicy-sweet mix of flavors without a lot of dicing and measuring.

beef and broccoli

prep: 25 minutes marinate: 20 minutes cook: 8 minutes
makes: 4 servings (1½ cups broccoli mixture and ½ cup noodles each)

39g
CARB. PER
SERVING

3	teaspoons cornstarch
1	tablespoon reduced-sodium soy sauce
3	cloves garlic, minced
¼	teaspoon crushed red pepper
12	ounces boneless beef top sirloin steak, bias-sliced ⅛ inch thick*
4	ounces Chinese egg noodles or whole wheat vermicelli
1	pound fresh broccoli
3	tablespoons bottled hoisin sauce
2	tablespoons water
2	teaspoons toasted sesame oil
1	tablespoon canola oil
¾	cup reduced-sodium beef broth
1	cup quartered and/or halved cherry tomatoes

1 In a medium bowl stir together 2 teaspoons of the cornstarch, the soy sauce, garlic, and crushed red pepper; add beef and stir to coat. Marinate at room temperature for 20 minutes.

2 Meanwhile, cook noodles according to package directions, except omit any salt; drain and set aside.

3 Cut broccoli into 2-inch florets. Peel stem and cut into ½-inch slices; set aside. For sauce, combine hoisin sauce, the water, sesame oil, and remaining 1 teaspoon cornstarch; set aside.

4 In an extra-large skillet or wok heat canola oil over medium-high heat. Add beef mixture; stir-fry for 1 to 2 minutes or until still slightly pink in center. Remove beef mixture; set aside.

5 Stir beef broth into skillet, scraping up any browned bits. Add broccoli; bring to boiling. Reduce heat to medium. Cover and cook for 3 to 4 minutes or until broccoli is crisp-tender.

6 Add sauce to broccoli; cook and stir until thickened. Add beef and tomatoes; heat through. Serve over cooked noodles.

nutrition facts per serving: 379 cal., 14 g total fat (4 g sat. fat), 48 mg chol., 532 mg sodium, 39 g carb. (8 g fiber, 7 g sugars), 26 g pro. exchanges: 1.5 vegetable, 2 starch, 2.5 lean meat, 1.5 fat.

*test kitchen tip: For easier slicing, freeze the beef for 30 to 60 minutes before slicing.

When you make your own taco seasoning mix, you can control the sodium that goes into it. That's just one of the many tricks this recipe calls on to make these nachos better for you.

23g CARB. PER SERVING

loaded nachos

prep: 30 minutes **bake:** 10 minutes
makes: 4 servings (16 chips, ¼ cup meat, ¼ cup cheese sauce, and ½ cup vegetables each)

8   6-inch corn tortillas, cut into 8 wedges each
    Nonstick cooking spray
2   teaspoons unsalted butter
1   tablespoon flour
¾   cup fat-free milk
½   cup shredded part-skim mozzarella cheese (2 ounces)
½   cup shredded reduced-fat cheddar cheese (2 ounces)
1   ounce fat-free cream cheese, softened
¼   teaspoon paprika
¼   teaspoon ground turmeric
8   ounces extra-lean ground beef
¼   cup water
1   recipe Homemade Taco Seasoning
1   cup chopped tomato (1 large)
½   cup chopped green or red sweet pepper (1 small)
¼   cup sliced green onions (2)
1   fresh jalapeño chile pepper, stemmed, seeded, and thinly sliced✷ (optional)
½   cup chunky mild salsa

1 Preheat oven to 375°F. Place tortilla wedges in a single layer on a large baking sheet. Coat wedges with cooking spray. Bake for 10 to 13 minutes or until wedges are crisp and golden brown on edges. Set aside.

2 Meanwhile, for cheese sauce, in a small saucepan melt butter over medium heat. Stir in flour until combined. Whisk in milk until smooth. Cook and stir until thickened and bubbly. Cook and stir for 2 minutes more. Stir in mozzarella cheese, cheddar cheese, cream cheese, paprika, and turmeric. Cook and stir over medium heat until cheese is melted and mixture is smooth. Reduce heat to low. Hold cheese sauce over low heat until needed, stirring occasionally.

3 Meanwhile, coat an unheated large skillet with cooking spray. Heat skillet over medium heat. Cook beef in skillet until browned, using a wooden spoon to break up meat as it cooks. Drain off fat. Stir the water and Homemade Taco Seasoning into meat in skillet. Cook and stir for 3 to 5 minutes more or until most of the water has evaporated.

4 To serve, arrange tortilla wedges on four plates. Top with meat mixture, cheese sauce, tomato, sweet pepper, green onions, and, if desired, chile pepper. Serve with salsa.

nutrition facts per serving: 291 cal., 11 g total fat (6 g sat. fat), 61 mg chol., 356 mg sodium, 23 g carb. (3 g fiber, 6 g sugars), 24 g pro. exchanges: 1 vegetable, 1 starch, 3 lean meat, 1 fat.

✷test kitchen tip: Because chile peppers contain volatile oils that can burn your skin and eyes, avoid direct contact with them as much as possible. When working with chile peppers, wear plastic or rubber gloves. If your bare hands do touch the peppers, wash your hands and nails well with soap and warm water.

homemade taco seasoning: In a small bowl stir together 2 teaspoons paprika, 1 teaspoon ground cumin, ½ to 1 teaspoon black pepper, ½ teaspoon ground coriander, ⅛ to ¼ teaspoon ground chipotle chile pepper, and ⅛ teaspoon cayenne pepper.

33g CARB. PER SERVING

Go ahead! Fork into the luscious layers of this all-time-favorite layered Italian dish—it's been revamped just for you!

classic lasagna

prep: 30 minutes   bake: 25 minutes   stand: 10 minutes
makes: 8 servings (⅛ of a 2-quart dish each)

12	ounces lean ground beef
½	cup chopped onion
½	cup finely chopped carrot
2	cloves garlic, minced
1	15-ounce can no-salt-added tomato sauce
1	6-ounce can no-salt-added tomato paste
½	cup water
1	teaspoon dried Italian seasoning, crushed
¼	teaspoon black pepper
9	lasagna noodles
1	egg, beaten
1	15-ounce carton light ricotta cheese or low-fat cottage cheese, drained
	Nonstick cooking spray
1	cup shredded part-skim mozzarella cheese (4 ounces)
¼	cup grated Parmesan or Romano cheese (1 ounce)
2	tablespoons snipped fresh parsley (optional)

1 Preheat oven to 375°F. For sauce, in a large saucepan cook beef, onion, carrot, and garlic over medium-high heat until meat is browned and vegetables are tender. Drain off fat. Stir in tomato sauce, tomato paste, the water, Italian seasoning, and pepper. Bring to boiling; reduce heat. Cover and simmer for 10 minutes, stirring occasionally.

2 Meanwhile, cook lasagna noodles according to package directions. Drain noodles; rinse with cold water. Drain well; set aside. For cheese filling, in a small bowl stir together egg and ricotta cheese.

3 Coat a 2-quart rectangular baking dish with cooking spray. Layer three noodles in the prepared dish. Spread with one-third of the cheese filling. Top with one-third of the sauce and one-third of the mozzarella. Repeat layers twice. Sprinkle with Parmesan.

4 Bake, covered, for 20 minutes. Uncover and bake for 5 minutes more or until heated through. Let stand for 10 minutes before serving. If desired, sprinkle with parsley.

nutrition facts per serving: 309 cal., 9 g total fat (5 g sat. fat), 81 mg chol., 326 mg sodium, 33 g carb. (3 g fiber, 9 g sugars), 25 g pro. exchanges: 0.5 vegetable, 2 starch, 2.5 lean meat, 0.5 fat.

The emerald green leaves and creamy white stalks of bok choy add enticing color to the dish, as well as fresh flavors reminiscent of celery, spinach, and cabbage. Pictured on page 276.

kung pao chicken

start to finish: 40 minutes

makes: 4 servings (⅔ cup chicken mixture and ⅓ cup brown rice each)

5   teaspoons reduced-sodium soy sauce

2   teaspoons dry sherry

2   teaspoons toasted sesame oil

10 ounces skinless, boneless chicken breast halves, cut into ½-inch pieces

3   tablespoons water

2   tablespoons rice vinegar

1   tablespoon packed brown sugar＊

1   teaspoon cornstarch

4   teaspoons canola oil

4   small dried red chile peppers, seeded and broken into small pieces (see tip, *page 280*)

4   green onions, cut into 1-inch pieces

2   cups coarsely chopped bok choy

2   teaspoons grated fresh ginger

1⅓ cups hot cooked brown rice

¼   cup chopped unsalted dry-roasted peanuts

1 In a medium bowl stir together 2 teaspoons of the soy sauce, the sherry, and sesame oil; add chicken and toss to coat. Marinate at room temperature 20 minutes. Meanwhile, for sauce, stir together the remaining 3 teaspoons soy sauce, the water, rice vinegar, sugar, and cornstarch; set aside.

2 In a large skillet heat 2 teaspoons of the canola oil over medium-high heat. Add marinated chicken; stir-fry until nearly cooked through. Remove chicken. Add the remaining 2 teaspoons oil. Add chile peppers and green onions; stir-fry 1 minute. Add bok choy and ginger; stir-fry 1 minute more. Add the sauce; cook until bubbly. Serve with hot cooked rice. Sprinkle with peanuts.

nutrition facts per serving: 303 cal., 13 g total fat (2 g sat. fat), 41 mg chol., 296 mg sodium, 24 g carb. (3 g fiber, 6 g sugars), 22 g pro. exchanges: 0.5 vegetable, 1.5 starch, 2.5 lean meat, 1.5 fat.

nutrition facts per serving with substitute: Same as original, except 292 calories, 21 g carb. (3 g sugars).

＊sugar substitutes: Choose from Splenda Granular, Sweet'N Low Brown, or Sugar Twin Granulated Brown. Follow package directions to use amount equivalent to 1 tablespoon granulated or brown sugar.

*If you don't have any Italian seasoning on hand, substitute
equal parts dried oregano and basil and a pinch of dried thyme
or dried rosemary.*

34g
CARB. PER
SERVING

chicken romano

prep: 20 minutes bake: 18 minutes
makes: 4 servings (1 chicken breast half, ⅓ cup spaghetti, and ⅓ cup sauce each)

Nonstick cooking
   spray
4 skinless, boneless
   chicken breast
   halves (1¼ to
   1½ pounds total)
1 egg white
1 tablespoon water
1¼ cups cornflakes,
   crushed (about
   ½ cup crushed)
2 tablespoons grated
   Romano cheese
½ teaspoon dried Italian
   seasoning
⅛ teaspoon black
   pepper
4 ounces dried
   multigrain spaghetti
1⅓ cups low-sodium
   tomato-base pasta
   sauce
   Shaved or grated
   Romano cheese
   (optional)
   Snipped fresh Italian
   (flat-leaf) parsley
   (optional)

1 Preheat oven to 400°F. Lightly coat a
15×10×1-inch baking pan with cooking
spray; set aside. Place each piece of chicken
between two pieces of plastic wrap. Using
the flat side of a meat mallet, pound chicken
breast halves until about ½ inch thick. Remove
plastic wrap. Set aside.

2 In a shallow dish use a fork to beat
together egg white and the water.
In another shallow dish combine crushed
cornflakes, the 2 tablespoons grated cheese,
the Italian seasoning, and pepper. Dip chicken
pieces, one at a time, into egg mixture, letting
excess drip off. Then dip chicken into cornflake
mixture, turning to coat. Place coated chicken
in the prepared baking pan.

3 Bake for 18 minutes or until chicken is no
longer pink. Meanwhile, cook spaghetti
according to package directions; drain. In a
small saucepan cook pasta sauce until heated
through, stirring occasionally.

4 To serve, divide cooked spaghetti among
four serving plates. Top with chicken and
pasta sauce. If desired, sprinkle with additional
cheese and/or parsley.

nutrition facts per serving: 362 cal., 6 g total fat
(1 g sat. fat), 85 mg chol., 405 mg sodium, 34 g carb. (4 g fiber,
5 g sugars), 41 g pro. exchanges: 2 starch, 5 lean meat.

*This dish can satisfy your craving for something rich
and creamy without undermining your aim to eat well.*

chicken and sweet pepper linguine alfredo

43g
CARB. PER
SERVING

start to finish: 25 minutes
makes: 4 servings (1⅓ cups each)

6 ounces dried whole
wheat linguine
2 teaspoons canola oil
1 medium red sweet
pepper, cut into thin
strips
2 medium zucchini
and/or yellow
summer squash,
halved lengthwise
and sliced (about
2½ cups)
8 ounces packaged
chicken stir-fry
strips＊
1 10-ounce container
refrigerated light
Alfredo pasta sauce
⅓ cup finely shredded
Parmesan, Romano,
or Asiago cheese
(optional)
2 teaspoons snipped
fresh thyme
⅛ teaspoon freshly
ground black
pepper

1 Break linguine in half. Cook linguine
according to package directions; drain.
Return to hot pan; cover and keep warm.

2 Meanwhile, heat 1 teaspoon of the oil in a
large skillet over medium-high heat. Add
sweet pepper; cook and stir for 2 minutes. Add
zucchini; cook and stir for 2 to 3 minutes more
or until vegetables are crisp-tender. Remove
from skillet.

3 Add remaining 1 teaspoon oil to skillet.
Add chicken to skillet. Cook and stir for
2 to 3 minutes or until no longer pink. Return
vegetables to skillet. Stir in pasta sauce;
heat through.

4 Add chicken-vegetable mixture, cheese
(if desired), and thyme to cooked linguine;
toss gently to coat. Sprinkle with black pepper.

nutrition facts per serving: 364 cal., 12 g total fat
(5 g sat. fat), 54 mg chol., 485 mg sodium, 43 g carb. (5 g fiber,
6 g sugars), 24 g pro. exchanges: 1 vegetable, 2.5 starch,
2 lean meat, 1.5 fat.

＊test kitchen tip: If you prefer, cut skinless,
boneless chicken breast halves into thin strips.

Keep the healthful theme going. Serve this favorite picnic dish with Two-Tone Potato Salad, page 371.

oven-fried parmesan chicken

prep: 30 minutes bake: 45 minutes
makes: 12 servings (1 piece each)

6g
CARB. PER
SERVING

½   cup refrigerated or
      frozen egg product,
      thawed, or 2 eggs,
      beaten
¼   cup fat-free milk
¾   cup grated Parmesan
      cheese
¾   cup fine dry bread
      crumbs
2   teaspoons dried
      oregano, crushed
1   teaspoon paprika
¼   teaspoon black pepper
12   meaty chicken pieces
      (breast halves, thighs,
      and drumsticks),
      skinned (5½ pounds
      total)
¼   cup butter, melted
      Snipped fresh
         oregano (optional)
      Lemon wedges
         (optional)

1 Preheat oven to 375°F. Grease two large shallow baking pans; set aside. In a bowl combine egg and milk. In a shallow dish combine Parmesan, bread crumbs, oregano, paprika, and pepper.

2 Dip chicken pieces into egg mixture; coat with crumb mixture. Arrange chicken pieces in prepared baking pans, making sure pieces do not touch. Drizzle chicken with melted butter.

3 Bake, uncovered, for 45 to 55 minutes or until chicken is tender and no longer pink (170°F for breasts; 180°F for thighs and drumsticks). Do not turn chicken pieces during baking. If desired, sprinkle with fresh oregano and serve with lemon wedges.

nutrition facts per serving: 198 cal., 9 g total fat (4 g sat. fat), 79 mg chol., 363 mg sodium, 6 g carb. (0 g fiber, 1 g sugars), 23 g pro. exchanges: 0.5 starch, 3 lean meat.

This version of the Mexican favorite is filled with beans and bursting with protein, fiber, and potassium. Plus, it's baked rather than fried, which cuts out loads of fat.

turkey and black bean chimichangas

33g CARB. PER SERVING

prep: 20 minutes bake: 15 minutes
makes: 6 servings (1 chimichanga each)

288

Nonstick cooking spray
6   10-inch low-carb whole wheat flour tortillas
8   ounces ground turkey breast
½   cup chopped onion
1   15-ounce can no-salt-added black beans, rinsed and drained, or 1¾ cup cooked black beans
1   14.5-ounce can no-salt-added diced tomatoes, drained
¼   cup bottled salsa
¼   cup snipped fresh cilantro
1   tablespoon lime juice
½   teaspoon ground cumin
½   cup shredded reduced-fat Monterey Jack cheese (2 ounces)
¼   cup light sour cream
2   tablespoons snipped fresh cilantro

1 Preheat oven to 425°F. Coat a baking sheet with cooking spray; set aside. Wrap the tortillas in foil. Heat in the oven for 5 minutes.

2 Meanwhile, in a large skillet cook turkey and onion until turkey is no longer pink and onion is softened, stirring to break up turkey as it cooks. Add black beans. Using a fork or potato masher, mash beans slightly. Stir in tomatoes, salsa, snipped cilantro, lime juice, and cumin. Heat through.

3 To assemble, spoon about ½ cup of the filling onto each tortilla just below the center. Fold bottom edge of each tortilla up and over filling. Fold opposite sides in and over filling. Roll up from the bottom. If necessary, secure rolled tortillas with wooden toothpicks. Place filled tortillas on prepared baking sheet, seam sides down. Lightly coat tops and sides of the filled tortillas with cooking spray.

4 Bake for 10 to 12 minutes or until tortillas are golden brown. Sprinkle chimichangas with cheese, sour cream, and cilantro.

nutrition facts per serving: 217 cal., 5 g total fat (1 g sat. fat), 28 mg chol., 430 mg sodium, 33 g carb. (18 g fiber, 3 g sugars), 23 g pro. exchanges: 1 vegetable, 2 starch, 2 lean meat.

Forget mixing and rolling the dough! Whole grain tortillas make a simple (and good-for-you) stand-in for the thin crust you crave.

thin-crust pepperoni and vegetable pizza

24g CARB. PER SERVING

prep: 25 minutes bake: 5 minutes per pizza
makes: 4 servings (½ pizza each)

⅓ cup chopped bottled roasted red sweet peppers

⅓ cup pizza sauce

2 teaspoons olive oil

½ cup sliced red onion (4)

½ cup chopped green sweet pepper (1 small)

½ cup sliced fresh mushrooms

2 10-inch whole grain tortillas

16 thin slices cooked turkey pepperoni (about ¼ cup)

1 cup shredded part-skim mozzarella cheese (4 ounces)

1 Place a pizza stone on the lowest rack of oven. Preheat oven to 450°F.

2 In a food processor or blender combine roasted red sweet peppers and pizza sauce. Cover and process or blend until smooth; set aside.

3 In a large skillet heat oil over medium-high heat. Add red onion, green sweet pepper, and mushrooms. Cook and stir about 5 minutes or until tender.

4 Divide pizza sauce mixture among tortillas, spreading evenly. Top with pepperoni and vegetable mixture. Sprinkle with cheese.

5 Transfer one of the pizzas to the hot pizza stone. ✳ Bake about 5 minutes or until edges of tortilla and the cheese are golden brown. Repeat with the remaining pizza.

nutrition facts per serving: 253 cal., 11 g total fat (4 g sat. fat), 25 mg chol., 625 mg sodium, 24 g carb. (4 g fiber, 3 g sugars), 14 g pro. exchanges: 0.5 vegetable, 1.5 starch, 1 medium-fat meat, 1 fat.

✳ test kitchen tip: To transfer the pizza to the hot stone, place pizza on a flat baking sheet; scoot pizza from baking sheet to pizza stone. When pizza is done, lift an edge of the pizza with a spatula, scoot the baking sheet under pizza, and lift it off the stone.

Many recipes for barbecued pork call for pork shoulder and can take hours to cook. Quick-cooking pork loin gets these meals in a bun to the table much more quickly.

barbecued pork sandwiches

prep: 25 minutes   cook: 15 minutes
makes: 6 servings (1 sandwich each)

Nonstick cooking spray
½   cup chopped onion
2   cloves garlic, minced
⅔   cup water
½   of a 6-ounce can tomato paste (⅓ cup)
2   tablespoons red wine vinegar
2   tablespoons packed brown sugar
1   tablespoon chili powder
1   teaspoon dried oregano, crushed
1   teaspoon Worcestershire sauce
¼   teaspoon cayenne pepper
    Dash bottled hot pepper sauce
12 ounces pork tenderloin
¾   cup chopped green sweet pepper
6   whole wheat hamburger buns, split and toasted
1   recipe Crunchy Cabbage Slaw

1 For sauce, lightly coat an unheated small saucepan with cooking spray. Heat saucepan over medium heat. Add onion and garlic; cook and stir about 5 minutes or until onion is tender. Stir in the water, tomato paste, vinegar, brown sugar, chili powder, oregano, Worcestershire sauce, cayenne pepper, and hot pepper sauce. Bring to boiling; reduce heat. Simmer, uncovered, about 10 minutes or until desired consistency, stirring occasionally.

2 Meanwhile, trim any fat from pork; cut pork into bite-size strips. Lightly coat an unheated large skillet with cooking spray. Heat skillet over medium-high heat. Add pork. Cook and stir for 2 to 3 minutes or until pork is slightly pink in center. Stir in the sauce and sweet pepper; heat through. Serve the meat mixture in toasted buns along with Crunchy Cabbage Slaw.

nutrition facts per serving: 240 cal., 3 g total fat (1 g sat. fat), 37 mg chol., 387 mg sodium, 35 g carb. (5 g fiber, 13 g sugars), 19 g pro. exchanges: 0.5 vegetable, 2 starch, 3.5 lean meat.

crunchy cabbage slaw: In a medium bowl combine half of a 14-ounce package shredded cabbage with carrot (coleslaw mix), 1 finely chopped fresh jalapeño chile pepper (see tip, *page 292*), and 2 tablespoons snipped fresh cilantro. In a small bowl whisk together ⅓ cup plain fat-free Greek yogurt, 2 tablespoons fat-free mayonnaise, 1½ teaspoons lime juice, ½ teaspoon ground cumin, and ⅛ teaspoon salt. Add to cabbage mixture; toss to coat. Cover and chill until serving time.

Whenever you gather friends for dinner, everyone winds up in the kitchen. Why not make stuffing and folding these rolls a team effort—you'll get the work done in less time and with more fun!

light and crisp egg rolls

23g
CARB. PER SERVING

prep: 30 minutes bake: 15 minutes
makes: 8 servings (1 egg roll each)

Nonstick cooking spray
2 teaspoons toasted sesame oil
8 ounces lean pork loin, cut into ½-inch pieces, or ground pork
½ cup chopped red sweet pepper
1 teaspoon grated fresh ginger or ¼ teaspoon ground ginger
1 clove garlic, minced
¾ cup finely chopped bok choy
½ cup chopped canned water chestnuts
1 medium carrot, coarsely shredded (½ cup)
¼ cup sliced green onions (2)
¼ cup bottled light Asian sesame ginger vinaigrette
8 egg roll wrappers

1 Preheat oven to 450°F. Lightly coat a large baking sheet with cooking spray; set aside. For filling, in a medium nonstick skillet heat oil over medium-high heat. Add pork, sweet pepper, ginger, and garlic. Cook for 3 to 4 minutes or until pork is no longer pink, stirring occasionally. If using ground pork, drain off fat. Add bok choy, water chestnuts, carrot, and green onions to pork mixture in skillet. Cook and stir about 1 minute more or until any liquid evaporates. Stir in vinaigrette. Cool filling slightly.

2 For each egg roll, place a wrapper on a flat surface with a corner pointing toward you. Spoon ⅓ cup of the filling across and just below center of each egg roll wrapper. Fold bottom corner over filling, tucking it under on opposite side. Fold side corners over filling, forming an envelope shape. Roll egg roll toward remaining corner. Moisten top corner with water; press to seal.

3 Place egg rolls, seam sides down, on the prepared baking sheet. Coat the tops and sides of the egg rolls with cooking spray. Bake for 15 to 18 minutes or until egg rolls are golden brown and crisp. Cool slightly before serving.

nutrition facts per serving: 167 cal., 4 g total fat (1 g sat. fat), 22 mg chol., 282 mg sodium, 23 g carb. (1 g fiber, 2 g sugars), 10 g pro. exchanges: 1.5 starch, 1 lean meat.

How can pork tacos fit into your meal plan? Simple—we used a relatively lean cut of meat (pork loin) rather than the higher-fat cut usually called for in this dish.

35g CARB. PER SERVING

pork and pineapple tacos

prep: 45 minutes marinate: 4 hours grill: 10 minutes stand: 30 minutes
makes: 8 servings (2 tacos each)

½ of a medium peeled and cored fresh pineapple
8 dried pasilla and/or guajillo chile peppers
¼ cup orange juice
¼ cup vinegar
4 cloves garlic, minced
½ teaspoon salt
½ teaspoon ground cumin
⅛ teaspoon ground cloves
2 pounds boneless pork loin, trimmed of fat and cut into ½-inch slices
16 6-inch corn tortillas
1 cup chopped onion (1 large)
2 tablespoons snipped fresh cilantro
8 lime wedges

*test kitchen tip: Because chile peppers contain volatile oils that can burn your skin and eyes, avoid direct contact with them as much as possible. When working with chile peppers, wear plastic or rubber gloves. If your bare hands do touch the peppers, wash your hands and nails well with soap and warm water.

1 Cut pineapple into ½-inch-thick slices, reserving juice; cover and chill pineapple and juice separately.

2 Remove stems and seeds from chile peppers.* Place peppers in a medium bowl and add enough boiling water to cover. Allow peppers to stand about 30 minutes or until soft; drain, discarding water.

3 In a food processor or blender combine chile peppers, any juice from the pineapple, the orange juice, vinegar, garlic, salt, cumin, and cloves. Cover and process or blend until nearly smooth.

4 In a 3-quart baking dish arrange pork slices in a single layer, overlapping slices as necessary. Pour chile pepper mixture over pork, spreading evenly. Cover and marinate in the refrigerator for 4 to 24 hours. Remove pork from marinade, discarding marinade. Wrap tortillas in foil.

5 For a charcoal grill, place tortilla packet on grill rack directly over medium coals. Place pork and pineapple slices on the grill rack alongside the foil packet directly over medium coals. Grill pork and pineapple slices, uncovered, for 5 to 6 minutes or until pork slices are slightly pink in the center and juices run clear (145°F), turning once. Grill tortilla packet for 10 minutes, turning once. (For a gas grill, preheat grill. Reduce heat to medium. Grill tortilla packet, pork, and pineapple as directed.)

6 Coarsely chop pork and pineapple and combine. Fill tortillas with pork and pineapple mixture. Sprinkle tacos with onion and cilantro. Serve with lime wedges.

nutrition facts per serving: 321 cal., 7 g total fat (2 g sat. fat), 71 mg chol., 233 mg sodium, 35 g carb. (6 g fiber, 5 g sugars), 30 g pro. exchanges: 0.5 fruit, 1.5 starch, 3.5 lean meat.

Once you get the hang of this recipe, substitute other vegetables you have on hand, such as broccoli, bok choy, mushrooms, peas, celery, and/or edamame.

spicy vegetable fried rice

31g
CARB. PER
SERVING

start to finish: 30 minutes
makes: 4 servings (1 cup each)

4   eggs
2   tablespoons water
    Nonstick cooking
      spray
1   tablespoon olive oil
1   tablespoon finely
      chopped, peeled
      fresh ginger
2   cloves garlic, minced
2   cups chopped napa
      cabbage
1   cup coarsely
      shredded carrots
1   cup fresh pea pods,
      trimmed
2   cups cooked brown
      rice
⅓   cup sliced green
      onions
2   tablespoons reduced-
      sodium soy sauce
1   to 2 teaspoons Asian
      chili sauce (sriracha
      sauce)
2   tablespoons snipped
      fresh cilantro
    Lime slices or
      wedges

1 In a small bowl whisk together eggs and the water. Coat an unheated extra-large nonstick skillet with cooking spray. Preheat skillet over medium heat. Pour in egg mixture. Cook, without stirring, until mixture begins to set on the bottom and around the edges. With a spatula or large spoon, lift and fold the partially cooked eggs so the uncooked portion flows underneath. Continue cooking over medium heat for 2 to 3 minutes or until egg mixture is cooked through but still glossy and moist, keeping eggs in large pieces. Carefully transfer eggs to a medium bowl; set aside.

2 In the same skillet heat oil over medium-high heat. Add ginger and garlic; cook for 30 seconds. Add cabbage, carrots, and pea pods; cook and stir for 2 minutes. Stir in cooked eggs, brown rice, green onions, soy sauce, and chili sauce; cook and stir about 2 minutes or until heated through. Top with cilantro. Serve with lime slices or wedges.

nutrition facts per serving: 250 cal., 9 g total fat (2 g sat. fat), 212 mg chol., 367 mg sodium, 31 g carb. (4 g fiber, 5 g sugars), 11 g pro. **exchanges:** 1 vegetable, 1.5 starch, 1.5 medium-fat meat, 0.5 fat.

When it comes to sensible eating, oven-baked beats deep-fried hands down. That's the secret to shaving fat and calories from this Mexican restaurant favorite.

17g
CARB. PER
SERVING

chiles rellenos

prep: 25 minutes bake: 15 minutes stand: 5 minutes
makes: 4 servings (1 dish each)

2 large fresh poblano chile peppers, Anaheim chile peppers, or green sweet peppers (8 ounces)
1 cup shredded reduced-fat Mexican-style cheese blend (4 ounces)
1 to 2 fresh jalapeño chile peppers, seeded and finely chopped (see tip, *page 292*)
1½ cups refrigerated or frozen egg product, thawed, or 6 eggs, beaten
⅓ cup fat-free milk
⅓ cup flour
½ teaspoon baking powder
¼ teaspoon cayenne pepper
 Picante sauce and/ or light sour cream (optional)

1 Preheat oven to 450°F. Halve the poblano, Anaheim, or sweet peppers and remove stems, ribs, and seeds (see tip, *page 292*). Immerse peppers in boiling water for 3 minutes; drain. Invert peppers onto paper towels to drain well. Place one pepper half in each of four greased 12- to 16-ounce au gratin dishes. Top each with cheese and jalapeño peppers.

2 In a medium bowl combine egg and milk. Add flour, baking powder, and cayenne pepper. Beat until smooth. Pour egg mixture evenly over peppers and cheese in dishes.

3 Bake, uncovered, about 15 minutes or until a knife inserted into the egg mixture comes out clean. Let stand about 5 minutes. If desired, serve with picante sauce and/or sour cream.

nutrition facts per serving: 203 cal., 5 g total fat (4 g sat. fat), 15 mg chol., 470 mg sodium, 17 g carb. (1 g fiber, 2 g sugars), 19 g pro. exchanges: 0.5 vegetable, 1 starch, 2 lean meat, 0.5 fat.

To make curly strips from egg roll wrappers, shape foil into small logs and place on a baking sheet. Drape the strips of egg roll wrappers over the foil logs; coat and bake as directed.

egg drop soup

prep: 25 minutes bake: 6 minutes
makes: 4 servings (1¾ cups soup and 1 tablespoon crispy strips each)

Nonstick cooking
    spray
1 egg roll wrapper,
    cut into thin 1- to
    1½-inch-long strips
6 cups low-sodium
    chicken broth
4 teaspoons reduced-
    sodium soy sauce
1 clove garlic, minced
¼ teaspoon ground
    white pepper
2 medium carrots
½ cup frozen baby
    sweet peas
8 teaspoons cornstarch
4 eggs
2 green onions,
    bias-sliced

1 Preheat oven to 375°F. Lightly coat a baking sheet with cooking spray. Place egg roll wrapper strips on prepared baking sheet. Lightly coat strips with cooking spray. Bake for 6 to 7 minutes or until lightly browned and crisp, stirring once after 3 minutes; set aside.

2 In a large saucepan combine 5 cups of the broth, the soy sauce, garlic, and pepper. Bring to boiling.

3 To make carrot flowers, using a paring knife or channel knife,✴ make four or five shallow lengthwise notches around each carrot; thinly slice carrot. (Or thinly slice carrots; cut each slice with a 1-inch or smaller flower-shape cutter.) Add carrots and peas to boiling broth; return to boiling.

4 Stir cornstarch into the remaining 1 cup broth; stir into soup. Reduce heat. Cook and stir until slightly thickened and bubbly; cook and stir for 2 minutes more. Remove from heat. Place eggs in a liquid measuring cup; use a fork to beat eggs. While gently stirring the broth, pour eggs in a thin stream into soup (eggs will form fine shreds).

5 To serve, ladle soup into bowls. Garnish individual servings with green onions. Serve with crisp egg roll wrapper strips.

nutrition facts per serving: 186 cal., 5 g total fat (2 g sat. fat), 212 mg chol., 559 mg sodium, 18 g carb. (2 g fiber, 4 g sugars), 15 g pro. exchanges: 0.5 vegetable, 1 starch, 1.5 lean meat, 0.5 fat.

✴test kitchen tip: A channel knife is a garnishing tool used to make thin strips of citrus peel and other garnishes.

Seared scallops, beef tenderloin steaks, lamb chops, lobster mac and cheese— all your dinner-party favorites are here. So when a special occasion rolls around, treat friends with dishes that offer good taste *and* good-for-you eating.

company-special

ent

coffee- and smoked
paprika-rubbed steak,
page 298

rées

If you can't find smoked paprika, use 1 teaspoon regular paprika and ½ teaspoon ground cumin instead. Pictured on page 297.

11g CARB. PER SERVING

coffee- and smoked paprika-rubbed steak

prep: 25 minutes chill: 2 hours broil: 17 minutes stand: 5 minutes
makes: 4 servings (3 ounces cooked meat, 2 vegetable skewers, and about 1 tablespoon dressing each)

1	**1-pound beef flank steak, trimmed of fat**
1	**tablespoon packed brown sugar***
1½	**teaspoons instant espresso coffee powder**
¾	**teaspoon sweet smoked paprika**
½	**teaspoon garlic powder**
½	**teaspoon salt**
⅛	**teaspoon freshly ground black pepper**
1	**zucchini, cut into 1-inch pieces**
16	**cherry tomatoes**
12	**to 16 fresh whole mushrooms**
1	**recipe Buttermilk Dressing**

1 Score both sides of steak in a diamond pattern by making shallow diagonal cuts at 1-inch intervals. In a small bowl combine brown sugar, espresso powder, paprika, garlic powder, salt, and pepper. Sprinkle evenly over both sides of steak; rub in with your fingers.

2 In a large saucepan bring a large amount of water to boiling. Add zucchini; cook for 2 minutes and drain. Thread tomatoes, mushrooms, and zucchini onto eight skewers.** Cover; chill steak and skewers for 2 hours to 24 hours.

3 Preheat broiler. Place steak on the unheated rack of a broiler pan. Broil 3 to 4 inches from heat for 17 to 21 minutes or until medium doneness (160°F), turning once. Add skewers to the broiler pan for the last 7 to 8 minutes of broiling or just until vegetables are tender, turning once. Transfer steak to a cutting board. Let stand for 5 minutes.

4 Thinly slice steak across the grain. Serve steak with vegetable skewers and Buttermilk Dressing.

nutrition facts per serving: 240 cal., 9 g total fat (3 g sat. fat), 73 mg chol., 523 mg sodium, 11 g carb. (2 g fiber, 8 g sugars), 28 g pro. exchanges: 1 vegetable, 0.5 carb., 3.5 lean meat, 0.5 fat.

buttermilk dressing: In a small bowl whisk together 2 tablespoons low-fat buttermilk, 2 tablespoons light mayonnaise or salad dressing, 1 tablespoon snipped fresh chives, 1 teaspoon cider vinegar, 1 teaspoon Dijon-style mustard, ⅛ teaspoon garlic powder, ⅛ teaspoon salt, and ⅛ teaspoon black pepper. Cover and chill for up to 2 days.

*sugar substitute: We do not recommend using a sugar substitute for this recipe.

**test kitchen tip: If using wooden skewers, soak them in enough water to cover for at least 30 minutes before broiling.

When you reduce balsamic vinegar as directed, it will become rich and syrupy—a perfect finishing touch to the beef tenderloin steak.

beef tenderloin with balsamic tomatoes

12g
CARB. PER
SERVING

start to finish: 25 minutes

makes: 2 servings (3 ounces cooked meat and ⅓ cup balsamic-tomato mixture each)

½ cup balsamic vinegar
⅓ cup coarsely
    chopped, seeded
    tomato
2 teaspoons olive oil
2 4-ounce beef
    tenderloin steaks,
    cut ¾ inch thick
1 teaspoon snipped
    fresh thyme

1 In a small saucepan bring vinegar to boiling. Reduce heat; simmer, uncovered, 5 minutes or until reduced to ¼ cup. Stir tomato into hot vinegar reduction.

2 Meanwhile, trim fat from steaks. Sprinkle steaks with a pinch each of salt and black pepper. In a large skillet heat oil over medium-high heat. Add steaks; reduce heat to medium. Cook to desired doneness, turning once; allow 7 to 9 minutes for medium rare (145°F) to medium (160°F).

3 To serve, spoon tomato and vinegar reduction over steaks. Sprinkle with thyme.

nutrition facts per serving: 275 cal., 12 g total fat (3 g sat. fat), 74 mg chol., 80 mg sodium, 12 g carb. (0 g fiber, 10 g sugars), 26 g pro. exchanges: 1 fruit, 3.5 lean meat, 1 fat.

With beef, mushrooms, pearl onions, and red wine, this recipe has all the hallmarks of Beef Burgundy, a classic French dish. Thanks to a few updates, this version is quicker, easier, and much better for you.

11g
CARB. PER
SERVING

beef with mushrooms and pearl onions

start to finish: 30 minutes
makes: 4 servings (½ steak and ⅔ cup sauce each)

company-special **entrées**

2 8-ounce boneless beef top loin steaks, cut ¾ to 1 inch thick
½ teaspoon cracked black pepper
¼ teaspoon salt
1 teaspoon olive oil
8 ounces fresh mushrooms, quartered
1 cup frozen pearl onions
4 cloves garlic, minced
¾ cup dry red wine
1 cup lower-sodium beef broth
2 tablespoons whole wheat flour
1 tablespoon snipped fresh parsley

1 Trim fat from steaks. Sprinkle steaks with the pepper and salt. Preheat a large skillet over medium-high heat. Add oil; swirl to lightly coat skillet. Reduce heat to medium. Add steaks; cook for 8 to 10 minutes or until medium rare (145°F), turning once. Transfer steaks to a tray or plate; cover with foil and let stand while preparing sauce.

2 For sauce, in the same skillet cook mushrooms and onions over medium-high heat about 5 minutes or until tender, stirring frequently. Add garlic. Cook for 1 minute more. Remove skillet from heat; add wine. Return skillet to heat. Boil gently, uncovered, for 5 minutes, stirring occasionally. Whisk together broth and flour; add to skillet. Cook and stir until sauce is thickened and bubbly; cook and stir for 1 minute more.

3 Return steaks to skillet; heat through, turning to coat steaks evenly with sauce. Cut steaks in half; transfer steaks and sauce to serving plates. Sprinkle with parsley.

nutrition facts per serving: 287 cal., 11 g total fat (4 g sat. fat), 64 mg chol., 330 mg sodium, 11 g carb. (2 g fiber, 3 g sugars), 28 g pro. exchanges: 1 vegetable, 0.5 starch, 3.5 lean meat, 1 fat.

Dreamy, creamy polenta—Italian comfort food—is a superlative substitute for mashed potatoes. Choose stone-ground whole grain polenta to up the nutritional ante.

grilled strip steaks with onion-pepper polenta

prep: 30 minutes   marinate: 1 hour   cook: 10 minutes
makes: 6 servings (1 steak portion and about ½ cup polenta each)

¼ cup balsamic vinegar
2 tablespoons water
2 tablespoons olive oil
1 tablespoon dried Italian seasoning, crushed
3 10-ounce beef top loin steaks (New York strip steaks), cut 1 inch thick, trimmed of fat, and halved crosswise
½ teaspoon salt
½ teaspoon freshly ground black pepper
   Nonstick cooking spray
1 recipe Onion-Pepper Polenta

1 In a large resealable plastic bag combine vinegar, the water, oil, and Italian seasoning. Add steaks. Seal bag and turn to coat steaks. Marinate in the refrigerator for 1 to 2 hours, turning bag occasionally.

2 Remove steaks from marinade, discarding any excess marinade. Sprinkle steaks with the salt and black pepper. Coat an indoor grill pan with cooking spray. Heat pan over medium-high heat.

3 Add steaks to pan. Cook for 10 to 12 minutes for medium rare (145°F) or 12 to 15 minutes for medium (160°F), turning steaks halfway through cooking and reducing heat to medium if steaks brown too quickly. Serve steaks with Onion-Pepper Polenta.

nutrition facts per serving: 327 cal., 12 g total fat (4 g sat. fat), 64 mg chol., 477 mg sodium, 22 g carb. (1 g fiber, 6 g sugars), 32 g pro. exchanges: 0.5 vegetable, 1.5 starch, 4 lean meat, 1 fat.

onion-pepper polenta: In a medium saucepan cook ½ cup chopped onion in 1 tablespoon olive oil over medium heat for 5 minutes, stirring occasionally. Add 1 red sweet pepper, chopped, and 2 cloves garlic, minced. Cook over medium-low heat for 10 minutes more or until onion is lightly browned and very tender, stirring occasionally. Add 2 cups fat-free milk and ¾ cup reduced-sodium chicken broth. Bring to boiling. Gradually stir in ¾ cup polenta (coarse cornmeal). Cook and stir over medium heat until simmering. Continue to simmer, uncovered, for 15 to 20 minutes or until creamy and thick, stirring frequently. Remove from heat. Just before serving, stir in ½ cup finely shredded Parmesan cheese and ¼ cup chopped fresh basil.

Precooking the potato, fennel, and onion in the microwave trims the time needed for pan-frying the tasty, golden-brown latkes.

rosemary-lemon lamb chops with latkes

prep: 20 minutes microwave: 4 minutes cook: 17 minutes
makes: 4 servings (2 lamb chops and 2 latkes each)

2 medium russet potatoes (about 10 ounces total)
1 medium fennel bulb
¼ cup finely chopped onion
1 tablespoon snipped fresh rosemary
4 cloves garlic, minced
1 teaspoon finely shredded lemon peel
¼ teaspoon salt
⅛ teaspoon black pepper
8 lamb rib chops, cut about 1 inch thick (2 to 2½ pounds total)
 Nonstick cooking spray
1 egg white, lightly beaten
¼ teaspoon salt
⅛ teaspoon black pepper
1 tablespoon canola oil

* test kitchen tip: To make quick work of shredding the potatoes and fennel, use a food processor fitted with a shredding blade.

1 Peel and coarsely shred the potatoes.* Trim the fennel bulb and cut out the core; coarsely shred the fennel bulb.* You should have 1½ cups each of potato and fennel. In a medium microwave-safe bowl combine potato, fennel, and onion. Cover with vented plastic wrap.

2 Microwave on 100 percent power (high) for 4 to 5 minutes or until vegetables are just tender, stirring once or twice. Drain off any liquid; set potato mixture aside to cool to room temperature.

3 In a small bowl combine rosemary, garlic, lemon peel, ¼ teaspoon salt, and ⅛ teaspoon pepper. Trim fat from lamb chops; sprinkle chops evenly with the rosemary mixture, rubbing in with your fingers.

4 Coat an unheated indoor grill pan with cooking spray. Heat over medium heat. Add the lamb chops. Cook to desired doneness, turning once halfway through cooking. Allow 12 to 14 minutes for medium rare (145°F) or 15 to 17 minutes for medium (160°F).

5 Meanwhile, add the egg white, ¼ teaspoon salt, and ⅛ teaspoon pepper to the potato mixture. Stir until well combined. Divide mixture into eight equal portions. Coat an unheated large nonstick skillet with cooking spray. Add the oil. Heat skillet over medium-high heat. Add potato portions to the hot skillet and flatten each portion into a circle about ½ inch thick.

6 Cook the potato latkes for 5 minutes or until golden brown, turning once halfway through cooking. Serve the latkes with the lamb chops.

nutrition facts per serving: 276 cal., 12 g total fat (3 g sat. fat), 64 mg chol., 400 mg sodium, 19 g carb. (4 g fiber, 1 g sugars), 23 g pro. exchanges: 1 starch, 3 lean meat, 1.5 fat.

The combo of sage, rosemary, and garlic is a perfect match for pork—especially when a little white wine enriches the flavors.

pork scaloppine in white wine sauce

8g CARB. PER SERVING

start to finish: 30 minutes

makes: 4 servings (3 ounces cooked meat and ¼ cup sauce each)

1   1-pound pork tenderloin
¼   teaspoon black pepper
3   tablespoons whole wheat flour
4   teaspoons olive oil
2   cloves garlic, minced
½   cup dry white wine or reduced-sodium chicken broth
2   teaspoons snipped fresh sage or ½ teaspoon dried sage, crushed
1   teaspoon snipped fresh rosemary or ¼ teaspoon dried rosemary, crushed
1   cup reduced-sodium chicken broth
2   tablespoons cold water
1   tablespoon cornstarch
2   tablespoons snipped fresh parsley (optional)

1 Trim fat from meat. Cut meat into ½-inch slices. Place each slice between two pieces of plastic wrap. Using the flat side of a meat mallet, pound meat lightly until ¼ inch thick. Remove plastic wrap. Sprinkle meat with pepper. Place flour in a shallow dish. Dip meat into flour, turning to coat evenly.

2 In an extra-large skillet heat 2 teaspoons of the oil over medium-high heat. Add half of the meat to skillet. Cook about 4 minutes or until meat is browned, turning once halfway through cooking. Remove meat from skillet; cover to keep warm.

3 Add the remaining 2 teaspoons oil to skillet; cook the remaining meat as directed. Remove from skillet; cover to keep warm.

4 For sauce, add garlic to the same skillet; cook and stir for 30 seconds. Add wine, sage, and rosemary; cook and stir for 2 minutes. Add broth; return meat to skillet. Bring just to boiling. Cook, uncovered, for 2 minutes. In a small bowl stir together the water and cornstarch; stir into broth mixture. Cook and stir for 2 minutes more.

5 Transfer meat to four serving plates; top with sauce. If desired, sprinkle with parsley.

nutrition facts per serving: 220 cal., 7 g total fat (1 g sat. fat), 73 mg chol., 199 mg sodium, 8 g carb. (1 g fiber, 1 g sugars), 25 g pro. **exchanges:** 0.5 starch, 3.5 lean meat, 0.5 fat.

Serve a simple salad, such as fresh spinach with red onion and balsamic vinaigrette, alongside these pretty slices.

mushroom-tomato-stuffed pork loin

10g
CARB. PER
SERVING

prep: 40 minutes roast: 40 minutes stand: 15 minutes
makes: 6 servings (⅙ of roast each)

1 large portobello mushroom (about 6 ounces) or 2 cups button mushrooms
½ of a medium fresh poblano chile pepper, seeded and chopped (see tip, *page 314*) (about ½ cup)
1 medium onion, chopped (½ cup)
3 cloves garlic, minced
2 teaspoons olive oil
¾ cup reduced-sodium chicken broth
¼ cup quick-cooking (hominy) grits
2 tablespoons snipped dried tomatoes (not oil-pack)
1 1½- to 2-pound boneless pork loin roast
¼ teaspoon black pepper

1 Remove stem from portobello mushroom if using; if desired, scrape out gills. Chop mushroom. (Or if using button mushrooms, chop mushrooms.) In a large nonstick skillet cook chopped mushrooms, chile pepper, onion, and garlic in hot oil over medium heat for 5 to 8 minutes or until tender, stirring occasionally. Remove mixture from skillet; set aside.

2 In the same skillet bring broth to boiling. Gradually stir in grits; stir in tomatoes. Reduce heat to low. Cook, uncovered, for 2 to 3 minutes or until thick, stirring frequently. Remove from heat and stir in mushroom mixture. Set aside.

3 Preheat oven to 350°F. Trim fat from roast. Place roast on cutting board with one end toward you. Using a long sharp knife, make a lengthwise cut 1 inch in from the left side of the roast, cutting down to about 1 inch from the bottom of the roast. Turn the knife and cut to the right, as if forming the letter L; stop when you get to about 1 inch from the right side of the roast.

4 Open up the roast so it lies nearly flat on the cutting board. Place a large piece of plastic wrap over the roast. Using the flat side of a meat mallet, pound meat to ¼- to ½-inch thickness. Discard plastic wrap. Spread mushroom mixture over meat, leaving a 1-inch border around the edge. Starting from one of the long sides, roll meat around filling. Using 100-percent-cotton kitchen string, tie securely at 1½-inch intervals. Sprinkle meat with black pepper. Place on a rack in a shallow roasting pan.

5 Insert an oven-going meat thermometer into center of meat. Roast, uncovered, for 40 to 45 minutes or until thermometer registers 145°F. Let stand for 3 minutes.

nutrition facts per serving: 209 cal., 6 g total fat (2 g sat. fat), 71 mg chol., 153 mg sodium, 10 g carb. (1 g fiber, 2 g sugars), 28 g pro. exchanges: 0.5 vegetable, 0.5 starch, 3.5 lean meat.

Fresh fennel adds a lightly sweet licorice note to this dish. Light sour cream adds body to the sauce without going overboard.

7g
CARB. PER
SERVING

sour cream—fennel pork tenderloins

prep: 20 minutes   cook: 10 minutes   roast: 25 minutes
makes: 8 servings (3 ounces cooked pork, about ⅓ cup fennel and onion, and 2 tablespoons sauce each)

2	medium fennel bulbs
2	1- to 1½-pound pork tenderloins
1	tablespoon snipped fresh rosemary
1	tablespoon fennel seeds, coarsely crushed (optional)
1	teaspoon salt
¼	teaspoon black pepper
2	tablespoons olive oil
1	medium onion, sliced
6	cloves garlic, minced
½	cup reduced-sodium chicken broth
½	cup dry vermouth or reduced-sodium chicken broth
¼	cup light sour cream

1 Preheat oven to 425°F. Trim and core fennel bulbs, reserving some of the leafy tops if desired. Cut each fennel bulb into thin wedges; set aside. Sprinkle pork with rosemary, fennel seeds (if using), salt, and pepper. In an extra-large straight-sided oven-going skillet brown pork on all sides in hot oil. Remove pork from pan; set aside.

2 Add fennel, onion, and garlic to skillet; cook about 4 minutes or until lightly browned, stirring occasionally. Remove skillet from heat; add broth, vermouth, and sour cream. Return to heat. Bring to boiling. Return pork to pan; transfer to preheated oven.

3 Roast, uncovered, for 25 to 30 minutes or until slightly pink in center (145°F). Cover with foil and let stand for 10 minutes. The temperature of the meat after standing should be 155°F. Serve pork with fennel, onion, and sauce. If desired, sprinkle with leafy fennel tops.

nutrition facts per serving: 206 cal., 7 g total fat (2 g sat. fat), 76 mg chol., 423 mg sodium, 7 g carb. (2 g fiber, 1 g sugars), 25 g pro. exchanges: 0.5 vegetable, 3.5 lean meat, 1 fat.

The nutty taste of cholesterol-fighting flaxseed meal blends beautifully with the almonds in this vegetable-packed Spanish sauce.

roast pork with romesco sauce

7g
CARB. PER SERVING

prep: 30 minutes   roast: 1 hour 15 minutes   stand: 15 minutes
makes: 8 servings (3 ounces cooked pork and ¼ cup sauce each)

1   tablespoon dried Italian seasoning, crushed
½   teaspoon black pepper
¼   teaspoon salt
1   2-pound boneless pork top loin roast (single loin), trimmed of fat
1   recipe Romesco Sauce

1 Preheat oven to 325°F. In a small bowl combine Italian seasoning, black pepper, and salt. Sprinkle over pork loin and rub in with your fingers. Place roast on a rack in a shallow roasting pan. Insert an ovenproof meat thermometer into center of roast.

2 Roast, uncovered, for 1¼ to 1½ hours or until thermometer registers 145°F. Remove from oven. Cover meat with foil; let stand for 15 minutes. The temperature of the meat after standing should be 155°F.

3 Meanwhile, prepare Romesco Sauce. To serve, slice pork and serve with sauce.

nutrition facts per serving: 230 cal., 10 g total fat (2 g sat. fat), 71 mg chol., 282 mg sodium, 7 g carb. (2 g fiber, 3 g sugars), 28 g pro. exchanges: 0.5 vegetable, 0.5 starch, 3.5 lean meat, 1 fat.

* test kitchen tip: To toast almonds, place almonds in a single layer in a shallow pan. Bake in 350°F oven for 5 to 10 minutes, shaking the pan once or twice.

romesco sauce: In a large skillet cook 1 large red sweet pepper, chopped; 1 medium onion, chopped; and 4 cloves garlic, minced, in 1 tablespoon hot olive oil over medium heat for 10 to 15 minutes or until onion is lightly browned and vegetables are very tender, stirring occasionally. Transfer mixture to a food processor or blender. Add one 14.5-ounce can fire-roasted diced tomatoes, drained; ½ cup slivered almonds, toasted;* ¼ cup red wine vinegar; 2 tablespoons flaxseed meal; 1 tablespoon snipped fresh Italian (flat-leaf) parsley; ⅛ teaspoon salt; and ⅛ teaspoon cayenne pepper to onion mixture. Cover and process or blend until nearly smooth, scraping sides of bowl as needed.

*Wine intensifies the flavor of savory braised dishes
like this one—without adding any fat.*

chicken cacciatore

prep: 40 minutes cook: 1 hour
makes: 4 servings (2 pieces chicken and 1⅔ cups vegetable sauce each)

⅓	cup flour
2	pounds chicken thighs and/or drumsticks, skinned (8 pieces)
¼	teaspoon kosher salt or sea salt
⅛	teaspoon freshly ground black pepper
2	tablespoons olive oil
4	small carrots, peeled and cut crosswise into thirds
3	stalks celery, cut crosswise into quarters
1	medium onion, coarsely chopped (½ cup)
8	cloves garlic, peeled and thinly sliced
¼	cup tomato paste
1	cup reduced-sodium chicken broth
1	cup dry red wine or cranberry juice
2	tablespoons white wine vinegar
6	medium roma tomatoes, coarsely chopped
1	tablespoon snipped fresh thyme or 1 teaspoon dried thyme, crushed
2	tablespoons freshly grated Parmesan cheese
2	tablespoons snipped fresh Italian (flat-leaf) parsley

1 Spread flour in a shallow dish. Season chicken pieces with the salt and pepper. Dip chicken in the flour, turning to coat evenly and gently shaking off excess.

2 In a 5-quart Dutch oven heat oil over medium-high heat. Add chicken pieces; cook about 6 minutes or until browned, turning occasionally.

3 Remove chicken from Dutch oven; set aside. Drain off fat, reserving 2 tablespoons in the Dutch oven. Add carrots, celery, onion, and garlic. Cook about 5 minutes or just until onion is tender, stirring occasionally.

4 Stir in tomato paste. Add broth, wine, and vinegar; bring to boiling. Add tomatoes and thyme. Return chicken to Dutch oven. Bring to boiling; reduce heat. Simmer, covered, for 60 to 70 minutes or until chicken and vegetables are tender.

5 To serve, place chicken, vegetables, and cooking juices on a serving platter. Sprinkle with Parmesan cheese and parsley.

nutrition facts per serving: 407 cal., 13 g total fat (3 g sat. fat), 109 mg chol., 600 mg sodium, 30 g carb. (6 g fiber, 11 g sugars), 32 g pro. exchanges: 2.5 vegetable, 1 carb., 4 lean meat, 2 fat.

Twenty minutes and one skillet are all you need to bring the flavors of pan-roasted chicken and fresh summer squash to your table.

pan-roasted chicken with shallots

9g
CARB. PER
SERVING

start to finish: 20 minutes
makes: 4 servings (1 breast half and about ⅓ cup vegetables each)

8   shallots or 1 large onion
4   medium skinless, boneless chicken breast halves (1 to 1¼ pounds total)
¼   teaspoon salt
⅛   teaspoon black pepper
1   tablespoon olive oil
1   medium zucchini, cut into julienne strips
¼   cup snipped fresh parsley

1 Peel shallots; halve small shallots and quarter large ones. If using onion, cut into thin wedges (you should have 1 cup shallots or onion wedges). Set aside. Sprinkle chicken with the salt and pepper. In a large skillet heat oil over medium-high heat. Reduce heat to medium. Add chicken; cook for 2 minutes.

2 Turn chicken. Add shallots to skillet. Cook for 8 to 10 minutes more or until chicken is no longer pink (170°F), stirring shallots frequently and turning chicken if necessary to brown evenly. If necessary, add additional oil to prevent sticking. Reduce heat to medium-low if chicken or shallots brown too quickly.

3 Transfer chicken and shallots to a serving platter. Cover to keep warm. Add zucchini to skillet. Cook and stir for 3 to 5 minutes or until crisp-tender. Add to platter with chicken. Sprinkle with parsley.

nutrition facts per serving: 193 cal., 5 g total fat (1 g sat. fat), 66 mg chol., 231 mg sodium, 9 g carb. (1 g fiber, 2 g sugars), 28 g pro. exchanges: 1 vegetable, 3.5 lean meat.

Kumquats may be mini in size, but they're mighty in flavor. The whole fruit is edible—rind, interior, and seeds—and brings sweet-tart appeal to the chutney.

chicken with spiced kumquat chutney

17g
CARB. PER SERVING

start to finish: 20 minutes
makes: 4 servings (1 chicken breast half and 3 tablespoons chutney each)

310

company-special entrées

1 recipe Spiced
  Kumquat Chutney
  Nonstick cooking
  spray
4 medium skinless,
  boneless chicken
  breast halves (1¼ to
  1½ pounds total)
¼ teaspoon salt
⅛ teaspoon black
  pepper
2 tablespoons chopped
  pistachio nuts

1 Prepare Spiced Kumquat Chutney; set aside. Coat a nonstick grill pan with cooking spray. Heat over medium-high heat. Sprinkle chicken with the salt and pepper and add to hot pan.

2 Cook for 10 to 12 minutes or until no longer pink (170°F), turning once halfway through cooking. Serve chutney over chicken. Sprinkle with pistachios.

nutrition facts per serving: 261 cal., 6 g total fat (1 g sat. fat), 82 mg chol., 242 mg sodium, 17 g carb. (3 g fiber, 12 g sugars), 34 g pro. exchanges: 1 fruit, 5 lean meat.

nutrition facts per serving with substitute: Same as original, except 250 cal., 14 g carb.

✱ sugar substitutes: Choose from Splenda Granular or Sweet'N Low bulk or packets. Follow package directions to use amount equivalent to 1 tablespoon sugar.

spiced kumquat chutney: In a small saucepan heat 2 teaspoons canola oil over medium heat. Add 2 green onions, thinly sliced; ¼ teaspoon ground ginger; ¼ teaspoon ground coriander; and ⅛ teaspoon ground cinnamon. Cook and stir for 1 minute. Stir in ½ cup chopped kumquats, ⅓ cup dried cranberries, 3 tablespoons water, 2 tablespoons cider vinegar, and 1 tablespoon sugar.✱ Bring to boiling; reduce heat. Cook, covered, over medium-low heat for 5 minutes, stirring once or twice. Remove from heat and set aside.

Remember that discarding the chicken skin also discards unwanted calories and fat.

cheese- and date-stuffed chicken breasts

10g CARB. PER SERVING

prep: 20 minutes bake: 15 minutes
makes: 4 servings (1 chicken breast each)

2 tablespoons pitted whole dates, chopped
4 small chicken breast halves (2 to 2½ pounds total), skinned
2 ounces goat cheese (chèvre), softened
2 tablespoons slivered almonds, toasted* and chopped
1 teaspoon snipped fresh thyme or rosemary
¼ teaspoon salt
¼ teaspoon black pepper
   Nonstick cooking spray
1 tablespoon honey
1 tablespoon lemon juice

1 Preheat oven to 375°F. Place dates in a small bowl; add enough boiling water to just cover dates. Let stand for 5 minutes. Meanwhile, using a sharp knife, cut a pocket in each chicken breast by cutting horizontally through the thickest portion to, but not through, the opposite side.

2 Drain liquid off dates. Add goat cheese, almonds, and thyme to dates and stir until combined. Spoon cheese mixture into pockets in chicken. If necessary, secure openings with wooden toothpicks. Sprinkle chicken with the salt and pepper.

3 Coat an unheated oven-going large nonstick skillet with cooking spray. Heat skillet over medium heat. Add chicken pieces to skillet, meaty sides down. Cook for 3 to 4 minutes or until browned. Turn chicken pieces. Bake for 15 to 18 minutes or until chicken is no longer pink (170°F). Meanwhile, in a small bowl combine honey and lemon juice. Brush over chicken for the last 2 to 3 minutes of baking.

nutrition facts per serving: 250 cal., 6 g total fat (3 g sat. fat), 92 mg chol., 294 mg sodium, 10 g carb. (1 g fiber, 8 g sugars), 37 g pro. exchanges: 0.5 carb., 5.5 lean meat.

*test kitchen tip: To toast almonds, place almonds in a single layer in a shallow pan and bake in a 350°F oven for 5 to 10 minutes, shaking pan once or twice.

Rubbing the Asian-inspired spice mixture beneath, rather than over, the skin allows the flavors and scents of the warm spices to permeate the entire bird.

spice-rubbed roast chicken

0g CARB. PER SERVING

prep: 20 minutes   roast: 1 hour 15 minutes   stand: 15 minutes
makes: 6 servings (5 ounces cooked chicken each)

company-special **entrées**

2   tablespoons snipped fresh cilantro
2   teaspoons finely shredded orange peel
½   teaspoon salt
½   teaspoon ground coriander
½   teaspoon ground ginger
¼   teaspoon black pepper
¼   teaspoon ground allspice
¼   teaspoon crushed red pepper
1   3½- to 4-pound whole roasting chicken
    Snipped fresh cilantro (optional)

1 Preheat oven to 375°F. In a small bowl combine the 2 tablespoons cilantro, the orange peel, salt, coriander, ginger, black pepper, allspice, and crushed red pepper. Rinse chicken body cavity; remove any excess fat from cavity. Pat chicken dry with paper towels.

2 Using your fingers, loosen chicken skin from breast meat and drumsticks. Spoon cilantro mixture under the skin, rubbing it evenly over the breast and drumstick meat. Skewer neck skin of chicken to back; tie legs to tail. Twist wing tips under back. Place chicken, breast side up, on a rack in a shallow roasting pan. Insert an ovenproof meat thermometer into the center of an inside thigh muscle, making sure tip does not touch bone.

3 Roast, uncovered, for 1¼ to 1¾ hours or until drumsticks move easily in their sockets and chicken is no longer pink (180°F). Cover and let stand for 15 minutes before serving. Remove skin and discard as you carve chicken.

nutrition facts per serving: 226 cal., 8 g total fat (2 g sat. fat), 107 mg chol., 292 mg sodium, 0 g carb. (0 g fiber, 0 g sugars), 34 g pro. exchanges: 5 lean meat.

With fresh baby spinach, blue cheese, and pears, no one will mistake this stylish turkey entrée for the Thanksgiving bird!

turkey steaks with spinach, pears, and blue cheese

start to finish: 20 minutes
makes: 4 servings (1 turkey steak and about ¾ cup spinach-pear mixture each)

8g
CARB. PER SERVING

- 2   8- to 10-ounce turkey breast tenderloins
- 1   teaspoon dried sage, crushed
- ¼   teaspoon salt
- ⅛   teaspoon black pepper
- 2   tablespoons butter
- 1   6-ounce package fresh baby spinach
- 1   large pear, cored and thinly sliced
- ¼   cup crumbled reduced-fat blue cheese (1 ounce)

1 Split tenderloins horizontally to make four ½-inch-thick steaks. Rub turkey with sage; sprinkle with salt and pepper. In an extra-large skillet cook steaks in 1 tablespoon of the butter over medium-high heat for 14 to 16 minutes or until no longer pink (170°F), turning once. (Reduce heat to medium if turkey browns too quickly.) Remove from skillet. Add spinach to skillet. Cook and stir until just wilted.

2 Meanwhile, in a small skillet cook pear slices in the remaining 1 tablespoon butter over medium to medium-high heat, stirring occasionally, about 5 minutes or until tender and lightly browned.

3 Serve turkey steaks with spinach and pear slices. Sprinkle with blue cheese.

nutrition facts per serving: 230 cal., 8 g total fat (5 g sat. fat), 89 mg chol., 357 mg sodium, 8 g carb. (2 g fiber, 4 g sugars), 31 g pro. exchanges: 1 vegetable, 0.5 fruit, 4 lean meat.

Thanks to garlic slivers and chile pepper pieces tucked into each turkey breast, plus a spicy-sweet glaze, this entrée bursts with fantastic flavors from all angles.

ginger-orange-glazed turkey breasts

prep: 25 minutes   marinate: 12 hours   roast: 45 minutes   stand: 5 minutes
makes: 8 servings (5 ounces cooked turkey each)

- 2   1½-pound skinless, boneless turkey breasts
- 2   cloves garlic, cut into 12 slivers total
- 1   to 2 small fresh red chile peppers, cut into 12 pieces*
- ¼   cup orange juice
- ¼   cup olive oil
- 1   cup low-sugar orange marmalade
- ½   cup finely chopped green onions (4)
- ½   cup orange juice
- 1   tablespoon grated fresh ginger
- 1   clove garlic, minced
- 1   tablespoon orange liqueur or orange juice
- 1   teaspoon black pepper
- ½   teaspoon salt
  Sliced green onion, chopped chile peppers,* and/or finely shredded orange peel (optional)

*test kitchen tip: Because chile peppers contain volatile oils that can burn your skin and eyes, avoid direct contact with them as much as possible. When working with chile peppers, wear plastic or rubber gloves. If your bare hands do touch the peppers, wash your hands and nails well with soap and warm water.

1 Using a sharp paring knife, cut 12 slits into the top of each turkey breast. Tuck a garlic sliver or a chile pepper piece into each slit, alternating garlic and chile pepper. Place turkey breasts side by side in a shallow glass baking dish.

2 In a small bowl combine the ¼ cup orange juice and the olive oil; pour over turkey. Cover; marinate in the refrigerator for 12 to 24 hours, turning occasionally.

3 For glaze, in a small saucepan combine marmalade, green onions, the ½ cup orange juice, the ginger, and minced garlic. Bring to boiling; reduce heat. Simmer, uncovered, 5 minutes. Remove from heat; stir in liqueur.

4 Preheat oven to 350°F. Remove turkey breasts from marinade; discard marinade. Arrange turkey breasts on a rack in a large roasting pan. Spoon some of the glaze over turkey breasts, being careful not to let the spoon touch the uncooked turkey. Sprinkle with the black pepper and salt.

5 Roast for 45 to 50 minutes or until an instant-read thermometer inserted into the thickest part of each turkey breast registers 160°F, spooning some of the remaining glaze over breasts every 15 minutes of roasting, each time being careful not to let the spoon touch the uncooked turkey. Let turkey stand for 5 minutes before slicing. If desired, garnish with additional sliced green onion, chopped chile peppers, and/or finely shredded orange peel.

nutrition facts per serving: 320 cal., 8 g total fat (1 g sat. fat), 105 mg chol., 231 mg sodium, 17 g carb. (0 g fiber, 12 g sugars), 42 g pro. exchanges: 1 carb., 6 lean meat.

make-ahead directions: If desired, prepare the glaze as directed in Step 3. Pour glaze into an airtight container. Cover and chill for up to 3 days. Before using, in a small saucepan reheat glaze over low heat.

Looking to impress? Guests know they're getting something special when you serve scallops. This zesty spiced version takes the seafood to the next level!

25g
CARB. PER
SERVING

seared scallops and spinach with pomegranate glaze

start to finish: 30 minutes
makes: 4 servings (3 scallops, ½ cup spinach, and 2 tablespoons sauce each)

316

12	large fresh or frozen sea scallops (about 1¼ pounds total)
¾	cup 100% pomegranate juice
2	tablespoons honey
½	teaspoon ground coriander
⅛	teaspoon ground cinnamon
1	tablespoon lemon juice
¾	teaspoon cornstarch
3	teaspoons vegetable oil
¼	teaspoon sugar
⅛	teaspoon black pepper
1	10-ounce package fresh baby spinach
	Pinch salt
	Pinch black pepper
¼	cup pomegranate seeds*

1 Thaw scallops, if frozen. Rinse scallops; pat very dry with paper towels. Remove and discard the small muscles if still attached. Set scallops aside.

2 For sauce, in a medium saucepan combine pomegranate juice, honey, coriander, and cinnamon; bring to boiling over medium-high heat. In a small bowl combine lemon juice and cornstarch; stir into boiling juice mixture. Boil gently, uncovered, 10 minutes or until reduced and slightly syrupy. Set aside.

3 Meanwhile, in an extra-large nonstick skillet heat 1 teaspoon of the oil over medium-high heat, brushing to coat the skillet. Sprinkle scallops with sugar and ⅛ teaspoon of the pepper. When skillet is very hot, add scallops; cook 2 minutes without stirring or turning (the scallops should be well seared). Turn scallops; cook 1 to 2 minutes more or just until scallops are opaque in the centers. Transfer to a plate.

4 Wipe skillet clean; add the remaining 2 teaspoons oil. Add spinach in batches; toss 1 to 2 minutes or until just slightly wilted. Season with the pinch each of salt and pepper.

5 Arrange scallops and spinach on four serving plates; drizzle with sauce. Sprinkle with pomegranate seeds..

nutrition facts per serving: 213 cal., 4 g total fat (0 g sat. fat), 34 mg chol., 651 mg sodium, 25 g carb. (2 g fiber, 16 g sugars), 19 g pro. exchanges: 1 vegetable, 1 fruit, 2.5 lean meat, 0.5 fat.

*test kitchen tip: Look for packages of fresh pomegranate seeds in your grocer's produce or freezer section.

When choosing dry white wine for enhancing this deluxe dish, pick a Sauvignon Blanc or Chardonnay in the $8 to $10 range.

seafood-stuffed shells

33g
CARB. PER
SERVING

prep: 45 minutes   bake: 30 minutes   stand: 10 minutes
makes: 6 servings (2 shells each)

1 pound fresh or frozen large shrimp in shells
12 dried jumbo shell macaroni
1 medium red sweet pepper, chopped
½ cup chopped sweet onion
1 tablespoon olive oil
3 cloves garlic, minced
⅓ cup dry white wine or reduced-sodium chicken broth
¾ cup reduced-sodium chicken broth
¼ cup flour
2 cups fat-free milk
8 ounces cooked crabmeat, coarsely chopped, or good-quality canned lump crabmeat, drained
2 tablespoons snipped fresh basil
1 tablespoon snipped fresh chives

1 Thaw shrimp, if frozen. Peel and devein shrimp; rinse with cold water and pat dry with paper towels. Coarsely chop shrimp and set aside. Meanwhile, cook pasta according to package directions; drain. Rinse with cold water; drain again.

2 Preheat oven to 350°F. In a large nonstick skillet cook sweet pepper and onion in hot oil over medium heat for 5 minutes, stirring occasionally. Add shrimp. Cook for 2 to 3 minutes more or until shrimp are opaque, stirring occasionally. Transfer shrimp mixture to a bowl.

3 For sauce, add garlic to the same skillet. Cook and stir for 30 seconds. Remove skillet from heat. Carefully add wine; return skillet to heat and cook for 1 to 2 minutes or until most of the wine is evaporated, stirring to scrape up browned bits from bottom of skillet. In a small bowl whisk together ¾ cup broth and flour. Add all at once to the skillet along with the milk. Cook and stir until thickened and bubbly.

4 Stir ⅔ cup of the sauce and the crab into the shrimp mixture. Spoon shrimp mixture evenly into the cooked shells and arrange shells in a 2-quart square baking dish. Pour remaining sauce over the shells.

5 Cover and bake for 30 to 35 minutes or until heated through. Let stand for 10 minutes. Sprinkle with basil and chives just before serving. Serve in shallow bowls.

nutrition facts per serving: 317 cal., 5 g total fat (1 g sat. fat), 154 mg chol., 325 mg sodium, 33 g carb. (1 g fiber, 7 g sugars), 31 g pro. exchanges: 2 starch, 3.5 lean meat.

You'll want to serve something refreshing after this luscious dish. Purchased angel food cake with light whipped topping and fresh fruit is just the ticket.

lobster mac and cheese casserole

prep: 20 minutes   cook: 17 minutes   bake: 15 minutes
makes: 6 servings (1 cup each)

1½ cups dried whole wheat rigatoni or rotini (6 ounces)
1 large lobster tail (8 to 10 ounces)
2 cups small broccoli florets
  Nonstick cooking spray
1 medium red sweet pepper, chopped (¾ cup)
⅓ cup chopped onion
1 6.5-ounce container light semisoft cheese with garlic and herb
2 cups fat-free milk
1 tablespoon flour
1 cup shredded reduced-fat Italian cheese blend (4 ounces)
½ teaspoon finely shredded lemon peel
¼ teaspoon black pepper
⅓ cup whole wheat or regular panko (Japanese-style bread crumbs)

1 Preheat oven to 375°F. In a 4-quart Dutch oven cook pasta according to package directions, adding the lobster tail for the last 7 minutes of cooking and adding the broccoli for the last 3 minutes of cooking. Drain and set aside. When lobster tail is cool enough to handle, remove the lobster meat and coarsely chop the meat.

2 Meanwhile, coat a large nonstick skillet with cooking spray; heat skillet over medium heat. Add sweet pepper and onion to skillet. Cook about 5 minutes or until tender, stirring frequently. Remove skillet from heat. Stir in semisoft cheese until melted.

3 In a medium bowl whisk together milk and flour until smooth. Add all at once to sweet pepper mixture. Cook and stir over medium heat until thickened and bubbly. Reduce heat to low. Stir in Italian cheese blend until melted. Stir in cooked pasta, broccoli, chopped lobster, lemon peel, and black pepper.

4 Transfer mixture to a 2-quart casserole. Sprinkle with panko. Bake for 15 to 20 minutes or until heated through and top is golden brown.

nutrition facts per serving: 322 cal., 10 g total fat (6 g sat. fat), 68 mg chol., 402 mg sodium, 35 g carb. (4 g fiber, 9 g sugars), 25 g pro. exchanges: 2 starch, 3 lean meat, 1 fat.

This company-perfect dish takes less than 1 hour start to finish. That means you can invite friends over for dinner tonight, even if you have to go to the grocery store first!

sicilian tuna with capers

1g CARB. PER SERVING

prep: 20 minutes marinate: 15 minutes broil: 8 minutes
makes: 4 servings (1 tuna steak and 2 tablespoons tomato mixture each)

4   fresh or frozen tuna steaks, cut 1 inch thick (about 1 pound total)
2   tablespoons red wine vinegar
1   tablespoon snipped fresh dill weed or 1 teaspoon dried dill weed
2   teaspoons olive oil
¼   teaspoon salt
⅛   teaspoon cayenne pepper
½   cup chopped tomato
1   tablespoon capers, drained
1   tablespoon chopped pitted ripe olives
1   clove garlic, minced
     Hot cooked rice (optional)
     Steamed baby bok choy (optional)

1 Preheat broiler. Thaw fish, if frozen. Rinse fish and pat dry with paper towels. For marinade, in a shallow dish combine vinegar, dill weed, oil, salt, and half of the cayenne pepper. Add fish to marinade in dish, turning to coat. Cover and marinate in the refrigerator for 15 minutes.

2 Meanwhile, in a small bowl stir together tomato, capers, olives, garlic, and the remaining cayenne pepper.

3 Drain fish, reserving marinade. Place fish on the greased unheated rack of a broiler pan. Broil 4 inches from the heat for 4 minutes. Turn fish and brush with all of the reserved marinade. Broil for 4 to 8 minutes more or until fish begins to flake when tested with a fork. Serve tuna topped with tomato mixture. If desired, serve over hot cooked rice with steamed baby bok choy.

nutrition facts per serving: 192 cal., 8 g total fat (2 g sat. fat), 43 mg chol., 271 mg sodium, 1 g carb. (0 g fiber, 1 g sugars), 27 g pro. exchanges: 4 lean meat.

12g
CARB. PER
SERVING

Pluck a few small fresh oregano leaves and toss them over the roasted red tomatoes for a red and green scene.

salmon with roasted tomatoes and shallots

prep: 20 minutes roast: 30 minutes
makes: 4 servings (3 ounces cooked salmon and ¾ cup tomato mixture each)

1	1-pound fresh or frozen salmon fillet, skinned if desired
⅛	teaspoon salt
⅛	teaspoon black pepper
	Nonstick cooking spray
4	cups grape tomatoes
½	cup thinly sliced shallots
6	cloves garlic, minced
2	tablespoons snipped fresh oregano or 1½ teaspoons dried oregano, crushed
1	tablespoon olive oil
¼	teaspoon salt
¼	teaspoon black pepper

1 Thaw salmon, if frozen. Rinse salmon and pat dry with paper towels. Sprinkle salmon with the ⅛ teaspoon salt and ⅛ teaspoon pepper. Preheat oven to 400°F.

2 Lightly coat a 3-quart baking dish with cooking spray. In the baking dish combine tomatoes, shallots, garlic, oregano, oil, ¼ teaspoon salt, and ¼ teaspoon pepper. Toss to coat.

3 Roast tomato mixture, uncovered, for 15 minutes. Place salmon, skin side down, on top of the tomato mixture. Roast, uncovered, for 15 to 18 minutes or until salmon flakes easily when tested with a fork.

4 Using two large pancake turners, transfer the salmon to a serving platter. Top with tomato mixture.

nutrition facts per serving: 320 cal., 19 g total fat (4 g sat. fat), 62 mg chol., 297 mg sodium, 12 g carb. (2 g fiber, 5 g sugars), 26 g pro. exchanges: 1.5 vegetable, 3.5 lean meat, 2.5 fat.

Some of the signature ingredients in a Greek salad—artichoke hearts, feta, olives, oregano, and lemon juice—freshen up a tuna casserole that will impress your guests.

greek tuna casserole

24g
CARB. PER
SERVING

prep: 20 minutes roast: 15 minutes bake: 40 minutes
makes: 6 servings (1 cup each)

Nonstick cooking spray
⅓ cup dried whole wheat orzo pasta
1 medium eggplant, ends trimmed, cut into 1-inch-thick slices
1 large red sweet pepper, stemmed, quartered, and seeded
2 tablespoons olive oil
1½ teaspoons finely shredded lemon peel
2 tablespoons lemon juice
1 clove garlic, minced
4 tablespoons snipped fresh oregano
½ teaspoon salt
¼ teaspoon black pepper
½ cup panko (Japanese-style bread crumbs)
3 5-ounce cans very low–sodium tuna (water pack), undrained, large pieces broken up
1 9-ounce package frozen artichoke hearts, thawed and quartered if needed
½ cup ripe olives, halved
¼ cup crumbled feta cheese

1 Preheat oven to 425°F. Coat a 1½-quart au gratin dish with cooking spray. Cook pasta according to package directions. Drain and set aside.

2 Line a 15×10×1-inch baking pan with foil. Lightly coat both sides of each eggplant slice with cooking spray. Place coated eggplant slices in the prepared baking pan. Add sweet pepper quarters to pan with eggplant slices. Roast, uncovered, 15 to 20 minutes or until eggplant begins to brown and peppers are just tender. Remove from oven; let cool. Cut eggplant and pepper pieces into ¾-inch cubes. Reduce oven temperature to 350°F.

3 For lemon dressing, in a small bowl whisk together olive oil, 1 teaspoon of the lemon peel, the lemon juice, and garlic. Whisk in 3 tablespoons of the oregano, the salt, and black pepper; set aside. In another small bowl combine panko, the remaining 1 tablespoon oregano, and the remaining ½ teaspoon lemon peel; set aside.

4 In a large bowl combine cooked orzo, eggplant, sweet pepper, tuna, artichoke hearts, olives, and feta. Stir in lemon dressing. Spoon mixture into the prepared baking dish. Cover with foil. Bake 35 to 40 minutes or until heated through. Sprinkle panko mixture over top. Bake, uncovered, 5 to 8 minutes more or until panko mixture is golden brown.

nutrition facts per serving: 239 cal., 8 g total fat (2 g sat. fat), 37 mg chol., 436 mg sodium, 24 g carb. (9 g fiber, 5 g sugars), 20 g pro. exchanges: 1 vegetable, 1 starch, 2 lean meat, 1 fat.

grilled flank steak salad,
page 324

322

meals for

Smart eating becomes a joy when you share good-for-you dishes with your favorite person. Sized for the two of you, these recipes bring flavors you'll love savoring together—whether you're looking for a quick weeknight meal or something special for date night.

two

31g
CARB. PER
SERVING

Flank steak, known for its full-throttle beefy flavor, hails from the belly of the animal. Don't skip the marinating—it helps tenderize the cut. Pictured on page 322.

grilled flank steak salad

prep: 30 minutes marinate: 30 minutes grill: 17 minutes
makes: 2 servings (3 ounces cooked steak, 1 cup greens, ½ cup vegetables, 1½ tablespoons dressing, and 1 breadstick each)

1 recipe Cilantro
    Dressing
8 ounces beef flank
    steak
2 small yellow and/or
    red sweet peppers,
    seeded and halved
1 ear of fresh sweet
    corn, husks and
    silks removed
2 green onions,
    trimmed
    Nonstick cooking
    spray
2 cups torn romaine
    lettuce
4 cherry tomatoes,
    halved
¼ of a small avocado,
    halved, seeded,
    peeled, and thinly
    sliced (optional)

1 Prepare Cilantro Dressing and divide it into two portions.

2 Trim fat from steak. Score both sides of steak in a diamond pattern by making shallow diagonal cuts at 1-inch intervals. Place steak in a resealable plastic bag set in a shallow dish. Pour one portion of the Cilantro Dressing over steak in bag; set aside remaining dressing portion. Seal bag; turn to coat steak. Marinate in refrigerator for 30 minutes.

3 Coat sweet peppers, corn, and green onions with cooking spray.

4 For a charcoal grill, place steak and corn on the grill rack directly over medium coals. Grill, uncovered, until steak is desired doneness and corn is tender, turning steak once halfway through grilling and turning corn occasionally. For steak, allow 17 to 21 minutes for medium rare (145°F) to medium (160°F). For corn, allow 15 to 20 minutes. Add sweet pepper halves to the grill for the last 8 minutes of grilling and green onions for the last 4 minutes grilling, turning frequently. (For a gas grill, preheat grill. Reduce heat to medium. Place meat and then vegetables on grill rack. Cover and grill as directed.)

5 Thinly slice steak against the grain. Coarsely chop sweet peppers and green onions; cut corn from cob.

6 Divide romaine lettuce between two bowls. Place sliced steak, grilled vegetables, tomatoes, and, if desired, avocado slices over lettuce. Drizzle salads with the reserved portion of the Cilantro Dressing.

cilantro dressing: In a blender or food processor combine 3 tablespoons lime juice; 2 tablespoons chopped shallot; 2 tablespoons snipped fresh cilantro; 1 tablespoon olive oil; 1 tablespoon water; 2 teaspoons honey; 1 large clove garlic, quartered; ½ teaspoon chili powder; ¼ teaspoon salt; and ¼ teaspoon ground cumin. Cover and blend or process until combined.

nutrition facts per serving: 337 cal., 12 g total fat (3 g sat. fat), 47 mg chol., 376 mg sodium, 31 g carb. (5 g fiber, 13 g sugars), 29 g pro. exchanges: 2 vegetable, 0.5 starch, 1 carb., 3.5 lean meat, 1.5 fat.

Hold the mustard, pickles, and ketchup! Fresh, vibrant Cucumber Sauce helps these cheese-studded burgers veer well off the beaten path.

14g
CARB. PER
SERVING

greek feta burgers

prep: 25 minutes   cook: 8 minutes
makes: 2 servings (1 burger and ½ bun each)

1   recipe Cucumber
    Sauce
8   ounces 93% or leaner
    ground beef
1   tablespoon crumbled
    reduced-fat feta
    cheese
1½ teaspoons snipped
    fresh Italian
    (flat-leaf) parsley
1   clove garlic, minced
⅛   teaspoon black
    pepper
1   whole wheat
    hamburger bun,
    split and toasted
½   cup fresh spinach
    leaves
2   tomato slices

1 Prepare Cucumber Sauce; set aside. In a medium bowl combine ground beef, cheese, parsley, garlic, and pepper. Shape mixture into two ½-inch-thick patties.

2 In a large nonstick skillet cook patties over medium-high heat for 8 to 10 minutes or until an instant-read thermometer inserted into side of each patty registers 160°F, turning once halfway through cooking.

3 Top each bun half with spinach. Top each with a burger, tomato slice, and half of the sauce.

nutrition facts per serving: 262 cal., 10 g total fat (4 g sat. fat), 66 mg chol., 361 mg sodium, 14 g carb. (2 g fiber, 3 sugars), 27 g pro. exchanges: 0.5 vegetable, 1 starch, 3 lean meat, 1 fat.

cucumber sauce: In a small bowl combine 3 tablespoons chopped, seeded cucumber; 2 tablespoons light sour cream; 1 clove garlic, minced; ½ teaspoon snipped fresh Italian (flat-leaf) parsley; ¼ teaspoon snipped fresh mint; and ⅛ teaspoon sea salt.

14g
CARB. PER SERVING

If you can't find an 8-ounce roast, buy a larger one and cut it up as necessary. Freeze the unused portion, well wrapped in freezer wrap, for up to 12 months.

slow-cooked beef with carrots and cabbage

prep: 20 minutes   cook: 7 to 8 hours (low) or 3½ to 4 hours (high) + 30 minutes (high)
makes: 2 servings (3 ounces cooked meat and ¾ cup vegetables each)

8   ounces boneless beef chuck roast
¼   teaspoon dried oregano, crushed
¼   teaspoon ground cumin
¼   teaspoon paprika
¼   teaspoon black pepper
⅛   teaspoon salt
    Nonstick cooking spray
3   medium carrots, cut into 2-inch pieces
2   small garlic cloves, minced
⅓   cup lower-sodium beef broth
2   cups coarsely shredded cabbage

1 Trim fat from roast. Combine oregano, cumin, paprika, pepper, and salt. Sprinkle mixture over meat; rub in. Coat a medium nonstick skillet with cooking spray; heat over medium heat. Add meat to skillet; brown on all sides.

2 Meanwhile, in a 1½- or 2-quart slow cooker combine carrots and garlic. Pour broth over carrots. Top with meat.

3 Cover and cook on low-heat setting for 7 to 8 hours or on high-heat setting for 3½ to 4 hours. If no heat setting is available, cook for 5 to 5½ hours.

4 If using low-heat setting, turn to high-heat setting (if no heat setting is available, continue cooking). Add cabbage. Cover and cook for 30 minutes more. Using a slotted spoon, transfer meat and vegetables to a serving platter.

nutrition facts per serving: 214 cal., 5 g total fat (2 g sat. fat), 50 mg chol., 379 mg sodium, 14 g carb. (5 g fiber, 7 sugars), 27 g pro. exchanges: 2 vegetable, 3.5 lean meat.

*Here's a quick version of pho, a fresh and
satisfying Vietnamese noodle soup.*

vietnamese-style beef
and noodle bowls

start to finish: 30 minutes
makes: 2 servings (1½ cups each)

2 ounces banh pho
   (Vietnamese wide
   rice noodles)
1 teaspoon chili oil
6 ounces beef flank
   steak or beef top
   round steak, cut
   into bite-size strips
1 stalk bok choy, stalk
   and leaf separated
   and each thinly
   sliced
¼ cup chopped red
   sweet pepper
1 teaspoon grated fresh
   ginger
1 clove garlic, minced
⅛ teaspoon crushed
   red pepper
½ cup lower-sodium
   beef broth
1½ teaspoons reduced-
   sodium soy sauce
¼ cup canned bean
   sprouts, drained
1 tablespoon snipped
   fresh basil
   Fresh basil leaves
   Lime wedges

1 Prepare noodles according to package
directions. Set aside.

2 Pour oil into a wok or large skillet. Preheat
over medium-high heat. Stir-fry beef for
1 minute. Add the stalk portion of the bok
choy, sweet pepper, ginger, garlic, and crushed
red pepper. Stir-fry for 1 to 2 minutes more or
until beef is browned on all sides. Push beef
from the center of the wok. Add beef broth
and soy sauce. Bring to boiling. Reduce heat
and stir meat into broth mixture. Cook and stir
for 1 to 2 minutes more or until beef is done.

3 Add noodles, bok choy leaf portion, bean
sprouts, and snipped basil to mixture in
wok; toss to combine. Ladle mixture into soup
bowls. Garnish with fresh basil leaves. Serve
with lime wedges.

nutrition facts per serving: 274 cal., 7 g total fat (2 g sat.
fat), 51 mg chol., 397 mg sodium, 31 g carb. (2 g fiber, 2 sugars),
21 g pro. exchanges: 2 starch, 2.5 lean meat.

39g CARB. PER SERVING

meals for two

The apple juice and apple jelly add a fruity-sweet counterpoint to the spicy flavors of ginger, garlic, and red pepper.

apple pork stir-fry

start to finish: 25 minutes

makes: 2 servings (1 cup pork-veggie mixture and ⅓ cup rice each)

2 tablespoons unsweetened apple juice

1½ tablespoons apple jelly

2 teaspoons reduced-sodium soy sauce

2 teaspoons reduced-sodium teriyaki sauce

⅛ to ¼ teaspoon crushed red pepper
   Nonstick cooking spray

½ cup red sweet pepper cut into bite-size strips

¼ cup sliced onion

¼ cup sliced celery

¼ cup matchstick-size apple strips

2 tablespoons canned sliced water chestnuts, drained

2 tablespoons shredded carrot

1 teaspoon grated fresh ginger

1 clove garlic, minced

2 teaspoons sesame oil

6 ounces boneless pork top loin chops, cut into thin bite-size strips

⅔ cup hot cooked brown rice

1 For sauce, in a small bowl combine apple juice, apple jelly, soy sauce, teriyaki sauce, and crushed red pepper; set aside.

2 Meanwhile, coat an unheated large nonstick skillet or wok with cooking spray. Preheat over medium-high heat. Add sweet pepper, onion, and celery to hot skillet. Cover and cook for 3 minutes, stirring occasionally. Add apple, water chestnuts, carrot, ginger, and garlic; cover and cook for 3 to 4 minutes more or until vegetables and apple are crisp-tender, stirring occasionally. Remove vegetable mixture from skillet.

3 Add sesame oil to the same skillet. Add pork strips. Cook and stir over medium-high heat for 2 to 3 minutes or until cooked through. Return vegetable mixture to skillet along with sauce mixture. Cook and stir for 1 to 2 minutes or until heated through. Serve stir-fry mixture with hot cooked rice.

nutrition facts per serving: 294 cal., 7 g total fat (1 g sat. fat), 35 mg chol., 498 mg sodium, 39 g carb. (4 g fiber, 16 sugars), 20 g pro. exchanges: 0.5 fruit, 2 starch, 2 lean meat, 0.5 fat.

Adding green onions and fresh cilantro or parsley at the end of the cooking time helps bring a burst of brightness to this long-simmered recipe.

cheesy ham and veggie bowls

 37g
CARB. PER SERVING

prep: 15 minutes cook: 6 to 7 hours (low) or 3 to 3½ hours (high) stand: 10 minutes
makes: 2 servings (1½ cups each)

1   small zucchini, chopped (1½ cups)

1½ cups frozen whole kernel corn

1   red sweet pepper, chopped (¾ cup)

½   of a medium fresh poblano chile pepper, seeded and thinly sliced∗

1½ ounces reduced-sodium ham, chopped

½   teaspoon smoked paprika

2   tablespoons water

⅓   cup thinly sliced green onions

¼   cup shredded reduced-fat cheddar cheese (1 ounce)

2   tablespoons snipped fresh cilantro or parsley

1   tablespoon fat-free milk

2   tablespoons shredded reduced-fat cheddar cheese

1 In a 2-quart slow cooker combine zucchini, corn, sweet pepper, poblano pepper, ham, and paprika. Drizzle the water over mixture in cooker.

2 Cover and cook on low-heat setting for 6 to 7 hours or on high-heat setting for 3 to 3½ hours. Stir in the green onions, ¼ cup cheese, the cilantro, and milk. Remove liner from cooker. Let stand, covered, for 10 minutes. Serve in bowls; top with remaining cheese.

nutrition facts per serving: 251 cal., 7 g total fat (4 g sat. fat), 26 mg chol., 364 mg sodium, 37 g carb. (5 g fiber, 9 sugars), 16 g pro. exchanges: 1 vegetable, 2 starch, 1.5 lean meat.

∗test kitchen tip: Because chile peppers contain volatile oils that can burn your skin and eyes, avoid direct contact with them as much as possible. When working with chile peppers, wear plastic or rubber gloves. If your bare hands do touch the peppers, wash your hands and nails well with soap and warm water.

No peeking, please! Avoid lifting the lid while the dumplings are in the slow cooker. Doing so will prevent them from cooking through.

meals for two

chicken and cornmeal dumplings

47g CARB. PER SERVING

prep: 25 minutes cook: 7 to 8 hours (low) or 3½ to 4 hours (high) + 20 to 25 minutes (high)
makes: 2 servings (1½ cups chicken mixture and 2 dumplings each)

2 medium carrots, thinly sliced (1 cup)
1 stalk celery, thinly sliced (½ cup)
⅓ cup fresh or frozen corn kernels
½ of a medium onion, thinly sliced
2 cloves garlic, minced
1 teaspoon snipped fresh rosemary or ½ teaspoon dried rosemary, crushed
¼ teaspoon black pepper
2 chicken thighs, skinned
1 cup reduced-sodium chicken broth
½ cup fat-free milk
1 tablespoon flour
1 recipe Cornmeal Dumplings
   Coarsely ground black pepper (optional)

1 In a 1½- or 2-quart slow cooker combine carrots, celery, corn, onion, garlic, rosemary, and the ¼ teaspoon pepper. Top with chicken. Pour broth over all in cooker.

2 Cover and cook on low-heat setting for 7 to 8 hours or on high-heat setting for 3½ to 4 hours. If no heat setting is available, cook for 5 to 5½ hours.

3 If using low-heat setting, turn to high-heat setting (if no heat setting is available, continue cooking). Remove chicken from cooker. Transfer chicken to a cutting board; cool slightly. When cool enough to handle, remove chicken from bones; discard bones. Chop chicken; return to mixture in cooker. In a small bowl whisk or stir milk and flour until smooth. Stir into mixture in cooker.

4 Using two spoons, drop Cornmeal Dumplings dough into four mounds on top of hot chicken mixture. Cover and cook for 20 to 25 minutes more or until a toothpick inserted into a dumpling comes out clean. (Do not lift cover during cooking.) If desired, sprinkle each serving with coarse pepper.

nutrition facts per serving: 369 cal., 10 g total fat (1 g sat. fat), 55 mg chol., 582 mg sodium, 47 g carb. (5 g fiber, 9 sugars), 24 g pro. exchanges: 1 vegetable, 2.5 starch, 2 lean meat, 1 fat.

cornmeal dumplings: In a medium bowl stir together ¼ cup flour, ¼ cup cornmeal, ½ teaspoon baking powder, and dash salt. In a small bowl combine 1 egg white, 1 tablespoon fat-free milk, and 1 tablespoon canola oil. Add egg mixture to flour mixture; stir just until moistened.

Skip happy hour! Get the chicken marinating, then go for a walk to enjoy some appetite-rousing together time. Once home, you'll be just a few minutes away from a great dinner.

9g
CARB. PER SERVING

chicken skewers with peach salsa

prep: 20 minutes   marinate: 2 hours   grill: 5 minutes
makes: 2 servings (1 skewer with ½ cup salsa each)

3   tablespoons rice vinegar
1   tablespoon reduced-sodium soy sauce
1   teaspoon packed brown sugar *
1   teaspoon grated fresh ginger
8   ounces skinless, boneless chicken breast halves, cut lengthwise into 1-inch strips
½   of a medium peach, pitted and chopped
2   tablespoons chopped red sweet pepper
2   teaspoons finely chopped red onion
2   teaspoons snipped fresh cilantro
½   teaspoon lime juice
¼   teaspoon finely chopped, seeded fresh jalapeño chile pepper (see tip, page 329)

1 In a large resealable plastic bag set in a shallow bowl combine rice vinegar, soy sauce, brown sugar, and ginger. Add chicken strips. Seal bag and turn to coat chicken. Marinate in the refrigerator 2 to 4 hours, turning bag occasionally.

2 Drain chicken, discarding marinade. Thread chicken onto two 10- to 12-inch-long skewers.

3 For a charcoal grill, place skewers on the grill rack directly over medium coals. Grill, uncovered, 5 to 7 minutes or until chicken is no longer pink, turning occasionally to brown evenly. (For a gas grill, preheat grill. Reduce heat to medium. Place chicken skewers on grill rack over heat. Cover and grill as directed.)

4 Meanwhile, for peach salsa, in a small bowl combine peach, sweet pepper, onion, cilantro, lime juice, and jalapeño pepper. Serve chicken skewers with peach salsa.

nutrition facts per serving: 171 cal., 1 g total fat (0 g sat. fat), 66 mg chol., 326 mg sodium, 9 g carb. (1 g fiber, 8 sugars), 27 g pro. exchanges: 0.5 fruit, 4 lean meat.

nutrition facts per serving with substitute: Same as original, except 162 cal., 325 g sodium, 7 g carb.

* sugar substitutes: Choose from Sweet'N Low Brown or Sugar Twin Granulated Brown. Follow package directions to use product amount equivalent to 1 teaspoon brown sugar.

Why wait for the holidays to enjoy turkey and stuffing? Here the dynamite duo becomes a hearty casserole you can enjoy—without a fat-and-calorie splurge—all year.

main-dish turkey stuffing

32g
CARB. PER
SERVING

prep: 30 minutes bake: 20 minutes
makes: 2 servings (1½ cups stuffing and about 3 tablespoons gravy each)

8   ounces skinless, boneless turkey breast tenderloin, cut into bite-size pieces
⅓   cup chopped celery
¼   cup chopped onion
¼   cup chopped carrot
1   clove garlic, minced
1   tablespoon light butter with canola oil
1½   teaspoons snipped fresh parsley
1   teaspoon snipped fresh oregano or ¼ teaspoon dried oregano, crushed
½   teaspoon snipped fresh thyme or ⅛ teaspoon dried oregano, crushed
¼   teaspoon poultry seasoning
⅛   teaspoon black pepper
1½   cups dried reduced-calorie whole wheat bread cubes
1   cup dried reduced-calorie white bread cubes
⅓   to ½ cup unsalted chicken stock
1   recipe Herbed Gravy

1 Preheat oven to 350°F. In a medium skillet cook turkey, celery, onion, carrot, and garlic in hot butter over medium heat for 7 to 10 minutes or until turkey is cooked through and vegetables are tender, stirring occasionally. Remove from heat; stir in parsley, oregano, thyme, poultry seasoning, and pepper.

2 In a medium bowl combine turkey mixture and bread cubes. Drizzle with enough chicken stock to moisten, tossing lightly to combine. Divide mixture between two 12-ounce individual casserole dishes.

3 Bake, covered, about 20 minutes or until heated through. Serve with Herbed Gravy.

nutrition facts per serving: 323 cal., 6 g total fat (2 g sat. fat), 74 mg chol., 495 mg sodium, 32 g carb. (7 g fiber, 5 sugars), 37 g pro. exchanges: 2 starch, 4 lean meat.

herbed gravy: In a small saucepan melt 2 teaspoons light butter with canola oil over medium heat. Stir in 1 tablespoon flour; cook and stir about 3 minutes or until flour begins to brown. Slowly whisk in ½ cup unsalted chicken stock. Cook and stir until thickened and bubbly. Reduce heat; cook and stir for 1 minute more. Stir in ½ teaspoon snipped fresh oregano or ⅛ teaspoon dried oregano, crushed, and ¼ teaspoon snipped fresh thyme or dash dried thyme, crushed.

1g CARB. PER SERVING

meals for two

This preparation works well with a variety of fish types; if halibut isn't available, substitute cod, grouper, red snapper, or sea bass.

garlic-basil halibut

start to finish: 20 minutes

makes: 2 servings (5 ounces cooked fish and about 2 cups zucchini each)

12 ounces fresh or frozen halibut steaks (about 1 inch thick)

2 tablespoons snipped fresh basil

1 tablespoon butter, melted

1 clove garlic, minced

⅛ teaspoon salt

⅛ teaspoon black pepper

1 recipe Zucchini Chips

1 Thaw fish, if frozen; rinse and pat dry with paper towels. If necessary, cut fish into two serving-size pieces. In a small bowl combine basil, melted butter, garlic, salt, and black pepper. Brush mixture over both sides of fish.

2 Place fish on the unheated rack of a broiler pan. Broil 4 inches from the heat for 8 to 12 minutes or until fish flakes easily when tested with fork, turning once. Serve with Zucchini Chips.

nutrition facts per serving: 241 cal., 10 g total fat (4 g sat. fat), 70 mg chol., 279 mg sodium, 1 g carb. (0 g fiber, 0 sugars), 36 g pro. exchanges: 5 lean meat.

zucchini chips: Preheat broiler. Line a 15×10×1-inch baking pan with parchment paper; set aside. In a medium bowl toss 8 ounces zucchini, bias-sliced ¼ inch thick; 8 ounces yellow summer squash, bias-sliced ¼ inch thick; and 1 teaspoon olive oil. Arrange vegetables in a single layer on the prepared baking pan. Broil vegetables 4 to 5 inches from the heat for 2 to 3 minutes or until tender. In a small bowl combine 1 teaspoon olive oil and 1 tablespoon lemon juice. Drizzle mixture over vegetables. Sprinkle with ⅛ teaspoon each salt and black pepper.

Tuna steaks rank among the most hearty and satisfying fish options around. They're also a great source of healthful omega-3 fatty acids.

tuna with sweet 'n' heat salsa

9g
CARB. PER SERVING

prep: 25 minutes   marinate: 30 minutes   grill: 6 minutes
makes: 2 servings (1 tuna steak and ⅔ cup salsa each)

2   5-ounce fresh or frozen tuna steaks, cut ¾ to 1 inch thick
½   teaspoon cumin seeds
½   teaspoon finely shredded lime peel
2   tablespoons lime juice
1   tablespoon canola oil
⅛   teaspoon crushed red pepper
⅛   teaspoon salt
1   recipe Sweet 'n' Heat Salsa
    Lime wedges (optional)

1 Thaw fish, if frozen. Rinse fish; pat dry. Place fish in a large resealable plastic bag. Set aside. In a small dry skillet heat cumin seeds over medium heat 1 to 2 minutes or until aromatic, shaking skillet occasionally. Crush cumin seeds in a mortar and pestle.

2 Combine crushed cumin seeds, the lime peel, lime juice, oil, crushed red pepper, and the salt. Pour over fish in bag; turn to coat fish. Seal bag. Marinate in the refrigerator for 30 to 60 minutes, turning bag occasionally.

3 Prepare Sweet 'n' Heat Salsa; set aside. Drain fish, discarding marinade. For a charcoal grill, place fish on the greased grill rack directly over medium coals. Grill, uncovered, for 6 to 10 minutes or until fish flakes easily, gently turning once halfway through grilling. (For a gas grill, preheat grill. Reduce heat to medium. Place fish on greased grill rack over heat. Cover and grill as directed.) Serve fish topped with salsa. If desired, serve with lime wedges.

nutrition facts per serving: 252 cal., 8 g total fat (1 g sat. fat), 63 mg chol., 202 mg sodium, 9 g carb. (2 g fiber, 6 sugars), 34 g pro. exchanges: 0.5 fruit, 4.5 lean meat, 0.5 fat.

sweet 'n' heat salsa: In a small bowl combine ¾ cup chopped, seeded watermelon; ½ cup chopped yellow or orange sweet pepper; 1 green onion, thinly sliced; 2 teaspoons snipped fresh mint; and ⅛ teaspoon crushed red pepper.

30g CARB. PER SERVING

Thai food is known for its multidimensional flavors. Here you'll enjoy nutty, sweet, spicy, and citrusy tastes all in one dish.

thai red snapper

prep: 20 minutes cook: 23 minutes
makes: 2 servings (1 fish fillet, 3 tablespoons sauce, and ⅔ cup rice each)

2 5- to 6-ounce fresh or frozen red snapper fillets or other firm-flesh white fish fillets
¼ teaspoon salt
¼ teaspoon black pepper
3 teaspoons canola oil
1 teaspoon grated fresh ginger
1 clove garlic, minced
½ teaspoon finely shredded lime peel
¼ teaspoon ground coriander
⅛ teaspoon crushed red pepper
¼ cup unsweetened light coconut milk
1 tablespoon snipped fresh basil
1 tablespoon snipped fresh cilantro
⅓ cup shredded red cabbage
⅓ cup jicama cut into matchstick-size pieces
1 recipe Jasmine Rice with Fresh Herbs
   Fresh basil and cilantro leaves (optional)

1 Thaw fish, if frozen. Rinse fish; pat dry with paper towels. Measure thickness of fish. Season fish with ⅛ teaspoon of the salt and ⅛ teaspoon of the black pepper. In a large skillet cook fish, skin sides down, in 2 teaspoons of the hot oil 4 to 6 minutes for each ½-inch thickness of fish or until skin is golden and crisp and fish flakes easily when tested with a fork, turning once halfway through cooking. Remove skin if desired.

2 Meanwhile, in a medium skillet cook ginger and garlic in remaining 1 teaspoon hot oil for 30 to 60 seconds or until aromatic. Stir in lime peel, coriander, crushed red pepper, and remaining ⅛ teaspoon salt and ⅛ teaspoon black pepper. Stir in coconut milk, snipped basil, and snipped cilantro. Heat through.

3 Serve fish with coconut milk sauce over cabbage and jicama. Serve with Jasmine Rice with Fresh Herbs. If desired, garnish with fresh basil and cilantro leaves.

nutrition facts per serving: 353 cal., 11 g total fat (3 g sat. fat), 52 mg chol., 532 mg sodium, 30 g carb. (1 g fiber, 1 sugars), 32 g pro. exchanges: 0.5 vegetable, 2 starch, 4 lean meat, 0.5 fat.

jasmine rice with fresh herbs: In a small saucepan bring ½ cup reduced-sodium chicken broth and 1 tablespoon unsweetened light coconut milk to boiling. Add ⅓ cup jasmine rice. Reduce heat. Simmer, covered, for 15 to 20 minutes or until all the liquid is absorbed. Stir in 2 teaspoons snipped fresh basil and 2 teaspoons snipped fresh cilantro.

Napa cabbage and spinach or romaine lettuce provide a filling (but low-cal) base for this colorful, Asian-inspired take on scallops.

scallop stir-fry salad

12g
CARB. PER SERVING

start to finish: 30 minutes
makes: 2 servings (1½ cups each)

6 ounces fresh or frozen bay scallops
1 tablespoon orange juice
1 tablespoon reduced-sodium soy sauce
1½ teaspoons rice vinegar or white wine vinegar
½ teaspoon toasted sesame oil
1 tablespoon cooking oil
½ cup fresh pea pods, strings and tips removed
½ of a medium red sweet pepper, cut into strips
¼ cup sliced green onions (2)
½ of a 12-ounce jar baby corn, rinsed and drained
1 cup shredded napa cabbage
1 cup shredded fresh spinach or romaine lettuce

1 Thaw scallops, if frozen. Rinse scallops; pat dry with paper towels. In a small bowl combine orange juice, soy sauce, vinegar, and sesame oil. Set aside.

2 In a medium skillet heat 2 teaspoons of the cooking oil over medium-high heat. Add scallops; stir-fry about 2 minutes or until scallops are opaque. Remove scallops from skillet.

3 Add remaining 1 teaspoon cooking oil to skillet. Add pea pods, sweet pepper, and green onions; stir-fry 2 to 3 minutes or until crisp-tender. Add cooked scallops, baby corn, and orange juice mixture to skillet; stir-fry 1 minute or until heated. Remove from heat.

4 In a large salad bowl combine napa cabbage and spinach. Top with scallop mixture; toss gently to combine.

nutrition facts per serving: 203 cal., 9 g total fat (1 g sat. fat), 28 mg chol., 633 mg sodium, 12 g carb. (4 g fiber, 0 g sugars) 18 g pro. exchanges: 2 vegetable, 2 lean meat, 2 fat.

Start a new trend with these fabulous side dishes that don't tip the scale on fat, carbs, and calories. From bright, colorful salads and veggies to hearty grain-based go-withs, these sides will complement the main dish and bring compliments to the cook.

simple

side

smoky baked beans,
page 360

dishes

5g
CARB. PER
SERVING

Mushrooms absorb water like a sponge.
To clean, gently wipe them off with a
damp paper towel.

asparagus
and wild mushrooms

prep: 20 minutes roast: 15 minutes
makes: 4 servings (5 asparagus spears and ⅓ cup mushrooms each)

3 cups halved cremini,
    stemmed shiitake,
    and/or button
    mushrooms
2 tablespoons white
    wine
2 teaspoons snipped
    fresh tarragon
1 pound fresh
    asparagus spears
1 tablespoon olive oil
¼ teaspoon salt
¼ teaspoon black
    pepper
  Snipped fresh
    tarragon (optional)

1 Preheat oven to 400°F. In a medium
    bowl toss together mushrooms, wine,
and 2 teaspoons tarragon; set aside.

2 Snap off and discard woody bases from
    asparagus. Place asparagus in a 15×10×1-
inch baking pan. Drizzle with oil and sprinkle
with the salt and pepper. Toss to coat.

3 Roast, uncovered, for 5 minutes. Add
    mushroom mixture to the pan; toss gently
to combine. Return to oven; roast about
10 minutes more or until asparagus is crisp-
tender. If desired, garnish with additional
fresh tarragon.

nutrition facts per serving: 64 cal., 4 g total fat (1 g sat.
fat), 0 mg chol., 151 mg sodium, 5 g carb. (2 g fiber, 2 g sugars),
4 g pro. exchanges: 1 vegetable, 1 fat.

If you don't have a fine-grate Microplane to shred the lemon peel, remove a strip with a vegetable peeler and finely chop it using a chef's knife.

lemon-dill cauliflower and broccoli

prep: 25 minutes grill: 20 minutes
makes: 4 servings (1 cup each)

2 cups cauliflower florets
2 cups broccoli florets
1 tablespoon olive oil
2 teaspoons snipped fresh dill weed or ½ teaspoon dried dill weed
¼ teaspoon finely shredded lemon peel
2 teaspoons lemon juice
1 small clove garlic, minced
⅛ teaspoon salt
⅛ teaspoon dry mustard
⅛ teaspoon black pepper
Fresh dill sprigs (optional)

1 Fold a 36×18-inch piece of heavy-duty foil in half to make an 18-inch square. Place cauliflower and broccoli in center of the foil square.

2 In a small bowl combine oil, dill, lemon peel, lemon juice, garlic, salt, mustard, and pepper; drizzle over vegetables. Bring up two opposite edges of the foil and seal with a double fold. Fold remaining ends to completely enclose the food, allowing space for steam to build.

3 For a charcoal grill, place foil packet on the grill rack directly over medium coals. Grill, uncovered, about 20 minutes or until vegetables are tender, turning packet once halfway through cooking and carefully opening packet to check doneness. (For a gas grill, preheat grill. Reduce heat to medium. Place foil packet on grill rack over heat. Cover and grill as above.) Remove from foil packet. If desired, garnish with fresh dill sprigs.

nutrition facts per serving: 60 cal., 4 g total fat (1 g sat. fat), 0 mg chol., 103 mg sodium, 6 g carb. (2 g fiber, 2 g sugars), 2 g pro. exchanges: 1 vegetable, 0.5 fat.

oven method: Preheat oven to 350°F. Prepare as directed through Step 2. Bake packet directly on the oven rack about 35 minutes or until vegetables are tender, turning packet once halfway through cooking and carefully opening packet to check doneness.

simple **side** dishes

4g
CARB. PER
SERVING

Lemon juice causes green vegetables to lose their luster. To keep the color of the Broccolini vibrant, serve lemon wedges alongside so that diners may add the juice just before eating.

broccolini with bacon and feta

start to finish: 15 minutes
makes: 6 servings (2 to 3 spears each)

1   pound Broccolini*
¼   cup dry white wine or reduced-sodium chicken broth
⅛   teaspoon black pepper
⅓   cup crumbled reduced-fat feta cheese
2   slices turkey bacon, cooked according to package directions and crumbled
     Lemon wedges

1 In a large skillet cook Broccolini, covered, in a small amount of boiling water for 6 to 8 minutes or until just tender. Drain off water. Add wine or broth and pepper. If using wine, add ⅛ teaspoon salt. Cook, uncovered, over medium heat for 2 to 3 minutes or until liquid is evaporated, stirring frequently to coat Broccolini evenly in the liquid.

2 Transfer Broccolini to a serving platter. Sprinkle with cheese and bacon. Serve with lemon wedges.

nutrition facts per serving: 64 cal., 2 g total fat (1 g sat. fat), 7 mg chol., 205 mg sodium, 4 g carb. (2 g fiber, 1 g sugars), 5 g pro. exchanges: 1 vegetable, 0.5 lean meat.

*test kitchen tip: If desired, substitute 1¼ pounds broccoli for the Broccolini. Trim off stems and discard; cut broccoli into florets. Cook as directed.

Sizzle prosciutto in a hot skillet and crumble like bacon.
Serve it over just about anything to add an irresistible finish.

brussels sprouts with crisp prosciutto

9g
CARB. PER SERVING

start to finish: 40 minutes
makes: 12 servings (¾ cup each)

2½ pounds Brussels
     sprouts
 1 tablespoon olive oil
 3 ounces thinly sliced
     prosciutto
 ½ cup thinly sliced
     shallots or chopped
     onion
 2 tablespoons butter
 ¼ teaspoon salt
 ¼ teaspoon freshly
     ground black
     pepper
 1 tablespoon red wine
     vinegar

1 Trim stems and remove any wilted outer leaves from Brussels sprouts; wash. Cut any large sprouts in half lengthwise.

2 In a covered large pot cook Brussels sprouts in enough boiling lightly salted water to cover for 6 to 8 minutes or just until tender (centers should still be slightly firm); drain. Spread Brussels sprouts in a shallow baking pan.

3 In an extra-large skillet heat oil over medium-high heat. Cook prosciutto, half at a time, in the hot oil until crisp. Remove from skillet. Add shallots and butter to skillet. Cook and stir over medium heat about 2 minutes or until shallots start to soften.

4 Add Brussels sprouts, salt, and pepper to skillet. Cook and stir about 6 minutes or until Brussels sprouts are heated through. Drizzle with vinegar; toss gently to coat. Transfer to a serving bowl. Top with prosciutto.

nutrition facts per serving: 91 cal., 5 g total fat (1 g sat. fat), 5 mg chol., 212 mg sodium, 9 g carb. (3 g fiber, 2 g sugars), 5 g pro. **exchanges:** 1 vegetable, 1 fat.

brussels sprouts with bacon: Prepare as directed, except substitute 4 slices bacon for the prosciutto and omit the olive oil. Cook bacon until crisp. Remove from skillet, discarding drippings. Drain bacon on paper towels; crumble bacon.

If you can't find baby carrots with tops, substitute packaged peeled fresh baby carrots.

8g
CARB. PER
SERVING

cinnamon-almond-topped carrots

prep: 15 minutes cook: 11 minutes
makes: 4 servings (½ cup carrots and 1 tablespoon almonds each)

simple side dishes

12   ounces baby carrots
       with tops
¼   cup slivered almonds
       Butter-flavor nonstick
       cooking spray
⅛   teaspoon ground
       cinnamon
1   tablespoon light
       butter, melted
       Fresh marjoram
       sprigs (optional)

1 Trim green tops of carrots to 1 inch. Scrub carrots. Halve any thick carrots lengthwise. Place a steamer insert in a large skillet or 4-quart Dutch oven with a tight-fitting lid. Add water to the skillet to just below the steamer insert. Bring water to boiling. Place carrots in the steamer insert. Cover and steam over medium heat for 8 to 10 minutes or until carrots are tender, adding more water as needed to maintain steam.

2 Place almonds in a small bowl. Lightly coat with cooking spray and sprinkle with cinnamon; toss gently to coat. In a medium nonstick skillet cook spiced almonds over medium heat for 3 to 5 minutes or until toasted, stirring occasionally. Remove from heat.

3 Transfer carrots to a serving platter; drizzle with melted butter. Toss to coat. Sprinkle with spiced almonds. If desired, garnish with marjoram.

nutrition facts per serving: 76 cal., 4 g total fat (1 g sat. fat), 4 mg chol., 91 mg sodium, 8 g carb. (3 g fiber, 4 g sugars), 2 g pro. exchanges: 1 vegetable, 1 fat.

You can use yellow beets exclusively in this dish; however, the red beets add a striking ruby color that looks as appealing as it tastes.

maple-orange roasted carrots and beets

16g
CARB. PER SERVING

prep: 10 minutes roast: 45 minutes
makes: 6 servings (⅓ cup each)

Nonstick cooking
     spray
6 medium carrots,
     peeled and cut into
     1- to 1½-inch pieces
12 ounces small red
     and/or yellow beets,
     trimmed, peeled,
     and quartered
¼ teaspoon salt
⅛ teaspoon black
     pepper
4 medium shallots,
     peeled and cut into
     ¾-inch wedges
2 tablespoons light
     stick butter (not
     margarine), cut up
½ teaspoon finely
     shredded orange
     peel
2 tablespoons orange
     juice
2 tablespoons light
     maple-flavored
     syrup

1 Preheat oven to 425°F. Coat a 3-quart rectangular baking dish with cooking spray. Arrange carrots and beets in a single layer in the prepared dish. Coat the vegetables with cooking spray and sprinkle with the salt and pepper. Toss to coat.

2 Cover with foil and roast for 20 minutes. Carefully uncover and stir in shallots. Replace cover and roast for 15 minutes more. Uncover and roast for 10 to 15 minutes more or until carrots and beets are tender. Add butter, orange peel, orange juice, and maple syrup to the dish. Toss vegetable mixture until butter is melted and vegetables are nicely coated. Serve warm.

nutrition facts per serving: 87 cal., 2 g total fat (1 g sat. fat), 5 mg chol., 227 mg sodium, 16 g carb. (4 g fiber, 10 g sugars), 2 g pro. exchanges: 1 vegetable, 0.5 carb., 0.5 fat.

21g
CARB. PER
SERVING

simple **side dishes**

*Although we've lightened this much-loved side dish,
it still has the homey appeal and great taste of the original.*

lightened-up traditional corn casserole

prep: 15 minutes bake: 1 hour
makes: 12 servings (½ cup each)

Nonstick cooking
 spray
30 saltine crackers,
 crushed (about
 1 cup)
2 tablespoons sugar✻
¼ teaspoon salt
¼ teaspoon black
 pepper
2 cups fat-free milk
¾ cup refrigerated or
 frozen egg product,
 thawed
2 tablespoons butter,
 melted
4 cups frozen whole
 kernel corn
Snipped fresh parsley

1 Preheat oven to 325°F. Coat a 2-quart rectangular baking dish with cooking spray.

2 In a bowl combine crushed crackers, sugar, salt, and pepper. Stir in milk, egg, and melted butter. Stir in frozen corn.

3 Pour corn mixture into the prepared baking dish. Bake for 1 to 1¼ hours or until a knife inserted in the center comes out clean. Sprinkle with parsley.

nutrition facts per serving: 119 cal., 3 g total fat (1 g sat. fat), 6 mg chol., 233 mg sodium, 21 g carb. (1 g fiber, 6 g sugars), 5 g pro. **exchanges:** 1 starch, 0.5 carb., 0.5 fat.

nutrition facts per serving with substitute: Same as original, except 112 cal., 19 g carb. (4 g sugars).

✻ sugar substitutes: Choose from Splenda Granular or Sweet'N Low bulk or packets. Follow package directions to use product amount equivalent to 2 tablespoons sugar.

Thanks to the citrus, herbs, and spice, a little dab of the spread goes a long way to butter up your corn on the cob.

corn on the cob with cilantro-lime butter

prep: 10 minutes cook: 5 minutes
makes: 8 servings (1 piece corn and about 1 teaspoon butter each)

9 g
CARB. PER SERVING

4   ears of fresh sweet corn, husked and scrubbed
3   tablespoons light butter, softened
1   tablespoon snipped fresh cilantro
¼   teaspoon salt
¼   teaspoon finely shredded lime peel
⅛   to ¼ teaspoon crushed red pepper

1 Carefully cut each ear of corn crosswise in half. In a Dutch oven cook corn, covered, in enough boiling water to cover for 5 to 7 minutes or until kernels are tender. Remove from water.

2 Meanwhile, in a small bowl combine butter, cilantro, salt, lime peel, and crushed red pepper. Serve with warm corn.

nutrition facts per serving: 58 cal., 3 g total fat (1 g sat. fat), 6 mg chol., 117 mg sodium, 9 g carb. (1 g fiber, 1 g sugars), 1 g pro. exchanges: 0.5 starch, 0.5 fat.

simple **side dishes**

15g
CARB. PER
SERVING

This side dish tastes great at room temperature, too. If you wish, let it stand at room temperature for 30 minutes before serving.

summer corn and tomatoes

prep: 15 minutes cook: 5 minutes
makes: 6 servings (½ cup each)

4   ears of fresh sweet corn or 2 cups frozen whole kernel corn, thawed
1   tablespoon butter
½   cup sliced green onions (4)
2   cloves garlic, minced
2   cups grape tomatoes or cherry tomatoes, halved
1   tablespoon red wine vinegar
¼   teaspoon salt
¼   teaspoon black pepper

If using fresh corn, remove and discard husks and cut corn from cobs; set aside. In a large skillet heat butter over medium heat. Add green onions and garlic; cook and stir about 1 minute or until onions and garlic are slightly softened. Add corn and tomatoes; cook and stir for 4 to 5 minutes or until vegetables are crisp-tender. Drizzle with vinegar and sprinkle with the salt and pepper.

nutrition facts per serving: 81 cal., 2 g total fat (1 g sat. fat), 5 mg chol., 120 mg sodium, 15 g carb. (2 g fiber, 3 g sugars), 2 g pro. exchanges: 1 starch.

Consider making a double batch of the herb butter. Freeze the extra and you'll be that much closer to serving this delectable dish next time you crave it.

haricots verts with herb butter

7g CARB. PER SERVING

prep: 15 minutes cook: 5 minutes

makes: 4 servings (1 cup beans and about 2 teaspoons butter each)

- 2 tablespoons butter, softened
- 1 tablespoon very finely chopped onion
- 2 teaspoons snipped fresh tarragon
- 1 clove garlic, minced
- ½ teaspoon finely shredded lemon peel
- ¼ teaspoon salt
- ¼ teaspoon black pepper
- 12 ounces fresh haricots verts or other thin green beans (4 cups)

1 In a small bowl by hand beat together butter, onion, tarragon, garlic, lemon peel, salt, and pepper. Cover and chill until ready to use.

2 Rinse beans; drain. If desired, trim tips off beans. Place a steamer basket in a large skillet. Add water to just below the bottom of basket. Bring water to boiling. Add beans to steamer basket. Cover skillet and steam for 5 to 6 minutes or until beans are crisp-tender. Drain.

3 To serve, place green beans on a serving platter or on four serving plates. Top with small dollops of the herbed butter. Spread butter over beans.

nutrition facts per serving: 80 cal., 6 g total fat (4 g sat. fat), 15 mg chol., 202 mg sodium, 7 g carb. (2 g fiber, 3 g sugars), 2 g pro. exchanges: 1 vegetable, 1 fat.

Keep the mushrooms spread in a single layer as they cook.
This will help each sauté evenly to the desired caramel color.

simple side dishes

5g
CARB. PER
SERVING

green beans with caramelized mushrooms

start to finish: 30 minutes
makes: 6 servings (½ cup each)

8   ounces fresh green
     beans, trimmed
1   8-ounce package
     sliced fresh
     mushrooms
2   teaspoons olive oil
¼   teaspoon salt
⅛   teaspoon black
     pepper
¼   cup chopped walnuts,
     toasted
¼   cup snipped fresh
     basil

1 In a large skillet cook beans, covered, in a small amount of boiling water for 6 to 8 minutes or until crisp-tender. Drain and rinse beans under cold water to stop cooking; drain again. Pat dry with paper towels.

2 Carefully wipe the skillet dry. In the same skillet cook mushrooms in hot oil over medium heat for 5 to 10 minutes or until tender and lightly browned, stirring occasionally. Add beans and sprinkle with the salt and pepper. Cook for 2 to 3 minutes or until beans are heated through, tossing frequently. Transfer bean mixture to a serving platter. To serve, sprinkle with walnuts and basil.

nutrition facts per serving: 66 cal., 5 g total fat (1 g sat. fat), 0 mg chol., 101 mg sodium, 5 g carb. (2 g fiber, 1 g sugars), 3 g pro. exchanges: 1 vegetable, 1 fat.

Porcini mushrooms, popular in Italian cooking, have a concentrated earthy and nutty appeal. Yes, they're pricey, but a small amount goes a long way to add richness and flavor.

porcini eggplant

prep: 15 minutes **roast:** 15 minutes **stand:** 15 minutes **cook:** 5 minutes
makes: 6 servings (½ cup each)

1 pound eggplant, peeled and cut into 1-inch cubes
2 tablespoons olive oil
¼ teaspoon salt
¼ teaspoon black pepper
½ ounce dried porcini mushrooms
⅓ cup balsamic vinegar
1 teaspoon snipped fresh thyme
½ cup grape tomatoes, quartered
1 tablespoon snipped fresh basil

1 Preheat oven to 425°F. Arrange eggplant in a 15×10×1-inch baking pan. Drizzle with olive oil and sprinkle with the salt and pepper. Toss to coat. Roast for 15 to 20 minutes or until tender and browned, stirring once or twice.

2 Meanwhile, place mushrooms in a small bowl. And 1 cup boiling water to bowl. Let stand for 15 minutes; drain water. Chop mushrooms.

3 In a small saucepan heat balsamic vinegar over medium heat until boiling; reduce heat. Simmer, uncovered, about 5 minutes or until reduced by half. Stir in mushrooms and thyme.

4 To serve, drizzle roasted eggplant with balsamic mixture. Combine grape tomatoes and basil. Sprinkle over the eggplant mixture.

nutrition facts per serving: 77 cal., 5 g total fat (1 g sat. fat), 0 mg chol., 103 mg sodium, 8 g carb. (3 g fiber, 4 g sugars), 1 g pro. **exchanges:** 1 vegetable, 1 fat.

*If you wish, stir together 2 tablespoons snipped fresh basil,
1 tablespoon finely shredded lemon peel, and 2 teaspoons
minced ginger to create a gremolata to sprinkle over the top.*

9g
CARB. PER
SERVING

peas, carrots, and mushrooms

start to finish: 25 minutes
makes: 6 servings (⅔ cup each)

simple **side dishes**

1 medium carrot, sliced
(½ cup)
1 10-ounce package
frozen peas
2 cups sliced fresh
mushrooms
2 green onions, cut into
½-inch pieces
1 tablespoon butter
1 tablespoon snipped
fresh basil or
½ teaspoon dried
basil, crushed
¼ teaspoon salt
Dash black pepper

1 In a covered medium saucepan cook
carrot in a small amount of boiling salted
water for 3 minutes. Add frozen peas. Return
to boiling; reduce heat. Cook about 5 minutes
more or until carrot and peas are crisp-tender.
Drain well. Remove carrot and peas from
saucepan; set aside.

2 In the same saucepan cook mushrooms
and green onions in hot butter until
tender. Stir in basil, salt, and pepper. Return
carrot and peas to saucepan; heat through,
stirring occasionally.

nutrition facts per serving: 69 cal., 3 g total fat (1 g sat.
fat), 5 mg chol., 229 mg sodium, 9 g carb. (3 g fiber, 3 g sugars),
4 g pro. exchanges: 0.5 vegetable, 0.5 starch, 0.5 fat.

make-ahead directions: Prepare as
directed through Step 1. Cool carrot mixture;
transfer to a storage container; seal. Cut up
green onions; place in a separate storage
container; seal. Chill carrot mixture and
green onions for 24 to 48 hours. To serve,
continue as directed in Step 2.

Yukon gold potatoes are a great choice for slimming down a potato recipe. With their buttery gold color and rich flavor, you won't need to use much fat to make them look and taste luscious.

12g
CARB. PER
SERVING

twice-baked potatoes

prep: 15 minutes bake: 1 hour 20 minutes stand: 15 minutes
makes: 4 servings (1 potato half each)

2 medium Yukon gold
  potatoes (12 to
  14 ounces total)
1 teaspoon olive oil
¼ teaspoon black
  pepper
⅛ teaspoon salt
1 to 2 tablespoons
  fat-free milk
1 tablespoon butter
  or olive oil
2 tablespoons light
  sour cream
1 tablespoon snipped
  fresh chives
2 tablespoons reduced-
  fat shredded
  cheddar cheese
  Snipped fresh chives
  (optional)

1 Preheat oven to 400°F. Scrub potatoes thoroughly with a brush; pat dry. Prick potatoes with a fork. Drizzle olive oil over each potato and sprinkle with half of the pepper and salt. Wrap each potato in foil. Bake potatoes about 1 hour or until tender. Remove and discard foil. Let potatoes stand about 15 minutes to cool slightly. Cut the potatoes in half lengthwise. Carefully scoop pulp out of each potato, leaving a ¼- to ½-inch shell; set potato shells aside.

2 Place potato pulp in a large bowl. Mash potato pulp with a potato masher or an electric mixer on low speed until nearly smooth. In a small saucepan heat milk and butter over medium heat until butter is melted. Pour milk mixture over mashed potatoes; beat until smooth. Stir in sour cream, the 1 tablespoon snipped chives, 1 tablespoon of the cheese, and remaining half of the pepper and salt. Mound mixture into reserved potato shells. Sprinkle with remaining cheese. Place potato halves in a single layer in a 2-quart square baking dish.

3 Bake, uncovered, about 20 minutes or until golden brown and heated through. If desired, garnish with snipped chives.

nutrition facts per serving: 105 cal., 5 g total fat (3 g sat. fat), 12 mg chol., 130 mg sodium, 12 g carb. (1 g fiber, 1 g sugars), 3 g pro. exchanges: 1 starch, 1 fat.

Panko is a delightfully coarse and crisp version of bread crumbs. You'll find panko either alongside bread crumbs at the supermarket or in the Asian food aisle.

spicy vegetable bake

prep: 25 minutes bake: 25 minutes
makes: 10 servings (¾ cup each)

Nonstick cooking
spray
1 tablespoon butter
1 tablespoon olive oil
3 tablespoons flour
1¼ cups fat-free milk
7 individually wrapped
slices 2% milk
cheddar cheese
(about 4½ ounces),
torn into pieces
1 medium fresh jalapeño
chile pepper, thinly
sliced (see tip,
page 360)
½ teaspoon salt
Dash freshly ground
black pepper
1 16-ounce package
peeled fresh baby
carrots
3 cups broccoli florets
3 cups cauliflower
florets
1 8-ounce can sliced
water chestnuts,
drained
½ cup whole wheat
panko (Japanese-
style bread crumbs)

1 Preheat oven to 375°F. Lightly coat a 2-quart oval or rectangular baking dish with cooking spray.

2 For cheese sauce, in a medium saucepan melt butter over medium heat. Add oil. Whisk in flour until dissolved. Whisk in milk. Cook and whisk until thickened and bubbly. Add torn cheese slices; cook and stir until cheese melts. Remove from heat. Stir in sliced chile pepper, salt, and black pepper.

3 In a Dutch oven bring 5 cups water to boiling. Add carrots; cook 4 minutes (water may not return to boiling). Add broccoli and cauliflower. Cook, uncovered, 4 minutes more. Drain in a colander set in a sink. In the Dutch oven combine vegetables and water chestnuts. Spoon into the prepared baking dish. Top with the cheese sauce. Sprinkle panko on top of the vegetables; coat with cooking spray. Bake 25 to 30 minutes or until vegetables are crisp-tender, cheese sauce is bubbly, and topping is golden brown.

nutrition facts per serving: 126 cal., 5 g total fat (2 g sat. fat), 11 mg chol., 374 mg sodium, 15 g carb. (3 g fiber, 6 g sugars), 6 g pro. exchanges: 0.5 milk, 2 vegetable, 0.5 fat.

Tote this peak-season combo to a cookout. It will go beautifully with grilled meat, poultry, and fish.

tri-color summer vegetables

6g CARB. PER SERVING

prep: 25 minutes cook: 8 minutes
makes: 6 servings (⅔ cup each)

simple side dishes

1   tablespoon butter
1¼   cups coarsely
      chopped yellow
      summer squash
1¼   cups coarsely
      chopped zucchini
1   cup frozen shelled
      sweet soybeans
      (edamame)
¾   cup coarsely chopped
      red sweet pepper
¾   cup thinly sliced red
      onion
2   cloves garlic, minced
1   tablespoon
      champagne vinegar
      or white wine
      vinegar
1½   teaspoons snipped
      fresh oregano
1   teaspoon snipped
      fresh thyme
¼   teaspoon salt
¼   teaspoon black
      pepper

1 In a large skillet heat butter over medium heat. Add yellow squash, zucchini, soybeans, sweet pepper, red onion, and garlic to butter. Cook and stir about 8 minutes or until vegetables are crisp-tender.

2 Stir in vinegar, oregano, thyme, salt, and black pepper. Serve immediately.

nutrition facts per serving: 61 cal., 3 g total fat (1 g sat. fat), 5 mg chol., 119 mg sodium, 6 g carb. (2 g fiber, 3 g sugars), 3 g pro. exchanges: 1 vegetable, 0.5 fat.

Coriander is a spice ground from the tiny dried fruit of a cilantro plant. Like fresh cilantro, it offers a pleasant lemony aroma.

coriander rice with zucchini

16g
CARB. PER SERVING

prep: 25 minutes   cook: 25 minutes   stand: 5 minutes
makes: 5 servings (⅔ cup each)

1   14.5-ounce can reduced-sodium chicken broth
½   cup uncooked basmati rice or brown basmati rice
1   clove garlic, minced
1   medium zucchini, quartered lengthwise, then cut crosswise into ½-inch slices (1¼ cups)
½   cup julienned carrots
2   tablespoons snipped fresh parsley
1   tablespoon snipped fresh mint
1½ teaspoons finely shredded lemon peel
1   tablespoon lemon juice
¼   teaspoon ground coriander
⅛   teaspoon black pepper

1 In a medium saucepan combine broth, rice, and garlic. Bring to boiling; reduce heat. Simmer, covered, for 15 minutes for white rice or 35 minutes for brown rice. Stir in zucchini and carrots. Cook, covered, about 10 minutes more or until rice is tender and liquid is absorbed. Remove from heat.

2 Let stand, covered, for 5 minutes. Stir in parsley, mint, lemon peel, lemon juice, coriander, and pepper.

nutrition facts per serving: 82 cal., 0 g total fat, 0 mg chol., 202 mg sodium, 16 g carb. (1 g fiber, 2 g sugars), 3 g pro.
exchanges: 1 starch.

simple **side dishes**

19g
CARB. PER
SERVING

For the cooked quinoa, bring 1¾ cups water to boiling. Add ¾ cup plus 2 tablespoons rinsed quinoa. Bring to boiling; reduce heat. Cover and simmer 15 minutes or until tender. Drain excess water if necessary.

butternut squash and quinoa pilaf

prep: 25 minutes **roast:** 30 minutes
makes: 8 servings (½ cup each)

4   cups peeled and
      cubed butternut
      squash
6   cloves garlic, minced
⅛   teaspoon crushed red
      pepper
5   teaspoons olive oil
¼   cup sliced almonds
2   cups cooked quinoa
1   tablespoon snipped
      fresh sage
½   teaspoon salt

1 Preheat oven to 425°F. In a large bowl combine butternut squash, garlic, and crushed red pepper. Drizzle with 2 teaspoons of the oil. Stir until squash is evenly coated. Spoon into a 15×10×1-inch baking pan. Roast 30 minutes, stirring once and adding the sliced almonds for the last 4 to 5 minutes of roasting.

2 In a large bowl combine quinoa, the remaining 3 teaspoons oil, the snipped sage, and salt. Stir in roasted squash and almonds. If desired, garnish with sage leaves.

nutrition facts per serving: 132 cal., 5 g total fat (1 g sat. fat), 0 mg chol., 152 mg sodium, 19 g carb. (3 g fiber, 2 g sugars), 4 g pro. **exchanges:** 1 starch, 1 fat.

Put the extra lima beans to good use—stir them into a pot of baked beans or use them to make hummus.

moroccan-style simmered beans

24g
CARB. PER
SERVING

prep: 15 minutes **cook:** 30 minutes
makes: 8 servings (½ cup each)

½ cup chopped sweet onion

1 medium carrot, chopped (½ cup)

2 teaspoons canola oil

1 clove garlic, minced

¼ teaspoon ground cumin

¼ teaspoon ground coriander

⅛ teaspoon crushed red pepper

⅛ teaspoon ground cinnamon

1 15-ounce can garbanzo beans (chickpeas), rinsed and drained

1 15-ounce can Great Northern beans, rinsed and drained

½ cup frozen baby lima beans

½ cup chopped tomatoes

⅓ cup water

1 tablespoon lemon juice

Ground cumin and/or crushed red pepper (optional)

1 In a large saucepan cook onion and carrot in hot oil over medium heat for 8 to 10 minutes or until very tender, stirring occasionally. Stir in garlic, the ¼ teaspoon cumin, the coriander, the ⅛ teaspoon crushed red pepper, and the cinnamon. Cook and stir for 1 minute.

2 Add garbanzo beans, Great Northern beans, lima beans, tomatoes, and the water. Bring to boiling; reduce heat. Cook, covered, for 20 minutes to blend flavors, stirring occasionally. Stir in lemon juice just before serving. If desired, sprinkle with additional cumin and/or crushed red pepper.

nutrition facts per serving: 127 cal., 2 g total fat (0 g sat. fat), 0 mg chol., 202 mg sodium, 24 g carb. (6 g fiber, 2 g sugars), 8 g pro. **exchanges:** 1.5 starch, 0.5 lean meat.

To turn up the heat on this fiber-packed three-bean bake, top it with fresh jalapeño slices just before serving. Pictured on page 339.

smoky baked beans

prep: 20 minutes bake: 1 hour
makes: 8 servings (½ cup each)

6 slices bacon, chopped
¾ cup chopped green
    sweet pepper
    (1 medium)
½ cup chopped onion
    (1 medium)
2 cloves garlic, minced
1 15-ounce can no-salt-
    added black beans,
    rinsed and drained
1 15-ounce can no-salt-
    added butter beans
    or cannellini beans
    (white kidney
    beans), rinsed and
    drained
1 15-ounce can no-salt-
    added red kidney
    beans, rinsed and
    drained
1 8-ounce can no-salt-
    added tomato sauce
¼ cup orange juice
2 tablespoons packed
    brown sugar*
1 tablespoon
    Worcestershire
    sauce
1 fresh jalapeño chile
    pepper, seeded and
    finely chopped**
1 slice crisp-cooked
    bacon, chopped
    (optional)

1 Preheat oven to 375°F. In a large skillet cook chopped bacon, sweet pepper, onion, and garlic over medium heat about 10 minutes or until bacon is crisp and onion is tender; drain.

2 In a large bowl combine bacon mixture, beans, tomato sauce, orange juice, brown sugar, Worcestershire sauce, and finely chopped chile pepper. Spoon mixture into a 1½-quart casserole.

3 Bake, covered, for 1 hour, stirring once halfway through baking. If desired, garnish with additional chopped cooked bacon.

nutrition facts per serving: 218 cal., 6 g total fat (2 g sat. fat), 9 mg chol., 168 mg sodium, 31 g carb. (10 g fiber, 7 g sugars), 11 g pro. exchanges: 2 starch, 0.5 lean meat, 0.5 fat.

nutrition facts per serving with substitute: Same as original, except 205 cal., 28 g carb.

✻ sugar substitutes: Choose from Sweet'N Low Brown or Sugar Twin Granulated Brown. Follow package directions to use product amount equivalent to 2 tablespoons brown sugar.

✻✻ test kitchen tip: Because chile peppers contain volatile oils that can burn your skin and eyes, avoid direct contact with them as much as possible. When working with chile peppers, wear plastic or rubber gloves. If your bare hands do touch the peppers, wash your hands and nails well with soap and warm water.

Divide into small portions and freeze leftover chipotle peppers in the adobo sauce. Stir one or two portions into chili and other dishes to add smoky, spicy flavor.

chipotle quinoa with beans

23g
CARB. PER SERVING

prep: 15 minutes **cook:** 16 minutes **stand:** 10 minutes
makes: 6 servings (⅔ cup each)

1 medium onion, chopped (½ cup)
1 tablespoon canola oil
2 cloves garlic, minced
1 14.5-ounce can reduced-sodium chicken broth
¾ cup quinoa,* rinsed and drained
1 small green sweet pepper, chopped (½ cup)
½ of a 15-ounce can no-salt-added black beans (¾ cup), rinsed and drained
1 teaspoon finely chopped canned chipotle pepper in adobo sauce (see tip, *opposite*)
1 medium tomato, seeded and chopped (⅔ cup)
¼ cup snipped fresh cilantro

1 In a large saucepan cook onion in hot oil over medium heat for 5 minutes, stirring occasionally. Add garlic; cook and stir for 30 seconds more. Add broth and quinoa. Bring to boiling; reduce heat. Simmer, covered, for 15 minutes.

2 Stir in sweet pepper, black beans, and chipotle pepper. Cook, covered, for 1 minute. Remove from heat. Let stand, covered, for 10 minutes. Stir in tomato and cilantro.

nutrition facts per serving: 146 cal., 4 g total fat (0 g sat. fat), 0 mg chol., 175 mg sodium, 23 g carb. (4 g fiber, 2 g sugars), 6 g pro. exchanges: 2 vegetable, 1 starch, 0.5 fat.

*test kitchen tip: Look for quinoa at health food stores or in the grains section of large supermarkets.

To cook regular brown rice, bring 2 cups water to boiling. Add 1 cup brown rice. Return to boiling; reduce heat. Simmer, covered, 45 minutes. Let stand 5 minutes. This yields 3 cups.

17g
CARB. PER
SERVING

spanish-style rice

start to finish: 25 minutes
makes: 5 servings (½ cup each)

2   teaspoons olive oil
½   cup chopped green
    sweet pepper
¼   cup chopped onion
½   to 1 medium fresh
    serrano chile
    pepper, chopped
    (see tip, *page 360*)
    (optional)
2   cloves garlic, minced
1   8.8-ounce pouch
    cooked brown rice
    or 2 cups cooked
    brown rice
½   cup chopped tomato
¼   cup chopped pitted
    green olives
¼   teaspoon salt
2   tablespoons snipped
    fresh cilantro

1 In a large skillet heat oil. Add sweet pepper, onion, and, if desired, serrano pepper to skillet. Cook over medium heat for 3 to 5 minutes or until vegetables are crisp-tender, stirring occasionally. Add garlic and cook for 1 minute more.

2 Stir in cooked rice, tomato, green olives, and salt. Cook and stir for 2 minutes or until heated through. Stir in cilantro and serve immediately.

nutrition facts per serving: 106 cal., 3 g total fat (0 g sat. fat), 0 mg chol., 122 mg sodium, 17 g carb. (1 g fiber, 1 g sugars), 2 g pro. exchanges: 1 starch, 0.5 fat.

Lightly coat the blades of your kitchen scissors with nonstick cooking spray to keep the sticky apricots from adhering to them.

indian basmati rice

prep: 30 minutes cook: 18 minutes
makes: 12 servings (½ cup each)

20g
CARB. PER
SERVING

½   cup chopped onion
       (1 medium)
1   tablespoon butter
1   cup basmati rice
⅔   cup snipped dried
       apricots
1   medium carrot,
       bias-sliced
1   teaspoon ground
       turmeric
½   teaspoon ground
       cumin
⅛   teaspoon crushed
       red pepper
1   14.5-ounce can
       reduced-sodium
       chicken broth
¼   cup water
1   6-ounce package
       frozen snow pea
       pods, thawed
2   tablespoons snipped
       fresh parsley
2   tablespoons slivered
       almonds, toasted

1 In a medium saucepan cook onion in hot butter over medium heat about 5 minutes or until onion is tender. Stir in uncooked rice. Cook and stir for 4 minutes. Stir in apricots, carrot, turmeric, cumin, and crushed red pepper.

2 Carefully stir broth and the water into rice mixture in saucepan. Bring to boiling; reduce heat. Cover and simmer for 18 to 20 minutes or until liquid is absorbed and rice is tender. Stir in pea pods and parsley. Sprinkle individual servings with almonds.

nutrition facts per serving: 100 cal., 2 g total fat (1 g sat. fat), 3 mg chol., 94 mg sodium, 20 g carb. (2 g fiber, 5 g sugars), 2 g pro. exchanges: 0.5 fruit, 1 starch.

Chèvre can be somewhat creamy, so it may seem a bit sticky when crumbling.

23g
CARB. PER
SERVING

lemon couscous with asparagus

start to finish: 15 minutes
makes: 6 servings (½ cup each)

364

12 ounces thin fresh
   asparagus spears,
   trimmed and cut
   into 1½- to 2-inch
   pieces
2 teaspoons cooking oil
1 cup reduced-sodium
   chicken broth
¼ teaspoon black
   pepper
⅔ cup whole wheat
   couscous
2 teaspoons finely
   shredded lemon
   peel
2 ounces semisoft goat
   cheese (chèvre),
   crumbled
2 tablespoons chopped
   fresh chives or
   thinly sliced green
   onion tops

1 In a large skillet cook asparagus in hot oil for 3 to 5 minutes or until lightly browned and crisp-tender.

2 Meanwhile, in a medium saucepan bring broth and pepper just to boiling; stir in couscous. Cover and remove from heat. Let stand for 5 minutes.

3 Fluff couscous mixture with a fork. Stir in lemon peel and asparagus. Transfer couscous mixture to a serving dish. Sprinkle with goat cheese and chives.

nutrition facts per serving: 156 cal., 5 g total fat (2 g sat. fat), 7 mg chol., 145 mg sodium, 23 g carb. (4 g fiber, 2 g sugars), 7 g pro. exchanges: 0.5 vegetable, 1.5 starch, 0.5 fat.

Because pine nuts are high in fat, they will turn rancid more quickly than other nuts. Keep them in the freezer for longer storage.

herbed pasta with pine nuts

prep: 20 minutes cook: 14 minutes
makes: 6 servings (½ cup each)

½ of a medium sweet onion, cut into thin wedges
1 tablespoon olive oil
1 medium red sweet pepper, cut into thin bite-size strips (1 cup)
3 cloves garlic, minced
3 ounces dried multigrain penne pasta (1 cup)
¼ teaspoon salt
⅛ teaspoon black pepper
2 tablespoons snipped fresh oregano
1 teaspoon snipped fresh rosemary or thyme
2 tablespoons pine nuts, toasted

1 In a large nonstick skillet cook onion wedges, covered, in hot oil over medium heat for 8 minutes, stirring occasionally. Uncover and add sweet pepper strips. Cook, uncovered, for 5 to 8 minutes more or until onion wedges are lightly browned and pepper strips are tender, stirring occasionally. Add garlic; cook and stir for 30 seconds more.

2 Meanwhile, cook pasta according to package directions. Drain pasta, reserving ¼ cup of the cooking liquid. Add pasta, reserved ¼ cup cooking liquid, the salt, and black pepper to vegetables in skillet. Cook and stir for 1 to 2 minutes or until well combined. Add oregano and rosemary; toss to coat. Divide pasta among six serving plates. Sprinkle with pine nuts.

nutrition facts per serving: 103 cal., 5 g total fat (0 g sat. fat), 0 mg chol., 105 mg sodium, 13 g carb. (2 g fiber, 2 g sugars), 3 g pro. exchanges: 1 starch, 1 fat.

Israeli couscous is beadier and larger than regular couscous,
so it takes a little longer to cook.

vegetable israeli couscous

17g
CARB. PER
SERVING

prep: 25 minutes **cook:** 20 minutes **chill:** up to 4 hours
makes: 8 servings (½ cup each)

1   cup Israeli couscous
1   medium yellow sweet
     pepper, coarsely
     chopped
1   medium zucchini,
     coarsely chopped
1   medium tomato,
     seeded and coarsely
     chopped
2   green onions, sliced
2   tablespoons lemon
     juice
2   tablespoons reduced-
     sodium chicken
     broth
1   tablespoon olive oil
1   tablespoon snipped
     fresh mint
1   clove garlic, minced
¼   teaspoon salt
¼   teaspoon black
     pepper
¼   cup crumbled feta
     cheese
     Fresh mint leaves

1 In a large saucepan bring 2 quarts lightly salted water to boiling.

2 Meanwhile, in a medium skillet toast the couscous over medium heat about 7 minutes or until golden brown, stirring frequently.

3 Add the couscous to the boiling water. Cook for 7 minutes. Add sweet pepper and zucchini. Return to boiling and cook about 5 minutes more or until couscous is tender. Drain and transfer to a large bowl. Stir in the tomato and green onions.

4 Meanwhile, in a small bowl mix together lemon juice, broth, olive oil, snipped mint, garlic, salt, and black pepper. Stir mixture into couscous mixture. Serve warm or cover and chill for up to 4 hours. To serve, sprinkle with feta cheese and garnish with fresh mint leaves.

nutrition facts per serving: 109 cal., 3 g total fat (1 g sat. fat), 4 mg chol., 211 mg sodium, 17 g carb. (2 g fiber, 2 g sugars), 3 g pro. **exchanges:** 0.5 vegetable, 1 starch.

16g
CARB. PER
SERVING

Fresh out of fresh basil? Use fresh oregano instead. If you're really in a bind, substitute fresh parsley and add ½ teaspoon crushed dried basil to the dressing.

fresh macaroni salad

prep: 25 minutes   chill: 4 hours
makes: 6 servings (¾ cup each)

1   cup dried multigrain
    elbow macaroni
    (3 ounces)
1   cup small fresh
    broccoli florets
½   cup sugar snap pea
    pods, trimmed and
    halved crosswise
½   cup chopped, drained
    bottled roasted red
    sweet peppers
2   green onions, thinly
    sliced (¼ cup)
½   cup plain fat-free
    yogurt
¼   cup light mayonnaise
2   tablespoons snipped
    fresh basil
2   tablespoons fat-free
    milk
2   cloves garlic, minced
1   teaspoon finely
    shredded lemon
    peel
⅛   teaspoon salt
    Dash black pepper
2   hard-cooked eggs,
    peeled and coarsely
    chopped (optional)
    Fat-free milk

1 In a medium saucepan cook macaroni according to package directions, adding broccoli and pea pods for the last 3 minutes of cooking. Drain pasta mixture. Rinse with cold water; drain again. In a large bowl combine pasta mixture, roasted peppers, and green onions.

2 For dressing, in a small bowl whisk together yogurt, mayonnaise, basil, the 2 tablespoons milk, the garlic, lemon peel, salt, and black pepper.

3 Pour dressing over pasta mixture. If desired, add chopped eggs. Toss lightly to coat. Cover and chill for 4 to 24 hours. Before serving, stir in additional milk, 1 tablespoon at a time, to moisten if necessary.

nutrition facts per serving: 114 cal., 4 g total fat (1 g sat. fat), 4 mg chol., 160 mg sodium, 16 g carb. (2 g fiber, 3 g sugars), 5 g pro. exchanges: 1 vegetable, 1 starch, 0.5 fat.

If you have a sweet tooth, roasted vegetables may help satisfy your craving! The roasting process teases out their natural sweetness.

pasta salad with roasted vegetables

start to finish: 45 minutes
makes: 8 servings (½ cup each)

14g
CARB. PER SERVING

1 medium onion, cut into thin wedges
3 tablespoons olive oil
1 medium yellow sweet pepper, cut into wedges
1 medium fresh poblano chile pepper, seeded and halved (see tip, *page 360*)
¾ cup grape tomatoes or cherry tomatoes
4 ounces dried whole wheat rotini pasta, dried whole grain penne pasta, or dried bow tie pasta (about 1½ cups)
½ teaspoon finely shredded lemon peel
2 tablespoons lemon juice
1 tablespoon snipped fresh oregano
2 teaspoons snipped fresh thyme
1 clove garlic, minced
¼ teaspoon salt
¼ teaspoon black pepper

1 Preheat oven to 400°F. In a 15×10×1-inch baking pan combine onion wedges and 1 tablespoon of the oil; toss to coat. Roast, uncovered, for 10 minutes. Add sweet pepper, poblano pepper, and tomatoes to pan. Stir to combine. Roast, uncovered, for 8 to 10 minutes more or until peppers are crisp-tender, stirring once. Remove pan from oven; set aside to cool slightly.

2 Meanwhile, cook pasta according to package directions. Drain well. Rinse well with cold water; drain again.

3 Coarsely chop cooled vegetables. In a large bowl combine pasta and vegetable mixture.

4 For dressing, in a screw-top jar combine lemon peel, lemon juice, remaining 2 tablespoons olive oil, oregano, thyme, garlic, salt, and black pepper. Cover and shake well. Pour dressing over pasta and vegetables; toss gently to combine. Serve immediately or cover and chill for up to 24 hours. Stir before serving.

nutrition facts per serving: 111 cal., 5 g total fat (1 g sat. fat), 0 mg chol., 76 mg sodium, 14 g carb. (2 g fiber, 2 g sugars), 3 g pro. **exchanges:** 0.5 vegetable, 0.5 starch, 1 fat.

For a Greek version of this family-friendly pasta salad, substitute green sweet pepper for the poblano, basil for the cilantro, and reduced-fat feta for the queso fresco.

20g CARB. PER SERVING

poblano pasta salad

prep: 20 minutes bake: 20 minutes stand: 20 minutes
makes: 6 servings (⅔ cup each)

1   medium fresh poblano chile pepper
1   medium red sweet pepper
½   of a medium sweet onion, cut into ½-inch slices
4   ounces dried whole wheat rotini pasta, dried whole grain penne pasta, or dried whole grain bow tie pasta (about 1⅔ cups)
¼   cup chopped tomatoes
2   tablespoons snipped fresh cilantro
2   tablespoons toasted pumpkin seeds (pepitas)
2   tablespoons red wine vinegar
1   tablespoon olive oil
1   clove garlic, minced
¼   teaspoon salt
⅛   teaspoon black pepper
1   ounce queso fresco, crumbled

1 Preheat oven to 425°F. Halve the poblano pepper (see tip, *page 360*) and sweet pepper. Remove seeds and membranes. Place poblano pepper, sweet pepper, and onion slices, cut sides down, on foil-lined baking sheet. Roast in oven about 20 minutes or until pepper skins and onion are lightly charred. Wrap peppers in the foil and let stand for 20 to 30 minutes or until cool enough to handle. Peel off skin. Coarsely chop peppers and onion.

2 Meanwhile, cook pasta according to package directions. Drain well. Rinse well with cold water; drain again.

3 In a large bowl combine cooked pasta, poblano pepper, sweet pepper, onion, tomatoes, cilantro, and pumpkin seeds. Set aside.

4 For dressing, in a screw-top jar combine vinegar, olive oil, garlic, salt, and pepper. Cover and shake well. Pour dressing over pasta and vegetables; toss gently to combine. Garnish each serving with a sprinkle of queso fresco.

nutrition facts per serving: 146 cal., 5 g total fat (1 g sat. fat), 3 mg chol., 138 mg sodium, 20 g carb. (2 g fiber, 3 g sugars), 5 g pro. exchanges: 1 vegetable, 1 starch, 1 fat.

Yukon gold potatoes share the spotlight with sweet potatoes in this take on one of America's favorite potluck salads.

two-tone potato salad

13g CARB. PER SERVING

prep: 25 minutes chill: at least 4 hours
makes: 6 servings (½ cup each)

6 ounces small (about 2-inch) Yukon gold potatoes, cut into ½-inch-thick wedges

1 6-ounce sweet potato, peeled and cut into 1-inch cubes

⅓ cup light mayonnaise

1 tablespoon Dijon-style mustard

1 tablespoon fat-free milk

2 teaspoons snipped fresh thyme or ½ teaspoon dried thyme, crushed

¼ teaspoon black pepper

1 stalk celery, thinly sliced

2 green onions, thinly sliced

2 slices turkey bacon, cooked according to package directions and chopped

1 In a large saucepan cook potatoes, covered, in enough boiling water to cover for 10 to 12 minutes or until just tender. Drain well; cool to room temperature.

2 Meanwhile, for dressing, in a large bowl combine mayonnaise, mustard, milk, thyme, and pepper. Add potatoes, celery, and green onions. Toss to coat. Cover and chill at least 4 hours or up to 24 hours. Gently stir in bacon just before serving.

nutrition facts per serving: 106 cal., 5 g total fat (1 g sat. fat), 10 mg chol., 248 mg sodium, 13 g carb. (2 g fiber, 2 g sugars), 2 g pro. exchanges: 1 starch, 1 fat.

Cut the extra jicama into ½-inch strips and serve on an appetizer platter alongside dips, spreads, and other vegetables.

jicama radish slaw

start to finish: 30 minutes

makes: 8 servings (½ cup each)

¼ cup snipped fresh
    cilantro
2   tablespoons rice
    vinegar
2   tablespoons toasted
    sesame oil
¼   teaspoon salt
⅛   to ¼ teaspoon
    crushed red pepper
½   of a medium jicama,
    peeled and cut into
    thin matchstick-size
    pieces (about 3 cups)
¾   cup radishes, trimmed
    and thinly sliced
½   cup julienne or
    packaged coarsely
    shredded fresh
    carrot
2   green onions, cut
    into 2-inch pieces
    and thinly sliced
    lengthwise
    Lime wedges
    (optional)

In a large bowl whisk together cilantro, vinegar, oil, salt, and crushed red pepper. Add jicama, radishes, carrot, and green onions. Toss to coat. Serve immediately or cover and chill for up to 2 hours. If desired, garnish with lime wedges.

nutrition facts per serving: 54 cal., 3 g total fat (1 g sat. fat), 0 mg chol., 86 mg sodium, 5 g carb. (3 g fiber, 2 g sugars), 1 g pro. exchanges: 0.5 vegetable, 0.5 fat.

8g
CARB. PER
SERVING

Add punch to the peach flavor of this dish by substituting peach vinegar for the white wine vinegar if you have some on hand.

peach and spinach salad with feta

start to finish: 15 minutes
makes: 4 servings (1¼ cups each)

6 cups packaged fresh
   baby spinach
1 recipe Honey-Mustard
   Vinaigrette
1 medium peach,
   pitted, or 1 apple,
   cored and thinly
   sliced
3 tablespoons crumbled
   reduced-fat feta
   cheese
1 tablespoon pine nuts,
   toasted

In a large bowl toss spinach with Honey-Mustard Vinaigrette. Divide spinach among four salad bowls. Top with peach or apple slices, feta cheese, and pine nuts.

nutrition facts per serving: 99 cal., 6 g total fat (1 g sat. fat), 2 mg chol., 234 mg sodium, 8 g carb. (3 g fiber, 3 g sugars), 4 g pro. exchanges: 1 vegetable, 1 fat.

honey-mustard vinaigrette: In a screw-top jar combine 2 tablespoons white wine vinegar, 1 tablespoon olive oil, 1 tablespoon finely chopped shallot, 2 teaspoons water, 1 teaspoon honey mustard, and ⅛ teaspoon salt. Cover and shake well.

*Some people love the peppery bite of arugula; some don't.
If you're in the latter camp, substitute fresh spinach.*

apple-tomato salad

14g
CARB. PER
SERVING

start to finish: 20 minutes
makes: 4 servings (1½ cups salad mixture and 1 tablespoon dressing each)

1 Arrange leaf lettuce, arugula, tomatoes, apple, and red onion on four salad plates. Sprinkle with blue cheese and pecans.

2 For dressing, in a screw-top jar combine vinegar, olive oil, honey, salt, and pepper. Cover and shake well. Drizzle dressing over salads.

- 2 cups green leaf lettuce, torn into bite size pieces
- 2 cups arugula
- 1 cup cherry tomatoes, halved
- 1 medium Fuji apple or green-skin apple, halved and thinly sliced
- ¼ of a medium red onion, thinly sliced
- 2 tablespoons crumbled blue cheese
- 4 teaspoons chopped pecans, toasted*
- 2 tablespoons cider vinegar
- 4 teaspoons olive oil
- 1 tablespoon honey
- ⅛ teaspoon salt
- ⅛ teaspoon black pepper

nutrition facts per serving: 128 cal., 8 g total fat (2 g sat. fat), 3 mg chol., 143 mg sodium, 14 g carb. (2 g fiber, 11 g sugars), 2 g pro. exchanges: 1 vegetable, 0.5 fruit, 1.5 fat.

✱test kitchen tip: To toast nuts in the oven, place them in a baking pan and bake in a 350°F oven about 10 minutes or until golden, stirring once or twice. Toast a cup or two at a time and store them in the freezer.

To seed tomatoes, cut them in half crosswise (across the "equator"). Squeeze the tomato gently over the sink until the seeds pop out. Or use your thumb to scoop out the seeds.

6g
CARB. PER SERVING

arugula salad with grilled eggplant

prep: 25 minutes **grill:** 6 minutes
makes: 6 servings (1 eggplant slice, 1 cup greens, ⅓ ounce goat cheese, ½ teaspoon pine nuts, and about 4 teaspoons dressing each)

1	teaspoon garlic powder
½	teaspoon black pepper
⅛	teaspoon salt
½	cup chopped, seeded tomatoes
2	tablespoons olive oil
1	tablespoon snipped fresh oregano
2	teaspoons snipped fresh thyme
2	teaspoons cider vinegar
6	½-inch-thick eggplant slices
3	cups baby spinach
3	cups arugula
2	ounces crumbled goat cheese (chèvre)
1	tablespoon pine nuts, toasted

1 In a small bowl combine garlic powder, pepper, and salt. For dressing, in another small bowl combine half of the garlic powder mixture, the tomatoes, 1 tablespoon of the oil, the oregano, thyme, and vinegar. Transfer mixture to a food processor or blender. Cover and process or blend until combined but still chunky. Set aside.

2 Brush eggplant slices with the remaining 1 tablespoon oil and sprinkle with the remaining garlic powder mixture.

3 For a charcoal or gas grill, place eggplant slices on the grill rack directly over medium heat. Grill, covered, for 6 to 8 minutes or just until tender and golden brown, turning once halfway through grilling.

4 To serve, arrange spinach and arugula on a serving platter or on six salad plates. Top with eggplant slices, goat cheese, and pine nuts. Spoon or drizzle tomato dressing over salads.

nutrition facts per serving: 112 cal., 9 g total fat (3 g sat. fat), 7 mg chol., 124 mg sodium, 6 g carb. (3 g fiber, 2 g sugars), 4 g pro. **exchanges:** 1.5 vegetable, 1.5 fat.

Here's how to bring a favorite steak-house salad home—with less fat and fewer calories and at a fraction of the price.

6g
CARB. PER
SERVING

classic wedge salad

start to finish: 20 minutes
makes: 6 servings (1 lettuce wedge and 2 tablespoons dressing each)

1 head iceberg lettuce, cut into 6 wedges
1 cup grape tomatoes, halved
2 green onions, sliced
2 slices bacon, crisp-cooked, drained, and coarsely crumbled
1 recipe Blue Cheese Dressing

Arrange lettuce wedges and grape tomatoes on six salad plates. Top with green onion and bacon. Drizzle with Blue Cheese Dressing.

nutrition facts per serving: 77 cal., 4 g total fat (2 g sat. fat), 9 mg chol., 201 mg sodium, 6 g carb. (2 g fiber, 4 g sugars), 4 g pro. exchanges: 1 vegetable, 1 fat.

blue cheese dressing: In a small bowl whisk together ¼ cup plain low-fat yogurt; 3 tablespoons crumbled blue cheese or reduced-fat blue cheese; 2 tablespoons light mayonnaise; 2 tablespoons buttermilk; 1 green onion, sliced; 2 cloves garlic, minced; ¼ teaspoon black pepper; and a pinch salt.

Panzanella, a rustic Italian bread salad, is usually made with day-old bread cubes and tomatoes. This version uses grapes and whole grain bread for a twist on tradition.

17g
CARB. PER SERVING

panzanella salad with a twist

start to finish: 25 minutes
makes: 6 servings (2 cups each)

simple **side dishes**

4 ounces whole grain baguette-style French bread, cut into ½-inch slices
1 clove garlic, halved
6 cups packaged fresh baby spinach or torn romaine lettuce
⅓ cup torn fresh basil
½ of a small red onion, cut into thin wedges
1½ cups halved seedless red grapes
¼ cup bottled reduced-calorie balsamic vinaigrette salad dressing

1 Preheat broiler. Place bread slices on a baking sheet. Broil 2 to 3 inches from the heat for about 3 minutes or until lightly toasted, turning once to toast both sides. Cool on a wire rack. Lightly rub bread slices with cut sides of garlic clove. Cut bread into cubes.

2 In a large salad bowl combine spinach and basil. Top with red onion, the bread cubes, and grapes. Drizzle with salad dressing and toss to coat. Serve immediately.

nutrition facts per serving: 99 cal., 2 g total fat (0 g sat. fat), 0 mg chol., 237 mg sodium, 17 g carb. (3 g fiber, 7 g sugars), 4 g pro. exchanges: 1 starch, 0.5 fat.

make-ahead directions:
Prepare bread cubes; store in an airtight container. In the salad bowl layer spinach, red onion, and grapes. Cover and chill salad for up to 4 hours. Top with basil and bread cubes and drizzle with salad dressing; toss to coat. Serve immediately.

One lemon yields about 3 tablespoons of lemon juice. Freeze the extra juice in a small freezer container and use it the next time you make this refreshing salad.

couscous salad platter

26g
CARB. PER
SERVING

prep: 15 minutes cook: 22 minutes stand: 5 minutes
makes: 4 servings (½ cup couscous mixture, ¼ cup cucumber, 2 tablespoons sweet pepper, and 1 tablespoon hummus each)

¾ cup Israeli (large pearl) couscous
1¼ cups reduced-sodium chicken broth
¼ cup chopped tomatoes
1 tablespoon snipped fresh mint
1 tablespoon lemon juice
⅛ teaspoon black pepper
1 cup sliced cucumber
½ cup bottled roasted red sweet peppers, cut into strips
8 pitted Kalamata olives (optional)
¼ cup purchased hummus

1 In a dry medium saucepan toast couscous over medium-low heat, stirring frequently, for 8 to 10 minutes or until golden brown. Remove from saucepan; set aside.

2 In the medium saucepan bring broth to boiling. Add couscous. Return to boiling; reduce heat. Simmer, covered, for 12 to 15 minutes or until liquid is absorbed. Remove from heat. Stir in tomatoes, mint, lemon juice, and black pepper. Cover and let stand for 5 minutes.

3 Transfer couscous to a small platter. Arrange cucumber, roasted red peppers, olives (if using), and hummus on or around couscous.

nutrition facts per serving: 138 cal., 1 g total fat (0 g sat. fat), 0 mg chol., 228 mg sodium, 26 g carb. (3 g fiber, 2 g sugars), 5 g pro. exchanges: 1 vegetable, 1.5 starch.

Appetizers and between-meal snacks sometimes get a bad rap from the diet police. These recipes prove that satisfying nibbles can fit into a healthful meal plan, especially when they're right-sized and made with just-right ingredients.

good-for-you

sna

fruity-limeade
slushy, *page 412*

cks

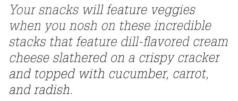

Your snacks will feature veggies when you nosh on these incredible stacks that feature dill-flavored cream cheese slathered on a crispy cracker and topped with cucumber, carrot, and radish.

21g
CARB. PER
SERVING

veggie-topped rye crisps

start to finish: 20 minutes
makes: 4 servings (2 topped crackers each)

½   cup light cream
     cheese spread,
     softened
½   teaspoon finely
     shredded lemon
     peel
½   teaspoon snipped
     fresh dill weed or
     ¼ teaspoon dried
     dill weed
1   small clove garlic,
     minced
8   3½×1½-inch crisp
     rye crackers
½   cup thin bite-size
     English cucumber
     strips
½   cup coarsely
     shredded carrot
¼   cup thin bite-size
     radish strips

In a small bowl stir together cream cheese, lemon peel, dill, and garlic. Spread evenly on crackers. Top with cucumber, carrot, and radishes.

nutrition facts per serving: 144 cal., 5 g total fat (3 g sat. fat), 15 mg chol., 217 mg sodium, 21 g carb. (4 g fiber, 3 g sugars), 5 g pro. exchanges: 1.5 starch, 0.5 fat.

make-ahead directions: Prepare cream cheese mixture as directed. Transfer to an airtight container; cover. Store in the refrigerator for up to 2 days. Within 4 hours of assembling the crisps, cut up the vegetables and store, covered, in the refrigerator.

*Use a flatware teaspoon to hollow out the insides
of the tomatoes, being careful not to split the sides.*

caprese stuffed cherry tomatoes

7g
CARB. PER
SERVING

start to finish: 15 minutes
makes: 4 servings (6 stuffed tomatoes each)

24	cherry tomatoes
4	ounces part-skim mozzarella cheese
2	tablespoons snipped fresh basil
1	tablespoon white balsamic vinegar
¼	teaspoon black pepper

1 Using a sharp knife, cut off the top third of each cherry tomato on the stem end. Hollow out the cherry tomatoes; invert on paper towels to drain. Set aside.

2 Cut the mozzarella into 24 equal cubes. In a medium bowl combine the cheese cubes, basil, vinegar, and pepper. Stuff each tomato with a coated cheese cube.

nutrition facts per serving: 112 cal., 6 g total fat (3 g sat. fat), 15 mg chol., 190 mg sodium, 7 g carb. (1 g fiber, 5 g sugars), 8 g pro. exchanges: 1 vegetable, 1 medium-fat meat.

384

10g
CARB. PER
SERVING

Spoon the warm, chunky veggie topper on the crunchy cracker just before serving to keep it from getting soggy.

bruschetta planks

prep: 10 minutes   cook: 6 minutes
makes: 4 servings (1 cracker and ¼ cup topping each)

½   cup chopped red
      or yellow sweet
      pepper
½   cup chopped fresh
      button mushrooms
      or cremini
      mushrooms
¼   cup chopped onion
2   teaspoons olive oil
1   medium tomato,
      seeded and chopped
      (½ cup)
1   clove garlic, minced
2   tablespoons snipped
      fresh basil
4   thin whole grain
      flatbread crackers
1   ounce Parmesan
      cheese, thinly
      shaved

1 In a medium nonstick skillet cook sweet pepper, mushrooms, and onion in hot oil over medium heat for 5 to 7 minutes or until tender, stirring occasionally. Add tomato and garlic. Cook and stir for 1 minute more. Remove from heat. Stir in basil.

2 Spoon tomato mixture evenly on crackers. Top with shaved Parmesan cheese. Serve immediately.

nutrition facts per serving: 107 cal., 6 g total fat (2 g sat. fat), 5 mg chol., 157 mg sodium, 10 g carb. (2 g fiber, 3 g sugars), 4 g pro. exchanges: 1 vegetable, 0.5 starch, 1 fat.

Fiber-rich and wholly satisfying garbanzo beans are the main ingredient in this Middle Eastern spread, but it's the seasonings that help the hummus really take off.

hummus with roasted red peppers

17g
CARB. PER SERVING

prep: 20 minutes broil: 10 minutes
makes: 8 servings (¼ cup hummus and ½ cup vegetable dippers each)

2 medium red sweet peppers, quartered
4 unpeeled cloves garlic
1 15-ounce can no-salt-added garbanzo beans (chickpeas), rinsed and drained
2 tablespoons tahini (sesame seed paste)
1 tablespoon lemon juice
1 to 2 teaspoons bottled mild chile pepper sauce
¼ cup chopped fresh cilantro
4 cups assorted vegetable dippers, such as carrot sticks, celery sticks, and/or cherry tomatoes

1 Preheat the broiler. Place the pepper quarters on a foil-lined baking sheet. Wrap the garlic cloves in foil and place on the baking sheet with the peppers. Broil 4 to 5 inches from the heat for 10 to 15 minutes or until pepper skin is charred. Place on a wire rack and carefully wrap the pepper quarters in the foil. Let peppers and garlic stand until cool enough to handle.

2 When garlic is cool enough to handle, peel the garlic cloves and place in a food processor. Cover and process until finely chopped. When the peppers are cool enough to handle, peel off and discard the skins. (You should have about 1 cup of roasted peppers.) Add the peppers, garbanzo beans, tahini, lemon juice, and pepper sauce to the garlic in the food processor. Cover and process until smooth. Transfer to a serving bowl. Stir in cilantro. For best flavor, cover and refrigerate for at least 4 hours or up to 3 days. Serve with vegetable dippers.

nutrition facts per serving: 108 cal., 3 g total fat (0 g sat. fat), 0 mg chol., 53 mg sodium, 17 g carb. (4 g fiber, 4 g sugars), 5 g pro. exchanges: 0.5 vegetable, 1 starch, 0.5 fat.

Put these out at your next gathering. Everyone will thank you for offering something fresh, colorful, and healthful instead of the usual fat-and-calorie bomb.

mango and black bean salsa cups

18g
CARB. PER SERVING

good-for-you **snacks**

prep: 20 minutes
makes: 16 servings (¼ cup salsa and 8 scoop chips each)

1   15-ounce can no-salt-added black beans, rinsed and drained
1   medium papaya, halved, seeded, peeled, and chopped (1¼ cups)
1   medium mango, halved, peeled, pitted, and chopped (1 cup)
1   medium orange, sectioned and chopped*
⅓   cup chopped red onion
2   tablespoons orange juice*
2   tablespoons olive oil
2   tablespoons snipped fresh cilantro or parsley
1   tablespoon lime juice
½   teaspoon salt
¼   teaspoon black pepper
⅛   to ¼ teaspoon cayenne pepper (optional)
8   ounces scoop-shape baked tortilla chips
    Cilantro or parsley leaves (optional)

1 In a large bowl combine beans, papaya, mango, orange, and red onion. In a small bowl whisk together orange juice, olive oil, snipped cilantro, lime juice, salt, black pepper, and, if desired, cayenne pepper. Spoon orange juice mixture over bean mixture; toss to combine. Serve immediately or cover and chill for up to 24 hours.

2 To serve, spoon salsa into baked scoop chips. If desired, garnish cups with fresh cilantro or parsley leaves.

nutrition facts per serving: 126 cal., 5 g total fat (1 g sat. fat), 0 mg chol., 132 mg sodium, 18 g carb. (4 g fiber, 4 g sugars), 3 g pro. exchanges: 0.5 fruit, 0.5 starch, 1 fat.

*test kitchen tip: Section and chop the orange over a shallow dish; you should be able to reserve the juice for the 2 tablespoons needed in the recipe.

Rinsing the beans in cold water will stop the cooking process and leave them bright green and crisp-tender.

green beans with lemon-chili dip

prep: 20 minutes cook: 3 minutes
makes: 4 servings (¾ cup beans and 2 tablespoons dip each)

8 ounces fresh green
    beans, trimmed
½ cup light sour cream
2 tablespoons chopped
    green onion (1)
½ teaspoon finely
    shredded lemon
    peel
2 teaspoons lemon
    juice
1 clove garlic, minced
½ teaspoon chili
    powder

1 Leave beans whole. In a medium saucepan cook beans, covered, in a small amount of boiling water for 3 to 5 minutes or just until crisp-tender; drain. Rinse beans with cold water; drain well. Transfer to a serving bowl.

2 For dip, in a small bowl whisk together the sour cream, green onion, lemon peel, lemon juice, garlic, and chili powder. Serve beans✳ with sour cream mixture for dipping.

nutrition facts per serving: 54 cal., 3 g total fat (2 g sat. fat), 8 mg chol., 26 mg sodium, 7 g carb. (2 g fiber, 2 g sugars), 2 g pro. exchanges: 1 vegetable, 0.5 fat.

✳test kitchen tip: If desired, serve dip with roasted asparagus spears. To roast asparagus, preheat oven to 400°F. Snap off and discard woody bases from 8 ounces fresh asparagus spears; scrape off scales. Place asparagus in a 15×10×1-inch baking pan; drizzle with 1 teaspoon olive oil. Spread asparagus in a single layer. Roast, uncovered, for 10 to 12 minutes or until asparagus is crisp-tender.

One reason BLTs taste so good is the way mayonnaise marries the flavors. Thank goodness for light mayo, which does the trick without an overload of fat!

blt cups

start to finish: 20 minutes
makes: 4 servings (1 cup each)

5g
CARB. PER
SERVING

3 tablespoons light
mayonnaise
1 tablespoon fat-free
milk
½ teaspoon finely
shredded lemon
peel
1 clove garlic, minced
⅛ teaspoon black
pepper
3 cups chopped
romaine lettuce
1 cup cherry tomatoes
or grape tomatoes,
halved
2 slices turkey bacon,
cooked according to
package directions
and chopped
4 whole wheat
croutons, coarsely
crushed

1 In a small bowl stir together mayonnaise, milk, lemon peel, garlic, and pepper. Set aside.

2 In four wide 8-ounce glasses or serving dishes layer half the lettuce, half the tomatoes, and half the bacon. Top with half the mayonnaise mixture. Repeat layers once. Sprinkle with crushed croutons.

nutrition facts per serving: 83 cal., 6 g total fat (1 g sat. fat), 9 mg chol., 226 mg sodium, 5 g carb. (2 g fiber, 2 g sugars), 3 g pro. exchanges: 1 vegetable, 1 fat.

No mini peppers? You can substitute wedges of sweet pepper, but don't bake them quite as long.

10g
CARB. PER
SERVING

bbq chicken bites

prep: 15 minutes bake: 15 minutes
makes: 4 servings (4 stuffed pepper halves each)

Nonstick cooking
   spray
8 miniature red, yellow,
   and/or green sweet
   peppers or large
   fresh jalapeño chile
   peppers
½ cup shredded cooked
   chicken breast
¼ cup shredded
   reduced-fat cheddar
   cheese (1 ounce)
2 green onions, thinly
   sliced (¼ cup)
2 tablespoons snipped
   fresh cilantro
   (optional)
⅓ cup low-sodium
   barbecue sauce

1 Preheat oven to 350°F. Line a baking sheet with foil; coat foil with cooking spray. Set aside. Cut each pepper in half lengthwise (do not remove stem); remove seeds and membranes.✳ Place pepper halves, cut sides up, on prepared baking sheet. Set aside.

2 For filling, in a small bowl combine chicken, cheese, green onion, and, if desired, cilantro. Add barbecue sauce; stir until combined. Spoon chicken mixture evenly into pepper halves.

3 Bake for 15 to 20 minutes or until heated through and peppers are just tender.

nutrition facts per serving: 90 cal., 2 g total fat (1 g sat. fat), 20 mg chol., 87 mg sodium, 10 g carb. (1 g fiber, 7 g sugars), 8 g pro. exchanges: 0.5 vegetable, 0.5 carb., 1 lean meat, 0.5 fat.

✳test kitchen tip: If using jalapeño peppers, because chile peppers contain volatile oils that can burn your skin and eyes, avoid direct contact with them as much as possible. When working with chile peppers, wear plastic or rubber gloves. If your bare hands do touch the peppers, wash your hands and nails well with soap and warm water.

Nothing predictable here! Belgian endive and scooped-out zucchini slices make fun, unexpected dippers for the luscious salmon spread.

mediterranean salmon spread

prep: 15 minutes chill: 2 hours
makes: 4 servings (¼ cup spread, 4 zucchini slices, and 2 endive leaves each)

3 tablespoons light
   sour cream
2 teaspoons snipped
   fresh mint
⅛ teaspoon garlic
   powder
1 6-ounce pouch
   skinless, boneless
   pink salmon
⅓ cup bottled roasted
   red sweet pepper,
   drained and
   chopped
16 1-inch-thick diagonal
   slices zucchini, with
   centers hollowed
   out slightly
8 Belgian endive leaves
   Snipped fresh mint
   (optional)

1 In a small bowl combine sour cream, the 2 teaspoons mint, and the garlic powder. Stir in salmon and roasted sweet pepper. Cover and chill for 2 to 24 hours.

2 Stir spread. Spoon evenly onto zucchini slices and endive leaves. If desired, garnish with additional snipped mint.

nutrition facts per serving: 78 cal., 3 g total fat (1 g sat. fat), 18 mg chol., 227 mg sodium, 5 g carb. (1 g fiber, 2 g sugars), 9 g pro. exchanges: 1 vegetable, 1 lean meat.

good-for-you snacks

22g
CARB. PER
SERVING

An interesting play of textures can help a low-fat treat be highly satisfying. The chewy bagel, the creamy cheese, and the crunchy granola really make everything come together.

brown sugar–cinnamon cream cheese bagels

prep: 15 minutes chill: up to 2 hours

makes: 8 servings (½ of a mini bagel, 1 tablespoon cream cheese mixture, and 1 tablespoon granola each)

½ cup light tub-style cream cheese, softened

2 tablespoons fresh blueberries, mashed slightly

1½ tablespoons packed brown sugar✳

¼ teaspoon ground cinnamon

4 whole wheat mini bagels, split and toasted

½ cup low-fat granola

1 In a small bowl combine cream cheese, slightly mashed blueberries, brown sugar, and cinnamon. Beat with an electric mixer on medium speed until well combined. Cover and chill for up to 2 hours. Stir before using.

2 Spread on toasted mini bagel halves. Top each serving with 1 tablespoon granola.

nutrition facts per serving: 133 cal., 3 g total fat (2 g sat. fat), 10 mg chol., 191 mg sodium, 22 g carb. (3 g fiber, 8 g sugars), 5 g pro. exchanges: 1.5 starch, 0.5 fat.

✳ sugar substitute: We do not recommend using a sugar substitute for this recipe.

Once you discover chia seeds, you'll find other ways to use this fiber-rich food: Try sprinkling the seeds over hot cereals or into yogurt parfaits or incorporating them into baked goods.

blueberry oat–chia seed muffins

prep: 20 minutes bake: 10 minutes
makes: 18 servings (2 mini muffins each)

15g
CARB. PER SERVING

Nonstick cooking
    spray
1¼ cups flour
¾ cup regular rolled
    oats
⅓ cup sugar✻
2 tablespoons chia
    seeds, ground
2 teaspoons baking
    powder
¼ teaspoon salt
1 egg, beaten
¾ cup fat-free milk
¼ cup vegetable oil
¾ cup fresh blueberries

✻ sugar substitutes: Choose from Splenda Sugar Blend for Baking or Equal Sugar Lite. Follow package directions to use product amount equivalent to ⅓ cup sugar.

1 Preheat oven to 350°F. Lightly coat thirty-six 1¾-inch muffin cups with cooking spray or line with mini paper bake cups; set aside. In a large bowl combine flour, oats, sugar, chia seeds, baking powder, and salt. Make a well in the center of flour mixture; set aside.

2 In another bowl combine egg, milk, and oil. Add egg mixture all at once to flour mixture. Stir just until moistened (batter should be lumpy). Fold in blueberries.

3 Spoon a scant tablespoon batter into prepared muffin cups, filling each two-thirds full. Bake about 10 minutes or until a wooden toothpick inserted in centers comes out clean. Cool in muffin cups on a wire rack for 5 minutes. Remove from muffin cups. Serve warm or at room temperature. Serve within 1 day of preparation.

nutrition facts per serving: 108 cal., 4 g total fat (1 g sat. fat), 11 mg chol., 95 mg sodium, 15 g carb. (1 g fiber, 5 g sugars), 2 g pro. exchanges: 1 starch, 0.5 fat.

nutrition facts per serving with substitute: Same as original, except 102 cal., 13 g carb. (3 g sugars).

394

18g
CARB. PER
SERVING

If you have extra pumpkin, transfer it to an airtight container or freezer bag. Refrigerate for up to 1 week or freeze up to 3 months.

pumpkin spice dip

prep: 10 minutes

makes: 16 servings (2 tablespoons dip, ¼ of an apple, and 3 pretzel twists each)

3	ounces reduced-fat cream cheese (Neufchâtel), softened
¾	cup canned pumpkin
1	6-ounce carton vanilla fat-free yogurt
2	tablespoons packed brown sugar∗
1	teaspoon pumpkin pie spice
4	apples, sliced
48	honey-wheat braided pretzel twists

In a medium bowl beat cream cheese with an electric mixer until light and fluffy. Beat in pumpkin, yogurt, brown sugar, and pumpkin pie spice. Serve dip with apple slices and honey-wheat braided pretzel twists.

nutrition facts per serving: 93 cal., 2 g total fat (1 g sat. fat), 4 mg chol., 116 mg sodium, 18 g carb. (2 g fiber, 8 g sugars), 2 g pro. exchanges: 1 starch.

∗sugar substitute: We do not recommend using a sugar substitute for this recipe.

This luscious parfait makes a lovely snack, but it's also a good breakfast when you crave something sweet, light, and refreshing to jump-start your day.

berry yogurt parfaits

27g CARB. PER SERVING

prep: 20 minutes
makes: 4 servings (¼ cup yogurt, ⅓ cup berries, and ¼ cup cereal each)

1 cup plain fat-free Greek yogurt
2 tablespoons honey
1 teaspoon vanilla
½ teaspoon finely shredded lemon peel
½ cup fresh raspberries
½ cup fresh blackberries, halved if desired
½ cup fresh blueberries
1 cup multigrain oats and honey cereal
Lemon peel strips

1 In a small bowl combine yogurt, honey, vanilla, and shredded lemon peel. (If desired, the yogurt mixture can be stirred together ahead of time, covered, and chilled for several hours.)

2 Divide half of the yogurt mixture among four glasses or parfait dishes. Top with half of the berries and half of the cereal. Repeat layers. Serve immediately or cover and chill for up to 30 minutes. Garnish servings with lemon peel strips.

nutrition facts per serving: 129 cal., 0 g total fat, 0 mg chol., 75 mg sodium, 27 g carb. (4 g fiber, 18 g sugars), 6 g pro. exchanges: 0.5 milk, 0.5 fruit, 1 starch.

What's not to love? You can savor the satisfying flavor of apple pie with the delicate crispness of a snack chip.

crisp apple chips

31g
CARB. PER
SERVING

prep: 20 minutes bake: 2 hours
makes: 4 servings (about ¾ ounce chips each)

2 large apples, such
   as Braeburn, Jazz,
   Pink Lady, or Gala,
   cored
¼ cup sugar٭
2 teaspoons apple pie
   spice٭٭

1 Preheat oven to 200°F. Line two or three baking sheets with parchment paper; set aside.

2 Using a mandoline or a serrated knife, cut apples crosswise into ⅛-inch slices. Arrange slices in a single layer on baking sheets. In a small bowl combine sugar and apple pie spice. Sprinkle apple slices with half of the sugar mixture. Use a pastry brush to brush mixture over apple slices to cover evenly. (Or place the sugar mixture in a small sieve; holding the sieve over the apple slices, stir the mixture with a spoon to evenly disperse the sugar mixture over the apples.) Turn apple slices and repeat with remaining sugar mixture.

3 Bake for 2 to 2½ hours or until crisp, turning apple slices and rotating pans every 30 minutes. Cool completely on wire racks. Store apple slices in an airtight container for up to 1 week.

nutrition facts per serving: 116 cal., 0 g total fat, 0 mg chol., 2 mg sodium, 31 g carb. (3 g fiber, 25 g sugars), 0 g pro. exchanges: 1 fruit, 1 carb.

nutrition facts per serving with substitute: Same as original, except 67 cal., 19 g carb. (13 g sugars). exchanges: 0 carb.

٭sugar substitutes: Choose from Splenda Sugar Blend for Baking or C&H Light Sugar and Stevia Blend. Follow package directions to use product amount equivalent to ¼ cup sugar.

٭٭test kitchen tip: If desired, substitute 1¼ teaspoons ground cinnamon, ¼ teaspoon ground cloves, ¼ teaspoon ground nutmeg, and ¼ teaspoon ground allspice for the apple pie spice.

For a quick fix, skip the skewers and divide the fruit mixture among four bowls.

thai fruit skewers

prep: 20 minutes   chill: 1 hour
makes: 4 servings (2 skewers each)

½   cup reduced-fat or
     light unsweetened
     coconut milk
1   tablespoon finely
     shredded lime peel
⅛   teaspoon cayenne
     pepper
2   kiwifruits, peeled and
     quartered
4   to 6 1½-inch fresh
     peeled pineapple
     pieces
4   to 6 1½-inch fresh
     peeled papaya
     pieces
4   to 6 1½-inch fresh
     peeled mango
     pieces
¼   cup snipped fresh
     mint
¼   cup shredded
     coconut, toasted

1 In a medium bowl combine coconut milk, lime peel, and cayenne pepper. Add kiwifruit quarters and pineapple, papaya, and mango pieces. Toss to coat. Cover and chill for 1 to 4 hours, stirring occasionally.

2 Drain fruit, discarding coconut milk mixture. Thread fruit pieces alternately on eight 6-inch skewers. Sprinkle fruit with mint and coconut.

nutrition facts per serving: 112 cal., 4 g total fat (3 g sat. fat), 0 mg chol., 13 mg sodium, 21 g carb. (4 g fiber, 14 g sugars), 1 g pro. exchanges: 1 fruit, 0.5 carb., 0.5 fat.

Vary these treats each time you make them by substituting a sugar-free preserve of another fruit, such as peach, raspberry, or apple.

rice cakes with fire jelly

start to finish: 10 minutes
makes: 4 servings (3 topped mini cakes each)

⅓ cup sugar-free apricot preserves
2 teaspoons minced fresh jalapeño chile pepper✱
12 miniature salt-and-pepper rice cakes, such as Quaker Quakes brand
⅓ cup fat-free tub-style cream cheese
1 teaspoon snipped fresh rosemary

In a small bowl combine preserves and chile pepper. Spread rice cakes with cream cheese; top with preserves mixture. Sprinkle with rosemary.

nutrition facts per serving: 56 cal., 1 g total fat (0 g sat. fat), 2 mg chol., 200 mg sodium, 12 g carb. (0 g fiber, 1 g sugars), 3 g pro. exchanges: 1 starch.

✱ test kitchen tip: Because chile peppers contain volatile oils that can burn your skin and eyes, avoid direct contact with them as much as possible. When working with chile peppers, wear plastic or rubber gloves. If your bare hands do touch the peppers, wash your hands and nails well with soap and warm water.

This quick snack makes a lovely side dish or dessert, too.
For eye candy, garnish each serving with a lemon peel twist.

cottage cheese
with raspberry honey

start to finish: 15 minutes
makes: 4 servings (²/₃ cup each)

2 cups fresh
  raspberries
2 tablespoons honey
1 teaspoon finely
  shredded lemon
  peel
2 cups low-fat cottage
  cheese
2 tablespoons roasted,
  salted sunflower
  kernels

1 Place 1 cup of the raspberries in a food processor; cover and process until pureed. Strain raspberry mixture through a fine-mesh sieve. In a small bowl combine the raspberry puree, honey, and shredded lemon peel.

2 Divide cottage cheese among four bowls. Top with raspberry-honey mixture; gently stir once or twice. Top with the remaining 1 cup raspberries and the sunflower kernels.

nutrition facts per serving: 169 cal., 4 g total fat (1 g sat. fat), 5 mg chol., 476 mg sodium, 20 g carb. (4 g fiber, 15 g sugars), 16 g pro. exchanges: 1 fruit, 2 lean meat, 0.5 fat.

Depending on what's looking best at the market, reverse the colors of the fruit and try blood oranges paired with yellow grapefruit.

citrus fruit bowl

27g
CARB. PER
SERVING

start to finish: 10 minutes
makes: 4 servings (1 cup fruit slices, ½ tablespoon honey, ½ tablespoon cheese, and ¾ teaspoon mint each)

3 oranges, peeled and
   sliced crosswise
1 pink grapefruit,
   peeled and sliced
   crosswise
2 tablespoons honey
2 tablespoons
   crumbled fat-free
   feta cheese
1 tablespoon snipped
   fresh mint

Arrange orange and grapefruit slices in four shallow bowls. Drizzle with honey; sprinkle with feta cheese and snipped fresh mint. If desired, cover and chill for up to 4 hours before serving.

nutrition facts per serving: 110 cal., 0 g total fat, 0 mg chol., 32 mg sodium, 27 g carb. (3 g fiber, 22 g sugars), 2 g pro.
exchanges: 1 fruit, 1 carb.

These sweet-hot nuts are so addictively tasty, you might want to present them in ¼-cup portions to keep count of how much you're eating.

13g
CARB. PER
SERVING

brown sugar–cayenne roasted nuts

start to finish: 45 minutes
makes: 16 servings (¼ cup each)

good-for-you snacks

1   egg white
1   tablespoon water
4   cups raw whole
     cashews, whole
     almonds, walnut
     halves, and/or
     pecan halves
3   tablespoons packed
     brown sugar ✳
1   tablespoon ground
     cumin
2   teaspoons chili
     powder
1   teaspoon garlic salt
⅛   teaspoon cayenne
     pepper

1 Preheat oven to 300°F. In a bowl combine egg white and the water; beat with a fork until frothy. Add nuts; toss to coat. Let stand for 5 minutes.

2 Meanwhile, in a large plastic bag combine brown sugar, cumin, chili powder, garlic salt, and cayenne pepper. Add nuts; shake well to coat. Spread nuts evenly in a 15×10×1-inch baking pan.

3 Bake for 35 to 40 minutes or until nuts are toasted and coating is dry, stirring twice. Transfer to a large sheet of foil. Cool completely. Store in an airtight container at room temperature for up to 5 days or freeze for up to 3 months.

nutrition facts per serving: 206 cal., 16 g total fat (3 g sat. fat), 0 mg chol., 72 mg sodium, 13 g carb. (1 g fiber, 4 g sugars), 7 g pro. exchanges: 1 starch, 0.5 lean meat, 2.5 fat.

nutrition facts per serving with substitute: Same as original, except 200 cal., 11 g carb. (2 g sugars).

✳ sugar substitutes: Choose from Sweet'N Low Brown or Sugar Twin Granulated Brown. Follow package directions to use product amount equivalent to 3 tablespoons brown sugar.

Stash a batch of this tasty combo in the freezer so it's handy when you crave something crunchy.

sweet and spicy wasabi snack mix

15g CARB. PER SERVING

prep: 15 minutes bake: 30 minutes
makes: 14 servings (½ cup each)

2½   cups crispy corn and rice cereal
2   cups pretzel sticks
1   cup wasabi-flavor dried peas
¾   cup whole almonds
¼   cup light butter
2   tablespoons rice vinegar
4   teaspoons sesame seeds
1   tablespoon reduced-sodium soy sauce
½   teaspoon ground ginger
¼   teaspoon cayenne pepper
½   cup snipped dried apricots

1 Preheat oven to 300°F. In a large bowl combine cereal, pretzel sticks, dried peas, and almonds. Set aside. In a small saucepan heat and stir butter, vinegar, sesame seeds, soy sauce, ginger, and cayenne over medium-low heat until butter melts. Drizzle butter mixture over cereal mixture; stir gently to coat. Transfer mixture to a 15×10×1-inch baking pan.

2 Bake about 30 minutes or until mixture is almost dry and almonds are lightly toasted, stirring twice. Stir in apricots. Spread mixture on a large piece of foil to cool. Store in an airtight container at room temperature for up to 3 days or in the freezer for up to 1 month.

nutrition facts per serving: 127 cal., 7 g total fat (2 g sat. fat), 4 mg chol., 194 mg sodium, 15 g carb. (2 g fiber, 4 g sugars), 3 g pro. exchanges: 1 starch, 1 fat.

The sweet-and-salty flavor of classic kettle corn comes through in this baked popcorn treat. Using brown sugar gives the coating a caramel flavor.

17g
CARB. PER
SERVING

kettle-style caramel corn

prep: 10 minutes bake: 20 minutes
makes: 11 servings (1 cup each)

404

½ cup packed brown
    sugar*
3 tablespoons tub-style
    vegetable oil spread
½ teaspoon salt
1 teaspoon vanilla
12 cups air-popped
    popcorn

1 Preheat oven to 300°F. In a small saucepan combine brown sugar, vegetable oil spread, and ¼ teaspoon of the salt; cook and stir over medium heat just until boiling and sugar is dissolved. Stir in vanilla.

2 Place popcorn in a shallow roasting pan. Drizzle brown sugar mixture over popcorn; toss to coat. Bake, uncovered, for 20 minutes, stirring once. Sprinkle with the remaining ¼ teaspoon salt. Transfer to a large piece of foil or a large roasting pan; let cool for 1 hour. Immediately place in an airtight container; cover and store at room temperature for up to 2 days.

nutrition facts per serving: 95 cal., 3 g total fat (1 g sat. fat), 0 mg chol., 134 mg sodium, 17 g carb. (1 g fiber, 10 g sugars), 1 g pro. exchanges: 1 starch, 0.5 fat.

nutrition facts per serving with substitute: Same as original, except 79 cal., 131 mg sodium, 11 g carb. (4 g sugars).

*sugar substitute: Choose Splenda Brown Sugar Blend. Follow package directions to use product amount equivalent to ½ cup brown sugar.

Leave the spiced peanuts on the supermarket shelf. Next time you want to serve something nutty and crunchy, present this more healthful option.

toasted chickpeas

14g CARB. PER SERVING

prep: 15 minutes roast: 32 minutes
makes: 6 servings (2½ tablespoons each)

1	15-ounce can no-salt-added garbanzo beans (chickpeas), drained
4	teaspoons olive oil
½	teaspoon paprika
¼	teaspoon salt
¼	teaspoon garlic powder
¼	teaspoon ground cumin
⅛	teaspoon black pepper
	Dash cayenne pepper

1 Preheat oven to 450°F. Rub garbanzo beans with a paper towel to dry well and to remove the thin skins. Place in a 9×9×2-inch baking pan. Drizzle with olive oil; stir to coat.

2 Roast, uncovered, for 20 minutes, stirring once. Remove from the oven and stir. Sprinkle with paprika, salt, garlic powder, cumin, black pepper, and cayenne pepper. Stir to coat evenly. Return to oven. Roast for 12 to 14 minutes more or until dried and crispy, stirring once. Cool completely before eating. Chickpeas can be stored in an airtight container overnight.

nutrition facts per serving: 104 cal., 4 g total fat (0 g sat. fat), 0 mg chol., 115 mg sodium, 14 g carb. (3 g fiber, 0 g sugars), 4 g pro. exchanges: 1 starch, 0.5 fat.

Turn on the exhaust fan while you pop the corn. The fumes from the chili oil can be strong.

garlic-chili popcorn

start to finish: 10 minutes
makes: 3 servings (3 cups each)

1   teaspoon chili oil
½   cup unpopped
     popcorn
¼   cup grated Parmesan
     cheese
½   teaspoon garlic
     powder

1 In a stove-top popcorn popper or large heavy saucepan heat chili oil over medium-high heat. Add popcorn; cover. Stir popcorn or shake pan constantly until popcorn has stopped popping.

2 Transfer popcorn to a large bowl. In a small bowl combine the Parmesan cheese with the garlic powder. Sprinkle cheese mixture over hot popcorn; toss well to coat popcorn. Serve immediately.

nutrition facts per serving: 150 cal., 5 g total fat (1 g sat. fat), 6 mg chol., 102 mg sodium, 26 g carb. (5 g fiber, 0 g sugars), 6 g pro. exchanges: 1.5 starch, 1 fat.

Tasty frozen yogurts abound at shops popping up everywhere, but when you make the treat yourself, you can ensure it fits right into your meal plan.

honeyed greek frozen yogurt

22g
CARB. PER SERVING

prep: 15 minutes freeze: 4 hours
makes: 8 servings (½ cup each)

3 cups plain fat-free Greek yogurt
½ cup buttermilk
½ cup honey
1 tablespoon lemon juice
1 vanilla bean, split lengthwise
   Fresh mint leaves

1 In a medium bowl combine yogurt, buttermilk, honey, and lemon juice. Scrape the seeds from the vanilla bean and add to the yogurt mixture; discard bean. Stir yogurt mixture to combine. Transfer to a 1½- to 2-quart ice cream freezer. Freeze according to manufacturer's directions. Transfer to a freezer container and ripen for 4 hours in the freezer.

2 If needed, let stand 10 minutes to soften slightly before serving. Garnish servings with mint leaves.

nutrition facts per serving: 118 cal., 0 g total fat, 1 mg chol., 50 mg sodium, 22 g carb. (0 g fiber, 22 g sugars), 8 g pro.
exchanges: 1 milk, 0.5 carb.

Not only do bananas provide lots of potassium to help lower your blood pressure, they also help improve your body's ability to absorb vitamins and minerals, especially calcium.

20g CARB. PER SERVING

frozen chocolate-banana bites

prep: 15 minutes freeze: 1 hour
makes: 4 servings (½ banana each)

good-for-you snacks

2 medium bananas
1½ ounces dark chocolate pieces (about ⅓ cup)

1 Peel bananas. Slice bananas into ½-inch-thick pieces. Line a baking sheet with waxed paper. Arrange banana pieces in a single layer on the prepared baking sheet.

2 In a heavy small saucepan melt chocolate over low heat. Cool slightly. Place melted chocolate in a small resealable plastic bag. Seal bag and snip off a tiny corner. Drizzle chocolate over banana slices. Cover and freeze for 1 to 2 hours or until frozen.

3 Divide banana pieces among four freezer containers or small resealable freezer bags. Freeze for up to 3 days.

nutrition facts per serving: 112 cal., 4 g total fat (0 g sat. fat), 1 mg chol., 1 mg sodium, 20 g carb. (2 g fiber, 12 g sugars), 1 g pro. exchanges: 1 fruit, 1 high-fat meat, 1 fat.

If you like piña colada, be sure to try the coconut-flavor yogurt option. When it's melded with the fruits, the hint of coconut will take you to tropical island heaven!

tropical smoothie

25g
CARB. PER SERVING

prep: 15 minutes freeze: 4 hours
makes: 4 servings (¾ cup each)

1 small banana, peeled and cut up
3 cups frozen mixed fruit blend (pineapple, strawberries, mango, and/or peaches)
1 6-ounce carton vanilla or coconut fat-free yogurt
¾ to 1 cup diet tropical blend carrot-based drink
   Pineapple wedges (optional)

1 Freeze banana pieces in a resealable freezer bag about 4 hours or until frozen.

2 In a blender combine frozen banana and frozen fruit blend. Add yogurt and ¾ cup of the tropical drink. Cover and blend until smooth, adding more tropical drink as needed to reach desired consistency. Divide mixture among four glasses. If desired, garnish each serving with a pineapple wedge.

nutrition facts per serving: 107 cal., 0 g total fat, 3 mg chol., 33 mg sodium, 25 g carb. (2 g fiber, 19 g sugars), 2 g pro. exchanges: 1 fruit, 0.5 starch.

test kitchen tip: For single-serving smoothies, prepare recipe and freeze in individual portions. Let individual portions stand at room temperature for about 20 minutes before serving, stirring occasionally after mixture begins to thaw.

8g
CARB. PER
SERVING

*When fresh sweet cherries are in
season, halve and pit a few to use
in combination with the berries.*

fruity applesauce pops

prep: 25 minutes freeze: overnight
makes: 16 servings (1 pop each)

1   32-ounce jar
     unsweetened
     applesauce
2   cups assorted fresh
     berries, such
     as raspberries,
     blackberries,
     blueberries, and
     sliced strawberries

In a large bowl stir together the applesauce
and berries. Spoon into 16 freezer pop
containers. Cover and freeze overnight. (Or
spoon into 5-ounce paper cups. Cover cups
with plastic wrap; secure wrap with tape or a
rubber band. Insert a flat wooden crafts stick
through the plastic wrap into applesauce
mixture in each cup. Freeze overnight.)

nutrition facts per serving: 32 cal., 0 g total fat, 0 mg
chol., 1 mg sodium, 8 g carb. (1 g fiber, 6 g sugars), 0 g pro.
exchanges: 0.5 fruit.

Who needs ice cream or sherbet when you can beat the heat and satisfy your sweet tooth with something so much better for you?

frozen fruit cup

prep: 15 minutes freeze: 4 hours stand: 30 minutes
makes: 8 servings (½ cup each)

2   cups chopped
      cantaloupe
2   cups coarsely
      chopped fresh
      strawberries
1   cup fresh raspberries
1   cup fresh
      blackberries, halved
2   tablespoons sugar*
½   teaspoon finely
      shredded lemon
      peel

1 In a large bowl combine cantaloupe, strawberries, raspberries, blackberries, sugar, and lemon peel. Transfer 2 cups of the mixture to a food processor. Cover and process until mixture is smooth. Return to whole fruit mixture.

2 Divide mixture into eight 4-ounce individual storage containers or small glasses or paper cups. Freeze for 4 to 24 hours or until frozen.

3 To serve, let frozen mixture stand for 30 to 40 minutes or until slightly thawed and slushy.**

nutrition facts per serving: 53 cal., 0 g total fat, 0 mg chol., 7 mg sodium, 13 g carb. (3 g fiber, 10 g sugars), 1 g pro.
exchanges: 1 fruit.

nutrition facts per serving with substitute: Same as original, except 141 cal., 10 g carb. (6 g sugars).

*sugar substitutes: Choose from Splenda Granular, Equal bulk or packets, or Sweet'N Low bulk or packets. Follow package directions to use product amount equivalent to 2 tablespoons sugar.

**test kitchen tip: To serve more quickly, run the bottom of an individual container under hot water for 30 seconds. Transfer one serving to a small microwave-safe bowl. Microwave on 100 percent power (high) for 45 seconds to 1 minute or until partially thawed, breaking up with a fork after 30 seconds.

Fresh lime ramps up the refreshing citrusy appeal of the cherry-limeade drink mix, and the berries add a delightfully sweet contrast. Pictured on page 381.

fruity-limeade slushy

start to finish: 10 minutes
makes: 4 servings (1½ cups each)

good-for-you snacks

1 lime
3 cups water
4 2.2-gram packets
    low-calorie cherry-
    limeade drink mix
3 cups ice
2 cups frozen mixed
    berries
4 lime slices

Finely shred 1 teaspoon peel from the whole lime. Squeeze juice from the lime into a blender. Add lime peel, the water, and dry drink mix to lime juice in blender. Cover and blend until drink mix is dissolved. Add ice and mixed berries. Cover and blend until mixture is combined and ice is crushed. Pour into four glasses. Garnish with lime slices.

nutrition facts per serving: 50 cal., 0 g total fat, 0 mg chol., 6 mg sodium, 12 g carb. (3 g fiber, 6 g sugars), 1 g pro.
exchanges: 0.5 fruit, 0.5 carb.

Using frozen fruit instead of ice helps pack some major flavor and nutrients into this frosty and fresh snack drink.

pineapple-melon slushy

23g
CARB. PER
SERVING

prep: 20 minutes freeze: 2 hours
makes: 4 servings (1¼ cups each)

3 cups cubed
  honeydew melon
1½ cups cold water
½ cup orange juice
½ 16-ounce package
  frozen pineapple
  chunks (2 cups)
  Orange peel twists

1 Place melon chunks in a 13×9×2-inch baking pan. Freeze about 2 hours or until solidly frozen.

2 Place the water, orange juice, and about ⅓ cup of the fruit in a blender. Cover and process until smooth. Gradually add remaining fruit, processing after each addition until smooth. Divide among four tall glasses. Garnish each serving with an orange peel twist.

nutrition facts per serving: 96 cal., 0 g total fat, 0 mg chol., 30 mg sodium, 23 g carb. (2 g fiber, 19 g sugars), 1 g pro. exchanges: 1.5 fruit.

Plan ahead! Keep something sensible on hand to satisfy your craving for a sweet treat so you won't be tempted with less-healthful options. Thanks to the right ingredients, these cookies and bars will fit your dietary goals.

favorite cook

fruited oatmeal cookies,
page 416

ies
&bars

Love oatmeal cookies? You'll like them even more when they're chock-full of sweet dried fruits and rich, flavorful walnuts. Pictured on page 415.

17g
CARB. PER
SERVING

fruited oatmeal cookies

prep: 25 minutes bake: 9 minutes per batch
makes: 48 servings (1 cookie each)

2 cups rolled oats
  Nonstick cooking
    spray
½ cup butter, softened
1½ cups packed brown
    sugar*
¾ teaspoon baking soda
¼ teaspoon salt
¼ teaspoon ground
    allspice
1 6-ounce carton plain
    low-fat yogurt
½ cup refrigerated or
    frozen egg product,
    thawed, or 2 eggs,
    lightly beaten
1 teaspoon vanilla
2¼ cups flour
¼ cup snipped dried
    apricots
¼ cup currants
¼ cup chopped walnuts,
    toasted

1 Preheat oven to 375°F. Spread oats in a shallow baking pan. Bake about 10 minutes or until toasted, stirring once; set aside. Lightly coat cookie sheet with cooking spray; set aside.

2 In a large mixing bowl beat butter with an electric mixer on medium speed for 30 seconds. Add brown sugar, baking soda, salt, and allspice; beat until combined. Beat in yogurt, eggs, and vanilla. Beat in as much of the flour as you can with the mixer. Using a wooden spoon, stir in oats, apricots, currants, walnuts, and any remaining flour. Drop dough by rounded teaspoons 2 inches apart on prepared cookie sheet.

3 Bake for 9 to 11 minutes or until edges and bottoms are browned. Transfer cookies to a wire rack; let cool. To store, place cookies in an airtight container; cover. Store at room temperature for up to 3 days or freeze for up to 3 months.

nutrition facts per serving: 101 cal., 3 g total fat (1 g sat. fat), 5 mg chol., 55 mg sodium, 17 g carb. (1 g fiber, 8 g sugars), 2 g pro. exchanges: 0.5 starch, 0.5 carb., 0.5 fat.

nutrition facts per serving with substitute: Same as original, except 90 cal., 53 mg sodium, 13 g carb. (4 g sugars).

*sugar substitute: Choose Splenda Brown Sugar Blend. Follow package directions to use product amount equivalent to 1½ cups brown sugar.

Substitute other dried fruits depending on what you crave: snipped dried apricots or dried cranberries will also work well with the flavors here.

carrot raisin cookies

14g
CARB. PER SERVING

prep: 30 minutes **bake:** 8 minutes per batch
makes: 36 servings (1 cookie each)

½   cup butter, softened
1   cup packed brown
      sugar✳
2   teaspoons baking
      soda
1   teaspoon ground
      cinnamon
1   teaspoon ground
      ginger
¼   teaspoon salt
1   egg
¼   cup unsweetened
      applesauce
1   teaspoon vanilla
2   cups whole wheat
      flour
1   cup finely shredded
      carrots (2 medium)
¾   cup raisins
¾   cup finely chopped
      walnuts

1 Preheat oven to 375°F. In a large bowl beat butter with an electric mixer on medium speed for 30 seconds. Add brown sugar, baking soda, cinnamon, ginger, and salt; beat until combined. Beat in egg, applesauce, and vanilla. Beat in as much of the flour as you can. Stir in any remaining flour, the carrots, raisins, and walnuts just until combined.

2 Drop dough by slightly rounded teaspoons 2 inches apart onto ungreased cookie sheets. Bake for 8 to 9 minutes or until edges are firm. Transfer cookies to a wire rack; cool completely. To store, layer between sheets of waxed paper in an airtight container; cover. Store in the refrigerator for up to 3 days or freeze for up to 3 months.

nutrition facts per serving: 98 cal., 4 g total fat (2 g sat. fat), 12 mg chol., 115 mg sodium, 14 g carb. (1 g fiber, 8 g sugars), 2 g pro. exchanges: 0.5 starch, 0.5 carb., 0.5 fat.

nutrition facts per serving with substitute: Same as original, except 88 cal., 113 mg sodium, 11 g carb. (5 g sugars). exchanges: 0 carb., 1 fat.

✳sugar substitute: Choose Splenda Brown Sugar Baking Blend. Follow package directions to use product amount equivalent to 1 cup brown sugar.

11g
CARB. PER
SERVING

These heavenly puffs of yum are a diabetes-smart way to enjoy one of the world's all-time-best flavor duos.

chocolate-coconut macaroons

prep: 30 minutes **bake:** 15 minutes **stand:** 25 minutes
makes: 18 servings (1 macaroon each)

2   egg whites
½   teaspoon vanilla
⅛   teaspoon cream of tartar
     Dash salt
⅔   cup sugar✱
¾   cup shredded coconut
2   ounces dark chocolate or semisweet chocolate, coarsely grated

1 Preheat oven to 325°F. Line two cookie sheets with parchment paper; set aside. In a large mixing bowl beat egg whites, vanilla, cream of tartar, and salt with an electric mixer on high speed until soft peaks form (tips curl). Gradually add sugar, about 1 tablespoon at a time, beating until stiff peaks form (tips stand straight). Gently fold in ½ cup of the coconut and the chocolate.

2 Drop mixture into a total of 18 mounds on the prepared cookie sheets, using 2 tablespoons of the egg white mixture for each mound and leaving about 1 inch between the mounds. Sprinkle tops with remaining ¼ cup coconut. Place cookie sheets on separate oven racks. Bake for 15 minutes. Rotate cookie sheets in oven by putting cookie sheet that was on top rack on bottom rack and bottom-rack cookie sheet on top rack. Turn off oven; let macaroons dry in oven for 25 minutes. Transfer macaroons to a wire rack and let cool.

✱ sugar substitute: We do not recommend using a sugar substitute for this recipe.

nutrition facts per serving: 72 cal., 3 g total fat (2 g sat. fat), 0 mg chol., 28 mg sodium, 11 g carb. (1 g fiber, 11 g sugars), 1 g pro. exchanges: 1 carb., 0.5 fat.

For easy cleanup, place the baked cookies on a cooling rack over waxed paper. Drizzle the glaze over the cookies, allowing the excess to drip onto the waxed paper instead of your countertop!

almond-chocolate-cherry cookies

14g
CARB. PER
SERVING

prep: 30 minutes chill: 1 hour bake: 10 minutes per batch
makes: 32 servings (1 cookie each)

- 6 tablespoons butter, softened
- ¾ cup granulated sugar*
- 1 egg
- 1 egg yolk
- 1 teaspoon vanilla
- 1 ounce sweet baking, bittersweet, or semisweet chocolate, melted and cooled slightly
- 1⅓ cups flour
- ½ cup dried cherries
- ⅓ cup sliced almonds
- 1 recipe Chocolate-Almond Glaze

1 In a medium bowl beat butter with an electric mixer on medium-high speed about 2 minutes or until smooth. Add granulated sugar, beating until creamy. Beat in egg, egg yolk, and vanilla until combined. Stir in melted chocolate. Stir in flour. Fold in dried cherries and almonds. Cover and chill dough for 1 hour.

2 Preheat oven to 350°F. Line cookie sheets with parchment paper; set aside. Shape dough into 1-inch balls. Place balls about 1 inch apart on prepared cookie sheets. Bake for 10 to 12 minutes or until centers are set. Transfer cookies to wire racks; cool completely.

3 Drizzle Chocolate-Almond Glaze over cooled cookies. Let stand until glaze is set. To store, layer cookies between sheets of waxed paper in an airtight container; cover. Store in the refrigerator for up to 3 days or freeze for up to 3 months.

nutrition facts per serving: 88 cal., 4 g total fat (2 g sat. fat), 18 mg chol., 25 mg sodium, 14 g carb. (0 g fiber, 9 g sugars), 1 g pro. exchanges: 0.5 starch, 0.5 carb., 0.5 fat.

nutrition facts per serving with substitute: Same as original, except 81 cal., 11 g carb. (6 g sugars).

*sugar substitute: Use Splenda Sugar Blend. Follow package directions to use product amount equivalent to ¾ cup granulated sugar.

chocolate-almond glaze: In a small saucepan combine ½ ounce sweet baking, bittersweet, or semisweet chocolate and 1½ teaspoons butter. Heat and stir over low heat until melted and smooth. Remove from heat. Stir in ½ cup powdered sugar, 1 tablespoon fat-free milk, and a dash of almond extract until smooth.

Another time, try dried cherries instead of the dried cranberries and toasted pecans in place of the almonds.

8g
CARB. PER
SERVING

cranberry-almond slice-and-bake cookies

prep: 25 minutes chill: about 2 hours bake: 8 minutes per batch
makes: 48 servings (1 cookie each)

⅔ cup butter, softened
1 8-ounce can almond paste
¼ cup granulated sugar*
1 teaspoon baking powder
¼ teaspoon salt
¼ cup refrigerated or frozen egg product, thawed, or 1 egg
2 teaspoons finely shredded orange peel (optional)
2 cups flour
⅓ cup dried cranberries, finely chopped
¼ cup toasted almonds, very finely chopped
1 recipe Orange Glaze (optional)

1 In a large bowl beat butter with an electric mixer on medium speed for 30 seconds. Add almond paste, sugar, baking powder, and salt; beat until well combined. Beat in egg and, if desired, the 2 teaspoons orange peel. Beat in as much of the flour as you can. Stir in any remaining flour, the cranberries, and the almonds.

2 Divide dough in half. Shape each dough portion into an 8-inch-long log. Wrap logs in plastic wrap. Chill about 2 hours or until firm enough to slice.

3 Preheat oven to 350°F. Cut logs crosswise into ¼-inch-thick slices. Place slices 1 inch apart on ungreased cookie sheets.

4 Bake for 8 to 10 minutes or until edges are firm and centers are set. Transfer cookies to a wire rack and let cool. If desired, drizzle with Orange Glaze. To store, layer unglazed cookies between sheets of waxed paper in an airtight container; cover. Store at room temperature for up to 3 days or freeze for up to 3 months. If desired, drizzle with glaze before serving.

nutrition facts per serving: 73 cal., 4 g total fat (2 g sat. fat), 7 mg chol., 45 mg sodium, 8 g carb. (0 g fiber, 3 g sugars), 1 g pro. exchanges: 0.5 starch, 0.5 fat.

nutrition facts per serving with substitute: Same as original, except 72 cal., 8 g carb. (3 g sugars).

*sugar substitutes: Choose from C&H Light Sugar and Stevia Blend, Splenda Sugar Blend for Baking, or Sun Crystals Granulated Blend. Follow package directions to use product amount equivalent to ¼ cup granulated sugar.

orange glaze: In a small bowl combine ½ cup powdered sugar and ¼ teaspoon finely shredded orange peel. Using 2 to 3 teaspoons orange juice or fat-free milk, stir in enough to make drizzling consistency.

Need a pick-me-up? A soft sugar cookie and a cup of coffee or tea is one of the best ways to beat the late-afternoon blahs.

soft sugar cookies

11g
CARB. PER SERVING

prep: 25 minutes   bake: 14 minutes per batch   cool: 1 minute
makes: 48 servings (1 cookie each)

½   cup butter, softened
4   ounces cream cheese, softened
1¾ cups sugar✶
1   teaspoon baking soda
1   teaspoon cream of tartar
⅛   teaspoon salt
3   egg yolks
½   teaspoon vanilla
1¼ cups all-purpose flour
½   cup white whole wheat flour

✶sugar substitutes: Choose from Splenda Sugar Blend for Baking or Sun Crystals Granulated Blend. Follow package directions to use product amount equivalent to 1¾ cups sugar. Bake as directed, except reduce baking time to 12 to 14 minutes.

1 Preheat oven to 300°F. In a large mixing bowl beat butter and cream cheese with an electric mixer on medium to high speed for 30 seconds. Add sugar, baking soda, cream of tartar, and salt. Beat mixture until combined, scraping sides of bowl occasionally. Beat in egg yolks and vanilla. Beat in as much of the all-purpose flour and white whole wheat flour as you can with the mixer. Stir in any remaining flour with a wooden spoon.

2 Shape dough into balls that are 1 inch in diameter. Place balls 2 inches apart on ungreased cookie sheets.

3 Bake for 14 to 16 minutes or until edges are set;✶ do not let edges brown. Cool cookies for 1 minute on cookie sheet. Transfer cookies to a wire rack and let cool.

nutrition facts per serving: 73 cal., 3 g total fat (2 g sat. fat), 19 mg chol., 57 mg sodium, 11 g carb. (0 g fiber, 7 g sugars), 1 g pro. exchanges: 0.5 starch, 0.5 fat.

nutrition facts per serving with substitute: Same as original, except 62 cal., 7 g carb. (4 g sugars).

You'll have an easier time bypassing those doughnuts a coworker brought in when you know one of these gems waits in your lunch bag.

9g
CARB. PER
SERVING

molasses cookies

prep: 30 minutes chill: 1 hour bake: 7 minutes per batch
makes: 48 servings (1 cookie each)

⅓ cup margarine, softened
⅔ cup packed dark brown sugar*
1 teaspoon baking soda
1 teaspoon ground ginger
½ teaspoon ground cinnamon
¼ cup refrigerated or frozen egg product, thawed, or 1 egg
¼ cup mild molasses
1½ cups all-purpose flour
½ cup white whole wheat flour
 Nonstick cooking spray
2 tablespoons granulated sugar**
½ teaspoon ground cinnamon

1 In a large mixing bowl beat margarine with an electric mixer on medium to high speed for 30 seconds. Add brown sugar, baking soda, ginger, and ½ teaspoon cinnamon. Beat mixture until combined. Beat in egg and molasses. Beat in as much of the all-purpose and white whole wheat flour as you can with the mixer. Stir in any remaining flour with a wooden spoon. Cover and chill in the refrigerator for 1 hour.

2 Lightly coat cookie sheet with cooking spray; set aside. Preheat oven to 350°F.

3 Shape dough into balls that are slightly less than 1 inch in diameter. In a small dish combine the granulated sugar and ½ teaspoon cinnamon. Roll balls in sugar-cinnamon mixture. Place balls 2 inches apart on prepared cookie sheet. Flatten each ball to a ½-inch thickness with bottom of a glass, dipping glass in the sugar mixture if it sticks. Bake for 7 minutes or until edges are set. Remove from cookie sheet; transfer cookies to a wire rack and let cool.

nutrition facts per serving: 48 cal., 1 g total fat (0 g sat. fat), 0 mg chol., 45 mg sodium, 9 g carb. (0 g fiber, 5 g sugars), 1 g pro. exchanges: 0.5 starch.

nutrition facts per serving with substitute: Same as original, except 44 cal., 44 mg sodium, 7 g carb. (3 sugars).

*sugar substitute: Choose Splenda Brown Sugar Baking Blend. Follow package directions to use product amount equivalent to ⅔ cup brown sugar. Baking time may need to be decreased slightly.

**sugar substitute: We do not recommend using a sugar substitute for granulated sugar used to coat the cookies.

These two-tone brownies are so rich and luscious, no one will believe how low in fat and calories they are.

17g
CARB. PER
SERVING

peanut butter swirl chocolate brownies

prep: 25 minutes bake: 20 minutes
makes: 20 servings (1 brownie each)

Nonstick cooking
   spray
¼ cup butter
¾ cup sugar✱
⅓ cup cold water
¾ cup refrigerated or
   frozen egg product,
   thawed, or 3 eggs,
   lightly beaten
¼ cup canola oil
1 teaspoon vanilla
1¼ cups flour
1 teaspoon baking
   powder
¼ cup creamy peanut
   butter
½ cup unsweetened
   cocoa powder
¼ cup miniature
   semisweet
   chocolate pieces

1 Preheat oven to 350°F. Line a 9×9×2-inch baking pan with foil, extending foil up over the edges of the pan. Lightly coat foil with cooking spray. Set aside.

2 In a medium saucepan melt butter over low heat; remove from heat. Whisk in sugar and the water. Whisk in egg, oil, and vanilla until combined. Stir in 1 cup of the flour and the baking powder until combined. (Batter will be thin at this point.) Place peanut butter in a small bowl; gradually whisk in ½ cup of the batter until smooth. Set aside. In another small bowl combine the remaining ¼ cup flour and the cocoa powder; stir into the plain batter. Stir chocolate pieces into chocolate batter; pour chocolate batter into prepared pan.

3 Drop peanut butter batter in small mounds over chocolate batter in pan. Using a thin metal spatula, swirl batters together. Bake for 20 to 25 minutes✱ or until top springs back when lightly touched and a toothpick inserted near the center comes out clean. Cool completely in pan on a wire rack. Cut into 20 bars.

nutrition facts per serving: 151 cal., 8 g total fat (3 g sat. fat), 6 mg chol., 61 mg sodium, 17 g carb. (0 g fiber, 10 g sugars), 3 g pro. exchanges: 1 carb., 1.5 fat.

nutrition facts per serving with substitute: Same as original, except 140 cal., 13 g carb. (6 g sugars).

✱sugar substitutes: Choose from Splenda Sugar Blend or Sun Crystals Granulated Blend. Follow package directions to use product amount equivalent to ¾ cup sugar. Decrease baking time to 15 to 18 minutes or until top springs back when lightly touched and a toothpick inserted near the center comes out clean.

Canned pumpkin is sometimes used to stand in for some of the fat and eggs in baked goods; however, there's a trick to getting just the right proportions. Our Test Kitchen nailed it in these bars!

red velvet pumpkin bars

prep: 30 minutes bake: 25 minutes
makes: 24 servings (1 bar each)

2 teaspoons all-purpose flour
1½ cups all-purpose flour
1⅓ cups granulated sugar ✱
½ cup whole wheat flour
3 tablespoons unsweetened cocoa powder
1 teaspoon baking soda
½ teaspoon salt
½ teaspoon pumpkin pie spice
1 15-ounce can pumpkin
1 5.3- to 6-ounce carton plain fat-free Greek yogurt
½ cup refrigerated or frozen egg product, thawed
⅓ cup canola oil
1 tablespoon red food coloring
1½ teaspoons vanilla
1 teaspoon cider vinegar
1 1.3-ounce envelope whipped dessert topping mix
¼ cup whipped light cream cheese
3 tablespoons fat-free milk
2 tablespoons powdered sugar
½ teaspoon vanilla Unsweetened cocoa powder

1 Preheat oven to 350°F. Coat a 15×10×1-inch baking pan with *nonstick cooking spray.* Gently wipe pan interior with a paper towel so bottom and sides are evenly coated with spray. Dust with the 2 teaspoons all-purpose flour; set aside.

2 In a large bowl sift together the 1½ cups all-purpose flour, granulated sugar, whole wheat flour, the 3 tablespoons cocoa powder, baking soda, salt, and pumpkin pie spice.

3 In a medium bowl combine pumpkin, yogurt, egg, canola oil, food coloring, the 1½ teaspoons vanilla, and the vinegar. Add to flour mixture, stirring just until combined. Spread into the prepared baking pan.

4 Bake 25 to 30 minutes or until a toothpick inserted near the center comes out clean. Cool in pan on a wire rack. Cut into 24 bars.

5 For topping, in a medium bowl combine dessert topping mix, cream cheese, milk, powdered sugar, and the ½ teaspoon vanilla. Beat with an electric mixer on high speed until stiff peaks form (tips stand straight). Cover and chill until needed.

6 To serve, top each bar with a tablespoon-size dollop of the topping. Sprinkle with additional cocoa powder.

nutrition facts per serving: 137 cal., 4 g total fat (1 g sat. fat), 1 mg chol., 128 mg sodium, 24 g carb. (1 g fiber, 14 g sugars), 3 g pro. exchanges: 1.5 starch, 1 fat.

nutrition facts per serving with substitute: Same as original, except 120 cal., 18 g carb. (8 g sugars). exchanges: 1 starch.

✱ sugar substitutes: Choose from Splenda Sugar Blend or C&H Light Sugar & Stevia Blend. Follow package directions to use product amount equivalent to 1⅓ cups granulated sugar.

15g
CARB. PER
SERVING

With all the supersize muffins out there, portion control can be a challenge. These let you enjoy the flavors of a blueberry muffin and easily keep track of what you eat.

blueberry muffin bars

prep: 25 minutes bake: 30 minutes
makes: 32 servings (1 bar each)

Nonstick cooking
  spray
1¾ cups quick-cooking
  rolled oats
¾ cup all-purpose flour
¾ cup whole wheat
  flour
¾ cup packed brown
  sugar∗
1 teaspoon apple pie
  spice
½ cup light butter
  (1 stick)
½ cup coarsely chopped
  slivered almonds
1 cup sugar-free
  blueberry preserves
½ teaspoon almond
  extract

∗ sugar substitute: We do not recommend using a sugar substitute for the brown sugar for this recipe.

1 Preheat oven to 350°F. Line a 13×9×2-inch baking pan with foil, extending foil up over the edges of the pan. Lightly coat foil with cooking spray; set aside.

2 In a large bowl combine oats, all-purpose flour, whole wheat flour, brown sugar, and apple pie spice. Using a pastry blender, cut in light butter until mixture is crumbly. Transfer ¾ cup of the crumb mixture to a small bowl; stir in almonds. Set aside.

3 Press remaining crumb mixture into the bottom of the prepared pan. Bake for 10 minutes.

4 In a small bowl stir together the preserves and almond extract. Carefully spread preserves evenly over crust. Sprinkle with reserved crumb mixture; press lightly.

5 Bake for 20 to 25 minutes or until top is lightly browned. Cool completely in pan on wire rack. Lift from pan using foil and cut into bars. Wrap remaining bars in foil to store.

nutrition facts per serving: 89 cal., 3 g total fat (1 g sat. fat), 4 mg chol., 18 mg sodium, 15 g carb. (1 g fiber, 5 g sugars), 2 g pro. exchanges: 0.5 fruit, 0.5 starch, 0.5 fat.

Cooks tend to bring their most diet-undoing desserts to the potluck table. Why not offer these creamy bars and treat diners to something more healthful they can enjoy?

raspberry-lemon cheesecake bars

prep: 30 minutes bake: 40 minutes chill: 2 hours
makes: 16 servings (1 bar each)

⅔ cup flour
⅔ cup ground unsalted pretzels (about 1¾ cup pretzels)
3 tablespoons packed brown sugar∗
½ cup light butter with canola oil, melted
12 ounces reduced-fat cream cheese (Neufchâtel), softened
¼ cup granulated sugar∗
1½ teaspoons vanilla
1 teaspoon finely shredded lemon peel
¾ cup refrigerated or frozen egg product, thawed, or 3 eggs, beaten
1 cup fresh raspberries
2 tablespoons powdered sugar

1 Preheat oven to 350°F. Grease an 8×8×2-inch baking pan or line pan with foil, extending foil up over the edges of the pan; set aside. In a medium bowl stir together flour, ground pretzels, and brown sugar. Stir in light butter just until combined. Press crumbs into the bottom of the prepared pan. Bake for 15 minutes.

2 Meanwhile, in a medium bowl beat cream cheese with an electric mixer on medium speed just until smooth. Beat in granulated sugar, vanilla, and lemon peel until light and fluffy. Gradually add egg, beating on low speed just until combined. Spread cream cheese mixture over partially baked crust. Sprinkle with raspberries.

3 Bake for 25 to 30 minutes or until cream cheese layer is set. Cool completely in pan on a wire rack. Cover and chill for 2 to 24 hours before serving. Dust with powdered sugar before serving. Cut into bars to serve. Store in the refrigerator.

nutrition facts per serving: 148 cal., 6 g total fat (3 g sat. fat), 16 mg chol., 178 mg sodium, 18 g carb. (1 g fiber, 8 g sugars), 4 g pro. exchanges: 1 starch, 1 fat.

nutrition facts per serving with substitutes: Same as original, except 141 cal., 177 mg sodium, 15 g carb. (6 g sugars).

∗sugar substitutes: Choose Sweet'N Low Brown to substitute for the brown sugar. Choose Splenda Sugar Blend for Baking or Equal Sugar Lite to substitute for the granulated sugar. Follow package directions to use product amounts equivalent to 3 tablespoons brown sugar and ¼ cup granulated sugar.

Lining the baking pan with foil makes lifting the uncut baked brownies from the pan easy.

layered brownies

prep: 30 minutes bake: 25 minutes
makes: 24 servings (1 brownie each)

⅔ cup packed brown
sugar✳

⅔ cup tub-style
vegetable oil spread

¼ teaspoon baking soda

¾ cup refrigerated or
frozen egg product,
thawed, or 3 eggs,
lightly beaten

2 cups flour

1½ cups quick-cooking
rolled oats

¼ cup granulated
sugar✳

¼ cup canola oil

3 tablespoons
unsweetened cocoa
powder

½ teaspoon baking
powder

2 tablespoons miniature
semisweet
chocolate pieces

2 tablespoons chopped
walnuts

2 tablespoons quick-
cooking rolled oats

✳ sugar substitutes: Choose
Splenda Brown Sugar Blend for
the brown sugar. Choose Splenda
Granular or Sweet'N Low bulk or
packets for the granulated sugar.
Follow package directions to use
product amounts equivalent to
⅔ cup brown sugar and ¼ cup
granulated sugar.

1 Preheat oven to 350°F. Line a 9×9×2-inch
baking pan with foil, extending foil up
over the edges of the pan. Lightly grease the
foil. Set aside.

2 For crust, in a large mixing bowl beat
brown sugar, vegetable oil spread,
and baking soda with an electric mixer on
medium speed until well mixed, scraping bowl
occasionally. Beat in ¼ cup of the egg product
or one of the eggs. Beat in 1½ cups of the
flour. Stir in the 1½ cups oats.

3 Set aside ½ cup of the oat mixture. Spread
the remaining oat mixture into the bottom
of the prepared pan. Bake about 12 minutes or
just until crust is set.

4 Meanwhile, in a medium bowl whisk
together the remaining ½ cup egg
product or 2 eggs, the granulated sugar, and
oil. Stir in the remaining ½ cup flour, the cocoa
powder, and baking powder. Stir in semisweet
chocolate pieces. Pour evenly over partially
baked crust. If necessary, gently spread with a
metal spatula. Stir nuts and the 2 tablespoons
oats into the reserved oat mixture (mixture
may be a little soft). Crumble over the top of
the mixture in the baking pan.

5 Bake for 13 to 15 minutes or until the top is
puffed and set. Cool completely in pan on
a wire rack. Using the edges of the foil, lift the
uncut brownies out of the pan; cut into bars. To
store, layer brownies between waxed paper in an
airtight container; cover. Store in the refrigerator
for up to 5 days or freeze for up to 3 months.

nutrition facts per serving: 163 cal., 8 g total fat (2 g sat.
fat), 0 mg chol., 75 mg sodium, 21 g carb. (1 g fiber, 9 g sugars),
3 g pro. exchanges: 1.5 carb., 1.5 fat.

nutrition facts per serving with substitutes: Same
as original, except 145 cal., 73 mg sodium, 16 g carb. (4 g sugars).
exchanges: 1 carb.

Stored in a single layer in an airtight container, these rich, nutty squares will keep at room temperature for up to 3 days. However, be sure to let the chocolate set before storing.

caramel-cashew blondies

26g
CARB. PER SERVING

prep: 20 minutes bake: 18 minutes
makes: 16 servings (1 bar each)

Nonstick cooking spray
1 cup packed brown sugar＊
½ cup light butter
½ cup refrigerated or frozen egg product, thawed, or 2 eggs, lightly beaten
2 tablespoons fat-free milk
1½ teaspoons vanilla
1 cup all-purpose flour
½ cup whole wheat pastry flour or whole wheat flour
¾ teaspoon baking powder
¼ teaspoon ground cinnamon
⅛ teaspoon baking soda
½ cup lightly salted dry-roasted cashews, chopped
1 ounce semisweet chocolate, melted
2 tablespoons sugar-free caramel-flavor ice cream topping

1 Preheat oven to 350°F. Line a 9×9×2-inch baking pan with foil, extending foil up over the edges of the pan. Coat the foil with cooking spray; set aside.

2 In a medium saucepan heat brown sugar and butter over medium heat until butter melts and mixture is smooth, stirring constantly. Remove from heat. Cool slightly. Stir in eggs until well combined. Stir in milk and vanilla. Stir in all-purpose and whole wheat flours, baking powder, cinnamon, and baking soda. Spread batter in prepared baking pan. Sprinkle with cashews.

3 Bake for 18 to 20 minutes or until edges are browned and a toothpick inserted near center comes out clean. Cool in pan on a wire rack.

4 To serve, lift uncut bars from pan using foil. Drizzle the top with melted chocolate. If necessary, stir to soften caramel topping. Drizzle the top with caramel topping. Cut into 16 bars to serve.

nutrition facts per serving: 167 cal., 6 g total fat (3 g sat. fat), 8 mg chol., 110 mg sodium, 26 g carb. (1 g fiber, 15 g sugars), 3 g pro. exchanges: 1 starch, 1 carb., 1 fat.

nutrition facts per serving with substitute: Same as original, except 145 calories, 106 mg sodium, 18 g carb. (7 g sugars). exchanges: 0 carb.

＊sugar substitute: Choose Splenda Brown Sugar Blend. Follow package directions to use product amount equivalent to 1 cup brown sugar.

lemony tea cake,
page 434

delightful

des

Chocolate pie, bread pudding, cheesecake, baklava, custard—if you thought these and other desserts were off limits, take a peek into this chapter. Each recipe proves you can end your meal on a sweet high *and* follow your meal plan.

serts

delightful desserts

Save prep time by purchasing a container of chopped fresh pineapple instead of cleaning and chopping a whole one.

tropical cake squares

prep: 40 minutes bake: 18 minutes cool: 5 minutes
makes: 24 servings (1 frosted cake square and 2 tablespoons topping each)

Nonstick cooking
   spray
1 package 2-layer-size
   sugar-free yellow
   cake mix
1 teaspoon water
6 egg whites or ¾ cup
   refrigerated or
   frozen egg product,
   thawed
⅓ cup canola oil
1¼ cups plain fat-free
   Greek yogurt
6 ounces fat-free cream
   cheese, softened
⅓ cup sugar✱
1½ teaspoons vanilla
1 cup chopped fresh
   pineapple
1 cup fresh blueberries
½ cup shredded
   coconut, toasted

1 Preheat oven to 325°F. Coat a 15×10×1-inch baking pan with cooking spray; line with parchment paper. Set aside.

2 In a large bowl combine cake mix, the water, egg whites, and oil. Mix according to package directions. Pour batter into the prepared pan, using the back of a spoon to spread evenly. Bake about 18 minutes or until a toothpick inserted in the center comes out clean. Cool in pan on a wire rack for 5 minutes. Invert pan and cake together; remove pan. Cool cake completely on wire rack. Carefully remove parchment paper.

3 Meanwhile, in a food processor or blender combine yogurt, cream cheese, sugar, and vanilla. Cover and process or blend until smooth, stopping occasionally to scrape sides and push mixture into blades. Transfer to a small bowl. Chill until needed.

4 To serve, cut cake into 2½-inch squares. Spoon 1 tablespoon of the cream cheese mixture onto each square. Top each square with about 1½ tablespoons fruit and 1 teaspoon toasted coconut.

nutrition facts per serving: 130 cal., 5 g total fat (2 g sat. fat), 1 mg chol., 210 mg sodium, 20 g carb. (0 g fiber, 5 g sugars), 4 g pro. exchanges: 1 starch, 1 fat.

nutrition facts per serving with substitute: Same as original, except 120 cal., 18 g carb. (3 g sugars).

✱sugar substitutes: Choose from Splenda Granular, Equal Classic Spoonful or packets, or Sweet'N Low bulk or packets. Follow package directions to use product amount equivalent to ⅓ cup sugar.

Use a long serrated knife to carefully cut this stacked cake into wedges. Between cuts, wipe the knife clean with a damp paper towel. Pictured on page 430.

33g CARB. PER SERVING

lemony tea cake

prep: 40 minutes   stand: 30 minutes   bake: 18 minutes   cool: 10 minutes
makes: 12 servings (1 wedge each)

3	eggs
1½	cups flour
2	tablespoons poppy seeds
1½	teaspoons baking powder
¾	cup fat-free milk
2	individual-size bags green tea
3	tablespoons butter, cut up
2	tablespoons honey
1	tablespoon finely shredded lemon peel
1	teaspoon vanilla
¾	cup sugar∗
¼	cup pomegranate seeds
2	teaspoons finely shredded lemon peel
1	tablespoon lemon juice
1	tablespoon honey
1	5- to 6-ounce carton plain fat-free Greek yogurt
1	cup frozen light whipped dessert topping, thawed
¼	cup pomegranate seeds

1 Allow eggs to stand at room temperature for 30 minutes. Meanwhile, grease and lightly flour two 8-inch round cake pans; set pans aside. In a bowl combine flour, poppy seeds, baking powder, and ¼ teaspoon *salt;* set aside.

2 Preheat oven to 350°F. In a small saucepan bring milk just to boiling; remove from heat. Add tea bags. Cover; let steep for 4 minutes. Remove and discard tea bags, pressing out any liquid from the bags. Add butter, 2 tablespoons honey, 1 tablespoon lemon peel, and the vanilla to the hot milk mixture and stir until well combined. Set aside.

3 In a large mixing bowl beat eggs with an electric mixer on high speed about 4 minutes or until thick. Gradually add sugar, beating on medium speed for 4 to 5 minutes or until light and fluffy. Add the flour mixture; beat on low to medium speed just until combined. Add milk mixture and beat until combined. Pour batter evenly into the prepared pans.

4 Bake for 18 to 22 minutes or until a toothpick comes out clean. Cool cakes in pans on wire racks for 10 minutes. Remove from pans; cool on wire racks.

5 For filling, combine 2 teaspoons lemon peel, the lemon juice, and 1 tablespoon honey. Stir in yogurt until smooth. Fold in dessert topping. Cover; chill until ready to use.

6 To assemble cake, place one of the cooled cake layers on a cake plate. Spread top evenly with half of the filling. Top with second cake layer and spread top with remaining filling. Sprinkle with pomegranate seeds.

nutrition facts per serving: 201 cal., 6 g total fat (3 g sat. fat), 54 mg chol., 149 mg sodium, 33 g carb. (1 g fiber, 19 g sugars), 5 g pro. exchanges: 1 starch, 1 carb., 1 fat.

nutrition facts per serving with substitute: Same as original, except 182 cal., 27 g carb. (13 g sugars).

∗sugar substitutes: Choose from Splenda Blend for Baking or Sun Crystals Sugar Blend for Baking. Follow package directions to use product amount equivalent to ¾ cup sugar.

No frosting needed! When you invert the cake, the sweet, caramelly pecans and oranges make an irresistible topper.

upside-down orange carrot cake

prep: 25 minutes bake: 30 minutes
makes: 10 servings (1 wedge each)

1   tablespoon canola oil
    or cooking oil
2   tablespoons packed
    brown sugar✱
¼   cup coarsely chopped
    pecans, lightly
    toasted
1   orange, peeled, thinly
    sliced, and seeded
¾   cup all-purpose flour✱✱
¼   cup yellow cornmeal
½   cup granulated
    sugar✱
1½ teaspoons pumpkin
    pie spice
1   teaspoon baking
    powder
⅛   teaspoon salt
1   cup finely shredded
    carrot
⅓   cup refrigerated or
    frozen egg product,
    thawed, or 3 egg
    whites, lightly
    beaten
¼   cup canola oil
¼   cup fat-free milk
    Orange peel twists
    (optional)

✱ sugar substitutes: We
do not recommend sugar
substitute for the brown sugar.
Choose Splenda Sugar Blend
for Baking to substitute for
the granulated sugar. Follow
package directions to use
product amount equivalent to
½ cup granulated sugar.

1 Preheat oven to 350°F. Pour the 1 tablespoon oil into an 8×1½-inch round cake pan; tilt pan to coat bottom evenly with oil. Sprinkle brown sugar evenly in pan. Top with pecans. Arrange orange slices on pecans. Set aside.

2 In a medium bowl combine flour, cornmeal, granulated sugar, pumpkin pie spice, baking powder, and salt. Add carrot, eggs, the ¼ cup oil, and the milk. Stir just until combined. Spread mixture evenly over orange slices in pan.

3 Bake for 30 to 35 minutes or until a toothpick inserted near center comes out clean. Cool in pan on a wire rack for 5 minutes. Loosen sides of cake from pan; invert cake onto a serving plate. Serve warm. If desired, garnish with orange peel twists.

nutrition facts per serving: 191 cal., 9 g total fat (1 g sat. fat), 0 mg chol., 81 mg sodium, 26 g carb. (1 g fiber, 15 g sugars), 3 g pro. exchanges: 1.5 carb., 1.5 fat.

nutrition facts per serving with substitute: Same as original, except 176 cal., 21 g carb. (10 g sugars).

✱✱ test kitchen tip: You can substitute whole wheat pastry flour or white whole wheat flour for up to half of the total all-purpose flour used.

Buttermilk—or cultured low-fat milk—gives this pound cake a tangy taste and tender crumb.

31g
CARB. PER
SERVING

cranberry-smothered white chocolate pound cake

prep: 25 minutes   stand: 30 minutes   bake: 30 minutes   cool: 15 minutes
makes: 16 servings (1 slice cake and about 1½ tablespoons compote each)

⅔   cup buttermilk
4   egg whites
    Nonstick cooking
      spray for baking
2   cups flour
½   teaspoon baking
      powder
¼   teaspoon baking soda
¼   teaspoon salt
¾   cup granulated sugar✱
½   cup shortening
1   teaspoon vanilla
2   ounces white
      chocolate (with
      cocoa butter),
      melted and cooled
1   recipe Cranberry-
      Orange Compote

1 Allow buttermilk and egg whites to stand at room temperature for 30 minutes. Preheat oven to 325°F. Coat a 10-inch fluted tube pan with cooking spray for baking; set aside. In a medium bowl stir together flour, baking powder, baking soda, and salt; set aside.

2 In a large mixing bowl beat granulated sugar and shortening with an electric mixer on medium speed about 5 minutes or until light and fluffy. Beat in vanilla. Add egg whites, one at a time, beating well after each addition. Beat in the melted white chocolate.

3 Alternately add flour mixture and buttermilk to shortening mixture, beating on low speed after each addition just until combined. Pour batter into prepared pan, spreading top evenly. Bake for 30 to 35 minutes or until a wooden skewer inserted in the center of cake comes out clean. (Cake will appear shallow in the pan.) Cool in the pan on a wire rack for 15 minutes. Invert cake onto a wire rack and cool completely.

4 To serve, cut cake into 16 slices and top with Cranberry-Orange Compote.

nutrition facts per serving: 205 cal., 7 g total fat (2 g sat. fat), 1 mg chol., 93 mg sodium, 31 g carb. (1 g fiber, 18 g sugars), 3 g pro. exchanges: 2 carb., 1.5 fat.

nutrition facts per serving with substitutes: Same as original, except 185 cal., 24 g carb. (11 g sugars).

cranberry-orange compote: In a small saucepan combine 1 cup fresh cranberries, ¼ cup dried cranberries, ¼ cup orange juice, and 2 tablespoons packed brown sugar.✱ Bring to boiling, stirring constantly; reduce heat. Simmer, uncovered, about 5 minutes or until mixture is thickened and liquid is syrupy, stirring occasionally. Meanwhile, peel, seed, and section 2 medium oranges. Gently stir orange sections into cooked cranberry mixture. Serve warm or at room temperature. Just before serving, stir in 1 kiwifruit, peeled and chopped.

✱sugar substitutes: Choose Splenda Sugar Blend for Baking to substitute for the granulated sugar. Choose from Sweet'N Low Brown or Sugar Twin Granulated Brown to substitute for the brown sugar. Follow package directions to use product amounts equivalent to ¾ cup granulated sugar and 2 tablespoons brown sugar.

For a little spice that's extra nice, give each cake a sprinkling of pumpkin pie spice just before serving.

gingerbread cupcakes with marshmallow cream cheese frosting

26g
CARB. PER SERVING

prep: 15 minutes bake: 15 minutes cool: 5 minutes
makes: 15 servings (1 cupcake each)

Nonstick cooking
   spray for baking
¼ cup butter, softened
2 tablespoons light
   stick butter (not
   margarine), softened
¼ cup sugar*
2 teaspoons pumpkin
   pie spice
1½ teaspoons baking
   powder
¼ teaspoon baking soda
½ cup refrigerated or
   frozen egg product,
   thawed, or 2 eggs
1 cup water
½ cup mild-flavor
   molasses
1¾ cups flour
3 ounces reduced-fat
   cream cheese
   (Neufchâtel),
   softened
2 tablespoons butter,
   softened
½ cup marshmallow
   creme

1 Preheat oven to 350°F. Line fifteen 2½-inch muffin cups with paper bake cups. Spray paper bake cups with cooking spray; set aside.

2 In a mixing bowl beat butter and light butter together with an electric mixer on medium speed for 30 seconds. Add sugar, pumpkin pie spice, baking powder, and baking soda. Beat until combined, scraping sides of bowl. Beat in eggs.

3 In a medium bowl whisk together water and molasses. Alternately add flour and molasses mixture to the butter mixture, beating on low speed after each addition just until combined. Spoon batter evenly into prepared muffin cups, filling each about two-thirds full.

4 Bake for 15 to 20 minutes or until a toothpick inserted in centers comes out clean. Cool on a wire rack for 5 minutes. Carefully remove cupcakes from pans; cool on a wire rack.

5 In a bowl beat cream cheese and 2 tablespoons butter until well combined and smooth. Stir in marshmallow creme. Spread or pipe on top of cooled cupcakes. Store frosted cupcakes in the refrigerator.

nutrition facts per serving: 174 cal., 7 g total fat (4 g sat. fat), 18 mg chol., 150 mg sodium, 26 g carb. (0 g fiber, 12 g sugars), 3 g pro. exchanges: 1 starch, 1 carb., 1 fat.

nutrition facts per serving with substitute: Same as original, except 169 cal., 24 g carb. (10 g sugars). exchanges: 0.5 carb.

*sugar substitute: Use Splenda Sugar Blend for Baking. Follow package directions to use product amount equivalent to ¼ cup sugar.

You'll have plenty of tea bags left to enjoy the herbal tea as a beverage. Drink up! Rose hips contain lycopene, believed to be a cancer fighter.

33g
CARB. PER
SERVING

grilled angel food cake with strawberry sauce

prep: 25 minutes cook: 5 minutes
makes: 6 servings (1 cake slice, ¼ cup ice cream, and about ⅓ cup sauce each)

¾	cup water
1	hibiscus and rose hip herbal tea bag
2½	cups small fresh strawberries, hulled
1	tablespoon sugar∗
1½	teaspoons cornstarch
1	tablespoon tub-style vegetable oil spread
6	ounces purchased angel food cake, cut into 6 equal slices
	Butter-flavor nonstick cooking spray
1½	cups light strawberry ice cream
	Fresh mint leaves (optional)

1 In a small saucepan bring water just to boiling. Remove from heat; add tea bag. Cover; steep for 5 minutes. Remove tea bag, pressing out tea; discard tea bag.

2 Meanwhile, in a small bowl mash 1 cup of the strawberries until well mashed. Thinly slice remaining berries. Add the sugar and cornstarch to the mashed berries and stir until combined. Add to the brewed tea in the saucepan. Cook and stir until thickened and bubbly. Cook and stir for 2 minutes more. Remove from heat and stir in the vegetable oil spread and sliced strawberries. Set aside to cool slightly.

3 Lightly coat both sides of the cake slices with cooking spray. Heat an indoor grill pan or griddle over medium-high heat. Add cake slices. Cook for 2 to 3 minutes or until cake is golden, turning once halfway through cooking.

4 To serve, place a cake slice in each of six dishes. Spoon strawberry sauce over cake. Top each with a ¼-cup scoop of ice cream. If desired, garnish with fresh mint leaves.

nutrition facts per serving: 171 cal., 3 g total fat (1 g sat. fat), 6 mg chol., 258 mg sodium, 33 g carb. (2 g fiber, 21 g sugars), 4 g pro. exchanges: 0.5 fruit, 1.5 carb., 0.5 fat.

nutrition facts per serving with substitute: Same as original, except 164 cal., 32 g carb. (19 g sugars).

∗sugar substitutes: Choose from Splenda Granular, Sweet'N Low bulk or packets, or Equal Spoonful or packets. Follow package directions to use product amount equivalent to 1 tablespoon sugar. If using Equal, add to the sauce with the vegetable oil spread.

Eating sensibly at your next gathering will be easier when you know that you have this rich and refreshing dessert waiting in the freezer for your finale.

lemon-blueberry angel cake dessert

prep: 25 minutes freeze: 4 hours
makes: 12 servings (½ cup each)

½ of a 7- to 8-inch
purchased angel
food cake (5 ounces)
1 8-ounce tub light
cream cheese
1½ teaspoons finely
shredded lemon
peel
2 tablespoons lemon
juice
1½ cups frozen light
whipped dessert
topping, thawed
2 cups fresh
blueberries
Lemon peel strips
(optional)

1 Cut cake into ½-inch cubes. (You should have about 4½ cups cubes.) Place half of the cubes in a 2-quart soufflé dish.

2 In a medium bowl beat cream cheese with an electric mixer on medium speed until smooth. Add lemon juice, beating until smooth. Stir in finely shredded lemon peel. Fold in about ¼ cup of the dessert topping until combined. Fold in the remaining dessert topping. Divide the mixture in half; stir 1½ cups of the blueberries into one portion of the cream cheese mixture. Spoon over cake cubes in dish. Top with the remaining cake cubes and the remaining plain cream cheese mixture. Cover and freeze about 4 hours or until firm.

3 Sprinkle with the remaining blueberries before serving. If desired, garnish with lemon peel strips.

nutrition facts per serving: 100 cal., 4 g total fat (3 g sat. fat), 9 mg chol., 177 mg sodium, 14 g carb. (1 g fiber, 8 g sugars), 3 g pro. exchanges: 1 carb., 0.5 fat.

28g
CARB. PER
SERVING

delightful desserts

For tender apple chunks, use McIntosh apples. For firm chunks, choose Jonathan, Braeburn, Cortland, or Empire.

apple-nut wedges

prep: 25 minutes bake: 25 minutes
makes: 8 servings (1 wedge and about 1 tablespoon topping each)

Nonstick cooking
   spray
1 egg
2 egg whites
⅔ cup packed brown
   sugar✳
1 teaspoon vanilla
⅓ cup flour
¾ teaspoon baking soda
⅛ teaspoon salt
2 large apples, cored
   and chopped (2 cups)
½ cup chopped walnuts
   or pecans, toasted
½ cup light sour cream
¼ cup vanilla low-fat
   yogurt sweetened
   with artificial
   sweetener
½ teaspoon vanilla

1 Preheat oven to 325°F. Coat a 9-inch pie plate with cooking spray; set aside.

2 In a large bowl combine egg, egg whites, brown sugar, and the 1 teaspoon vanilla. Beat with an electric mixer on medium speed about 1 minute or until smooth. In a small bowl stir together flour, baking soda, and salt. Add flour mixture to egg mixture; stir just until combined. Fold in apples and nuts. Spread batter evenly in the prepared pie plate.

3 Bake for 25 to 30 minutes or until center is set. Cool slightly on a wire rack. Meanwhile, for topping, in a small bowl whisk together sour cream, yogurt, and the ½ teaspoon vanilla.

4 To serve, cut dessert into eight wedges. Serve warm. Spoon about 1 rounded tablespoon of the topping over each serving.

nutrition facts per serving: 186 cal., 7 g total fat (1 g sat. fat), 31 mg chol., 195 mg sodium, 28 g carb. (1 g fiber, 22 g sugars), 4 g pro. exchanges: 2 carb., 1 fat.

nutrition facts per serving with substitute: Same as original, except 155 calories, 190 mg sodium, 18 g carb. (12 g sugars). exchanges: 1 carb.

✳sugar substitute: Choose Splenda Brown Sugar Blend. Follow package directions to use product amount equivalent to ⅔ cup brown sugar.

Grab your pastry blender or two knives to cut the butter into the flour mixture.

mocha shortcakes with white chocolate peppermint mousse

32g
CARB. PER SERVING

prep: 25 minutes bake: 10 minutes
makes: 10 servings (1 shortcake and ¼ cup mousse each)

1 cup all-purpose flour
⅓ cup whole wheat pastry flour
¼ cup unsweetened cocoa powder
3 tablespoons packed brown sugar∗
2 teaspoons baking powder
2 teaspoons instant espresso coffee powder
⅛ teaspoon salt
2 tablespoons butter
2 tablespoons light stick butter (not margarine)
½ cup fat-free half-and-half
¼ cup refrigerated or frozen egg product, thawed, or 1 egg, lightly beaten
2 tablespoons reduced-calorie or sugar-free chocolate-flavor syrup
2½ cups frozen light whipped dessert topping, thawed
½ teaspoon peppermint extract
2 ounces white baking chocolate, grated
4 sugar-free or regular striped round peppermint candies, coarsely crushed

1 Preheat oven to 375°F. Grease a large baking sheet; set aside. In a large bowl combine flours, cocoa powder, brown sugar, baking powder, espresso powder, and salt. Cut in butters until mixture resembles coarse crumbs. In a bowl combine half-and-half, egg, and chocolate syrup. Add to flour mixture. Stir just until combined.

2 Using a scant ¼ cup, drop dough into 10 mounds 2 inches apart on prepared baking sheet. Bake for 10 to 12 minutes or until tops are set and edges are firm. Transfer cakes to a wire rack; cool.

3 For mousse, in a bowl combine dessert topping and peppermint extract, folding gently to combine.

4 To serve, split shortcakes in half horizontally. Place shortcake bottoms on 10 plates. Top with half of the mousse and half of the white chocolate. Add shortcake tops and top each with remaining mousse. Sprinkle with remaining white chocolate and the crushed mints.

nutrition facts per serving: 207 cal., 8 g total fat (6 g sat. fat), 12 mg chol., 177 mg sodium, 32 g carb. (2 g fiber, 8 g sugars), 3 g pro. exchanges: 1 starch, 1 carb., 1.5 fat.

nutrition facts per serving with substitute: Same as original, except 191 cal., 28 g carb. (4 g sugars), 4 g pro.

∗sugar substitutes: Choose from Sweet'N Low Brown or Sugar Twin Granulated Brown. Follow package directions to use product amount equivalent to 3 tablespoons brown sugar.

You can bake these tender cakes ahead and freeze them in a freezer container for up to 1 month.

sunshine cupcakes

prep: 30 minutes stand: 30 minutes bake: 10 minutes
makes: 24 or 20 servings (1 cupcake each)

1   cup egg whites
       (7 to 9 large eggs)
¾   cup sifted cake flour
1   cup sugar✴
2   teaspoons vanilla
1   teaspoon cream of
       tartar
3   egg yolks
1   recipe Lemon Fluff
       Fresh raspberries
       (optional)
       Lemon peel strips
       (optional)

lemon fluff: In a bowl fold together ½ of an 8-ounce container frozen light whipped dessert topping, thawed; ½ teaspoon finely shredded lemon peel; and 1 tablespoon lemon juice just until combined.

1 In a very large bowl allow egg whites to stand at room temperature for 30 minutes. Meanwhile, sift cake flour and ½ cup of the sugar together three times. Line twenty-four 2½-inch muffin cups with paper bake cups;✴ set aside.

2 Preheat oven to 375°F. Add vanilla and cream of tartar to egg whites; beat with an electric mixer on medium to high speed until soft peaks form (tips curl). Gradually add the remaining ½ cup sugar, beating until stiff peaks form (tips stand straight). Sift about one-fourth of the flour mixture over egg white mixture; fold in gently. Repeat sifting and folding with the remaining flour mixture, using one-fourth of the flour mixture each time. Transfer half of the egg white mixture to another bowl; set both bowls aside.

3 In a bowl beat egg yolks on high speed 5 minutes or until thick and lemon color. Fold egg yolk mixture into one portion of the egg white mixture. Alternately spoon dollops of yellow and white batters into bake cups, filling cups two-thirds full. Gently cut through batters with a knife.

4 Bake for 10 to 12 minutes or until cakes spring back when lightly touched near centers. Remove from cups; cool on a wire rack. Frost with Lemon Fluff. If desired, garnish with raspberries and lemon peel strips. Store cupcakes in the refrigerator.

nutrition facts per serving: 72 cal., 1 g total fat (1 g sat. fat), 23 mg chol., 18 mg sodium, 14 g carb. (0 g fiber, 9 g sugars), 2 g pro. exchanges: 0.5 starch, 0.5 carb.

nutrition facts per serving with substitute: Same as original, except 28 mg chol., 22 mg sodium, 11 g carb. (6 g sugars).

✴sugar substitutes: Choose from Splenda Sugar Blend for Baking or Sun Crystals Granulated Blend. Follow package directions to use product amount equivalent to 1 cup sugar and line only 20 muffin cups with paper bake cups

Call on a food processor to grind the nuts—but don't overdo it. Use quick start-and-stop pulses just until the nuts are ground (and before they turn into nut butter).

coconut-blueberry cheesecake bars

11g CARB. PER SERVING

prep: 30 minutes bake: 26 minutes chill: 3 hours
makes: 32 servings (1 bar each)

⅓   cup butter
¾   cup finely crushed graham crackers
½   cup flour
½   cup flaked coconut
½   cup ground pecans
¾   cup sugar*
1½ 8-ounce packages reduced-fat cream cheese (Neufchâtel), softened
1   cup refrigerated or frozen egg product, thawed, or 4 eggs, lightly beaten
1   tablespoon brandy or fat-free milk
1   teaspoon vanilla
2   cups blueberries

1 Preheat oven to 350°F. Lightly grease a 13×9×2-inch baking pan; set aside.

2 For crust, in a small saucepan heat butter over medium heat until the color of light brown sugar. Remove from heat.

3 In a bowl combine graham crackers, flour, coconut, pecans, and ¼ cup of the sugar. Stir in butter. Press onto bottom of prepared pan. Bake for 8 to 10 minutes or until lightly browned.

4 Meanwhile, in large mixing bowl beat cream cheese and the remaining ½ cup sugar until combined. Add eggs, brandy, and vanilla. Beat until combined. Pour over hot crust. Sprinkle with blueberries.

5 Bake for 18 to 20 minutes or until center appears set. Cool in pan on a wire rack. Cover; chill for 3 hours. Cut into bars. Store, covered, in the refrigerator.

nutrition facts per serving: 109 cal., 6 g total fat (3 g sat. fat), 13 mg chol., 79 mg sodium, 11 g carb. (1 g fiber, 7 g sugars), 2 g pro. exchanges: 1 carb., 1 fat.

nutrition facts per serving with substitute: Same as original, except 93 cal. 7 g carb. (3 g sugars). exchanges: 0.5 carb.

✳ sugar substitutes: Choose from Splenda Granular or Sweet'N Low bulk or packets. Follow package directions to use product amounts equivalent to ¼ cup and ½ cup sugar).

At the end-of-year holidays, this seasonally flavored cheesecake will delight everyone at the table, especially those who are watching what they eat.

28g
CARB. PER
SERVING

pumpkin cheesecake

prep: 30 minutes bake: 60 minutes cool: 45 minutes chill: 4 hours
makes: 12 servings (1 wedge each)

Nonstick cooking spray
1   cup finely crushed
    chocolate graham
    crackers
2   tablespoons sugar∗
2   tablespoons butter,
    melted
2   8-ounce packages
    reduced-fat cream
    cheese (Neufchâtel),
    softened
1   12.3-ounce package
    firm silken-style
    tofu (fresh bean
    curd), well drained
1   6-ounce carton plain
    fat-free Greek yogurt
¾   cup sugar∗
1   tablespoon cornstarch
2   egg whites
2   tablespoons vanilla
1   15-ounce can pumpkin
2   teaspoons ground
    cinnamon
½   teaspoon ground
    ginger
½   ounce semisweet
    chocolate, melted,
    or 2 tablespoons
    chocolate-flavor
    syrup

∗ sugar substitutes: Choose
from Splenda Granular or
Sweet'N Low bulk or packets.
Follow package directions to use
product amounts equivalent to
2 tablespoons and ¾ cup sugar.

1 Preheat oven to 350°F. Coat a 9-inch
springform pan with cooking spray.
For crust, in a small bowl combine crushed
graham crackers, the 2 tablespoons sugar,
and the butter. Press crumb mixture onto
the bottom of the prepared pan. Bake for
10 minutes. Cool completely in pan on a wire
rack. Reduce oven temperature to 325°F.

2 In a large bowl combine cream cheese,
tofu, yogurt, the ¾ cup sugar, and the
cornstarch. Beat with an electric mixer on
medium speed just until combined and
mixture is nearly smooth. Add egg whites
and vanilla, beating just until combined. Set
aside 2 cups of the cream cheese mixture.
Stir pumpkin, cinnamon, and ginger into the
remaining cream cheese mixture. Spread
the pumpkin mixture over the cooled crust.
Carefully spoon the reserved 2 cups cream
cheese mixture over the pumpkin mixture;
spread evenly over the pumpkin mixture.

3 Bake in the 325°F oven for 50 to 60 minutes
or until a 2½-inch area around the outside
edge appears set when gently shaken.

4 Cool in pan on a wire rack for 15 minutes.
Using a thin metal spatula, loosen the
cheesecake from the side of the pan. Cool
for 30 minutes more. Remove side of the
springform pan. Cool completely. Cover and
chill for 4 to 24 hours before serving.

5 To serve, cut into wedges. Drizzle
each wedge with melted chocolate or
chocolate syrup.

nutrition facts per serving: 259 cal., 13 g total fat
(7 g sat. fat), 33 mg chol., 216 mg sodium, 28 g carb. (2 g fiber,
21 g sugars), 8 g pro. exchanges: 2 carb., 1 lean meat, 2.5 fat.

nutrition facts per serving with substitute: Same
as original, except 209 cal., 16 g carb. (8 g sugars). exchanges:
1 carb.

Who needs heavy, dense, and wholly unhealthful cheesecake when this light, luscious version fits into your meal plan?

fluffy peppermint cheesecake

prep: 30 minutes bake: 40 minutes cool: 45 minutes chill: at least 4 hours
makes: 12 servings (1 wedge each)

1¼ cups finely crushed low-fat graham crackers
¼ cup flaxseed meal
⅓ cup tub-style vegetable oil spread, melted
1 8-ounce package reduced-fat cream cheese (Neufchâtel), softened
1 7-ounce jar marshmallow creme
1 6-ounce carton plain fat-free Greek yogurt
½ teaspoon peppermint extract
¾ cup refrigerated or frozen egg product, thawed, or 3 eggs, lightly beaten
1½ cups frozen light whipped dessert topping, thawed
1 recipe Chocolate Lace Shards

1 Preheat oven to 375°F. For crust, in a bowl combine crushed graham crackers and flaxseed meal. Stir in melted vegetable oil spread. Press the crumb mixture onto the bottom and about 2 inches up the sides of an 8- or 9-inch springform pan; set aside.

2 For filling, in a large mixing bowl beat cream cheese, marshmallow creme, yogurt, and peppermint extract with an electric mixer until smooth. Stir in eggs just until combined.

3 Pour filling into crust-lined pan. Place the pan in a shallow baking pan. Bake for 40 to 45 minutes for the 8-inch pan, 35 to 40 minutes for the 9-inch pan, or until a 2½-inch area around the outside edge appears set when gently shaken.

4 Cool in pan on a wire rack for 15 minutes. Using a small sharp knife, loosen the crust from the sides of the pan; cool for 30 minutes. Remove side of pan; cool cheesecake completely on rack. Cover and chill for at least 4 hours before serving.

5 To serve, spread half of the dessert topping in a thin layer on top of the cheesecake. Sprinkle with any remaining crushed peppermint candies. Spoon the remaining dessert topping around the top edge of the cheesecake and top the topping with Chocolate Lace Shards.

nutrition facts per serving: 258 cal., 12 g total fat (5 g sat. fat), 14 mg chol., 212 mg sodium, 31 g carb. (1 g fiber, 16 g sugars), 6 g pro. exchanges: 2 carb., 2.5 fat.

chocolate lace shards: Crush 6 sugar-free striped round peppermint candies; set aside. Melt 1 ounce semisweet chocolate over low heat. Cool slightly. Place melted chocolate in a resealable plastic bag. Seal bag and snip off a tiny corner of the bag. On a sheet of waxed paper or parchment paper pipe chocolate in squiggles, forming a 6-inch circle. Sprinkle with some of the crushed peppermint candies. When set, gently cut into 12 wedges (most will break; that's OK).

13g
CARB. PER
SERVING

Cooks love no-bake cheesecakes because they're so easy to make. Cooks with an eye toward healthful eating will love this slimmed-down version even more.

orange-swirled cheesecake

prep: 30 minutes chill: 4 hours
makes: 12 servings (1 wedge each)

3¾ teaspoons unflavored gelatin
1 teaspoon finely shredded orange peel (set aside)
½ cup orange juice
⅓ cup fat-free milk
1 8-ounce package reduced-fat cream cheese (Neufchâtel), softened
2½ cups plain low-fat Greek or fat-free Greek yogurt
½ cup sugar*
1 teaspoon vanilla
Orange paste food coloring**
Fresh raspberries and/or orange peel curls (optional)

*sugar substitutes: Choose from Splenda Granular or Equal Spoonful or packets. Follow package directions to use product amount equivalent to ½ cup sugar.

**test kitchen tip: If you don't have paste food coloring, you can use 4 drops yellow and 1 drop red liquid food colorings to get an orange color.

1 In a small saucepan sprinkle 2½ teaspoons of the gelatin over the orange juice; let stand for 5 minutes. Heat and stir orange juice mixture over low heat just until gelatin is dissolved. Remove from heat and cool for 5 minutes.

2 In another small saucepan sprinkle remaining 1¼ teaspoons gelatin over the milk; let stand for 5 minutes. Heat and stir over low heat just until gelatin is dissolved. Remove from heat; cool 5 minutes.

3 In a large bowl beat cream cheese with an electric mixer on medium speed until smooth. Beat in yogurt, sugar, and vanilla until smooth. Remove ½ cup of the cream cheese mixture and add it to the milk mixture, whisking until smooth. Gradually beat orange juice mixture into the remaining cream cheese mixture until smooth. Tint to a light orange color with the orange food coloring. Stir in the 1 teaspoon orange peel.

4 Spoon half of the orange cream cheese mixture into a 7- to 8-inch springform pan. Spoon half of the white cream cheese mixture into mounds over orange cream cheese mixture. Using a thin-bladed narrow metal spatula or a table knife, swirl white mixture into orange mixture. Repeat layering and swirling remaining orange mixture and white mixture. Cover and chill for 4 to 24 hours or until set.

5 To serve, using a small sharp knife, loosen cheesecake from sides of springform pan; remove side of pan. If desired, garnish with fresh raspberries and/or orange peel curls. To serve, cut cheesecake into 12 wedges.

nutrition facts per serving: 126 cal., 5 g total fat (3 g sat. fat), 17 mg chol., 85 mg sodium, 13 g carb. (0 g fiber, 13 g sugars), 7 g pro. exchanges: 1 carb., 1 lean meat, 0.5 fat.

nutrition facts per serving with substitute: Same as original, except 97 cal., 6 carb. (5 g sugars). exchanges: 0.5 carb.

Key lime pie–flavor yogurt and light whipped dessert topping help put this classic on the list of diabetes-friendly desserts you can enjoy.

key lime pie

prep: 30 minutes bake: 8 minutes chill: 4 hours 30 minutes
makes: 8 servings (1 slice each)

17g
CARB. PER
SERVING

1½ cups small pretzel
     twists
2   tablespoons sliced
     almonds, toasted
3   tablespoons butter,
     melted
1   4-serving-size
     package sugar-free,
     lime-flavor gelatin
1   cup boiling water
2   6-ounce cartons
     low-fat Key lime
     pie–flavor yogurt
½   of an 8-ounce
     container frozen
     light whipped
     dessert topping,
     thawed
1   teaspoon finely
     shredded lime peel
     Shredded lime
     peel and/or fresh
     raspberries
     (optional)

1 Preheat oven to 350°F. For crust, in a food processor combine pretzels and sliced almonds; cover and process until finely crushed. Add butter; cover and process until combined. Press pretzel mixture onto the bottom and up the sides of a 9-inch pie plate. Bake for 8 to 10 minutes or until lightly browned. Cool on a wire rack.

2 Place gelatin in a medium bowl. Add the boiling water and stir until gelatin is dissolved (about 2 minutes). Cover and chill about 30 minutes or until mixture is partially set (the consistency of unbeaten egg whites). Fold in yogurt, whipped topping, and the 1 teaspoon lime peel. Pour into cooled crust.

3 Chill for at least 4 hours. If desired, top with additional shredded lime peel and/or raspberries to serve.

nutrition facts per serving: 153 cal., 7 g total fat (5 g sat. fat), 13 mg chol., 180 mg sodium, 17 g carb. (0 g fiber, 10 g sugars), 3 g pro. exchanges: 0.5 starch, 0.5 carb., 1.5 fat.

It's not too good to be true! This impressive pie is every bit as wonderful as the popular restaurant version that inspired it.

silky chocolate pie

prep: 25 minutes   chill: 27 hours   cool: 15 minutes
makes: 10 servings (1 wedge each)

5   cups plain low-fat or fat-free yogurt✶ or 2 cups plain fat-free Greek yogurt✶✶
1   envelope unflavored gelatin
½   cup fat-free milk
½   of an 8-ounce package reduced-fat cream cheese (Neufchâtel), softened
4   ounces semisweet chocolate, chopped
½   cup sugar✶✶✶
½   teaspoon vanilla
1   purchased reduced-fat graham cracker crumb pie shell
¾   cup frozen light whipped dessert topping, thawed (optional)
Chocolate curls (optional)

1 For yogurt cheese, line a yogurt strainer, sieve, or small colander with three layers of 100-percent-cotton cheesecloth or a clean paper coffee filter. Suspend lined strainer over a large bowl. Spoon yogurt into the strainer. Cover with plastic wrap. Chill for 24 hours. Discard liquid. You should have 2 to 2½ cups yogurt cheese. Set yogurt cheese aside.

2 In a small saucepan sprinkle gelatin over milk; let stand for 5 minutes. Heat and stir milk mixture over low heat just until gelatin is dissolved. Gradually whisk in cream cheese until melted. Add chocolate; heat and stir over low heat until chocolate is melted. Remove from heat. Stir in sugar and vanilla. Transfer mixture to a large bowl; cool for 15 minutes.

3 Stir about one-fourth of the yogurt cheese or Greek yogurt into the chocolate mixture until smooth. Fold in the remaining yogurt cheese or Greek yogurt. Spread mixture evenly in the pie shell.

4 Cover pie loosely; chill for 3 to 24 hours before serving. Cut into wedges to serve. If desired, top each serving with dessert topping and chocolate curls.

nutrition facts per serving: 235 cal., 9 g total fat (4 g sat. fat), 9 mg chol., 140 mg sodium, 31 g carb. (1 g fiber, 23 g sugars), 7 g pro. exchanges: 0.5 milk, 1.5 carb., 1.5 fat.

nutrition facts per serving with substitute: Same as original, except 201 cal., 23 g carb. (14 g sugars). exchanges: 1 carb.

✶✶✶sugar substitutes: Choose from Splenda Granular or Sweet'N Low bulk or packets. Follow package directions to use product amount equivalent to ½ cup sugar.

✶test kitchen tip: Be sure to use a brand of yogurt that contains no gums, gelatin, or fillers. These ingredients may prevent the whey from separating from the curd to make the yogurt cheese.

✶✶test kitchen tip: If you use Greek yogurt, omit Step 1.

Create a different dessert each time you make this recipe by using different flavors of low-fat or light ice cream.

banana split ice cream pie

27g
CARB. PER
SERVING

prep: 20 minutes bake: 5 minutes freeze: 4 hours
makes: 10 servings (1 wedge each)

1   purchased reduced-
     fat graham cracker
     crumb pie shell
2   tablespoons
     refrigerated or
     frozen egg product,
     thawed, or 1 egg
     white, lightly beaten
1½ cups low-fat or light
     chocolate ice cream,
     softened
1½ cups low-fat or light
     vanilla ice cream,
     softened
1   large banana, sliced
1   cup sliced fresh
     strawberries
2   tablespoons light
     chocolate-flavor
     syrup
⅔   cup frozen light
     whipped dessert
     topping, thawed
     (optional)

1 Preheat oven to 375°F. Brush pie shell with egg. Bake for 5 minutes. Cool on a wire rack. Spread chocolate ice cream in the bottom of the cooled pie shell. Spread vanilla ice cream evenly over chocolate ice cream. Cover and freeze for at least 4 hours or up to 1 week.

2 To serve, arrange banana and strawberry slices over ice cream layers. Drizzle with chocolate syrup. Cut pie into wedges to serve. If desired, top each serving with whipped topping.

nutrition facts per serving: 167 cal., 5 g total fat (2 g sat. fat), 6 mg chol., 115 mg sodium, 27 g carb. (1 g fiber, 16 g sugars), 3 g pro. exchanges: 2 carb., 0.5 fat.

Select firm, plump plums that yield slightly when gently pressed. Don't worry if bloom (a grayish cast) has developed on the skin— it's natural and will not affect the quality.

23g
CARB. PER
SERVING

country-style peach-plum tart

prep: 25 minutes bake: 30 minutes
makes: 10 servings (1 wedge tart and 1 tablespoon topping each)

delightful desserts

Flour
1   recipe Cornmeal Pastry
1   tablespoon cornstarch
1   teaspoon finely shredded lemon peel
¼   teaspoon ground cinnamon or ground nutmeg
4   medium plums, halved, pitted, and sliced
3   medium peaches, halved, pitted, and sliced
¼   cup honey
    Fat-free milk
10 tablespoons frozen fat-free whipped dessert topping, thawed

1 Preheat oven to 375°F. Line a baking sheet with foil; sprinkle lightly with flour. Place Cornmeal Pastry on foil. Slightly flatten dough ball. Using a rolling pin, roll dough from center to edges into a 12-inch circle. Set aside.

2 In a large bowl stir together cornstarch, lemon peel, and cinnamon. Add plum slices and peach slices. Toss to coat. Drizzle with honey; toss gently to coat. Mound fruit mixture in center of pastry circle, leaving a 2-inch border around the edges. Fold border up over fruit slices, pleating dough as needed. Brush pastry lightly with milk.

3 Bake for 30 to 40 minutes or until fruit slices are tender and pastry is lightly browned. If necessary to prevent fruit from drying out, cover tart with foil for the last 10 to 15 minutes of baking. Cool for 30 minutes and serve warm. (Or cool completely.) Cut into 10 wedges and serve with whipped topping.

nutrition facts per serving: 150 cal., 5 g total fat (1 g sat. fat), 0 mg chol., 102 mg sodium, 23 g carb. (2 g fiber, 7 g sugars), 2 g pro. exchanges: 0.5 fruit, 1 starch, 1 fat.

cornmeal pastry: In a medium bowl stir together 1 cup flour, ⅓ cup yellow cornmeal, and ¼ teaspoon salt. Using a pastry blender, cut in ⅓ cup chilled tub-style vegetable oil spread until pieces are pea size. Sprinkle 1 tablespoon cold water over part of the flour mixture; gently toss with a fork. Push moistened dough to the side of the bowl. Repeat moistening flour mixture, using 1 tablespoon cold water at a time, until all flour mixture is moistened (3 to 4 tablespoons cold water total). Shape dough into a ball.

If you don't have a sifter, you can use a fine-mesh sieve to give the pies a light dusting of powdered sugar.

bananas foster mini pies

prep: 30 minutes   chill: 1 hour   bake: 15 minutes
makes: 12 servings (1 mini pie each)

⅓   cup butter, softened
1   tablespoon
     granulated sugar*
¼   teaspoon salt
1   egg
2   tablespoons cold
     water
1½ cups flour
1   banana, chopped
     (about ¾ cup)
¼   cup sugar-free
     caramel-flavor ice
     cream topping
¼   cup chopped pecans,
     toasted
1   tablespoon bourbon
¼   teaspoon ground
     cinnamon
1   tablespoon butter,
     melted
2   teaspoons powdered
     sugar

1 Line a baking sheet with parchment paper; set aside. In a large bowl beat the ⅓ cup butter with an electric mixer on medium to high speed for 30 seconds. Add granulated sugar and salt. Beat for 3 minutes on medium speed. Add egg and the water; beat until combined. Beat in as much of the flour as you can. Stir in any remaining flour. Shape dough into a disk. Wrap in plastic wrap; chill about 1 hour or until easy to handle.

2 Preheat oven to 400°F. For filling, in a bowl combine banana, ice cream topping, pecans, bourbon, and cinnamon.

3 On a lightly floured surface roll the dough to ⅛ inch thick. Using a 4-inch round cutter, cut dough into rounds, rerolling scraps as necessary. Place about 1 tablespoon of the filling in the center of each round. Brush edges of pastry circles with a little water. Fold each circle in half over filling; press edges to seal. Place pies on prepared baking sheet. Brush pies with the 1 tablespoon melted butter.

4 Bake about 15 minutes or until lightly browned. Sift powdered sugar over pies. Serve warm.

nutrition facts per serving: 165 cal., 8 g total fat (4 g sat. fat), 32 mg chol., 118 mg sodium, 20 g carb. (1 g fiber, 3 g sugars), 3 g pro. exchanges: 1 starch, 1.5 fat.

nutrition facts per serving with substitute: Same as original, except 161 cal., 19 g carb. (2 g sugars). exchanges: 1 fat.

*sugar substitutes: Choose from Splenda Granular, Truvia Spoonable, or Sweet'N Low packets or bulk. Follow package directions to use product amount equivalent to 1 tablespoon granulated sugar.

delightful desserts

27 g
CARB. PER
SERVING

Peaches and nectarines can be used interchangeably. If using peaches, remove the fuzzy peels before slicing.

nectarine blueberry crisp

prep: 25 minutes **bake:** 35 minutes
makes: 8 servings (2/3 cup each)

4   cups sliced fresh
     nectarines
5   tablespoons packed
     brown sugar∗
¼   cup whole wheat
     flour or all-purpose
     flour
½   teaspoon ground
     cinnamon
1   cup fresh or frozen
     unsweetened
     blueberries or
     blackberries, thawed
¼   cup water
2/3 cup quick-cooking
     rolled oats
2   tablespoons butter,
     cut up
1/3 cup chopped
     pistachios or
     walnuts

1 Preheat oven to 375°F. For fruit filling, in a large bowl combine nectarine slices, 3 tablespoons of the brown sugar, 2 tablespoons of the flour, and the cinnamon. Add blueberries and the water; toss to combine. Spoon mixture into a 2-quart square baking dish.

2 For topping, in a medium bowl stir together oats, remaining 2 tablespoons brown sugar, and remaining 2 tablespoons flour. Using a pastry blender, cut in the butter until mixture is crumbly. Sprinkle topping onto fruit in dish. Top with nuts.

3 Bake for 35 to 40 minutes or until the fruit filling is bubbly and topping is lightly browned. Cool slightly on a wire rack; serve warm.

nutrition facts per serving: 166 cal., 6 g total fat (2 g sat. fat), 8 mg chol., 24 mg sodium, 27 g carb. (3 g fiber, 16 g sugars), 3 g pro. exchanges: 0.5 fruit, 1 starch, 0.5 carb., 1 fat.

nutrition facts per serving with substitute: Same as original, except 152 cal., 22 mg sodium, 22 g carb. (12 g sugars).

∗sugar substitute: Choose Splenda Brown Sugar Blend. Follow package directions to use product amount equivalent to 5 tablespoons brown sugar.

To keep the pretty stem intact, insert an apple corer into the bottom of each pear to remove the core. If you do not have an apple corer, use a small paring knife.

gingered pears

26g CARB. PER SERVING

prep: 15 minutes cook: 7 minutes
makes: 4 servings (1 pear and about 1½ tablespoons sauce each)

453

4 small pears, cored (about 1½ pounds total)
2 tablespoons sugar✻
2 tablespoons water
1 teaspoon finely shredded lemon peel
2 tablespoons lemon juice
1 tablespoon butter
¼ teaspoon ground ginger
1 tablespoon chopped crystallized ginger

1 Fill a large Dutch oven with water to a depth of 1 inch. Bring water to boiling. Place a steamer basket in the Dutch oven. Place pears in the steamer basket. Cover and steam for 7 to 9 minutes or until fruit is tender. Remove fruit from steamer basket.

2 Meanwhile, for lemon sauce, in a small saucepan heat and stir sugar, water, lemon peel, lemon juice, butter, and ground ginger over medium heat until butter is melted and sugar is dissolved.

3 To serve, place pears in four dessert dishes. Divide lemon sauce among the dishes and sprinkle with crystalized ginger.

nutrition facts per serving: 122 cal., 3 g total fat (2 g sat. fat), 8 mg chol., 27 mg sodium, 26 g carb. (4 g fiber, 17 g sugars), 1 g pro. exchanges: 1 fruit, 0.5 carb., 0.5 fat.

nutrition facts per serving with substitute: Same as original, except 101 cal., 20 g carb. (12 g sugars). exchanges: 0 carb.

✻sugar substitutes: Choose from Splenda Granular, Truvia Spoonable, or Sweet'N Low packets or bulk. Follow package directions to use product amount equivalent to 2 tablespoons sugar.

Everyone will look forward to coming to the table when your home is filled with the enticing aromas of apples and cinnamon.

maple-glazed baked apples

prep: 20 minutes bake: 40 minutes
makes: 6 servings (1 apple and ½ tablespoon sauce each)

6   small apples (such as
    Jonathan, Jonagold,
    or Winesap)
½   cup apple juice
    or apple cider
2   tablespoons sugar-
    free maple-flavor
    syrup
1   tablespoon butter or
    tub-style vegetable
    oil spread
6   3-inch cinnamon
    sticks

1 Preheat oven to 350°F. Using a melon baller, core apples, leaving the bottoms intact. Using a small sharp knife, cut off a strip of peel around the top of each apple. Place apples in a 2-quart casserole or baking dish.

2 In a small saucepan combine apple juice, syrup, and butter. Bring to boiling. Pour hot juice mixture over apples. Insert a cinnamon stick into the center of each apple.

3 Bake for 40 to 45 minutes or until apples are tender, brushing tops of apples occasionally with juice mixture in casserole. To serve, remove the cinnamon sticks and spoon the juice mixture over the baked apples.

nutrition facts per serving: 69 cal., 2 g total fat (1 g sat. fat), 5 mg chol., 25 mg sodium, 14 g carb. (2 g fiber, 10 g sugars), 0 g pro. exchanges: 1 fruit, 0.5 fat.

The subtly sweet herb and nut pesto is a sensational partner for juicy grilled fruit. Another time, serve the pesto as a dip for a fresh fruit platter.

grilled plum and strawberry skewers with sweet mint pesto

12g
CARB. PER SERVING

prep: 20 minutes grill: 3 minutes
makes: 4 servings (2 skewers and 1 tablespoon pesto each)

⅔ cup lightly packed fresh mint leaves
¼ cup lightly packed fresh basil leaves
3 tablespoons pine nuts, toasted
½ teaspoon finely shredded orange peel
3 tablespoons orange juice
Dash salt
4 plums, pitted and each cut into six wedges (24 wedges total)
8 large strawberries
Nonstick cooking spray

1 For pesto, in a blender or food processor combine mint, basil, pine nuts, orange peel, orange juice, and salt. Cover and blend or process until smooth, stopping and scraping side as needed. Set aside.

2 Thread plum wedges and strawberries on eight 6-inch-long skewers.✱ Lightly coat fruit with cooking spray. For a charcoal grill, grill skewers on the grill rack directly over medium coals. Grill, uncovered, for 3 to 4 minutes or until heated through and grill marks are visible, turning occasionally to brown evenly. (For a gas grill, preheat grill. Reduce heat to medium. Place skewers on grill rack over heat. Cover and grill as directed.)

3 To serve, spoon pesto into a small bowl. Serve skewers with pesto.

nutrition facts per serving: 85 cal., 4 g total fat (1 g sat. fat), 0 mg chol., 36 mg sodium, 12 g carb. (1 g fiber, 9 g sugars), 3 g pro. exchanges: 1 fruit, 0.5 fat.

✱ test kitchen tip: If using wooden skewers, soak them in enough water to cover for at least 30 minutes before using.

Cuckoo for coconut? You'll be glad to know you can enjoy it in a dessert that won't derail your goal to eat right.

coconut-pumpkin bread pudding with coconut sauce

33g CARB. PER SERVING

prep: 25 minutes bake: 50 minutes
makes: 9 servings (½ cup bread pudding and 1½ tablespoons sauce each)

Nonstick cooking
spray
10 slices light Italian
bread, such as
Village Hearth
brand, cut into
½-inch cubes
½ cup flaked coconut
1 13.5- to 14-ounce can
unsweetened light
coconut milk
1⅓ cups fat-free milk
1 cup canned pumpkin
4 egg whites
1 tablespoon vanilla
½ cup sugar✳
1½ teaspoons pumpkin
pie spice
¼ teaspoon kosher salt
2 tablespoons sugar✳
2 teaspoons cornstarch
2 egg yolks, lightly
beaten
2 tablespoons flaked
coconut, toasted
1½ teaspoons butter
Flaked coconut,
toasted (optional)

1 Preheat oven to 300°F. Lightly coat a 2-quart square or rectangular baking dish with cooking spray; set aside.

2 In a large bowl toss bread cubes with the ½ cup coconut. Spread mixture in a single layer in a 15×10×1-inch baking pan. Bake for 15 to 20 minutes or until bread cubes are dry and lightly toasted, stirring once. Remove from oven; set aside. Increase oven temperature to 375°F.

3 In a very large bowl whisk 1 cup of the coconut milk, 1 cup of the fat-free milk, the pumpkin, egg whites, and vanilla. Whisk in the ½ cup sugar, the pumpkin pie spice, and ⅛ teaspoon of the kosher salt. Stir in toasted bread cube mixture.

4 Transfer mixture to the prepared baking dish. Bake for 35 to 40 minutes or until a knife inserted near the center comes out clean.

5 For the sauce, in a medium saucepan stir together the 2 tablespoons sugar, the cornstarch, and the remaining ⅛ teaspoon kosher salt. Whisk in the remaining coconut milk and the remaining ⅓ cup fat-free milk. Cook and stir over medium heat just until boiling. Gradually stir half of the hot milk mixture into the egg yolks. Add egg yolk mixture to coconut milk mixture in saucepan; cook and stir 2 minutes more. Serve sauce warm over bread pudding. If desired, top with additional toasted coconut.

nutrition facts per serving: 213 cal., 7 g total fat (5 g sat. fat), 43 mg chol., 257 mg sodium, 33 g carb. (3 g fiber, 22 g sugars), 7 g pro. exchanges: 1 starch, 1 carb., 0.5 lean meat, 1.5 fat.

nutrition facts per serving with substitute: Same as original, except 166 cal., 20 g carb. (9 g sugars). exchanges: 0 carb.

✳sugar substitutes: Choose from Splenda Granular, Truvia Spoonable or packets, or Sweet'N Low bulk or packets. Follow package directions to use product amounts equivalent to ½ cup and 2 tablespoons sugar. If using sugar substitute to make the sauce, stir sugar substitute, coconut, and butter into the sauce after cooking and removing from heat.

Nobody will believe that this warm, comforting whole grain pudding weighs in at less than 150 calories per serving.

caramel-pear bread pudding

28g
CARB. PER
SERVING

prep: 25 minutes   bake: 50 minutes   stand: 30 minutes
makes: 12 servings (½ cup each)

Nonstick cooking
   spray
8   slices whole grain
   white bread or
   whole grain wheat
   bread, cut into
   ½-inch pieces and
   dried∗
2   tablespoons tub-style
   vegetable oil spread,
   melted
2   large red-skin pears
¼   cup dried cranberries
   (optional)
2   cups fat-free milk
¾   cup refrigerated or
   frozen egg product,
   thawed, or 3 eggs,
   lightly beaten
⅔   cup sugar-free caramel
   ice cream topping
½   teaspoon ground
   cinnamon
½   cup coarsely chopped
   pecans, toasted∗∗
   (optional)

1 Preheat oven to 350°F. Lightly coat a 2-quart rectangular or square baking dish with cooking spray; set aside. In a large bowl toss together dried bread and melted vegetable oil spread until coated. Core and chop one of the pears and add to the bread mixture along with the cranberries (if using). Gently toss to combine. Transfer to prepared baking dish.

2 In a bowl whisk together milk, eggs, ⅓ cup of the caramel topping, and the cinnamon. Slowly pour milk mixture evenly over bread mixture in dish. Using the back of a spoon, gently press down on top of bread mixture.

3 Bake, uncovered, for 50 to 60 minutes or until a knife inserted near center comes out clean. Let stand on a wire rack for 30 minutes.

4 To serve, cut pudding into 12 portions and place on dessert plates. Quarter and core the remaining pear. Cut into very thin slices; place a few slices on top of each portion. If desired, sprinkle with pecans. Drizzle each serving with some of the remaining ⅓ cup caramel topping.

nutrition facts per serving: 147 cal., 2 g total fat (1 g sat. fat), 2 mg chol., 169 mg sodium, 28 g carb. (2 g fiber, 7 g sugars), 5 g pro. exchanges: 1 starch, 1 carb.

∗test kitchen tip: To dry bread cubes, preheat oven to 300°F. Place bread cubes in an ungreased 15×10×1-inch baking pan. Bake for 10 to 12 minutes or until bread cubes are dry and crisp, stirring once or twice. You should have about 5 cups dried bread cubes.

∗∗test kitchen tip: To toast nuts, spread nuts in a shallow pan. Bake in a 350°F oven for 5 to 10 minutes, shaking the pan once or twice.

Coffee lovers' dreams will come true when they spoon into the indulgent espresso swirls that top the creamy vanilla custard.

24g CARB. PER SERVING

coffee shop custard

prep: 20 minutes   stand: 5 minutes   chill: at least 4 hours 15 minutes
makes: 4 servings (½ cup each)

1   envelope unflavored gelatin
2   cups fat-free milk
3   egg yolks
⅓   cup sugar*
1½   teaspoons vanilla
1½   teaspoons instant espresso coffee powder
     Frozen light whipped dessert topping, thawed (optional)
     Ground cinnamon (optional)

1 In a small bowl sprinkle gelatin over ¼ cup of the milk. Let stand for 5 minutes. Meanwhile, in a medium saucepan whisk together egg yolks and sugar. Gradually whisk in remaining 1¾ cups milk. Cook and stir over medium heat until just boiling. Remove from heat. Gradually whisk about ½ cup of the hot milk mixture into the gelatin mixture. Whisk gelatin mixture into remaining milk mixture in saucepan. Place saucepan in a large bowl of ice water. Stir in vanilla. Stir for a few minutes to cool the mixture. Remove ½ cup of the mixture to a small bowl; stir in espresso powder until dissolved. Cover and set espresso mixture aside.

2 Pour the remaining mixture into four 6-ounce individual dishes, custard cups, or glasses. Cover dishes; chill for 15 to 20 minutes. Drizzle the espresso mixture over the custard mixture in dishes. Using a thin metal spatula, lightly swirl the espresso mixture into the top of the custard.** Cover dishes loosely and chill for at least 4 hours or until set. If desired, top with a little whipped dessert topping and sprinkle with cinnamon.

nutrition facts per serving: 177 cal., 3 g total fat (1 g sat. fat), 160 mg chol., 72 mg sodium, 24 g carb. (0 g fiber, 23 g sugars), 12 g pro. exchanges: 0.5 milk, 1 carb., 0.5 medium-fat meat.

nutrition facts per serving with substitute: Same as original, except 120 cal., 9 g carb. (9 g sugars). exchanges: 0 carb

*sugar substitutes: Choose from Splenda Granular or Sweet'N Low bulk or packets. Follow package directions to use product amount equivalent to ⅓ cup sugar.

**test kitchen tip: If bottom mixture is too firm to swirl, just drizzle coffee mixture over top of custard and spread to cover the top.

You can refrigerate these cuties up to 24 hours. They'll be ready for supper the next day!

raspberry tiramisu

prep: 15 minutes chill: 1 hour
makes: 2 servings (1 dessert each)

23g
CARB. PER
SERVING

¼ of a 3-ounce package
    ladyfingers, cubed
    (6 halves)
2   tablespoons espresso
    or strong coffee
¼ cup reduced-fat
    cream cheese
    (Neufchâtel)
¼ cup light sour cream
2   tablespoons sugar*
1   teaspoon vanilla
¼ cup raspberries
    Fresh mint sprigs
    and/or raspberries
    (optional)

1 Divide half of the ladyfinger cubes between two 5- to 6-ounce dessert dishes. Drizzle ladyfinger cubes with half of the espresso. Set aside.

2 In a medium bowl stir cream cheese to soften. Stir in sour cream, sugar, and vanilla. (Beat smooth with a wire whisk if necessary.) Stir in the ¼ cup raspberries with a wooden spoon, mashing slightly.

3 Spoon half of the cream cheese mixture over ladyfinger cubes. Add remaining ladyfingers and drizzle with remaining espresso. Top with remaining cream cheese mixture. Cover and chill for 1 to 24 hours. If desired, garnish with fresh mint sprigs and/or additional raspberries.

nutrition facts per serving: 170 cal., 7 g total fat (4 g sat. fat), 42 mg chol., 81 mg sodium, 23 g carb. (1 g fiber, 17 g sugars), 3 g pro. exchanges: 1.5 carb., 1.5 fat.

nutrition facts per serving with substitute: Same as original, except 127 calories, 12 g carb. (6 g sugars). exchanges: 1 carb.

*sugar substitutes:
Choose from Splenda Granular or Equal Spoonful or packets. Follow package directions to use product amount equivalent to 2 tablespoons sugar.

34g
CARB. PER
SERVING

Whipped dessert topping flavored with a surprise ingredient provides a creamy, airy, and moist counterpoint to the cake.

carrot cake parfaits

prep: 30 minutes bake: 20 minutes cool: 10 minutes
makes: 10 servings (1 parfait each)

1 cup flour
1 teaspoon ground cinnamon
½ teaspoon baking soda
½ teaspoon ground nutmeg
½ cup unsweetened applesauce
¼ cup granulated sugar∗
¼ cup packed brown sugar∗
1 egg, lightly beaten
2 tablespoons vegetable oil
2 cups shredded carrots (4 medium)
1 8-ounce container frozen fat-free whipped dessert topping, thawed
2 tablespoons pureed baby food carrots
¼ teaspoon ground ginger
1 cup chopped fresh pineapple
¼ cup finely chopped walnuts

1 Preheat oven to 350°F. Grease a 9-inch round baking pan; set aside. In a small bowl combine flour, cinnamon, baking soda, and nutmeg; set aside.

2 In a medium bowl stir together applesauce, granulated sugar, brown sugar, egg, and oil. Stir in shredded carrots. Add flour mixture, stirring just until combined. Spread batter in the prepared pan.

3 Bake for 20 to 25 minutes or until a toothpick inserted near the center comes out clean. Cool in pan on a wire rack for 10 minutes. Remove from pan. Cool completely on wire rack. Coarsely crumble cooled cake (the crumbles will be dense and moist).

4 In a medium bowl fold together dessert topping, baby food carrots, and ginger just until combined.

5 To assemble desserts, divide half of the crumbled cake among ten 6-ounce parfait glasses or dessert dishes. Top with half of the dessert topping mixture. Top with pineapple, the remaining crumbled cake, and the remaining dessert topping mixture. Sprinkle with walnuts.

nutrition facts per serving: 198 cal., 5 g total fat (1 g sat. fat), 21 mg chol., 101 mg sodium, 34 g carb. (2 g fiber, 14 g sugars), 3 g pro. exchanges: 1 starch, 1 carb., 1 fat.

nutrition facts per serving with substitutes: Same as original, except 182 cal., 100 mg sodium, 28 g carb. (9 g sugars). exchanges: 0.5 carb.

∗sugar substitutes: Choose Splenda Sugar Blend for Baking to substitute for the granulated sugar. Choose Splenda Brown Sugar Blend to substitute for the brown sugar. Follow package directions to use product amounts equivalent to ¼ cup of each sugar.

Ravioli for dessert? Indeed! Bite into one of these sweet pillows and revel in the fabulous chocolate–cream cheese filling.

chocolate ravioli

16g CARB. PER SERVING

start to finish: 30 minutes
makes: 10 servings (1 ravioli each)

Nonstick cooking
   spray
½ cup tub-style light
   cream cheese
2 tablespoons sugar✳
2 ounces milk chocolate
20 square wonton
   wrappers
1 tablespoon pine
   nuts, toasted and
   coarsely chopped

1 Preheat broiler. Coat a large baking sheet with cooking spray; set aside. For filling, in a small bowl stir together cream cheese and sugar until smooth. Set aside one-fourth of the chocolate. Finely chop the remaining chocolate; stir into cream cheese mixture.

2 Lay 10 of the wonton wrappers on a work surface. Spoon 1 tablespoon filling into the center of each wrapper. Lightly moisten the edges of each wrapper with water. Top each with another wonton wrapper, pressing edges to seal. If desired, use a fluted pastry wheel to trim edges of each square.

3 Place squares on prepared baking sheet. Coat the tops of the squares with nonstick spray. Broil 4 to 5 inches from heat about 2 minutes or until golden brown (do not turn).

4 Meanwhile, place the reserved milk chocolate in a small microwave-safe bowl. Microwave on 50 percent power (medium) for 1 minute. Stir until smooth. Drizzle chocolate over warm ravioli; sprinkle with toasted pine nuts.

nutrition facts per serving: 116 cal., 4 g total fat (3 g sat. fat), 9 mg chol., 157 mg sodium, 16 g carb. (0 g fiber, 6 g sugars), 3 g pro. exchanges: 1 carb., 0.5 fat.

nutrition facts per serving with substitute: Same as original, except 106 cal., 14 g carb. (4 g sugars).

✳sugar substitutes: Choose from Equal Spoonful or packets or Sweet'N Low bulk or packets. Follow package directions to use product amount equivalent to 2 tablespoons sugar.

Homemade chocolate ice cream becomes even more irresistible when you add bright, fresh strawberries and swirl in extra bits of chopped chocolate.

milk chocolate–strawberry ice cream

prep: 30 minutes cook: 15 minutes chill: 8 hours freeze: according to manufacturer's directions + 4 hours
makes: 10 servings (½ cup each)

6　ounces milk chocolate, chopped
2½　cups reduced-fat milk (2%)
½　cup sugar✳
2　eggs, lightly beaten
1　teaspoon vanilla
1　cup chopped fresh strawberries
　　Halved strawberries (optional)

1 Reserve ¼ cup of the chopped chocolate; cover and set aside. In a medium saucepan stir together the remaining chopped chocolate, the milk, and sugar. Cook over medium heat just until boiling, whisking constantly. Whisk about ½ cup of the milk mixture into the eggs. Return egg mixture to the remaining milk mixture in saucepan. Cook and stir for 1 minute (do not boil). Remove from heat and place saucepan in a large bowl half-filled with ice water; stir constantly for 2 minutes. Strain through a fine-mesh sieve into a bowl; stir in vanilla. Cover and chill for 8 to 24 hours.

2 Pour chilled mixture into a 1½-quart ice cream freezer. Freeze according to manufacturer's directions. Stir reserved ¼ cup chopped chocolate and the 1 cup strawberries into frozen ice cream. Transfer mixture to a 2-quart freezer container. Cover and freeze for 4 hours before serving. To serve, scoop into small dessert dishes. If desired, serve with a few strawberry halves.

nutrition facts per serving: 181 cal., 7 g total fat (5 g sat. fat), 51 mg chol., 55 mg sodium, 24 g carb. (1 g fiber, 23 g sugars), 5 g pro. exchanges: 1.5 carb., 1.5 fat.

nutrition facts per serving with substitute: Same as original, except 146 cal., 15 g carb. (14 g sugars). exchanges: 1 carb.

✳ sugar substitute: Choose Splenda Granular. Follow package directions to use product amount equivalent to ½ cup sugar.

19g CARB. PER SERVING

Try this refreshing recipe at the holidays—it's a great alternative to the rich and heavy sweets often served during that time of year.

frozen pumpkin slices

prep: 40 minutes bake: 10 minutes freeze: 4 hours stand: 30 minutes
makes: 12 servings (1 slice each)

4   2½-inch squares cinnamon graham crackers, crushed
¼   cup chopped pecans
2   tablespoons flour
1   teaspoon granulated sugar✳
¼   teaspoon salt
⅛   teaspoon ground cinnamon
2   tablespoons butter, melted
3   tablespoons dried egg whites, such as Just Whites
½   cup warm water
2   tablespoons lemon juice
¼   teaspoon cream of tartar
½   cup powdered sugar
1   15-ounce can pumpkin
1   5.3- to 6-ounce carton plain fat-free Greek yogurt, drained
1   teaspoon pumpkin pie spice
½   teaspoon ground cinnamon
1   8-ounce container frozen light whipped dessert topping, thawed

1 Preheat oven to 350°F. In a small bowl stir together crushed graham crackers, pecans, flour, sugar, salt, and the ⅛ teaspoon cinnamon; stir in melted butter. Spread in a 9×9×2-inch square baking pan. Bake for 10 minutes, stirring twice. Cool completely.

2 In a large bowl stir dried egg whites into the warm water; whisk with a fork. Let stand 2 minutes. Beat with an electric mixer on medium speed until dried egg whites are dissolved and mixture is frothy. Add lemon juice and cream of tartar. Gradually add powdered sugar, beating on high speed until stiff peaks form (tips stand straight).

3 In a medium bowl stir together pumpkin, yogurt, pumpkin pie spice, and the ½ teaspoon cinnamon. Gently fold egg white mixture into pumpkin mixture. Fold in whipped topping.

4 Lightly coat a 9×5×3-inch loaf pan with *nonstick cooking spray*. Sprinkle ⅓ cup of the graham cracker mixture in the bottom of the loaf pan. Spread 4 cups of the pumpkin mixture evenly over the graham cracker mixture. Evenly sprinkle the remaining graham cracker mixture over the pumpkin mixture in loaf pan, pressing in slightly. Top with the remaining pumpkin mixture, spreading evenly. Cover with plastic wrap. Freeze at least 4 hours or up to 24 hours.

5 To serve, invert loaf pan onto a chilled serving platter and pull on plastic wrap to remove loaf. Let stand at room temperature for 30 to 60 minutes before cutting into slices.

nutrition facts per serving: 133 cal., 6 g total fat (4 g sat. fat), 5 mg chol., 90 mg sodium, 19 g carb. (1 g fiber, 10 g sugars), 3 g pro. **exchanges:** 1 starch, 1 fat.

nutrition facts per serving with substitute: Same as original, except 132 cal., 18 g carb.

✳sugar substitutes: Choose from Splenda Granular or Sweet'N Low bulk or packets. Follow package directions to use product amount equivalent to 1 teaspoon granulated sugar.

Designed for the adult palate but irresistibly playful, these treats prove you're never too old to enjoy a frosty pop!

layered frozen chocolate coffee pops

prep: 20 minutes freeze: 12 hours
makes: 8 servings (1 pop each)

1	4-serving-size package fat-free sugar-free reduced-calorie white chocolate instant pudding mix
1¼	teaspoons instant espresso coffee powder
2	cups fat-free milk
8	5-ounce paper or plastic drink cups
⅓	cup fat-free sweetened condensed milk
¼	cup unsweetened cocoa powder
½	teaspoon instant espresso coffee powder
½	teaspoon vanilla
1½	cups water
8	flat wooden crafts sticks

1 In a medium bowl stir together pudding mix and the 1¼ teaspoons espresso powder. Add the 2 cups fat-free milk; whisk about 2 minutes or until smooth and thickened.

2 Evenly spoon the pudding mixture into the paper cups. Cover with foil and chill while preparing the second layer.

3 In a medium bowl whisk together the sweetened condensed milk, cocoa powder, the ½ teaspoon espresso powder, and the vanilla. Whisk in the water until combined. Remove foil from cups and carefully spoon the cocoa powder mixture evenly over the pudding layer.

4 Cover cups with foil again. Cut a slit in the foil over each cup and insert a wooden stick into each slit, pushing the stick down into the layers. Freeze at least 12 hours or until firm.

5 To serve, remove foil and tear away the paper cups or remove pops from plastic cups.

nutrition facts per serving: 78 cal., 0 g total fat, 1 mg chol., 206 mg sodium, 16 g carb. (1 g fiber, 12 g sugars), 4 g pro.
exchanges: 1 starch.

Drive past the ice cream shop and come home to a chocolate-peanut pop that's much better for you because of the banana that serves as its base.

18g CARB. PER SERVING

banana buster pops

prep: 20 minutes freeze: 30 minutes
makes: 4 servings (1 pop each)

4 teaspoons peanut butter

1 large banana, cut into 12 equal slices

4 6- to 8-inch white sucker sticks or wooden skewers

2 ounces milk chocolate or semisweet chocolate, melted

2 tablespoons finely chopped unsalted dry-roasted or cocktail peanuts

1 Line a baking sheet with waxed paper; set aside. Spoon ½ teaspoon of the peanut butter onto each of eight of the banana slices. Place four of the peanut butter–topped banana slices on the remaining four peanut butter–topped slices to make four stacks of two banana slices with peanut butter between and peanut butter on top. Place one of the remaining banana slices on top of each stack. Push a sucker stick or skewer all the way through the center of each banana stack.

2 Place melted chocolate in a shallow dish. Place peanuts in another shallow dish. Roll each banana stack in the melted chocolate. Use a thin metal spatula to help spread the chocolate into a thin, even layer over the stacks. Immediately roll in peanuts. Place on prepared baking sheet.

3 Freeze banana pops about 30 minutes or until firm. Serve straight from the freezer.

nutrition facts per serving: 165 cal., 9 g total fat (4 g sat. fat), 3 mg chol., 38 mg sodium, 18 g carb. (2 g fiber, 12 g sugars), 4 g pro. exchanges: 5 fruit, 0.5 carb., 0.5 high-fat meat, 1 fat.

When baked, wonton wrappers become crispy, pastrylike sheets. They add enticing texture to this creamy, fruity dessert.

wonton dessert stacks

26g
CARB. PER SERVING

start to finish: 20 minutes
makes: 4 servings (1 stack each)

Nonstick cooking
  spray
8 wonton wrappers
  Sugar
½ cup sliced fresh
  strawberries
2 kiwifruits, peeled and
  sliced
1 6-ounce carton
  low-fat lemon
  yogurt
2 fresh strawberries,
  cut in half

1 Preheat oven to 350°F. Line a large baking sheet with foil; lightly coat with cooking spray. Place wonton wrappers flat on the baking sheet; lightly coat with additional cooking spray. Sprinkle lightly with sugar. Bake for 6 to 8 minutes or until golden brown and crisp. Remove from oven; cool slightly.

2 Meanwhile, in a medium bowl combine the ½ cup sliced strawberries and the kiwifruit slices.

3 To assemble, place 1 baked wonton wrapper on each of four dessert plates. Top the wrappers with half of the yogurt. Divide the fruit mixture evenly among the stacks. Add another baked wonton to each stack. Top with remaining yogurt. Top each stack with a strawberry half.

nutrition facts per serving: 127 cal., 1 g total fat (0 g sat. fat), 4 mg chol., 118 mg sodium, 26 g carb. (2 g fiber, 14 g sugars), 4 g pro. exchanges: 0.5 fruit, 1.5 carb.

18g CARB. PER SERVING

delightful desserts

*Swapping flaky puff pastry for phyllo makes this
classic Greek sweet easier and quicker to prepare.*

almond baklava

prep: 25 minutes bake: 10 minutes
makes: 12 servings (2 triangles each)

1   sheet frozen puff
    pastry (½ of a
    17.3-ounce package)
¾   cup sliced or slivered
    almonds
5   tablespoons honey
¼   teaspoon vanilla
¼   teaspoon ground
    cinnamon

1 Thaw puff pastry according to package
directions. Preheat oven to 400°F. Using
a pizza cutter, cut pastry into six pieces (each
about 5 inches long and 3 inches wide). Place
pastry pieces on a baking sheet. Bake for 10 to
12 minutes or until golden. Using a wide metal
spatula, transfer pastry pieces to a wire rack.

2 Meanwhile, place almonds in a large
skillet; cook over medium heat about
8 minutes or until lightly browned, stirring
frequently. Set aside 2 tablespoons of the
almonds. In a small food processor combine
the remaining almonds, 3 tablespoons of the
honey, the vanilla, and cinnamon; cover and
process until ground into a thick mixture.

3 Gently split each slightly warm pastry
piece horizontally into two layers. Carefully
spoon almond mixture in small spoonfuls on
bottoms of pastry layers. Replace top layers of
pastry. Using a pizza cutter, cut each pastry in
half crosswise and then cut diagonally in half
to make four triangles per pastry.

4 Spoon the remaining 2 tablespoons honey
into a glass measuring cup. Microwave
on 100 percent power (high) about 10 seconds
or until thinned and a pourable consistency.
Drizzle the warm honey over the pastry triangles.
Sprinkle with the reserved 2 tablespoons
toasted almonds.

nutrition facts per serving: 173 cal., 11 g total fat
(2 g sat. fat), , 51 mg sodium, 18 g carb. (1 g fiber, 8 g sugars),
3 g pro. exchanges: 1 carb., 2.5 fat.

Present these gems after dinner with coffee. Hint: Lightly dampen your hands to make shaping the mixture into balls easier.

cashew truffles

9g CARB. PER SERVING

prep: 45 minutes freeze: 2 hours bake: 8 minutes stand: 30 minutes
makes: 20 servings (2 truffles each)

8 ounces bittersweet chocolate, chopped
½ cup fat-free half-and-half
1 tablespoon pure maple syrup
¾ cup whole cashews
¼ teaspoon coarse salt

1 Place chocolate in a medium bowl; set aside. In a small saucepan bring half-and-half just to boiling; pour over chocolate. Stir until chocolate is melted. Stir in maple syrup. Cover; freeze about 2 hours or until firm.

2 Meanwhile, preheat oven to 350°F. Place cashews on a shallow baking pan. Bake for 8 to 10 minutes or until golden, stirring once. Set aside 40 whole cashews. In a food processor combine the remaining cashews and the salt. Cover and process with several on/off turns until nuts are finely chopped. Transfer finely chopped nuts to a small bowl; set aside.

3 Divide chocolate mixture into 40 portions. Place a whole cashew in the center of one of the portions; shape into a ball. Roll ball in the chopped cashew mixture. Place on a baking sheet. Repeat to make 40 truffles total. Cover and chill until serving time. Let stand at room temperature for 30 minutes before serving. If desired, serve in small paper candy cups.

nutrition facts per serving: 93 cal., 7 g total fat (3 g sat. fat), 1 mg chol., 62 mg sodium, 9 g carb. (1 g fiber, 5 g sugars), 2 g pro. exchanges: 0.5 carb., 1.5 fat.

index

metric information

The charts on this page provide a guide for converting measurements from the U.S. customary system, which is used throughout this book, to the metric system.

Product Differences

Most of the ingredients called for in the recipes in this book are available in most countries. However, some are known by different names. Here are some common American ingredients and their possible counterparts:

- Sugar (white) is granulated, fine granulated, or caster sugar.
- Powdered sugar is icing sugar.
- All-purpose flour is enriched, bleached or unbleached white household flour or plain flour. When self-rising (self-raising) flour is used in place of all-purpose flour in a recipe that calls for leavening, omit the leavening agent (baking soda or baking powder) and salt.
- Light-color corn syrup is golden syrup.
- Cornstarch is cornflour.
- Baking soda is bicarbonate of soda.
- Vanilla or vanilla extract is vanilla essence.
- Green, red, or yellow sweet peppers are capsicums or bell peppers.
- Golden raisins are sultanas.

Volume and Weight

The United States traditionally uses cup measures for liquid and solid ingredients. The chart, *bottom right,* shows the approximate imperial and metric equivalents. If you are accustomed to weighing solid ingredients, the following approximate equivalents will be helpful.

- 1 cup butter, caster sugar, or rice = 8 ounces = ½ pound = 250 grams
- 1 cup flour = 4 ounces = ¼ pound = 125 grams
- 1 cup icing sugar = 5 ounces = 150 grams

Canadian and U.S. volume for a cup measure is 8 fluid ounces (237 ml), but the standard metric equivalent is 250 ml.

1 British imperial cup is 10 fluid ounces.

In Australia, 1 tablespoon equals 20 ml, and there are 4 teaspoons in the Australian tablespoon.

Spoon measures are used for smaller amounts of ingredients. Although the size of the tablespoon varies slightly in different countries, for practical purposes and for recipes in this book, a straight substitution is all that's necessary. Measurements made using cups or spoons always should be level unless stated otherwise.

Common Weight Range Replacements

Imperial / U.S.	Metric
½ ounce	15 g
1 ounce	25 g or 30 g
4 ounces (¼ pound)	115 g or 125 g
8 ounces (½ pound)	225 g or 250 g
16 ounces (1 pound)	450 g or 500 g
1¼ pounds	625 g
1½ pounds	750 g
2 pounds or 2¼ pounds	1,000 g or 1 Kg

Oven Temperature Equivalents

Fahrenheit Setting	Celsius Setting*	Gas Setting
300°F	150°C	Gas Mark 2 (very low)
325°F	160°C	Gas Mark 3 (low)
350°F	180°C	Gas Mark 4 (moderate)
375°F	190°C	Gas Mark 5 (moderate)
400°F	200°C	Gas Mark 6 (hot)
425°F	220°C	Gas Mark 7 (hot)
450°F	230°C	Gas Mark 8 (very hot)
475°F	240°C	Gas Mark 9 (very hot)
500°F	260°C	Gas Mark 10 (extremely hot)
Broil	Broil	Grill

*Electric and gas ovens may be calibrated using Celsius. However, for an electric oven, increase Celsius setting 10 to 20 degrees when cooking above 160°C. For convection or forced air ovens (gas or electric), lower the temperature setting 25°F/10°C when cooking at all heat levels.

Baking Pan Sizes

Imperial / U.S.	Metric
9×1½-inch round cake pan	22- or 23×4-cm (1.5 L)
9×1½-inch pie plate	22- or 23×4-cm (1 L)
8×8×2-inch square cake pan	20×5-cm (2 L)
9×9×2-inch square cake pan	22- or 23×4.5-cm (2.5 L)
11×7×1½-inch baking pan	28×17×4-cm (2 L)
2-quart rectangular baking pan	30×19×4.5-cm (3 L)
13×9×2-inch baking pan	34×22×4.5-cm (3.5 L)
15×10×1-inch jelly roll pan	40×25×2-cm
9×5×3-inch loaf pan	23×13×8-cm (2 L)
2-quart casserole	2 L

U.S. / Standard Metric Equivalents

⅛ teaspoon = 0.5 ml	
¼ teaspoon = 1 ml	
½ teaspoon = 2 ml	
1 teaspoon = 5 ml	
1 tablespoon = 15 ml	
2 tablespoons = 25 ml	
¼ cup = 2 fluid ounces = 50 ml	
⅓ cup = 3 fluid ounces = 75 ml	
½ cup = 4 fluid ounces = 125 ml	
⅔ cup = 5 fluid ounces = 150 ml	
¾ cup = 6 fluid ounces = 175 ml	
1 cup = 8 fluid ounces = 250 ml	
2 cups = 1 pint = 500 ml	
1 quart = 1 litre	